Fishes of the Gulf of Mexico

NUMBER TWENTY-TWO:
W. L. Moody, Jr., Natural History Series

SECOND EDITION

FISHES
of the
Gulf of Mexico

Texas, Louisiana, and Adjacent Waters

By H. Dickson Hoese and Richard H. Moore

With underwater photography by Farley Sonnier and drawings by Dinah Bowman

Texas A&M University Press
College Station

The paper used in this book meets the minimum requirements

of the American National Standard for Permanence

of Paper for Printed Library Materials, Z39.48-1984.

Binding materials have been chosen for durability.

Library of Congress Cataloging-in-Publication Data

Hoese, H. Dickson.

    Fishes of the Gulf of Mexico, Texas, Louisiana, and adjacent waters /
by H. Dickson Hoese and Richard H. Moore ; with underwater photography
by Farley Sonnier ; drawings by Dinah Bowman. — 2nd ed.

    p.   cm. — (W.L. Moody, Jr., natural history series ; no. 22)

    Includes bibliographical references and index.

    ISBN 0-89096-737-7 (cloth). — ISBN 0-89096-767-9 (paper)

    1. Marine fishes—Mexico, Gulf of—Identification. 2. Marine fishes—
Texas—Identification. 3. Marine fishes—Louisiana—Identification. 4. Fishes—
Mexico, Gulf of—Identification. I. Moore, Richard H., 1945– . II. Title.
III. Series.

QL621.56.H63   1998

597.177´364—dc21   97-26437

                                           CIP

*This book is affectionately dedicated
to Ruth Hoese and Robin Morris
for their assistance and tolerance
over many years.*

Contents

Illustrations

Preface to the Second Edition

Twenty years have passed since *Fishes of the Gulf of Mexico* first appeared, and with these years our knowledge of the varieties and biology of the fish life of the Texas and Louisiana coasts has increased. There have been over sixty species added to the list, including several that have just been scientifically described. The scientific names of other species, including some of the most common, have changed, as have the recommended common names (Robins et al. 1980, 1991) of several species, including, we are glad to say, the hardhead catfish.

We are very gratified at the response to this book, due in no small part to the work of the many independent students of fishes, whom we tried to acknowledge. We have also been motivated in our endeavor by the wide acceptance of the first edition and the many comments and words of encouragement we have received from readers.

Our knowledge of the biology of the fishes of the northwestern Gulf of Mexico has also increased dramatically. The task now is to include and synthesize the wealth of information produced since the first edition. Much of this new information is available through the greatly expanded bibliography found in this book. Much of the most recent research has concentrated on the largely unknown early life stages of common or commercially important species—but with increasing emphasis on physiology, genetics, and more microscopic forms of study. There has been relatively little new taxonomic information and a concurrent loss of interest in field and museum work. One result of this shift in emphasis has been the creation of so-called orphaned collections in which specimens once valued for distributional and taxonomic study are no longer available to researchers. The study of "Biodiversity" as a new environmental imperative—or even as a fad—depends on such collections, and we hope that the future will bring renewed awareness of the value of properly maintained museum collections to current and future researchers. Collections under the care of Mike Fitzsimmons at the Louisiana State University Museum of Natural History stand out as an exception to this trend and have incorporated other collections, such as that formerly maintained at the University of Southwestern Louisiana. Texas A&M and Tulane Universities have also maintained their extensive collections, and the recently consolidated collections at the Texas Memorial Museum (Austin), which contains collections formerly housed at Rockport (Texas Parks and Wildlife Department) and Port Aransas (University of Texas Marine Science Institute), will also be an asset to future researchers once these are fully organized and cataloged. At the same time technology has made access easier to more distant collections. Many museums are now on-line, and their data may be accessed via the internet. While no substitute for the actual examination of specimens, the internet has provided us a means to acquire up-to-date information on several questionable records.

Lastly we have assembled over two hundred new or better pictures of the fishes. We have tried to keep as close as possible to the first edition's format and its objective of bridging the imaginary barrier between the technical and the popular, while trying always to remember that fish are fish.

While the basic coverage of the second edition remains unchanged from the first, we have attempted to make it more useful to users peripheral to the northwestern Gulf of Mexico and have included more common eastern Gulf and Atlantic species in the keys and descriptions. Many of these species closely resemble western gulf or Gulf of Mexico forms, and we hope this will help reduce confusion as well as facilitate the documentation of actual range extensions and incursions of several extralimital species into our waters.

The following table summarizes the habitat of species added now and in the past. The additions primarily reflect increased scientific effort in previously overlooked or disregarded areas and not any sudden shift in the actual composition of the ichthyo-

	Estuarine/ Freshwater Species	Coastal Demersal Species	Coastal Pelagic Species	Offshore/ Tropical Reef Dwellers	Deep (>100F)/ Epipelagic Species	Total
species listed by Hoese (1958)	111 (26%)	147 (35%)	63 (15%)	43 (10%)	65 (15%)	429
species added in Hoese and Moore (1977)	2 (3%)	16 (26%)	6 (10%)	37 (60%)	1 (2%)	62
species added since 1977	5 (8%)	8 (13%)	9 (15%)	21 (34%)	18 (30%)	61
Total	118 (21%)	171 (31%)	78 (14%)	101 (18%)	84 (15%)	552

fauna. The relatively few additions to the estuarine/freshwater category, for instance, demonstrate that the species composition of these habitats was relatively well known prior to 1958. Increased interest in offshore reef habitats is reflected in the greater percentages of additions in these categories from the 1970s through the present. Similarly, research in offshore waters is shown by the high percentage added in this category in the 1980s and 1990s. There is a need for a boom comparable to this on these offshore and deeper-living species.

Ichthyology classes at Coastal Carolina University and the University of Southwestern Louisiana have been a great help to us in preparing the second edition, as have the libraries at both institutions. Ruth Grundy, librarian at the University of Texas Marine Science Laboratory at Port Aransas has been especially helpful, for there is no way that we could have found, much less included, the many journal papers, reports, theses, dissertations, and other sources of information important to this subject without her help.

We had a particularly sad loss in the early death of our colleague Farley Sonnier in 1987. Reviewing his slide collection while preparing the second edition revealed that he was at the peak of his photographic skills at the time of his death, almost as if the fish posed to be framed by him. The reader will note improved photographs of many local species that were taken by Farley, even though he had turned his attention to other geographic areas. His contribution to Gulf of Mexico oceanography has been acknowledged by the naming of Sonnier Bank, located at 28° E 15′ N latitude, 92° E 25′ W longitude.

Again great credit goes to the many individuals who have done the basic research on Gulf fishes, sometimes at loss of life, as in Jeff Render's case. Other premature deaths, especially that of Elmer Gutherz, have hurt the field. We will no doubt overlook some very important workers who have contributed to this book. George K. Reid, who introduced H. Dickson Hoese to the study of fishes, was inadvertently omitted from the first edition. Other individuals who have helped us include, in no particular order, Robert S. Jones, Scott Holt, Don Hockaday, Joe and Anna Herring, Butch Pelligrin, Claude Boudreaux, Frank Truesdale, Dave Nieland, Chuck Wilson, Tony Reisinger, the late Mike Russell, Guthrie Perry, Bennie Rohr, Nate Sanders and Perry Thompson, Mark Schexnayder, Mark Konikoff, Stephen Hein, Ed Moss, and Jennifer Gatens (who scanned the original text making our task of revision that much easier). For important pictures (some carried forward from the first edition) we especially thank, again in no particular order, William D. Anderson, Jr., Steve Bortone, Steve Frishman, Mark Konikoff, Stu Strothers, Scott and Joan Holt, Darryl Felder, and Robert Parker, as well as Jerry Retzloff and Bill Wert of the Lone Star Brewery's Buckhorn Museum for permission to photograph several excellent models and fish mounts in their collection, and especially Tommy Rauch who provided the spectacular picture of Hypsoblennius invemar. Diane Rome Peoples allowed us to use her drawing of the bonefish. We are grateful also to Mike Fitzsimmons at the LSU Museum, Dean Henderson at the Texas Memorial Museum, and Barry Chernoff at the Field Museum of Natural History who provided access to or information about the specimens in their care. Bruce Thompson of the LSU Coastal Fisheries Institute has been free with his valuable information on offshore as well as some inshore species. The Texas State Aquarium in Corpus Christi, the Aquarium of the Americas in New Orleans, and the Mississippi Marine Education Center in Ocean Springs are important resources from which we acquired some of the pictures appearing in this book. Jim Prappas and the Texas State Aquarium staff were particularly helpful. Many aquaria have been established in recent years and provide excellent places to view fish, although frequently fatter than their wild cousins, and are important educational places.

C'est lui, en esprit, vol travers Jackaman's, Picket Fence,
Church Steeple, Twin Sisters, Hartley's et Lonesome Place

June, 1997

Preface to the First Edition

This work was originally begun by Moore in 1970 as an update and expansion of Hoese's (1958a) "A Partially Annotated Checklist of the Marine Fishes of Texas" (Moore, 1975b). Hoese, who at that time was involved in studies of large numbers of underwater photographs of fishes taken by Sonnier, was invited to participate and did so. Finally, Sonnier also joined the effort, which by this time had been expanded to cover Louisiana as well as Texas. With access to Sonnier's collection of excellent underwater photographs, we began a serious effort to fill the longstanding need for an illustrated guide to the marine fishes of Texas and Louisiana, with some thought of further expansion to cover all temperate and subtropical fishes in the Gulf of Mexico. Although two publications have appeared since we commenced work (Parker, Moore, and Galloway, 1972, 2d ed. 1975; and Walls, 1975), we have continually felt that our objective was still a valid one.

Rather than simply compiling records of fishes from existing literature, we attempted to verify every species of fish which had been reported by examining specimens and sometimes correcting previous misidentifications. Towards this ultimate goal, which was not completely possible, we traveled thousands of miles; collected thousands of fishes, mostly from the states of Texas, Louisiana, Mississippi, and Florida, from the upper estuaries to the outer continental shelf; and examined hundreds of preserved museum specimens. We are indebted to many people in these states, especially those from the Louisiana Wild Life and Fisheries Commission, the Texas Parks and Wildlife Department, the Florida Department of Natural Resources, and the National Marine Fisheries Service Laboratory at Pascagoula. We journeyed and collected from the following vessels and boats: *Oregon II* (National Marine Fisheries Service), *Longhorn* and *Lorene* (University of Texas Marine Science Institute); *Penaeid, Kalypseaux, Squalid* (University of Southwestern Louisiana); *Ms. Coastal* (Coastal Carolina College); *Skimmer I* and *Skimmer II* (U.S. Fish and Wildlife Service); *Loverly* (Grady Loftin); *Capt. Anderson IV; Capt. Juel I* (Captain Frank Juel); and *Charlene* (Great Atlantic Shrimp Co.).

During our travels we were impressed by the access we were allowed to materials, information (some of which has not been published), and specimens which were necessary for study and for many of the illustrations. We were especially dependent on the extensive collections of Tulane University which have been built up by Royal D. Suttkus and his students, but we also could not have done without the collections from Texas A&I University at Kingsville, the Louisiana Wild Life and Fisheries Commission Laboratory at Grande Terre, and the Texas Parks and Wildlife Department Marine Laboratory at Rockport. Of paramount importance to the preparation of the book was help from the University of Texas Marine Science Institute (UTMSI) at Port Aransas and the University of Southwestern Louisiana (USL), whose collections, vessels, personnel, libraries, and other facilities were heavily relied upon throughout the work.

The illustrations by Dinah Bowman were made possible through a loan from the Texas A&M University Sea Grant Program. The University of Southwestern Louisiana Foundation and the USL Department of Biology provided some funds for the final typing, and other clerical work was performed by the staffs at Port Aransas and USL. Classes in fish ecology at UTMSI and in ichthyology and marine biology at USL assisted in providing specimens and checking out the keys. Some specimens were made available during studies for the Environmental Protection Agency, the U.S. Fish and Wildlife Service, and the Bureau of Land Management.

The photographs were taken by the authors except for the following: tarpon was taken by Joyce Teerling; Spanish flag by Steve Bortone; cottonmouth jack, yellowtail bass, spreadfin skate, and marbled puffer by Scott Holt; Atlantic bonito by Stu Strothers; bighead sea robin, wenchman, chub mackerel and cownose ray by Mark Konikoff; tilefish by Steve Frishman; and hatchet marlin by Pete Laurie of the South Carolina Wildlife and Marine Resources Department. Mounted specimens were photographed at the Houston Museum of Natural History; the Louisiana Wild Life and Fisheries Commission Museum in New Orleans; and the taxidermy shop of A. R. Brundrett and Mrs. Pete's Restaurant in Port Aransas.

The drawing of the white marlin and the outline drawings in the family accounts were modified from Greenwood et al. (1966) and other sources by Dickie Hoese. The map of the northern Gulf of Mexico was drawn by Karen Dupont. Unpublished taxonomic information was provided by Margaret Bradbury (Ogcocephalidae), James Dooley (Branchiostegidae), Steve Bortone (*Diplectrum*), and Mark Leiby (*Bascanichthys*). The vernacular Cajun French names were provided mainly by Clovis Toups, Ted Falgout, and Hampton Hebert, and Henry Hildebrand supplied the Spanish names.

While we cannot thank everyone who helped in various important ways, we want to mention, in no particular order, Scott Williams, Joyce Teerling, Wayne Wiltz, John Voorhies, Ernest Simmons, Clark Hubbs, Johnie Tarver, Lynn and Grady Loftin, Faust Parker, Mark Konikoff, Tom Bright, Victor Springer, Rick Minkler, Elmer Gutherz, Perry Thompson, Don Gibson, Elgie Wingfield, Don Gooch, Geraldine Ard, Jo Ann Page, Al Chaney, Michael Stevenson, Gay Fay Kelly, Wayne Forman, Mikey and Teresa Thibodeaux, Ray and

Waneta Torres, John Thompson, Curly Wohlschlag, Carl Oppenheimer, Pat Parker, Johnny Holland, Susan and Patty Herring, Guthrie Perry, Peter Perceval, Dwight Leach, Russ Miget, Gary Powell, John Durrell, Frank Schwartz, Wayne Trahan, and the many others whose names we either missed or forgot in our haste.

Several special acknowledgments are necessary: Ruth Hoese, who fed and tolerated us (and our ichthyological preoccupations) and who also helped in numerous ways throughout the work on the book; Rez Darnell and John McEachran, of Texas A&M University, who spent many hours reviewing the manuscript and illustrations; Nettie Voorhies, who typed the final draft and provided other invaluable and necessary help during the latter stages; and Robin Morris, who helped with the index. Sonnier particularly expresses his thanks to Tenneco Oil Company for the occasional supply of diesel fuel and emergency evacuation of injured diving personnel.

We are also indebted to the many people cited in the bibliography who have collectively done most of the work. We have talked to many of them at one time or another in person and their knowledge and assistance have helped with the originality of the book.

While most of the keys are originally constructed, we have relied on previous keys for help since a good key should be perpetuated. The family keys were modifications of the well established keys by Bigelow and Schroeder for elasmobranchs and Jordan and Evermann for bony fishes. A book is never really finished, or never should be, but we are proud of the time we have spent in this endeavor because it gave us a different perspective, showed us how much we have yet to learn about the Gulf of Mexico and its fish fauna. Little did we know, when we began, how much work would be involved, how many people would help and be affected by the work, and how much fun and frustration it would be. In closing, we know that this book will not be considered as an end, but hope that it will be an impetus for future exploration and inquiry into the fishes of the Gulf of Mexico.

Fishes of the Gulf of Mexico

How to Use This Book

This guide consists of three major sections to aid you in identifying fishes:

(1) identification plates,
(2) keys to fish families, and
(3) accounts or descriptions of each family and species of fish.

Each identification plate is numbered. When you identify a fish by its picture, turn to the corresponding species number in the accounts for a description of that fish.

The keys provide a step-by-step method of identifying families of fishes, giving the page numbers on which accounts for each family begin. When you identify a fish's family by means of the keys, turn to the page number given for a description and a generalized line drawing of that family. Then use the species keys and descriptions that follow the family introduction to identify the fish more closely.

Further information on how to use this book is given in the chapter Identifying Fishes.

Introduction

Fishes are the most numerous group of vertebrates. Among the various divisions of the subphylum Vertebrata, fishes are the only type of organism classified into more than one of the major subdivisions known as classes. Zoologists consider "the fishes" to include the classes of cartilaginous and bony fishes together. Presently there are at least twenty thousand known species of fishes, and some ichthyologists suspect there may be as many as thirty thousand. On the Texas and Louisiana coasts we have counted nearly 550 species, a number also reached by Murdy (1983). The exact total number depends on how far offshore one stops the count.

Why are there more fishes than mammals, birds, reptiles, or amphibians? Part of the answer lies in the fact that fishes are the only group of vertebrates that spend their entire lives in the waters occupying approximately 70 percent of the earth's surface. Furthermore, fishes, unlike most terrestrial vertebrates, live in a truly three-dimensional environment. They are not confined to living upon the surface or limited to brief excursions away from the surface, as most other vertebrates are. Because of this freedom, it has been said that some fishes are like birds—in which case others are like opossums, snakes, horned toads, turtles, lizards, or flying squirrels. The variety of forms and lifestyles exhibited by fishes far exceeds the variety among terrestrial vertebrates, but we are only gradually finding out about the many ways in which fishes go about their day-to-day lives. While no single species of fish ranges from the surface of the ocean to its greatest depths, the ability of fishes in general to exploit all levels of their environment allows a much greater diversity of habitats and therefore of species occupying those habitats.

Fishes are important to our lives in many ways. They provide us with food and relaxation. Any angler knows that fishing is an educational, relaxing sport as well as one that may provide a delicious dinner. In addition scientists gain knowledge from fishes. Besides those who study fishes and their habits to provide people with a greater abundance of food, other scientists use fishes in their experiments because of the variety of responses that the many species exhibit and the ease with which some species may be maintained in the laboratory. Because fishes represent the "simplest" vertebrates, scientists—including medical researchers—can study many of the same systems as are found in humans but in a much less complicated organism.

Aquaria, ranging from modest goldfish bowls to elaborate tanks stocked with exotic, colorful tropical fishes, provide entertainment and education to thousands of people. Technology has taken "fish watching" out of the living room, and with the help of scuba equipment people are now able to observe fish relatively undisturbed in their natural habitat. Popular places for this sport include the South Texas and Florida panhandle jetties, grass beds, and offshore reefs and oil platforms.

Purpose and Scope

This book is meant for fishermen, fish watchers, and scientists—for anyone interested in fishes, especially those fishes that live in the salt water of the northwestern Gulf of Mexico adjacent to Texas and Louisiana. It is only slightly less useful to people living in adjacent Gulf states and Mexico, and is still helpful on the southern U.S. Atlantic Coast as far north as Cape Hatteras, North Carolina, and many species included range farther north.

One of our largest problems in designing this book was defining the area of coverage. Since boundary lines in the ocean are seldom precise, it was obvious that no single book could be complete. To keep ours to a manageable size and because of our greater familiarity with the area, we decided to focus on the northwestern Gulf. We originally attempted to include in this guide all temperate and subtropical fishes of the entire Gulf as well as tropical species most likely to be encountered in the northern Gulf. This has become increasingly difficult with new discoveries, but most species, especially those most likely to be encountered, are represented. Because this fauna is largely continuous from Cape Hatteras to Cape Canaveral, Florida, and from northwestern Florida to southern Texas and Mexico (see the map), the coverage of the book is actually much greater. To assist users outside the northwestern Gulf, we have included in the keys many fish species that occur in the northeastern Gulf or on the southeastern U.S. coast but which we do not treat in detail (these species are also listed in appendix 1). North of Cape Hatteras the fish fauna becomes quite different, but many of these cold temperate species move south of Cape Hatteras, especially in the winter. Hildebrand and Schroeder's *Fishes of Chesapeake Bay* (1928), which has been revised by Murdy et al. (1997), serves as the best single authority on these cold temperate species that occur in warmer waters.

The fish fauna of the deeper waters of the Gulf of Mexico is poorly known. Because this is primarily a guide for identifying marine fish found over the continental shelf, most of these deepwater inhabitants were also excluded, but again we have included most of their families in the Keys to the Families as well as providing a list of slope and deep-sea fishes that occasionally venture onto the continental shelf (appendix 2). Some

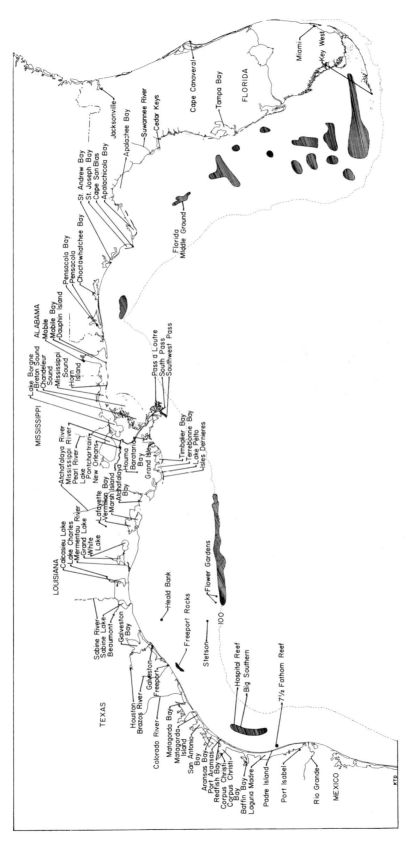

The Northern Gulf of Mexico (shaded areas designate major reefs)

deeper-dwelling members of families common on the outer shelf are included in the family keys, but not in the family descriptions. Occurrences of slope species on the shelf are most common where the slope is steepest, as off the Mississippi Delta, or where submarine canyons (Mississippi Canyon, just west of the delta, and DeSoto Canyon, off the Florida panhandle) intrude into the shelf. More slope species do this than were previously realized, some perhaps regularly and in numbers, but we cannot include all of the offshore pelagic and slope species, partly because this information has not been totally analyzed.

Freshwater fishes that are resident in low-salinity waters are included, and we mention other less common intruders from fresh water. Many freshwater species may tolerate salinities up to ten parts per thousand and thus may be found in bays, especially after floods (Renfro, 1959). Extensive floods in 1973–75 and again in the 1990s were especially effective. Species not found in this book and suspected of being freshwater fishes may be identified by consulting the references on freshwater fishes listed in the bibliography (Blair et al., 1968; Douglas, 1974; Eddy and Underhill, 1978; Hubbs et al., 1991; Lee et al., 1980; Page and Burr, 1991). A list of freshwater fishes that commonly venture into brackish or salt water is given in appendix 3, while a list of saltwater fishes that may occasionally be found in inland fresh waters is given in appendix 4.

While the idea of a single book that pleases everybody may seem too ambitious an undertaking, we felt that this was a better goal than making it either too simple or too complex. By producing a book aimed more toward the technical, we hope that this book provides a resource serving the needs of anyone seriously interested in our marine fishes while remaining attractive to readers of less technical inclination.

Ecology and Life History

Many features of the marine environment affect the lives of fishes. Time and space prevent a thorough description of environmental factors, and the serious student should consult one of the more general books on ichthyology such as Bone et al. (1996), Lagler et al. (1977), Moyle and Cech (1996), or some of the papers cited in the species accounts. Older works by Marshall (1971), Nikolskii (1963), and Norman and Greenwood (1975) still provide useful insights into specialized topics as well as into how relationships among different groups of fishes were formerly regarded.

The northwestern Gulf of Mexico provides a variety of environments for fishes. Indeed, it is arguably true that the Texas and Louisiana coasts contain as great a variety of marine and estuarine environments as any comparable length of coastline in the United States (Stickney, 1984; Britton and Morton, 1989). Including the area across to Florida further increases the diversity. Several natural gradients contribute to this diversity of habitats. First, as one travels along the coastline from the Mississippi River to the Rio Grande, rainfall and river output decrease and temperature slightly increases. These variations result in low salinities (less than ten parts per thousand) in the marshes and bayous of western Louisiana, the Mississippi River mouth (the influence of which extends well into the Gulf itself and even, at times, westward to Texas), and East Texas; moderate salinities along much of the central Texas coast and the east-central Louisiana coast; and often hypersaline conditions (over forty parts per thousand) in South Texas bays and lagoons. The seasonal extremes also vary regularly, with Port Isabel remaining subtropical for a great part of the year while salt waters on the East Texas and Louisiana coasts are usually colder in winter. During especially cold winters, salt waters even into Mexico have been known to freeze. To the east the characteristic cordgrass (Spartina) marshes typical of temperate estuaries are present. Extensive beds of turtle grass (Thalassia testudinum) occur in the Chandeleur Islands, and mixed Spartina-mangrove marshes extend from Barataria Bay to the Isles Dernieres. There are turtle grass beds as well in the southern Laguna Madre and Redfish Bay (part of the Corpus Christi–Aransas Bay complex), and historically there was a tiny one in western Galveston Bay. Grass beds dominated by species other than turtle grass are found at times in Lake Pelto and behind the Timbalier Islands. Turtle grass beds are found only where salinity does not fall below twenty-five parts per thousand (ideally thirty [Zieman, 1975]), while mangroves are limited by temperatures below 20°C (68°F). Because severe freezes as occurred in 1989 kill them, mangroves are limited in distribution to south of about 29°20' N (Kuentzler, 1974; Sherrod and McMillan, 1985) except in the Chandeleurs, where low winter temperatures are buffered by a large expanse of water between the islands and the mainland.

A second gradient is bottom composition. The greater riverine input found in the Gulf along the Louisiana and East Texas coasts results in large amounts of fine-grained sediments being transported into the Gulf in these regions. Conversely, coarser-grained sandy sediments become more common off the arid South Texas coast. Bottom sediments also become less sandy and more muddy as one progresses away from the barrier islands, although considerable sand exists on the Louisiana shelf. These changes help distinguish the inshore "white shrimp grounds" from the farther offshore "brown shrimp grounds" (Hildebrand, 1954; Chittenden and McEachran, 1976), but there are many exceptions. Rocky reefs occur on the forty-fathom contour off Texas and on most of the continental shelf off Louisiana, especially near the slope. These reefs furnish a hard bottom substrate for many invertebrates and so provide food and habitat for species of tropical reef fish that are not commonly found in the inshore shallow zones.

From east of the Mississippi Delta to about off Pensacola, the shelf is largely composed of coarse sand, with many areas of hard bottoms and accumulations of shells, not unlike the bottom off the coast of the southeastern United States but very different from that of most of the western Gulf. The Florida west coast consists largely of limestone and derived detrital sediments, which have favored the spread of many coral reef fishes northward. Just as some coarse sediment and rock occur on the northwestern Gulf shelf, some fine sediment and mud occur on the northeastern Gulf shelf, especially off the larger rivers. These variations contribute significantly to habitat diversity and to the accompanying diversity among the fishes and other organisms occupying the habitats.

A third important gradient is variation in depth from the shore to the edge of the continental shelf; the shelf is often divided into inner, middle, and outer zones, which differ in depth, temperature regime, and bottom type. Temperature variation is always less at the bottom than at the surface, and deeper waters and offshore habitats generally have less variable temperatures and salinities than do shallower waters. Surface temperature decreases offshore in the summer, but sometimes in winter a reverse temperature gradient is found in which offshore temperatures are higher than those inshore. Temperatures at the Flower Garden reefs and similar adjacent reefs are almost always above 20°C (68°F), at least at the bottom, allowing corals and coral reef fishes to live on these reefs, the most northerly living reefs in the Gulf of Mexico. As noted, there is a general correlation of sediment type with depth.

Currents play an important role in effecting the distribution of marine and estuarine fishes. Aside from bay shore forms like killifishes and silversides, most "estuarine" species actually spawn in the Gulf of Mexico and depend on seasonal, often wind-driven currents to transport their larvae and young into estuarine nursery areas. Offshore species, especially the tropical offshore reef fauna, are also highly dependent on currents. The major oceanographic feature of the Gulf of Mexico, the Loop Current, brings Caribbean waters into the Gulf through the Straits of Yucatán. The current proceeds northward into the central Gulf and then deflects to the east, traveling south parallel to the Florida west coast and exiting through the Straits of Florida. Occasional "rings" of tropical water separate from the northern end of the loop and these may drift into the western Gulf. The Loop Current contains a rich variety of larval tropical fishes, some of which settle and grow on the reefs of the eastern Gulf, while eddies bring additional tropical species into the western Gulf. These currents aid recruitment and may play a major role in determining long-term trends in tropical fish population dynamics, but it is also certain that many species of tropical fish reproduce in offshore Gulf waters and so Gulf populations are to some degree self-sufficient. The Loop Current may further be an important geographic isolating mechanism, separating eastern and western Gulf populations of inshore fishes and resulting in a degree of endemism found in the western Gulf (Shipp, 1992).

Extreme conditions of temperature, salinity, or dissolved oxygen as well as the occurrence of natural or human-induced toxic substances may cause spectacular die-offs of fishes. "Red tides" (Gunter et al., 1948; Riley et al., 1989) and more recently "brown tides" (Buskey and Hyatt, 1995) result from blooms of microscopic plankton, which consume available oxygen and in red tides produce nerve toxins that kill large numbers of fishes. Red tides are rare in the western Gulf, but one occurred in 1935 off South Texas (Gunter, 1951) and others have been reported for Offats Bayou on Galveston Island (Connell and Cross, 1950). A repeat of the 1935 incident with large mortalities of fishes occurred a half-century later in 1986. Brown tides increase turbidity, but their effect on fish is uncertain and an important area of study. An unusual kill in Galveston Bay was due to the formation of gas bubbles in the bloodstreams of fish (gas bubble disease), probably as a result of very high oxygen concentrations, caused by a plankton bloom, which suddenly dropped, allowing some gas to come out of solution in the blood (Renfro, 1963). Other mortalities or narcotic effects, called "jubilees," from low oxygen occasionally occur in several localities, most famously in Mobile Bay in May, 1973.

Other significant causes of fish mortalities are extreme freezes, which occur with varying severity about every decade. Possibly because northers hit the coast around the Corpus Christi area more abruptly and with more rapid temperature changes than to the northeast, more fish are killed there, although severe freezes may kill fish across the whole southern U.S. coastline and other factors may be important. Severe South Texas freezes have reduced populations of some species, including some game fishes, and recovery may take several years (see Gunter, 1952a, and Brongersma-Sanders, 1957, for a list of older works). Severe killing freezes were absent for two decades (1962–83), but another occurred in 1989. Species killed in Texas are given by McEachron et al. (1994).

Besides severe temperature changes, subtler and longer-term changes may cause population shifts from more tropical to more temperate species or vice versa. These changes are most noticeable when tropical species, which are rare inshore, become common along the South Texas coast (Moore, 1975a). While it has been thought that temperature has been rising, some tropical species, such as tarpon and snook, were more common in 1900 than in 1950. Commercial fisheries for snook existed before the 1920s in Texas, and until recently the only records of snook in Louisiana, with some marketed, were early in the century. Tarpon, Texas, was the original name of Port Aransas; today the fish is rarely caught there. Although factors other than temperature may have caused the disappearance of these species, they serve as an example of how populations of coastal marine fishes fluctuate. Recently, both tarpon and snook have shown a resurgence. Many other examples of such population changes have occurred over the last twenty years.

Floods, although spectacular in their impact on attached animals, seem mostly to run fish offshore and wash freshwater fish into the estuaries (Gunter, 1952b; Hoese, 1960; Russell, 1977). Freshwater river and marsh fishes do not seem to be adapted to open bay conditions, with few exceptions, so even during strong flooding, as occurred in Texas in 1957 and Louisiana in 1973 and 1975, the bays still contain mostly marine species such as croaker, menhaden, and saltwater killifishes. Saltwater fishes tend to predominate as long as some marine-derived salt remains in the water. Otherwise, our accounts would have to be increased by one hundred or so species. The Mississippi River and lately the Atchafalaya River release so much water that estuarine conditions may sometimes be found ten to twenty miles offshore from their mouths. At flood times freshwater fishes such as carp, pirate perch, and many others may be found in the Gulf, although in fresh water.

Hurricanes are another major type of climatic event in the northwestern Gulf of

Introduction

Mexico. Storm surge waves may rarely kill or injure many fishes, but the greater effect of the surge is to raise water levels in the bays, resulting in greater than normal discharges, which sweep large numbers of fish and invertebrates both into and out of the bays. Longer-term effects are produced from the lowered salinities resulting from heavy rainfall that often accompanies hurricanes. An exception was Hurricane Andrew in 1992, which seemed to have killed every shallow-water species in its path as it landed near Atchafalaya Bay (Harris and Darensbourg, 1992). Although this was popularly blamed on low oxygen, the species killed and the physical conditions do not support that hypothesis. Usually there is little direct storm-induced fish mortality. The effects of hurricanes on the Texas and Louisiana marine and estuarine fauna are little known; however, there are several theories (Matlock, 1987), such as that storms enhance red drum recruitment.

Hypersalinity (greater than normal oceanic salinities) has caused great mortality of fishes in the Laguna Madre, because except for a few killifishes all fishes are killed by salinity increases to about twice seawater strength (i.e., to seventy parts per thousand). Extensive mortalities occurred in the Laguna Madre in the 1930s and 1940s, but since completion of the Intracoastal Waterway to Brownsville in 1948, sufficient water exchange has prevented the development of excessive hypersalinity. Similar mortalities occur in the Laguna Madre de Tamaulipas just south of the Rio Grande mouth (Hildebrand, 1969). Probably more important are shifts in the amount of fresh water reaching the bays. When freshwater inflow is reduced because of drought or the use of inland water, more freshwater-intolerant (stenohaline) species such as pigfish, most sharks, and sea basses take the place of more freshwater-tolerant (euryhaline) species. Some of these effects are discussed by Copeland (1966) and correlations have been found between abundance of some species, such as redfish, and amount of fresh water (Funicelli, 1984; Powell, 1977; Beckman, 1989).

The fish fauna of the northwestern Gulf of Mexico may be divided into temperate and tropical components, with a fuzzy dividing line (as discussed in the following section on zoogeography), and certain habitats, especially the offshore reefs, have a truly distinctive group of fishes. The inshore Gulf and estuarine habitats appear to share a common fauna, but some species are largely, if not entirely, restricted to particular habitats and may be regarded as "indicator species." Often assemblages of two or more species are more characteristic of a given habitat than is any one species. Thus, the coastal marshes of Louisiana and East Texas, with low-salinity to almost fresh water, are characterized by such species as gar, killifish, mullet, and blue catfish. Salt marshes are characterized by several species of killifish and others. Mullet, speckled trout, redfish, and certain gobies are most commonly found on grass flats, while toadfish, clingfish, and other gobies are found on oyster beds.

Natural rocky areas are absent from inshore areas, except for one or two small ones off Atchafalaya Bay and Port Mansfield (7 1/2 Fathom Reef); however, piers, jetties, and bulkheads provide suitable habitat for such species as sheepshead, crested blennies, hairy blennies, frillfin gobies, and belted sand bass.

The low-salinity (oligohaline) bay communities are dominated by sciaenids like croaker, spot, and sand trout; anchovies; mullet; and, in areas receiving enough fresh water, menhaden. The hypersaline bays of South Texas contain no distinctive species, only a greatly reduced component of the general estuarine community found in lower salinities, such as mullet, black drum, redfish, and speckled trout. In the shallow Gulf, the surf zone with its open, sandy bottom characteristically contains fishes such as the Gulf whiting and the Atlantic threadfin. Outside this zone the bottom usually becomes rapidly muddier, and the characteristic fish are the star drum, silver trout, and longspine porgy. Farther offshore toward the middle shelf, the number of sciaenids is drastically reduced, and the fish community is dominated by small serranids, shoal flounders, and blackfin searobins. The middle and outer shelves have been increasingly explored, as fisheries have moved out, but this is still a relatively unknown area. The results of exploratory fishing expeditions by the Bureau of Commercial Fisheries (now the National Marine Fisheries Service) are described by Springer and Bullis (1956) and Bullis and Thompson (1965). Much of this material is still being studied, and information from these older, as well as more recent, collections is found in many reports throughout the literature.

The offshore reefs, with their more tropical fauna, support such distinctive forms as butterflyfishes, angelfishes, damselfishes, wrasses, parrotfishes, and several species of tropical sea basses. Juveniles of some of these species may occur inshore around the jetties and pilings of South Texas and some of the inshore oil platforms. The advent of scuba diving has allowed more attention to be paid to these areas and has resulted in the addition of many tropical fish species to our fauna (Bright and Cashman, 1974; Sonnier et al., 1976; Rezak et al., 1985; Dennis and Bright, 1988a, b; Rezak et al., 1990).

Life histories of many inshore fishes can be easily characterized because these species are estuarine-dependent (or, as recently suggested, opportunistic), which means they spend part or all of their lives in the estuaries. A typical estuarine-dependent species spawns in the Gulf of Mexico, and the larvae are presumably then carried toward shore by currents. By the time the young are big enough to swim, they are near the mouths of estuaries, which they then enter. The young fish remain in the estuaries for about one year, taking advantage of the protection and greater availability of food that estuarine habitats afford. Most estuarine-dependent species grow rapidly and reach maturity at one year of age although some take several years. They may then remain in the estuary, migrate to sea to spawn (returning to the estuary between spawnings), or migrate from the shallow estuaries to spend the rest of their lives in the deeper Gulf of Mexico. Of course, some fishes may spend their entire life cycle in the estuaries, while others that typically occur farther offshore may never be found in the bays. Many species in which adults live and spawn on the outer continental shelf live on the inner or middle shelf as young.

The reader is referred to the cited references for specific life history patterns or details; however, in appendix 5 we have included a list of spawning or birthing seasons for some of the most common inshore and estuarine species.

Zoogeography

While ecology is the study of the interrelationships between organisms and their environment (including other organisms), zoogeography is focused on why species are distributed as they are, especially in reference to past distributions of habitats and to other closely related species. As such, zoogeography and ecology are close sciences, with ecology concentrating more on the effects of current environmental conditions while zoogeography seeks to explain current distributions by the effects of past conditions.

The recent evolutionary history of the geography of the northwestern Gulf is peculiarly tied to two features: the Florida peninsula and the Mississippi River. If the Florida peninsula had never existed, there would be no barrier between the Atlantic Coast and the northern Gulf of Mexico, and the identification of fishes would be somewhat simpler since both coasts would share an uninterrupted fauna. However, the Florida peninsula not only physically separates the waters of Gulf of Mexico from those of the Atlantic; it also interposes a warm-water tropical environment and fauna between two temperate areas. In addition, the Florida peninsula has not always exerted the same influence on fish distribution that it does today, so to understand its modern role, we must look at its history.

During the Pleistocene, that period of the last two and a half million years when the climate has alternately warmed and cooled, at least four major glacial periods have alternated with warmer interglacial periods like the one we are presently experiencing. During the glacial periods, much of North America was covered with ice and sea level was lowered some one hundred meters, exposing most of the continental shelf. Conversely, during warmer interglacial periods, sea level rose and the peninsula was often at least partially submerged, making the Atlantic and Gulf more continuous.

During glacial periods, rivers running into the shrunken Gulf cut their valleys deeply in the soft coastal plain/continental shelf sediments, creating offshore canyons. Decreases in precipitation caused rivers to shrink and run clear (Fisk, 1944). While enclosed estuaries were rare, brackish water was probably found out into the Gulf near the mouths of rivers. As the sea level rose, last beginning about fifteen thousand years ago, precipitation and runoff both increased, leaving estuarine and nearshore sediments and fossils on the shelf as the shoreline advanced to its present level. Old oyster reefs, often covered by more recent sediments brought in by rivers, formed one type of offshore hard substrate. In addition, rock forced up by salt domes formed the bases of offshore coral reefs or "snapper banks." These areas of shale, limestone, and other hard substrates in the northwestern Gulf are now well mapped and the fishes on many of these have been fairly well studied (Rezak et al., 1985; Dennis and Bright, 1988b). Elsewhere the shelf is monotonously flat except where it is covered by newer sediment or where erosion has removed these deposits.

The glacial periods produced reductions in seawater temperature that allowed the movement of temperate species farther south than they occur today. During these cooler times the tropical fauna was pushed southward into the Caribbean; however, relict populations of some tropical fishes may have remained and been cut off from more southerly populations by the Gulf Stream (Walters and Robins, 1961).

Today the warm southern Florida coast prevents the free interchange of temperate fishes between the Atlantic and Gulf coasts and the temperate populations on either side of the peninsula have grown somewhat apart since the times when cooler temperatures extended below southern Florida. In warmer times a northward-displaced tropical fauna may have separated the temperate faunas even more than is the case today, pushing them northward and westward around Florida (Dahlberg, 1970). At the same time, higher sea levels created islands in what is now southern Florida, where small relict populations of some temperate species could have become isolated from those near the mainland (Springer, 1959).

The present temperature regime of the Northern Hemisphere is such that freezing temperatures seldom extend into the Rio Grande Valley of Texas or south of middle Florida. In the waters of the Gulf of Mexico the 20°C (68°F) winter isotherm falls at about those same places. Although this line may not represent the precise cause of change from temperate to tropical fauna, it closely approximates the midpoint of the area where such change occurs. To the south the tropical fauna comes closer to shore, eventually pinching the temperate fauna out of existence, while to the north it is pushed farther offshore until it disappears on the Atlantic side of Florida. On the Gulf side of that peninsula, the tropical fauna pushes up to near the northern shore, where it is kept offshore by cold winters and possibly by competition with temperate fishes better adapted to cooler waters. Therefore, at Miami and at Tampico, Mexico, most fishes are similar to those to the south, but at Jacksonville, Cedar Key, and Corpus Christi, most species are similar to those to the north. Year-to-year and longer-term fluctuations result in movement of the demarcation line, so that in warm years more tropical fishes may occur at Port Aransas (Moore, 1975a).

In the cooler temperate area, members of the croaker family (Sciaenidae) predominate, while in the tropical Gulf the grunts (Haemulidae) and mojarras (Gerreidae) are most abundant. Offshore, especially around reef structures, a well-developed tropical fauna exists. Young and larvae of some species, probably from adults on those reefs, make their way inshore in the warmer months and may be found around jetties, piers, and other structures where the water is relatively warm, clear, and salty.

Inside the Gulf the tail end of the temperate fauna is nearly continuous from the Florida panhandle to Texas. However, notable exceptions exist. Fish species that are apparently limited to the northeastern Gulf are either anadromous species, such as sturgeon, which range only as far west as the vicinity of the Mississippi River, or an uncertain but increasing number of tropical species, which are more common in the northeastern Gulf, due to the Loop Current and the more favorable reef-type habitats found there (Smith, 1976). Lesser quantities of these habitats west of the delta provide at least temporary homes for this type of organism and the more we look the more we find, but they may not have regular residents with significant populations. A combination of local spawning and recruitment of new larvae from the southern Gulf may be operating, but the relative contribution of each is a difficult question and probably varies with different species and in different years. Some eastern Gulf species, such as the southern puffer, separate more temperate forms in the northwestern Gulf from those on the southeastern Atlantic Coast (Shipp and Yerger, 1969; Springer, 1959; Williams, 1983).

The second major influence on the zoogeography of the northern Gulf of Mexico has been the Mississippi River. Most of the water from the river, after it leaves the delta, drifts westward carrying some of its load of silt and clay. To the west of the river's mouth the quantity of silt and clay is greater, the sand finer and darker because of the presence of heavy minerals, and the amount of fresh water greater than to the east. Except for Mobile Bay, Apalachicola Bay, and a few small estuaries east of the Mississippi, bay waters across the north-central Gulf are clear and salty, and much of the bay bottoms is covered by submerged plants, especially turtle grass and shoal grass, *Halodule wrighti*. As a result, the visitor to bays on either side of the Mississippi River will find them considerably different. Offshore in the eastern Gulf, less of the coarser sand has been covered by mud. In the northwestern Gulf, attached vegetation is rare, and turtle grass is found only in small stands in the saltier bays. The very large stand of it behind the Chandeleur Islands, part of an old Mississippi River delta, is in clear, salty water seldom affected by the river.

The effect of bottom type on fish distribution is exemplified by the distribution of the longspine porgy, *Stenotomus caprinus* (Caldwell, 1955a). It is absent from limestone bottoms off the west coast of Florida and Yucatán but it occurs on muddier (or mixed sand and mud) sediments from the Florida panhandle around the Gulf to Campeche. Many other distributions are similar; some species are more common on the northwest side of the Gulf because they require either mud or fine sand, and others are more common in the northeast because they need coarse sand and shell. Other species are distributed according to different patterns that fit their history combined with current conditions.

Related distributional patterns with little-understood causes are exhibited by a few species (perhaps as high as twenty taxa, but many have not been studied in this regard) that are split between the northeastern and northwestern Gulf (McClure and McEachran, 1992). These species pairs are included in the keys and are noted in the species distributions. The most noteworthy fact is that the split between closely related (sibling) species generally occurs either at the Mississippi Delta or to the east near Mobile Bay but never to the west. Although an unknown or mythical barrier has been postulated, consideration of glacial events may help explain the phenomenon. During glacial periods, the deltas of the Mobile and all rivers to the west into Texas would have produced a formidable barrier, with the only clear water and possibly warmer waters on the continental slope of what is now the west Florida shelf. Modern distributions of fishes that moved north as glaciers retreated might have been stopped at barriers or adjusted to those relict habitats (sediments) left by glacial rivers. The combination of the rivers' effect added to that of the Florida peninsula as a terrestrial barrier and the Loop Current favoring eastward dispersal (Shipp, 1992) in explaining modern distributions is an exciting area of investigation but a difficult one to resolve.

These events occurred several times during the Pleistocene, but the periods involved never lasted more than a few thousand years at any one time. Recent studies have tended to remove the distinction between temperate fishes on opposite sides of the Florida peninsula because the differences in populations ranging from, for example, Chesapeake Bay to Texas are clinal, with no clear breaks. That is, the differences between a fish at Cedar Key and one at Jacksonville are no greater than those between fish at Jacksonville and Savannah or Cedar Key and Panama City. Judging from speciation rates (the time it takes two populations to grow far enough apart to become incapable of interbreeding), indirectly measured in freshwater fishes, the period of time that Gulf and Atlantic populations have been split by the emergence of the Florida peninsula is probably inadequate for us to expect distinct species to have occurred on either side, and recent studies have synonymized most Atlantic-Gulf sibling species. Isolation in the Gulf is still not absolute as evidenced by the discovery of Gulf butterfish off the Atlantic Coast after a cold wave (Perschbacher et al., 1979). The fishes are still adjusting.

This brings up the question of what distinguishes species of marine fishes. Obviously, such different species as croaker and pigfish do not interbreed with each other, but a problem arises in knowing whether a group of similar fishes ranging, for instance, from Cape Cod to Rio de Janeiro is an interbreeding unit throughout. In the Caribbean and the Gulf of Mexico, these populations are split east to west as well as north to south, further complicating the problem. Some species are continuous in the temperate-to-tropical waters of the Western Hemisphere, while some northern species are replaced in the Caribbean or other areas to the south by a similar species. If the members of such a species pair are more closely related to one another than to any other species (meaning that they share the most recent common ancestor), they are called sibling species. Examples of sibling species also occur between the Atlantic and the Gulf for temperate species (such as the seatrouts *Cynoscion regalis* and *C. arenarius*) or between the Gulf and the Caribbean for tropical species (such as the small sea basses *Serranus subligarius* and *S. flaviventris*). Whether sibling species actually interbreed or not is difficult to prove since their distributions rarely overlap and so taxonomists traditionally have based species on morphological differences. However, newly developed genetic/biochemical techniques can demonstrate the degree of genetic similarity between two populations or species (i. e., King et al., 1991) and lead to reappraisals of traditional taxonomy, such as suggesting that the *Cynoscion* species mentioned are not really distinct (Weinstein and

Yerger, 1976). While these differences are significant to biologists, it remains to be proven whether the differences are of equal importance to the fish themselves. Questions along this line are found in species discussions.

Conservation

"They were preaching extermination at that time," writes Percy Viosca (1942) about the philosophy of fishery management followed in the early part of the century. Conservation of fishes in both Texas and Louisiana has generally followed the pattern set elsewhere, moving with the interests of the groups with the most political power. The reasons behind this pattern are partly based on scientific conclusions. The subject is controversial, full of misinformation, somewhat peripheral to our purpose, but crucially important to the future of fisheries and of the fishes themselves. Emerging analyses of fisheries economics and sociology-anthropology are being pursued and we can only encourage the reader to take our brief discussion as a beginning and to question objectively the points that we and others raise.

One might expect the conservation history of the area to consist of battles between special interest groups, and indeed, such has often been the case, especially between sporting anglers and commercial fishermen. Until recently, this has been most evident in Texas, where the tourist business is relatively large, commercial and sport-fishermen seek the same fishes, and sportfishermen have been well organized, politically astute, and well moneyed. Economic arguments have been used, but these vary widely— from sportfishing being seen as an order of magnitude greater than commercial fishing based on monies spent to near equal estimates for the two, and even to sportfishing adding very little actual value, being a luxury in which money spent is left over after the essentials and could be spent on anything.

In Texas, red drum and speckled trout were made game fishes in 1981 and gill netting for all species was banned in 1988, putting pressure on other species, especially black drum and flounder. An unprecedented constitutional amendment banned nets in Florida in 1994. Gill nets have just been outlawed in Louisiana, ironically at a time when most species seem especially common. For a century articles have been found in coastal Texas newspapers claiming that the commercial fishermen are ruining fishing, although there has been little evidence to support this claim. One study found only a local reduction in bays where net fishing was common compared to those where it was prohibited (Matlock et al., 1977). Also sport catches for most species in recent years usually have been much greater than the commercial take. The difficult question is showing what effect this has both on subsequent immediate fish catches and on later recruitment.

Therefore, in Texas the commercial fisherman has gradually been squeezed out in all but a few areas. In Louisiana the conflict was less pronounced, probably because of a lack of tourism, a more depressed economy, and the difficulty of access to coastal waters. As commercial fishing has become steadily more restricted, continental slope species—many not covered here—have come to be marketed increasingly. Also as the oil industry expanded in the early 1980s, sportfishing expanded proportionately, although it declined somewhat in the oil bust after 1985. Then came the blackened redfish craze, which involved fishing schools of mature redfish offshore with purse seines, a graphic image on television. Public concern, coupled with a three-decades-long scientific concern with fishing mortality and the perceived relationship between spawning stock and subsequent recruitment, resulted in many restrictions being established. (See Frank and Leggett, 1994, for a review of many fisheries questions. Ditton et al., 1992, give some information on Texas sport fishery management, and Fritchey, 1994, offers the viewpoint of the commercial fisherman. Hairston, 1989, reviews many pitfalls of ecological experiments and Peters, 1991, gives an overall critique of ecology, including fisheries problems.)

The greatest problem facing managers is separating natural fluctuations (as if no fishing mortality occurred) from those caused by the fishery. Species populations naturally wax and wane and up-to-date databases are short for Gulf fishes. More recent collections independent of fishery data and highly restricted sport catch databases are generally less than two decades old. While some biologists argue that population fluctuations are the product of overfishing, others consider these to reflect natural cycles. For example, low catches during the drought of the 1950s are contrasted with higher ones of the wetter early 1970s and 1990s. According to NMFS data, commercial shark catches increased in the latter part of the 1980s, while sport catches were trending down. Shark catches in the northern Gulf have decreased since 1989 (Russell, 1993). While there have been decreases in the take of bluefin tuna, a species considered in trouble by many biologists based also on small catches of larvae, yellowfin tuna catches increased in the 1980s (O'Connor, 1987; Southeast Fisheries Science Center, 1992). This latter report considered redfish overexploited based on the 1980s declining catches, but recent Louisiana data indicate that this is not true. White marlin and sailfish catches have declined since the 1970s, and while blue marlin were high in the 1980s, catches dropped in the latter part of the decade (Pristas and Avrigan, 1993).

Data recently published in Texas (Parks and Wildlife Management Series), suggest that there may be enhancement of stocks in wet years, while showing clear evidence for the effect of the freezes of 1983 and 1989, a phenomenon already shown by Gunter (1952a) and others. This is a general phenomenon with many unanswered questions about degree of effect with different species. Redfish seem to have been more common in the wetter years of the 1990s, showing patterns that may become clearer with additional data and interpretation. What may be the largest redfish year class ever occurred after Hurricane Beulah in 1967 (Matlock, 1987), which was particularly wet. Some biologists have suggested that changes in environmental factors may affect the young fish in the estuaries and may be the main factor regulating year-class strength. Water use in Texas rivers has been a problem for the estuaries, because of the evidence of its positive influence, often from floods, on fish production (Powell, 1977; Armstrong, 1979, 1982). Besides showing evidence of preferences of certain species for particular salinity regimes, these and other studies support the hypothesis of wet years enhancing fish production. However, the data do not explain all or even most variation, and this is a complex and little-understood subject.

Criticisms are emerging about preoccupation with spawning stock size, along the lines that such observers are confusing fish in their reproductive capacities with lions when they are actually like weeds. Most marine fishes produce such large quantities of spawn that even small changes in mortality of earlier life stages have profound effects on the larger sizes we see. Sharks and rays produce relatively few offspring and would be expected to be more like the mammal model. Even these, however, produce many more young than survive to reproduce.

The redfish craze stimulated better understanding of the life history of both red and black drum. Both produce millions of eggs per female in the Gulf, with larvae and then juveniles growing in the estuaries. Maturity comes in three to five years, and with it comes movement offshore to be incorporated into large schools, susceptible to capture by purse seines; these fish may live and reproduce for about two decades (Beckman et al., 1989, 1990). This is in contrast to the seatrouts, among other species, which mature rapidly and live shorter lives.

Commercial fishermen seeking food fishes in the area historically relied primarily on trotlines, beach seines, gill nets, trammel nets, and hooks and lines. Basically, the fishes of interest to sport anglers are the same, although a few species are not common to both fisheries. The main species sought inshore are trout, redfish, and flounder, while offshore the focus is on mackerel, the billfishes, red snapper, and menhaden. Probably more pinfish and hardhead catfish are caught by sportfishermen, but these do not usually find their way onto such lists. Offshore fisheries using trawls for croaker and purse nets for menhaden are usually not in conflict with sportfishermen, although a few of the favored sport fish are taken by both methods. Small fishes have increasingly become important as bait, especially killifishes, croakers, pinfish, and a few others. Previously mullet was the main fish bait species.

A number of species have been spawned successfully, providing for some hope of mariculture and other uses (see, for example, Arnold et al., 1988). Although a few red drum are commercially produced, there is uncertainty about the future of the industry. Texas has been extensively stocking that species, but it is not yet clear what effect this is having on populations.

Another potential problem has been concern about overfishing of menhaden. These fish occur in large schools, mostly on the western Louisiana and eastern Texas coasts. Used for oil and fish meal, they are caught by large vessels that send out small boats to lay purse nets around the tremendous schools that occur very close to the shore. Such a fishery is thought to be overexploited easily because of the small area involved, the schooling habits of the fish, and the ease with which schools can be observed from aircraft. We wrote in 1977 that the northern Gulf menhaden catch appeared to have peaked; however, the maxima did not occur until the mid-1980s and subsequently has increased again. As is true of most stocks, they are more resilient than has been predicted.

One management technique first used in Texas is the building of so-called artificial reefs to enhance fishing. These reefs are composed either of oyster shells placed in bays to form oyster reefs or of old car bodies, concrete blocks, pipes, or other structures, including World War II–vintage Liberty ships, to introduce hard substrates into an otherwise sandy or muddy environment. The theory is that these reefs somehow add to the numbers of catchable fishes. This may be due to increased surface area allowing attached invertebrate populations to concentrate the production of the rich surrounding waters. Some species such as speckled trout, redfish, and drum may congregate around artificial reefs inshore, and snapper, grouper, and a few other pelagic species, especially jacks, concentrate around these structures offshore, in places easily located by fishermen. Again there has been concern about overfishing of groupers and snappers because new technologies make them more vulnerable to capture. Solitary species such as jewfish, the behavior and biology of which suggest that they could be susceptible, are rarer, but snapper populations appear resilient and have increased in recent years. Huntsman (1992) brought up the debatable proposition that marine species may be endangered rather than merely overfished but also discusses the reasonable idea of marine reserves to ensure refugia for species that might have problems.

Both Texas and Louisiana have programs for using old petroleum platforms for this purpose. Some four thousand or more oil platforms built mostly off Louisiana since World War II provide a reef habitat, but one extending the whole height of the water column. Popular belief has it that some fishes were not present on the coast before these installations went in and that others have become much more common; however, with one possible exception—the tessellated blenny—it is certain that these species were in fact on the coast before the oil industry, although its installations have facilitated their dispersal across the shelf and have provided a hard substrate at the surface where none existed offshore before. There is some evidence that some schooling fishes may use such structures for orientation, while others more closely tied to structure gain food from attached organisms. Like a coral reef, an oil platform may concentrate nutrients and those animals that exploit it. While there are never as many kinds of fishes associated with these artificial structures as there are with natural reefs, the few species are often very abundant and thereby easy prey for fishermen.

Some habitats have received special protection or recognition. The Flower Garden Banks National Marine Sanctuary, and the Barataria-Terrebonne, Galveston, and Corpus Christi bays are included in the National Estuary Program.

In Texas an old problem has revolved around the so-called fish passes, or inlets to coastal lagoons. Because of well-developed barrier beaches and low river inflow, access between bay and Gulf has been difficult. During movements between these waters, fish must concentrate in the passageways, therefore packing the production of whole bay systems into small areas, an impressive sight and a phenomenon making these passes highly efficient places to harvest fish. Inlets in South Texas often fail, as did Fish Pass through Mustang Island, dredged in 1972 and closed by 1990. Nearby Packery Channel, opened in 1968 by hurricane Beulah, has closed since the 1972 dredging. Currently two artificial passes, Mansfield into the lower Laguna Madre, and Rollover into East Galveston Bay, have proven successful. A maintained ship channel into Matagorda Bay has stayed open, apparently at the expense of the natural channel.

It does not necessarily follow that creating more inlets (passes) means more fish. Certainly fishing is convenient and often better in the passes, but there is probably an optimum distance between inlets. The productive Laguna Madre has few inlets. Opening an inlet allows the intrusion of salt water with its fauna, and where the adjacent bay is low in salinity such an opening changes the fish fauna considerably. Such effects can be predicted by considering the general ecology of estuaries.

Another argument for the passes into the Laguna Madre has been that the inlets improve circulation, but that effect is slight. This history of creating inlets into the Upper Laguna Madre has been one of repetitive failure. One of the main reasons for building them has been to improve access to the Gulf by boats, since the natural unbroken stretch from Port Isabel to Port Aransas is a frustrating barrier to anyone attempting to move in a boat from the mainland to the Gulf. The early history of these inlets has been given by Gunter (1945b), Price (1952), and Hoese (1958b).

In Louisiana the problem has been the opposite: a more open and eroding coast, with much marsh converted to open water or tidal flats. Although some evidence exists that this is detrimental to fisheries production, other evidence does not support this, and many fisheries have been productive despite or because of the rapid changes that have occurred in the last two decades. Management of these low-salinity marshes has proceeded with the intent of enhancing the habitats of furbearers and waterfowl. Mostly this emphasis has meant blocking tidal creeks in brackish marshes with weirs to stabilize water levels and to cut down the intrusion of salt water (actually slightly brackish in most places) in large areas of marsh. The weirs, like the Texas passes, also tend to concentrate species, allowing the fishes to be collected easily, but it has been suggested this changes the concentrations of fishes reaching offshore areas. However, this effect is difficult to prove, because although weirs clearly impede migration, none are completely closed systems and they only semi-impound part of the coast producing these species. These marshes are burned in winter to favor tender, fast-growing plants as food for waterfowl and furbearers. The effects of such burning on fish are poorly known.

Another management technique, mitigation, is aimed at restoring or creating habitat to make up for that modified by development projects. In salt water most projects involve either intertidal marsh or subtidal grass beds. Both seem important as nurseries for many marine and estuarine fishes, although this conclusion may be colored by the large amount of recent research there. Sometimes plantings are made, but many such areas vegetate naturally if conditions (mainly relation to tide and protection from erosion) are suitable. Some success has been had, although many projects have been constructed in difficult places. Mitigation areas may not be as productive as natural areas, but many will evolve according to local conditions, mainly current, wind action, and local topography (Grove and Wilson, 1994).

Probably the greatest damage done to fisheries is the expansion into coast zones by real estate, industrial, oil, and agricultural interests. Shallow water, often with plant cover or interspersed with marshes, serves as a nursery ground for many fishes, and when it is removed, deepened, or built into, part of the potential of the coast to produce fish is destroyed. With predicted human population pressures, it seems likely that even with the best of management and protection, the capacity of the coast to produce fish will be reduced. This seems to have been the trend since civilization visited the coast, although this trend is not supported by much hard scientific data. Many species, mullet and menhaden among them, exploit to an unknown degree degraded habitats, such as ship channels, which clearly discriminate against other species. Even the most severely degraded habitat, the Houston Ship Channel—with no measurable dissolved oxygen in the 1950s—has shown signs of improvement (Guillen et al., 1994). Fish are now common there although they still shown a high percentage of anomalies, such as tumors, often a sign of environmental degradation (Sindermann, 1979; Smith and Guillen, 1994). Hypoxia (low oxygen) has typically occurred where excess nutrients, calm conditions allowing stratification, and high temperatures aid oxygen depletion (Renaud, 1986). Fish generally avoid such areas, but sometimes are trapped, as in blind canals, and extensive mortality may occur. In the Gulf, hypoxic zones form over large areas of the inshore continental shelf off Louisiana, especially after heavy Mississippi River floods. Some areas have also been found off Texas (Harper et al., 1981). The effect on future fish populations is unclear. Areas lost in production may be compensated for, at least somewhat, by large amounts of nutrients stimulating production. Although these so-called dead zones occurred historically, some speculation suggests that increased use of fertilizers has exacerbated the condition (Turner and Rabalais, 1991). The subject of toxicology is too vast to consider here, but some information may be found in Boesch and Rabalais (1987), Ward et al. (1979), and several toxicology books. Most work, however, has been on organisms other than fish.

In Louisiana, diversion projects from the Mississippi River are now attempting to mimic the historic wide distribution of fresh water, sediment, and nutrients present before the construction of levees, which were finalized after the great flood of 1927. Several projects now introduce Mississippi River water to adjacent watersheds, and more are planned. One that is controversial as this is written involves moving water at Bonnet Carré, a historic crevasse where water often moved into Lake Pontchartrain. The benefits seem to be increased production with added nutrients and other side effects in changing water quality, principally salinity but also turbidity. Some species, chiefly the clear-water, high-salinity types, are immediately discriminated against, although they may indirectly benefit from overall increased production.

Another effect presumed to be detrimental is bycatch, the original concern having been about sea turtles. An early paper by Gunter (1936) reflected this in its title. Although some unwanted catch occurs in all fisheries, the largest kill may be fish discarded from shrimp trawls. Again it is difficult to determine what the effects are beyond the obvious immediate mortality. Sediment is put into suspension, with nutrients, and in extreme cases clear bays are turned muddy. Standing crops of fishes may be reduced, but the amount of regeneration from release of nutrients into the near continual flood of new larvae from the Gulf is uncertain. Studies on menhaden caught by shrimping found no evidence of effect on commercial harvest, but croaker biomass may have decreased, perhaps due both to bycatch and to natural cycles. Bottom trawl catches were high in the wet years of the 1970s, decreasing since. However, data presented by Perret et al. (1993) do not support the hypothesis that shrimp trawling harms the fishes commonly caught. For whatever reason, most species seem to have increased. It will be interesting to see what happens from the effects of the wet years of the 1990s.

Seagulls and possibly other species may benefit from bycatch. Most inshore bycatch is composed of anchovies, menhaden, croaker, and sand trout, the last two being the species of which juveniles make up the largest concentration of open-bay bottom fishes. Juveniles of redfish, speckled trout, flounder, and black drum mostly occur in water too shallow to trawl, but larger juveniles may be taken in trawls, and the smaller fish are susceptible to capture in push nets used in grass beds to catch bait shrimp. Small red snapper are taken in Gulf shrimp trawls, which has caused concern, again for the quantity of spawning stocks. Whether large catches are simply the result of large year classes or actually cut subsequent recruitment of future year classes is a difficult question to answer. One study found no effect on fish from the three-month shrimp fishery closure and another found no difference in species composition between the 1940s and the 1970s. The central question would seem to be if removing the bycatch has significant effects, what is the effect of removing the shrimp, but not the bycatch? (See Adkins, 1993; Bryan et al., 1982; Guillory and Hutton, 1982; Guillory et al., 1985; Hoar et al., 1992; Watts and Pellegrin, 1982.)

Fortunately, because of their wide distribution, marine fishes have little potential for extinction (see Shipp, 1991, for one of the few discussions), but Gulf states and the federal government have listed a few marine species as threatened or in some category of special concern. One species so considered in Louisiana and Florida, the saltmarsh topminnow (*Fundulus jenkinsi*)—actually a more brackish-water than a marine species—has always been rare and hard to catch. Its rarity may be more a matter of our lack of skill than of its endangerment, since its habitat is mostly intact, and individuals are still caught from time to time. Rare species may not be any closer to extinction by virtue of their rarity than are the more common species, or they may indeed be on that road regardless of outside influence. However, limited distribution and small populations, which few marine species exhibit, might make them more susceptible to habitat degradation. Texas currently lists two estuarine species (opossum pipefish and river goby) as threatened and one (blackfin goby) as endangered. The two gobies are probably at the northern limit of their range on the Texas coast but might have been more common before extensive water use for irrigation. All three species are newly known within the state and may not be normal residents. Lists developed by other Gulf states and agencies contain only sturgeon for the northern Gulf, but some include a variety of species, including offshore groupers. One of the problems with the endangered species concept is the lack of separation of species that are normally rare from those that have been made rare by human activities.

Of course there are numerous other problems, such as how to place comparative values on various fisheries. This is further complicated by consideration of environments which are only aesthetically pleasing, and by lack of consideration of the possibility that due to excessive population (fishing) pressures, many problems are unsolvable from a biological standpoint, although it might be argued that the ultimate question is how many fish there are.

History of Ichthyological Research

Perhaps the earliest mention of fishes of the northwestern Gulf of Mexico that has come down to us is found in Joutel's journal of La Salle's last voyage (Joutel, 1714), noting the occurrence of gar, eels, mullet, herring (menhaden), flounder, seatrout, redfish, and "dorado" or gilt-head. La Salle's men caught these fish in nets, by gigging for flounder, and by picking up dead trout following a severe freeze in January, 1685, probably the first report of fish mortality due to cold on the Texas coast (see Gunter, 1952a, for a discussion of these freezes; regarding major ones since then, in 1962, 1983, and 1989, see Ecology section). Du Pratz (1774), perhaps based on Joutel's experience, included information about fishes from Louisiana. An early account of Mayan fishes was analyzed in the interesting paper by Baughman (1952).

While there was some early scientific work concerning the marine fishes of Texas in the nineteenth century, research and exploration in Louisiana lagged far behind that in the other coastal states, even nearby Florida. The visitor to Texas might die of thirst, but in Louisiana one would more likely be nearly eaten alive by insects or lost in the maze of marshes; these difficulties may explain the lack of historical fish collections in that state.

The United States–Mexican Boundary survey (Baird and Girard, 1854; Girard, 1858, 1859) collected forty-nine species of fishes from Brazos Santiago, the Rio Grande River mouth, Saint Joseph's Island (San Jose Island), Indianola, and Galveston. No further collections were reported until Jordan and Gilbert (1883) collected fifty-one species from Galveston, including snook, which is now rarely collected that far north. Meanwhile, Goode (1879) had described the Gulf menhaden, *Brevoortia patronus*, as a species distinct from the Atlantic menhaden, *B. tyrannus*.

The first extensive coastal collecting was done in late 1891 at Galveston and Corpus Christi by Evermann and Kendall (1894). These early collections consisted almost entirely of inshore fishes, although an active red snapper fishery added at least two offshore species. An interesting sidelight that occurred about that time was the introduction of salmon into Texas, and even a few into Louisiana (Baird, 1884). As could have been predicted, and no doubt was, those fish have not been seen since. The survival beyond a few months of red drum stocked in Texas, the first marine fish stocked since the salmon, is still uncertain, despite this drum being a native species.

The twentieth century brought little in the way of new fish investigations, although attention began to be paid to oysters and shrimp. The first marine laboratory on the northwestern Gulf was established in Cameron, Louisiana, in 1902. While it did collect fish, little information survived and local collections were confused with those from the Chandeleurs (Weymouth, 1910). The lab remained open for less than a decade but led to the establishment of the state coastal effort now under the Louisiana Wildlife and Fisheries Commission. A major contribution early in this century was a master's thesis from Tulane University (Raymond, 1905) which listed 117 species of fishes, mostly marine, from Louisiana and included most of the larger, most common inshore species as well as some offshore species and several rarely reported since. The last group included snook, *Centropomus undecimalis,* as a commercial species; red porgy, *Pagrus pagrus;* croaker, *Micropogon[ias] furnierei* (= *undulatus?*); tilefish, *Caulolatilus microps;* and luminous hake, *Steindachneria argentea.* Raymond also apparently has the only Louisiana record of the spottail pinfish, *Diplodus holbrooki,* although this may have come from the French Market in New Orleans and been caught to the east where it is common.

In 1917 the U.S. Bureau of Fisheries research vessel *Grampus* made several collections off the Texas coast, which provided material for descriptions of new species by Nichols and Breder (1922, 1924). Somewhat later, federally initiated studies both in Texas (Pearson, 1929) and in Louisiana (Gunter, 1938a) began emphasizing life histories and ecology instead of just the taxonomy of local fish species. Fowler (1933) reported on a small collection from Breton Island and Calcasieu Lake, one record being the unlikely report of dogfish *(Mustelus)* from the Calcasieu River. The only sharks known with certainty from these low-salinity waters are bull sharks.

During the 1930s two popular works on Texas and Louisiana fishes appeared (Burr, 1932; Gowanloch, 1933), the latter partly based on an earlier popular account of Louisiana fishes (Anonymous, 1917), as did the first of many papers by Gordon Gunter (1935) and Isaac Ginsburg (1931) on fishes of this area. Gunter and Ginsburg had the greatest influence on the first half-century of northern Gulf ichthyology.

Just before World War II, contributions to marine biology of Texas waters were made by Cross and Parks (1937) and Reed (1941). Their papers as well as an additional list by Woods (1942) included several species of marine fish that have only recently been rediscovered in the northwestern Gulf and others that have not been collected since or have become scarce. It is worth noting that many of these earlier records, which for years were considered doubtful, have now been reverified. Therefore, we should not automatically disregard these earlier works simply because some species are no longer found in this area.

After World War II, expansion of marine research was rapid, and especially so since our first edition appeared in 1977. References are too numerous to cite here but many are given in the bibliography and throughout the text. Before the war the Texas Game, Fish and Oyster Commission (now the Texas Parks and Wildlife Department) established a laboratory at Rockport, where the present facility was completed in 1948, and the University of Texas set up one in a similar time frame at Port Aransas. A lab at Grande Isle was maintained by Louisiana State University in summer from the late 1920s to the early 1950s, and the school has built the largest Louisiana staff studying fishes. Texas A&M conducted studies on the effect of oil on marine communities, mostly oysters, in the same locale through the 1950s. In the early 1950s Tulane University completed a biological survey of Lake Pontchartrain. Since that time Tulane has built the largest collection of fishes in the South, including many marine fishes. Also in the early 1950s, Texas A&M expanded its interest in the ocean, leading to an oceanographic fleet and marine laboratory at Galveston. In the late 1950s the University of Southwestern Louisiana built a fisheries field station on Vermilion Bay and began studies, and the Louisiana Wildlife and Fisheries Commission built a laboratory on Grand Terre Island. Nicholls State University began coastal studies in the mid-1960s (mostly on pond culture), and about 1967 the National Sea Grant Program funded studies aimed at the expansion of fisheries production. In the early 1970s Nicholls State built a field station at Fourchon near the mouth of Bayou LaFourche, and Pan American University (today known as the University of Texas–Pan American) established a similar structure on southern Padre Island. In 1980 the Louisiana Universities Marine Consortium (LUMCON) was formed, and the group developed a marine laboratory at Cocodrie and absorbed the facilities at Fourchon and Vermilion Bay. Today, Texas has a widespread state system, with a marine laboratory at Rockport, facilities on all major estuaries, a continental shelf research vessel, and two university-staffed marine laboratories with research vessels at Port Aransas and Galveston. Louisiana also has a state system of laboratories and vessels on most of its major estuarine systems.

The Gulf Coast Research Laboratory in Ocean Springs, Mississippi, has been conducting studies in Mississippi Sound and adjacent Gulf waters, maintains a large collection of marine fishes, and publishes Gulf Research Reports. The Alabama Marine Resources Laboratory has since the early 1960s been investigating coastal fisheries together with the laboratory established later on Dauphin Island and run by a consortium of Alabama universities. In western Florida, the laboratory of the Florida Department of Environmental Protection (formerly the State Board of Conservation) at Saint Petersburg operates inshore and offshore research vessels. The University of Florida operates a field station on Cedar Key, and Florida State University has a research facility and vessels at Turkey Point south of Tallahassee.

Although most of its efforts were dedicated toward shrimp research, and more recently habitats, the National Marine Fisheries Service Laboratory in Galveston has conducted some fish research. Similarly, the Environmental Protection Agency Laboratory at Gulf Breeze and the Marine Public Health Service Laboratory on Dauphin Island produce some information of value to the study of fish. The NMFS Laboratory in Pascagoula serves as a base for the research vessel *Oregon II*, which has ongoing programs studying commercial fishes of the northern Gulf. Similarly, the former Sports Fisheries Laboratory of the U.S. Fish and Wildlife Service at Panama City is now part of the National Marine Fisheries Service and that at Port Aransas is now part of the University of Texas Marine Science Institute, a body principally devoted to the study of reproduction in marine fishes. These are the main organizations, not including research foundations and consulting firms, currently conducting marine research. Students, fishermen, and other interested parties who need help with identification or need other information—and who themselves contribute to our knowledge—should find assistance at these places, and certainly many people at additional inland and smaller coastal universities are knowledgeable about marine fishes.

The literature on Gulf fishes has greatly expanded in the last two decades. Much of it can be found in the journal *Copeia,* the *Transactions of the American Fisheries Society,* local academy of science publications, and in many new national and international journals. Unfortunately *Contributions in Marine Science* (formerly *Publications of the Institute of Marine Science of the University of Texas*) ceased regular publication, but *Gulf of Mexico Science* (formerly *Northeast Gulf Science,* started in 1977) took its place in 1996.

Identifying Fishes

Fish come in a bewildering variety of shapes, forms, and sizes. The basic form of a fish requires little explanation, but for those unfamiliar with many of the terms used to describe fish, a glossary is included at the back of this book, along with drawings of some structures important in identification (figs. 7–12).

Three means of identifying fishes are provided here: the plates, the species accounts, and the keys. The plates are the simplest of the three means to use. We have attempted to obtain photographs of all species, showing the characteristics necessary for identification. Failing that, a drawing is included for species we were not able to photograph. While we attempted to photograph live or fresh fish, we sometimes had to settle for older preserved specimens. It should be remembered when consulting the figures that many fish are seen damaged and with faded colors and therefore may not be in the same condition as those in our photographs. Also, many fishes exhibit the ability to change their pigmentation, and natural variations in coloration may occur within a population and across a geographic area. Fish caught from clear water are usually lighter than those from more turbid areas. We have not illustrated continental slope or oceanic fishes that are less likely to occur on the shelf, although they may be included in the keys or descriptions. At this stage of exploration no book, however accurate otherwise, can be complete.

Often an unknown fish can be identified by comparing it with the illustrations of the types of fishes that are known and by deciding which of the known types most closely resembles the unknown one. At this point, not only the plates but also the species accounts or descriptions should be consulted. In some cases when several species closely resemble one another, we have included only a single plate, but the different forms are described in the text.

While we have tried to use the same general format for all species accounts, there are times when we have diverged from this format. Not all fishes have the same characteristics, so to save time and space we have chosen to abridge or alter the basic format whenever certain characteristics seemed to us inapplicable or unimportant. Full descriptions of most species are available in the literature cited.

The basic format for species accounts includes the common name of the species, its scientific name, and the name of the person or persons who first described it. Next follows a series of meristic counts (numbers of spines, rays, scales, and gill rakers), presented using standard abbreviations and terminology. Roman numerals refer to numbers of hard spines and Arabic numerals to numbers of soft rays. The last two soft rays are often joined at their bases and are counted as one. Commas indicate connections between spinous and soft-rayed parts of a fin, while a plus sign between the numbers indicates that the fins are separate. Abbreviations used are the following:

D. = dorsal fin,

A. = anal fin,

P. = pectoral fin,

Sc. = pored lateral line scales or the number of lateral scale rows in species that lack a complete lateral line (an obvious tube running along the side of most fishes; see glossary),

Gr. – gill rakers on the first (anteriormost) arch.

Unless otherwise noted, the total number of gill rakers on the first arch is given. The phrase "on lower limb" indicates that only the gill rakers on the lower limb (below the angle) of the gill arch are counted. A formula like "3 + 14" indicates that upper and lower limb gill rakers are given separately as the two numbers in the formula. Small knoblike rudiments at either end of the gill rakers are not counted. Various lengths, such as head length and standard length, are often useful in identifying fishes (see glossary). In any meristic count, a number in parentheses following a range of numbers indicates the most commonly encountered number in that range.

Following the meristic counts may be a description of the form and coloration of the fish, any other general information, and the species' geographic range. Regardless of what other species are discussed, the range given is only for the species first described unless otherwise specifically stated. Time and space do not permit us to include much information on food habits, life history, or ecology, for which the reader is referred to sources listed with the species. Finally, in parentheses, we have given the approximate maximum length the species is expected to attain in our area.

Two precautions are in order at this point. First, the maximum range says little about the density of a species within its range. Leim and Scott (1966) have listed several tropical species that occur as far north as Nova Scotia and Labrador. Because of the Gulf Stream it may be partly a matter of chance whether the northward limit for a species is North Carolina, Massachusetts, Nova Scotia, or Labrador. Where a species ranges through the Bahamian–West Indian–Caribbean tropical region, we have simply added "through the Caribbean" to the range. The Caribbean islands are more or less continuous with the Bahamas and share a similar fish fauna. Where the range extends north and south of the Gulf of Mexico, the range inside the Gulf is assumed to be over the entire Gulf unless otherwise qualified. In the western Atlantic many species range repetitiously "from Massachusetts to Brazil" because the warm Gulf Stream and Brazilian currents carry most species that far toward the poles, especially during the summer. Resident populations within this range are another matter, and these must be determined from the original works cited. Even within the range of resident, reproducing populations, species may be absent from long stretches of shoreline because of lack of proper habitats.

Second, the maximum sizes given are meant as rough guides to total length. Remember that fishes mature at smaller sizes, and they may never be seen at the given sizes. These sizes should tell the reader whether a fish is a giant or a midget. For exact sizes, scientific publications or the less precise fishing records published annually by most state conservation agencies and gamefishing organizations should be consulted.

Although the metric system is becoming more of a reality in the United States, we have retained the familiar English measurements, giving metric equivalents for most. Because of differences between the two systems, the equivalents are not precise, and we have rounded off the metric measurements. For reference, there are 25.4 millimeters (mm) or 2.54 centimeters (cm) to the inch and 3 feet, 3.4 inches in a meter (m); there are about 454 grams (g) in a pound and 2.2 pounds in a kilogram (kg).

The third means of identification is found in the keys. A key is a concise, systematic means for identifying an organism by comparing its features with a pair of statements and by following the directions given with the choice that best describes the animal.

An example of a key that could be used to identify vehicles familiar to everyone follows:

1	Propelled by internal combustion engine	(go to) 2
	Propelled by muscular effort of the rider	(go to) 3
2	Vehicle with two wheels	motorcycle
	Vehicle with four wheels	automobile
3	Vehicle with three wheels	tricycle
	Vehicle with two wheels	bicycle

Rather obviously, this key is good only for identifying motorcycles, automobiles, tricycles, and bicycles. A unicycle, a steam-powered locomotive, or a military tank could not be identified or would be incorrectly identified. Common sense and experience are the most useful aids for identifying any unknown fish. We hope this book can help readers gain that experience through careful use of the keys, descriptions, and illustrations.

Scientific and Common Names of Fishes

We have used both scientific (Latin) and common names following the American Fisheries Society's "List of Common and Scientific Names of Fishes from the United States and Canada" (Robins et al., 1991). While standardization of common names is valuable, and although we have given the AFS common names first in the species accounts, many of the AFS names are not in routine use among the people who encounter the fish, especially in our area of coverage. When local usage has provided a fish with another frequently used name, we give that local name after the AFS name. The names in parentheses are interesting and may be commonly used in Florida or on the Atlantic coast, but not in our region. For example, redfish is the name locally used more often, instead of red drum or channel bass; and speckled trout, instead of spotted trout or the less frequent names spotted weakfish or spotted squeteague. Some AFS common names are simply not realistic for this area, being seldom heard outside museums and ichthyology labs; however, the 1991 edition of the AFS list pays closer attention to local usage than did previous editions.

Scientific names usually agree with the AFS list or with a more recent revision of the group if such exists. Scientific (or Linnaean) names are intended to provide scientists around the world with a single name for every species of organism, while local or common names vary tremendously. (Consider again the cases of the redfish and the speckled trout, or the overly general names like perch, minnow, and sand shark.) Scientific names also reflect the degrees by which different species are related. Closely related species are placed in the same genus and share a generic or "first" name: the speckled trout is *Cynoscion nebulosus,* the sand trout is *Cynoscion arenarius.* More distantly but still closely related species are placed in the same family. Trout, redfish, croaker, drum, and whiting are all in different genera but within the same family, the Sciaenidae.

The way in which a species receives its proper scientific name is governed by a complex set of rules. Sometimes scientists decide that a certain species belongs in a different genus, that two forms formerly considered separate species are really identical and should have the same name, or that one variable species actually consists of two or more different forms, which require distinct names. In any case, scientific names can and do change, often more frequently than common names. Such changes can be very confusing to the layman, and even to the scientist, as it is often difficult to keep up with the latest changes in the literature.

Recognized but still unnamed species are treated in the text by listing "sp." after the proper genus. These are in the process of being formally described.

In appendix 6 we have listed some French names used in the Cajun culture in Louisiana and East Texas. This is not a complete list, but even French-speaking fishermen use English names for many marine fishes. Some names (for example, *truite, plie, requin*) are derived from European French, but others *(poisson arme, crapaud mer)* are original. Wherever we could decipher the word's meaning, we spelled the name in correct French. The list takes no account of changes in pronunciation, which varies along the coast. A few of the names had to be spelled phonetically, pending understanding of the words. A few Spanish common names in use in Mexico and less commonly in Texas are listed in appendix 7.

Plates for Identifying Fishes

1. Nurse shark

3. Sand tiger; sand shark

2. Whale shark

4. Common thresher

5a. Great white shark, adult

5b. Great white shark, juvenile

6. Shortfin mako

7. Tiger shark

8. Lemon shark

9. Finetooth shark; blueback shark

10. Atlantic sharpnose shark

11. Smalltail shark

12. Silky shark

13. Sandbar shark; brown shark

14. Dusky shark; sand shark

15. Bull shark

16. Blacknose shark

17. Spinner shark

18. Blacktip shark

19. Bonnethead; bonnetnose

21. Scalloped hammerhead

22. Florida smoothhound

23. Smooth dogfish

25. Atlantic angel shark

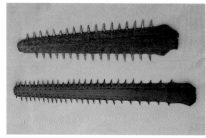

26-27. Sawfish saws: largetooth (above), smalltooth (below)

27. Smalltooth sawfish

28. Atlantic guitarfish

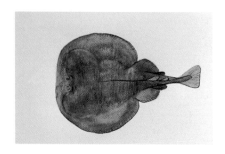

29. Atlantic torpedo

30. Lesser electric ray

31. Spreadfin skate

32. Rosette skate

33. Clearnose skate

34. Roundel skate

35. Yellow stingray

36. Atlantic stingray; stingaree

37. Bluntnose stingray

38. Roughtail stingray

39. Southern stingray

40. Smooth butterfly ray

41. Cownose ray

42. Spotted eagle ray; duck-billed ray

43. Bullnose ray

44. Manta; devil ray

46. Atlantic sturgeon

47. Longnose gar

48. Alligator gar

49. Spotted gar

50. Tarpon

51. Ladyfish; tenpounder; skipjack

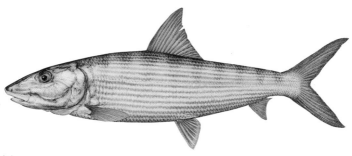

52. Bonefish

53. American eel; congo

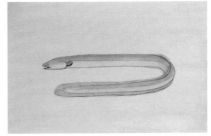

54. Ridged eel

55. Blacktail moray

56. Blackedge moray

57. Honeycomb moray

58. Purplemouth moray

59. Spotted moray

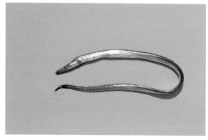

60. Freckled pike-conger, silver conger

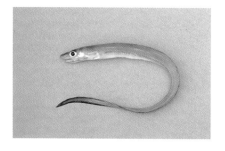

61. Yellow conger

62. Margintail conger

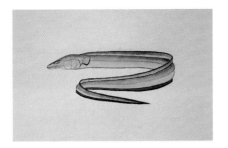

63. Threadtail conger

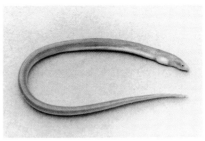

64. Speckled worm eel; white eel

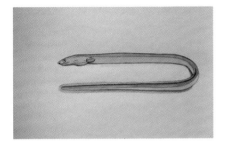

65. Key worm eel

66a. Shrimp eel

66b. Palespotted eel

67. King snake eel

68. Stippled spoon-nose eel

69. Sooty eel

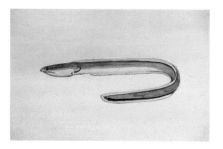

70. Shortbelly eel

71. Round herring

72. Dwarf herring

73. Atlantic thread herring; hairyback

74. Spanish sardine

75. Scaled sardine

76. Alabama shad

77. Skipjack herring

78. Gulf menhaden

79. Finescale menhaden

81. Threadfin shad

82. Gizzard shad

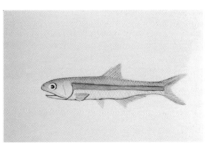

84. Bay anchovy

85. Cuban anchovy

86. Striped anchovy

87. Dusky anchovy

88. Snakefish   89. Inshore lizardfish

90. Red lizardfish; rockspear   91. Sand diver

92. Offshore lizardfish   93. Largescale lizardfish

94. Smallscale lizardfish   95. Blue catfish

96. Hardhead catfish; tourist trout; TR

97. Gafftopsail catfish; gafftop

98. Atlantic midshipman

99. Leopard toadfish

100. Gulf toadfish; oyster dog

101. Sargassumfish

102. Striated frogfish

103. Singlespot frogfish

104. Longlure frogfish

105. Slantbrow batfish

106. Spotted batfish

107. Pancake batfish

109. Antenna codlet

110. Luminous hake

111. Gulf hake

112. Spotted hake

113. Southern hake

114. Blackedge cusk-eel

115. Mottled cusk-eel

116. Bank cusk-eel

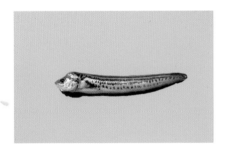

117. Crested cusk-eel

118. Blotched cusk-eel

119. Bearded brotula

121. Gold brotula

122. Pearlfish

123. Mountain mullet; freshwater mullet

124. White mullet

125. Striped mullet

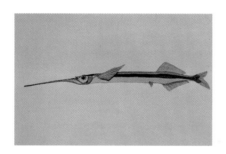

127. Flying halfbeak

128. American halfbeak

129. Ballyhoo

131. Smallwing flyingfish

132. Sailfin flyingfish

133. Oceanic two-wing flyingfish

134. Blackwing flyingfish

135. Bluntnose flyingfish

136. Margined flyingfish

137. Spotfin flyingfish

139. Keeltail needlefish

138. Atlantic flyingfish

140. Atlantic needlefish; needlegar; saltwater gar

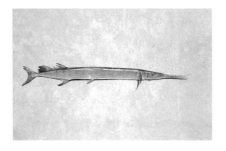

141. Flat needlefish

142. Houndfish

143a. Striped killifish

143b. Longnose killifish

144. Saltmarsh topminnow

145a. Gulf killifish, male

145b. Gulf killifish, female

146a. Bayou killifish, male

146b. Bayou killifish, female

147. Diamond killifish

148. Rainwater killifish

149a. Sheepshead minnow, male

149b. Sheepshead minnow, female

150a. Sailfin molly, male

150b. Sailfin molly, female

151. Mosquitofish

152. Least killifish

153. Rough silverside

155. Inland silverside

156. Tidewater silverside

158. Longspine squirrelfish

157. Longjaw squirrelfish

159. Squirrelfish

160. Dusky squirrelfish

162. Blackbar soldierfish

164. Trumpetfish

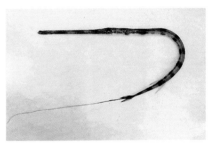

165. Bluespotted cornetfish

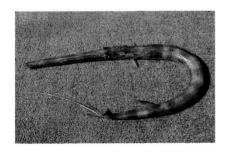

166. Red cornetfish

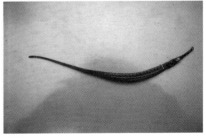

167. Opossum pipefish

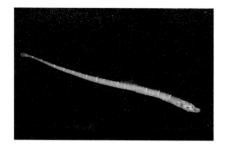

168. Fringed pipefish

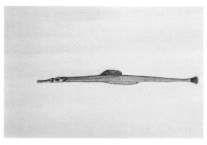

169. Texas pipefish

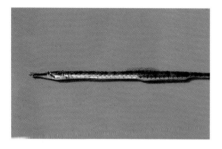

170a. Gulf pipefish, male

170b. Gulf pipefish, female

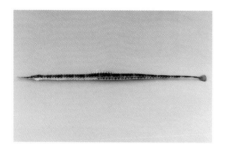

171. Chain pipefish

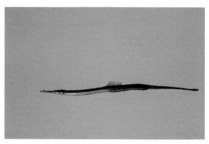

172. Dusky pipefish

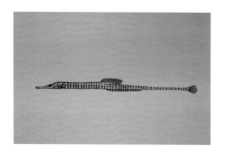

173. Sargassum pipefish

174. Dwarf seahorse

177. Common snook; robalo; saltwater pike

175. Lined seahorse

179. Striped bass

181. Yellowtail bass

182. Spanish flag

183. Creole fish

185. Wrasse bass

188. Longtail bass

190a. Yellowtail hamlet

190b. Butter hamlet

190c. Barred hamlet

191. Sand perch

192. Dwarf sand perch

193. Blackear bass

194. Belted sandfish; belted sand bass

196. Tattler

197. Pygmy sea bass

198. Gulf black sea bass

199. Rock sea bass

201. Graysby

200. Bank sea bass; rock squirrel

202. Coney

203. Warsaw grouper; black jewfish

204. Yellowedge grouper

205. Snowy grouper

206. Marbled grouper

207. Jewfish; spotted jewfish

208. Speckled hind; calico grouper

209. Red grouper

210. Rock hind; calico grouper

211. Red hind; strawberry grouper

212. Nassau grouper

213. Comb grouper

214. Gag

216a. Scamp, light phase

216b. Scamp, dark phase

217. Tiger grouper

218. Yellowfin grouper

219. Black grouper

220. Whitespotted soapfish

222. Greater soapfish

223. Bigeye

224. Short bigeye

225. Swordtail jawfish

226. Spotfin jawfish

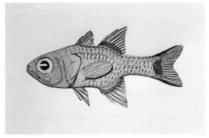

227. Freckled cardinalfish

229. Bridle cardinalfish

231. Flamefish

232. Twospot cardinalfish

233. Sand tilefish

234. Tilefish

236. Blackline tilefish

238. Anchor tilefish

239. Bluefish

240a. Cobia; ling, adult

240b. Cobia; ling, juvenile

242. Sharksucker

243. Remora

244. Whalesucker

246. Spearfish remora

247. Marlinsucker

248. Leatherjack; leatherjacket

249. Rainbow runner

250. Florida pompano

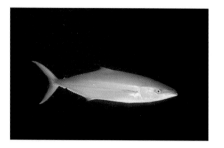

251a. Permit, adult

251b. Permit, juvenile

252. Palometa; longfinned pompano

253. Almaco jack

254. Lesser amberjack

255. Greater amberjack

256. Banded rudderfish   257. African pompano

258. Atlantic moonfish   259b. Lookdown, juvenile

259a. Lookdown, adult

260. Rough scad

261a. Round scad; cigarfish

261b. Mackerel scad

262. Bigeye scad

263. Atlantic bumper

264a. Bluntnose jack, adult

264b. Bluntnose jack, juvenile

265. Cottonmouth jack

266. Bar jack

267. Yellow jack

268. Blue runner

269. Black jack

270. Crevalle; common jack

271. Horse-eye jack

272. Dolphin; mahi-mahi

273. Pompano dolphin; blue dolphin

274. Vermilion snapper; bastard snapper; B-liner

275. Queen snapper; ball bat

276. Wenchman

278. Yellowtail snapper

279. Lane snapper; candy snapper

281a. Red snapper, adult

281b. Red snapper, juvenile

282. Cubera snapper

283. Mutton snapper

284. Gray snapper; black snapper; mangrove snapper

285. Schoolmaster

286. Dog snapper

288. Tripletail

289. Yellowfin mojarra

290. Mottled mojarra

291. Irish pompano

292. Spotfin mojarra

293. Silver jenny

294. Flagfin mojarra

295. Tomtate

296. Striped grunt

297. Cottonwick

298. Sailor's choice

299. White grunt

300. Spanish grunt

301. Barred grunt

302. Pigfish

303. Burro grunt

304. Porkfish

305. Black margate

306. Longspine porgy

307. Spottail pinfish

308. Pinfish; pin perch

309. Sheepshead

310. Red porgy; silver snapper; white snapper

311a. Littlehead porgy

311b. Sheepshead porgy

313. Campeche porgy

314. Whitebone porgy

316. Knobbed porgy

315. Jolthead porgy

317. Grass porgy

318. Atlantic threadfin; eight-fingered threadfin

319. Sand drum

320. Northern kingfish; king whiting

321. Southern kingfish; sea mullet

322. Gulf kingfish; Gulf whiting

323. Black drum

324. Atlantic croaker

325. Reef croaker

326. Spotted seatrout; speckled trout

327. Sand seatrout; sand trout; white trout

328. Silver seatrout

329. Red drum; redfish

330. Spot; flat croaker

331. Star drum

332. Banded drum; banded croaker

333. Silver perch

334. Cubbyu

335. Blackbar drum

337a. Spotted drum, adult

336. Jackknife fish

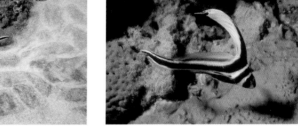

337b. Spotted drum, juvenile

338. Dwarf goatfish

339. Red goatfish

340. Yellow goatfish

341. Spotted goatfish

342. Bermuda chub

343. Yellow chub

347. Foureye butterflyfish

344. Redspotted hawkfish

346. Spotfin butterflyfish

348. Banded butterflyfish

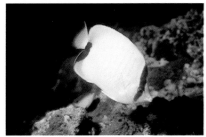

350. Reef butterflyfish

351. Cherubfish

352. Rock beauty

353. Queen angelfish

354. Blue angelfish

355a. French angelfish, adult

355b. French angelfish, juvenile

356. Gray angelfish

357. Yellowtail damselfish

358. Bicolor damselfish

359a. Threespot damselfish; yellow damselfish, adult

359b. Threespot damselfish; yellow damselfish, juvenile

360a. Cocoa damselfish, adult

360b. Cocoa damselfish, juvenile

362. Sergeant major

361. Dusky damselfish

363. Night sergeant

364. Blue chromis

365. Brown chromis

366. Purple reeffish

367. Yellowtail reeffish

368. Sunshinefish

369. Hogfish

370. Creole wrasse

371. Red hogfish

372. Spotfin hogfish

374. Pearly razorfish

373. Spanish hogfish

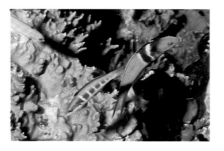

375. Bluehead

376. Puddingwife

377. Painted wrasse

378. Slippery dick

379. Yellowhead wrasse

380a. Queen parrotfish, male

380b. Queen parrotfish, female

381. Princess parrotfish, female above, male below

382. Bucktooth parrotfish

383a. Redband parrotfish, male

383b. Redband parrotfish, female

383c. Redband parrotfish, juvenile

384a. Stoplight parrotfish, male

384b. Stoplight parrotfish, female

385. Emerald parrotfish

386. Southern stargazer

387a. Lancer stargazer

387b. Freckled stargazer

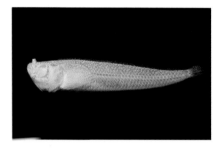
388. Speckled stargazer

392. Hairy blenny

393. Molly miller

394. Seaweed blenny

395. Redlip blenny

396. Striped blenny

397. Florida blenny

398. Crested blenny

400. Feather blenny

401. Freckled blenny

402. Tessellated blenny

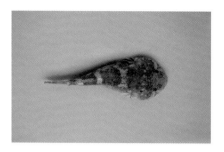

403. Skilletfish

404. Fat sleeper

405. Bigmouth sleeper

406. Emerald sleeper

407. Spinycheek sleeper

408. Blue goby

409. Spotted goby

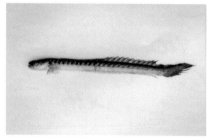

410. Violet goby

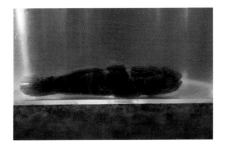

411. Frillfin goby

413. Twoscale goby

412. Neon goby

414. Code goby

415. Naked goby

416. Clown goby

417. Green goby

418. Ragged goby

419. Lyre goby

420. Highfin goby

421. Freshwater goby

422. Darter goby

424. Pink wormfish

426a. Atlantic spadefish; angelfish, adult

426b. Atlantic spadefish; angelfish, juvenile

427a. Blue tang, adult

427b. Blue tang, juvenile

428. Doctorfish

429. Ocean surgeon

430. Northern sennet

431. Guaguanche

432. Great barracuda

433a. Atlantic cutlassfish; ribbonfish, adult

433b. Atlantic cutlassfish; ribbonfish, close-up   434. Escolar

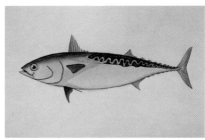

435. Chub mackerel   436. Frigate mackerel; frigate tuna

437. Bullet mackerel   438. Wahoo

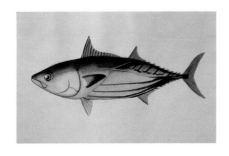

439. Skipjack tuna   440. Little tuna; bonito

441. Bluefin tuna

442. Blackfin tuna

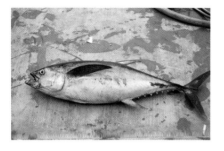

443. Yellowfin tuna

444. Atlantic bonito

445. King mackerel; kingfish (below);
Spanish mackerel (above)

447. Cero

448a. Swordfish, adult

448b. Swordfish, juvenile

449. Sailfish

450. Blue marlin

451. White marlin

452. Longbill spearfish

454. Harvestfish

455. Gulf butterfish

460. Black driftfish

462. Man-of-war fish

466. Slender searobin

465. Flying gurnard

467. Mexican searobin

468. Bandtail searobin

469. Shortwing searobin

470. Bluespotted searobin

471. Bighead searobin

472. Bigeye searobin

473. Blackwing searobin

474. Leopard searobin

475. Northern searobin

476. Horned searobin

477. Blackbelly rosefish

478. Longspine scorpionfish

480. Spotted scorpionfish

479. Spinycheek scorpionfish

481. Hunchback scorpionfish

482. Barbfish

483. Smoothhead scorpionfish

484. Twospot flounder

486. Ocellated flounder

487. Three-eye flounder

488. Gulf flounder

489. Broad flounder

490. Southern flounder

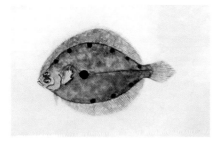

491. Spiny flounder

492. Sash flounder

493. Spotfin flounder

494. Mexican flounder

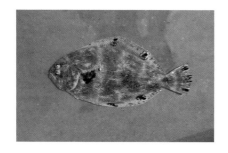

495. Fringed flounder

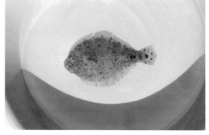

497. Shoal flounder

498. Dusky flounder

499. Horned whiff

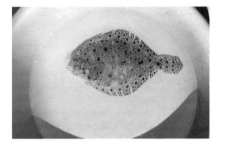

500. Spotted whiff

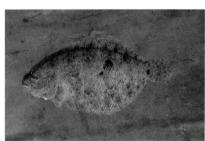

501a. Bay whiff, adult

501b. Bay whiff, juvenile

502a. Fringed sole

502b. Naked sole

503. Lined sole

504. Hogchoker

506. Pygmy tonguefish

507. Spottedfin tonguefish

508a. Blackcheek tonguefish; patch, adult

508b. Blackcheek tonguefish; patch, juvenile

509. Offshore tonguefish; patch

510. Deepwater tonguefish

511. Longtail tonguefish

512. Black durgon; black triggerfish

514. Gray triggerfish

513. Queen triggerfish

515. Sargassum triggerfish

516. Ocean triggerfish

518. Scrawled filefish

519. Unicorn filefish

520. Orange filefish

522. Whitespotted filefish

521. Dotterel filefish

524. Fringed filefish

523. Orangespotted filefish

525. Planehead filefish

526. Pygmy filefish

527. Scrawled cowfish

529. Smooth puffer

528. Smooth trunkfish

531. Marbled puffer

530. Sharpnose puffer

532. Bandtail puffer

533. Checkered puffer

534. Southern puffer

535. Least puffer

536. Striped burrfish

537. Porcupinefish

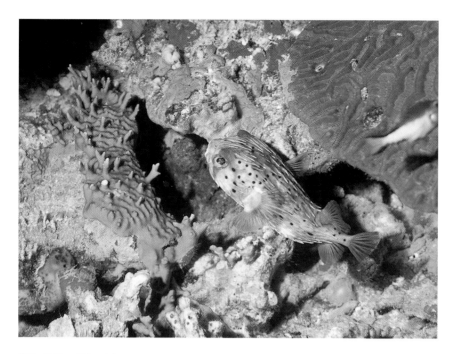

538a. Balloonfish, adult

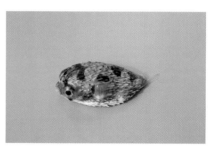

538b. Balloonfish, juvenile

540. Ocean sunfish

539. Sharptail mola

Keys to the Families

Included in these keys are all families of fishes that are likely to be encountered over the continental shelf of the northwestern Gulf of Mexico and a number of families that normally dwell in deeper water but may at times be found over the shelf, some perhaps regularly. These deeper-dwelling families, which are not further discussed, include the Hexanchidae, Argentinidae, Macrorhamphosidae, Zeidae, Macrouridae, Percophidae, Callionymidae, Lophiidae, Polymixiidae, Caproidae, Pleuronectidae, Chlorophthalmidae, Merlucciidae, and Triacanthodidae. They are illustrated in appendix 8. Cartilaginous fishes (sharks, skates, and rays) are easily distinguished from the bony fishes. Members of the former group have five, six, or seven gill openings, while the bony fishes possess only a single gill opening covered by a bony operculum.

Key to the Families of Shallow-Water Cartilaginous Fishes

1. Gill openings partly or wholly lateral; pectoral fins not attached to head in front of gills. Order Selachii, sharks 2

   Gill openings wholly ventral; pectoral fins attached to head in front of gills. Order Batoidei, rays 12

2. Anal fin present 3

   Anal fin absent 11

3. Gill openings six or seven ... family HEXANCHIDAE, cow sharks

   Gill openings five 4

4. At least half of base of first dorsal fin posterior to origin of pelvic fins 5

   Base of first dorsal fin terminates over or well before origin of pelvic fins 6

5. Anterior margin of nostril with well-developed barbel ... family GINGLYMOSTOMATIDAE, nurse sharks (p. 125)

   Anterior nostril without barbel ... family RHINCODONTIDAE, whale sharks (p. 125)

6   Head flattened and extended with eyes on lateral margins ... family SPHYRNIDAE, hammer-head sharks (p. 131)
     Head pointed, not expanded 7
7   Caudal fin lunate ... family LAMNIDAE, mackerel sharks (p. 127)
     Caudal fin not lunate, with upper lobe longer than lower lobe 8
8   Caudal fin one-half total length or more ... family ALOPIIDAE, thresher sharks (p. 126)
     Caudal fin length much less than one-half total length 9
9   Fifth gill opening well in front of origin of pectoral; no nictitating membrane on eye ... family ODONTASPIDIDAE, sand tigers (p. 126)
     Fifth gill opening over or behind origin of pectoral; eye with nictitating fold
     or membrane 10
10   Spiracle oval; teeth small, low, and rounded, with three cusps ... family TRIAKIDAE, smooth dogfishes (p. 133)
     Spiracle, if present, a narrow slit; teeth bladelike, with one cusp ... family CARCHARHINIDAE, requiem sharks (p. 128)
11   Trunk rounded; eyes lateral; anterior margins of pectorals not overlapping gill openings ... family SQUALIDAE, spiny dogfishes (p. 134)
     Trunk flattened; eyes dorsal; anterior margins of pectorals overlapping gill openings ... family SQUATINIDAE, angel sharks (p. 134)
12   Snout prolonged as a narrow blade with teethlike structures ... family PRISTIDAE, sawfishes (p. 134)
     Snout pointed or rounded, not as above 13
13   Electric organs present between head and forward extension of pectorals;
     skin of disc naked 19
     Electric organs not present; skin with spines, thorns, or scales (denticles) 14
14   Dorsal and caudal fins well developed, supported by horny rays; tail merges gradually with body ... family RHINOBATIDAE, guitarfishes (p. 135)
     Dorsal and caudal fins, if present, not supported by horny rays; tail distinct from body 15
15   Eyes and spiracles on top of head; no subrostral lobe or fin 16
     Eyes and spiracles on side of head; anterior part of pectorals forming a separate lobe or lobes ... family MYLIOBATIDAE, mantas and eagle rays (p. 139)
16   Two dorsal fins and caudal present ... family RAJIDAE, skates (p. 136)
     Dorsal fins not present, caudal reduced or absent 17
17   Disc less than 1.3 times as broad as it is long, tail spine present 18
     Disc more than 1.5 times as broad as it is long; tail spine usually absent ... family GYMNURIDAE, butterfly rays (p. 139)
18   Caudal fin moderately developed; entire disc rounded ... family UROLOPHIDAE, round stingrays
     Caudal fin tapering to a whiplike filament; portions of disc variously angled, never com-pletely rounded ... family DASYATIDAE, stingrays (p. 138)

19 Disc wider than it is long; anterior margin nearly straight ... family TORPEDINIDAE, electric rays (p. 135)

Disc narrower than it is long; anterior margin rounded ... family NARCINIDAE, electric rays (p. 136)

Key to the Families of Bony Fishes

13 Gill membranes broadly joined to isthmus; gill openings restricted to sides of body 14

Gill membranes free from isthmus, gill openings ventral as well as on sides of body 19

14 Snout tubular; body covered with bony plates . . . family SYNGNATHIDAE, pipefishes and seahorses (p. 186)

Snout not tubular 15

15 Dorsal fins two, with the anterior of spines, posterior of soft rays . . . family BALISTIDAE, triggerfishes and filefishes (p. 305)

Dorsal fin continuous, of soft rays only 16

16 Teeth in jaws separate; body encased in bony plates . . . family OSTRACIIDAE, trunkfishes (p. 309)

Teeth in jaws confluent into one or two plates in each jaw 17

17 Caudal fin present 18

Caudal fin absent . . . family MOLIDAE, ocean sunfishes (p. 313)

18 Jaws divided by median suture; body naked or covered by prickles . . . family TETRA-ODONTIDAE, puffers (p. 309)

Jaws not divided by median suture; body covered by thornlike spikes . . . family DIODONTIDAE, porcupinefishes and burrfishes (p. 312)

19 Upper jaw prolonged into a sword . . . family XIPHIIDAE swordfish (p. 200)

Upper jaw not prolonged into sword . . . family STROMATEIDAE, butterfishes (p. 283)

20 Adipose fin present 21

Adipose fin absent 25

21 Head scaled on sides 22

Head naked 23

22 Maxillary rudimentary or obsolete . . . family SYNODONTIDAE, lizardfishes (p. 158)

Maxillary well developed . . . family CHLOROPHTHALMIDAE, greeneyes

23 Body naked 24

Body scaled . . . family ARGENTINIDAE, smelts

24 Nostrils with barbels . . . family ICTALURIDAE, freshwater catfishes (p. 160)

Nostrils without barbels . . . family ARIIDAE, sea catfishes (p. 161)

25 Dorsal fin followed by series of detached finlets . . . family SCOMBERESOCIDAE, sauries

Dorsal fin not followed by detached finlets 26

26 Dorsal fin single, composed of soft rays (first ray may be modified and spinelike) 27

Dorsal fins two, the first of spines, the second chiefly of soft rays, or single dorsal preceded by free spines 40

27 Tail heterocercal 28

Tail not heterocercal 29

28 Body covered with diamond-shaped ganoid scales . . . family LEPISOSTEIDAE, gars (p. 143)

Body with six series of large shields, otherwise naked . . . family ACIPENSERIDAE, sturgeons (p. 142)

29 Body naked; caudal produced . . . family FISTULARIIDAE, cornetfishes (p. 186)

	Body scaled; caudal not produced 30
30	Pectoral fins inserted high, near axis of body; lateral line along sides of body 31
	Pectoral fins inserted below axis of body 33
31	Both jaws produced; teeth tricuspid; pectorals not overly developed ... family BELONIDAE, needlefishes (p. 177)
	One or both jaws not produced; teeth conical; pectorals elongate 32
32	Lower jaw elongate, much longer than upper ... family EXOCOETIDAE, halfbreaks (p. 173)
	Lower jaw not elongate, nearly subequal ... family EXOCOETIDAE, flyingfishes (p. 173)
33	Head more or less scaly 34
	Head naked 36
34	Third anal ray not branched; anal fin of male modified as an intromittent organ ... family POECILIIDAE, livebearers (p. 180)
	Third anal ray branched; anal fin of male not modified but similar to that of female 35
35	Teeth in jaws conical; interior (ventral) arms of maxillaries directed anteriorly, often with hooks; maxilla twisted, not straight ... family FUNDULIDAE, killifishes (p. 178)
	Teeth in jaws compressed, with three cusps; dorsal processes of maxillaries expanded medially, nearly meeting at midline; maxilla twisted, not straight ... family CYPRINODONTIDAE, pupfishes (p. 180)
36	Gular plate present 37
	Gular plate absent 38
37	Last ray of dorsal fin produced ... family MEGALOPIDAE, tarpons (p. 144)
	Last ray of dorsal fin not produced ... family ELOPIDAE, tenpounders (p. 145)
38	Lateral line developed ... family ALBULIDAE, bonefish (p. 145)
	Lateral line not developed 39
39	Mouth small to moderate ... family CLUPEIDAE, herrings (p. 152)
	Mouth large ... family ENGRAULIDAE, anchovies (p. 156)
40	Dorsal fin preceded by free spines ... family AULOSTOMIDAE, trumpetfish (p. 185)
	Dorsal fins two 41
41	Pectoral fin with lowermost rays detached and filamentous ... family POLYNEMIDAE, threadfins (p. 238)
	Pectoral fin entire 42
42	Snout tubular ... family MACROHAMPHOSIDAE, snipefishes
	Snout not tubular 43
43	Teeth strong, unequal; mouth large; lateral line present ... family SPHYRAENIDAE, barracudas (p. 273)
	Teeth small or wanting; mouth small; lateral line obsolete 44
44	Dorsal spines four; anal spines three ... family MUGILIDAE, mullets (p. 171)
	Dorsal spines four to eight; anal spine single ... family ATHERINIDAE, silversides (p. 182)
45	Gill openings in front of pectoral fin 46
	Gill openings behind pectoral fin 95

46   Body more or less scaly or armed with bony plates 47

Body scaleless, smooth or armed with tubercles, prickles, or scattered plates 92

47   Ventral fins separate 48

Ventral fins united; gill membranes joined at isthmus; no lateral line . . . family GOBIIDAE, gobies (p. 267)

48   Suborbital with bony stay; cheek sometimes mailed 49

Suborbital without bony stay; cheek never mailed 50

49   Pectoral fin with detached rays . . . family TRIGLIDAE, searobins (p. 287)

Pectoral fin entire . . . family SCORPAENIDAE, scorpionfishes (p. 291)

50   Spinous dorsal transformed into sucking disc . . . family ECHENEIDAE, sharksuckers (p. 213)

Spinous dorsal not sucking disc 51

51   Anal fin preceded by two free spines (obsolete in very large fish, often connected by membrane in young fish) with no more than one finlet 52

Anal fin not preceded by free spines 53

52   Scales small or absent; teeth, if present, not caninelike; preopercle entire; caudal peduncle with scutes . . . family CARANGIDAE, jacks (p. 215)

Scales moderate; teeth caninelike; preopercle serrate; caudal peduncle not scaled . . . family POMATOMIDAE, bluefish (p. 212)

53   Dorsal spines present, all or nearly all disconnected from each other 54

Dorsal spines, if present, all or nearly all connected by membranes 56

54   Body elongate, spindle-shaped, nearly square in cross section . . . family RACHYCENTRIDAE, cobia (p. 213)

Body oblong, ovate, or compressed 55

55   Gill membranes free from isthmus . . . family CENTROLOPHIDAE, ruffs (p. 285)

Gill membranes connected to isthmus . . . family EPHIPPIDAE, spadefishes (p. 271)

56   Dorsal and anal each with one or more detached finlets 57

Dorsal and anal each without finlets 58

57   Caudal fin lunate . . . family SCOMBRIDAE, mackerels and tunas (p. 275)

Caudal fin forked, not lunate . . . family TRICHIURIDAE (in part, incl. GEMPYLIDAE), escolars and oil fish (p. 274)

58   Lateral line armed posteriorly with a sharp, movable spine . . . family ACANTHURIDAE, surgeonfishes (p. 272)

Lateral line not armed posteriorly 59

59   Throat with two long barbels, dorsal fins two . . . family MULLIDAE, goatfishes (p. 245)

Throat without barbels 60

60   Nostril single on each side; lateral line interrupted . . . family POMACENTRIDAE, damselfishes (p. 251)

Nostril double on each side 61

61   Lateral line extending to tip of middle rays of caudal 62

Lateral line not extending onto caudal fin 64

62   Anal spines one or two . . . family SCIAENIDAE, croakers (p. 239)

Anal spines three 63

63 Dorsal fins two, separate ... family CENTROPOMIDAE, snook (p. 190)

    Dorsal fin single, continuous ... family HAEMULIDAE, grunts (p. 231)

64 Gills three and one-half, with slit behind the last arch small or absent 65

    Gills four, with long slit behind last arch 67

65 Mouth vertical; dorsal fin divided ... family URANOSCOPIDAE, stargazers (p. 260)

    Mouth not vertical; dorsal continuous 66

66 Teeth in each jaw united, forming beak ... family SCARIDAE, parrotfishes (p. 258)

    Teeth in jaws separate, or nearly so; anterior teeth more or less canine ... family LABRIDAE, wrasses (p. 255)

67 Teeth setiform, brushlike; soft fins scaled 68

    Teeth not setiform 70

68 Dorsal continuous 69

    Dorsal divided ... family EPHIPPIDAE, spadefishes (p. 271)

69 No spine at angle of preopercle ... family CHAETODONTIDAE, butterflyfishes (p. 247)

    Spine at angle of preopercle ... family POMACANTHIDAE angelfishes (p. 249)

70 Body deeper than long, covered with rough scales; dorsal spines eight; anal spines three; soft fins very long ... family CAPROIDAE, boarfishes

    Body longer than it is deep 71

71 Gill membranes broadly joined to isthmus; no lateral line ... family ELEOTRIDAE, sleepers (here included in GOBIIDAE) (p. 265)

    Gill membranes free from isthmus, or nearly so 72

72 Premaxillaries excessively protractile ... family GERREIDAE, mojarras (p. 230)

    Premaxillaries moderately or not protractile 73

73 Lateral line incomplete, running close to dorsal fin ... family OPISTOGNATHIDAE, jawfishes (p. 208)

    Lateral line, if present, not as above 74

74 Pseudobranchiae absent or covered by skin ... family CORYPHAENIDAE, dolphins (p. 223)

    Pseudobranchiae developed 75

75 Spinous dorsal with two or three short spines only; anal spines absent ... family SERRANIDAE (in part, GRAMMISTIDAE), soapfishes (p. 192)

    Spinous dorsal, if present, not as above; anal spines absent or present 76

76 Opercle ending in long scaly flap; snout depressed and spatulate; mouth large, lower jaw projecting; anal spines absent ... family PERCOPHIDAE, flatheads

    Opercle not ending in a scaly flap; snout not greatly depressed; anal spines present 77

77 Dorsal fin continuous, with spines few and slender; maxillary usually with enlarged tooth behind; anal fin long and even; upper and lower rays of caudal often produced 78

    Dorsal fin continuous or divided, not as above 79

78 Pectoral fin broad, with lower rays thickened and not branched ... family CIRRHITIDAE, hawkfishes (p. 247)

Pectoral fin narrow at base, with lower rays branched like upper ones . . . family MALA-CANTHIDAE, tilefishes (p. 210)

79 Caudal peduncle not slender; scales well developed; dorsal fin with distinct spines; anal with at least one spine, soft rays usually few (perchlike fishes) 80

Caudal peduncle slender; scales various but usually not ctenoid; dorsal spines various; anal fin long (mackerellike fishes) 89

80 Maxillary not sheathed by preorbital or only partially covered by edge of latter 81

Maxillary slipping beneath preorbital when mouth is closed; opercle without spines 86

81 Anal spines two and rarely three; body not elongate . . . family APOGONIDAE, cardinalfishes (p. 209)

Anal spines three, never two 82

82 Vomer, and usually palatines, with teeth 83

Vomer toothless . . . family LOBOTIDAE, tripletail (p. 229)

83 Anal fin shorter than dorsal; head not covered with rough scales 84

Anal fin scarcely shorter than dorsal, similar in appearance; head covered with rough scales . . . family PRIACANTHIDAE, bigeyes (p. 207)

84 Dorsal fins separate 85

Dorsal fin continuous   family SERRANIDAE, sea basses (p. 172)

85 Lateral line not extending onto caudal fin . . . family ACROPOMATIDAE, temperate ocean basses (p. 192)

Lateral line extending nearly to end of caudal fin . . . family MORONIDAE, temperate basses (p. 191)

86 Teeth in jaws incisorlike; intestine elongated; herbivorous fishes with moderately protractile premaxillaries . . . family KYPHOSIDAE, chubs (p. 246)

Teeth in jaws not incisorlike; intestine of moderate length; carnivorous fishes 87

87 Vomer with teeth, sometimes small; maxillary long . . . family LUTJANIDAE, snappers (p.224)

Vomer toothless; palatines and tongue also without teeth 88

88 Teeth on sides of jaws not molar; preopercle serrate . . . family HAEMULIDAE, grunts (p. 231)

Teeth on side of jaws molar; preopercle entire . . . family SPARIDAE, porgies (p.234)

89 Dorsal fin divided, spines six to eight 90

Dorsal fin not divided, spines three or four . . . family BRAMIDAE, pomfrets (p. 224)

90 Jaws with canines . . . family POMATOMIDAE, bluefish (p. 212)

Jaws without canines 91

91 Caudal peduncle square, with at least two lateral keels . . . family ARIOMMATIDAE, driftfishes (p. 284)

Caudal peduncle compressed, without lateral keels . . . family NOMEIDAE, man-of-war fishes (p. 286)

92 Breast with a sucking disc . . . family GOBIESOCIDAE, clingfishes (p. 265)

Breast without a sucking disc 93

93 Gill membranes broadly attached to isthmus . . . family CALLIONYMIDAE, dragonets

	Gill membranes free or nearly free of isthmus 94
94	Anal preceded by two free spines . . . family CARANGIDAE, jacks (p. 215)
	Anal without free spines . . . family SCOMBRIDAE, mackerels and tunas (p. 275)
95	Gill openings behind or in upper axil of pectorals . . . family OGCOCEPHALIDAE, batfishes (p. 164)
	Gill openings in or behind lower axil of pectorals 96
96	Head laterally compressed; no pseudobranchiae . . . family ANTENNARIIDAE, frogfishes (p. 163)
	Head depressed; pseudobranchiae present . . . family LOPHIIDAE, goosefishes
97	Eyes asymmetric, both on same side of head 98
	Eyes symmetrical, one on each side of head 101
98	Margin of preopercle free, not covered with skin or scales 99
	Margin of preopercle covered with skin and scales 100
99	Eyes on left side . . . family BOTHIDAE, lefteyed flounders (p. 294)
	Eyes on right side . . . family PLEURONECTIDAE, righteyed flounders
100	Eyes on right side . . . family ACHIRIDAE, soles (p. 302)
	Eyes on left side . . . family CYNOGLOSSIDAE tonguefishes (p. 303)
101	Ventral fins with or without a spine, soft rays more than five 102
	Ventral fins with or without spines, soft rays less than five 111
102	No true (hard) spines in fins 103
	At least some fins with true (hard) spines 109
103	Anterior dorsal fin a single elongate ray widely separated from rest of fin and fitting into a mid-dorsal groove when depressed . . . family BREGMACEROTIDAE, codlets (p. 166)
	Anterior dorsal originating at rear of or behind head, not widely separated from following rays 104
104	Top of skull with more or less well developed V-shaped ridges, the point of the V directed anteriorly 105
	Top of skull without V-shaped ridges 106
105	Anus and urogenital pore close together, caudal fin developed . . . family MERLUCCIIDAE, merlucid hakes
	Anus and urogenital pore widely separated in adults, the anus located between the pelvic fin bases; caudal fin absent . . . family STEINDACHNERIDAE, luminous hakes (p. 167)
106	Caudal fin absent . . . family MACOURIDAE, grenadiers
	Caudal fin present 107
107	Anal fin single . . . family PHYCIDAE (subfamily Gaidropsarinae)
	Anal fin in two parts 108
108	Head of vomer with well-developed teeth, swimbladder not attached to skull . . . family GADIDAE, cods
	Head of vomer toothless or with only minute teeth, anterior projections of swimbladder attached to skull . . . family MORIDAE, morid cods
109	Chin with two long barbels . . . family POLYMIXIIDAE, beardfishes

Chin without barbels 110

110 Body covered with firm, serrated scales; anal spines four; dorsal spines not greatly elongated ... family HOLOCENTRIDAE, squirrelfishes (p. 183)

Body covered with small scales or naked; dorsal spines elongated ... family ZEIDAE, dories

111 Gill openings behind pectoral fin 112

Gill openings before pectoral fin 113

112 Gill openings behind and above pectorals; mouth small ... family OGCOCEPHALIDAE, batfishes (p. 164)

Gill openings behind and below pectoral; mouth large ... family ANTENNARIIDAE, frogfishes (p. 163)

113 Upper jaw prolonged into bony sword ... family ISTIOPHORIDAE, billfishes (p. 280)

Upper jaw not prolonged into sword 114

114 Dorsal fin with spines or simple rays 115

Dorsal fin with soft rays only 122

115 Pectoral fin divided into two parts, one very long ... family DACTYLOPTERIDAE, flying gurnards (p. 287)

Pectoral fin not divided 116

116 Dorsal spines two to four; gills three 117

Dorsal spines numerous; gills four 118

117 Ventral fins not reduced to single spine ... family BATRACHOIDIDAE, toadfishes (p. 162)

Ventral fins reduced to single spine ... family TRIACANTHODIDAE, spikefishes

118 Gill membranes broadly connected, attached to isthmus or not 119

Gill membranes separate, joined to isthmus ... family DACTYLOSCOPIDAE, sand stargazers (p. 260)

119 Gill openings moderate or large 120

Gill openings small, reduced to oblique slits before pectorals ... family MICRODESMIDAE, wormfishes (p. 271)

120 Scales cycloid ... family LABRISOMIDAE, labrisomids (p. 261)

Body naked, a few scales in some species 121

121 Dorsal spines more than 20; conical teeth ... family CHAENOPSIDAE, pikeblennies (p. 261)

Dorsal spines fewer than 20; teeth comblike ... family BLENNIDAE, combtooth blennies (p. 262)

122 Dorsal fin subdivided into two or three parts of unequal height; ventral fins inserted below eyes ... family PHYCIDAE, hakes (p. 167)

Dorsal fin single, of uniform height; ventral fins inserted in advance of eyes, almost on the chin 123

123 Caudal fin joined to dorsal and anal fins ... family OPHIDIIDAE, cusk-eels (p. 168)

Caudal fin distinct ... family BYTHITIDAE, viviparous brotulids (p. 170)

Sharks, Skates, and Rays

(Elasmobranchiomorphi: Chondrichthyes)

Although not the most primitive (oldest) of fishes—ancestors of lampreys and hagfishes are the most ancient—the elasmobranchs are very old and probably have changed little in millions of years. They are characterized by having a cartilaginous skeleton and five to seven pairs of gill slits not covered by an opercle. Their skin is composed of tiny placoid scales (dermal denticles), which give it a sandpaper consistency. These scales can be used to identify species. The number and shape of teeth may also be used to distinguish species. Some of the more distinctive teeth are illustrated in figure 1.

Sharks and rays have been considered as separate groups, but the distinction is artificial, there being some intermediate forms such as angel sharks. Because of their size and deadliness, sharks have always attracted interest. The reproductive methods of the elasmobranchs may be their most interesting facet, however. All species have internal fertilization; the males have on the pelvic fins a pair of claspers that transfer sperm. Most species are viviparous or ovoviviparous, giving birth to few young, but a few species, such as the cat shark and the skates, deposit eggs in capsules. The species with perhaps the most spectacular reproduction method are the sand tiger and a few others, in which a single young develops in a uterus and feeds on eggs produced by the mother, which pass from the ovary into the mouth of the fetus (oviphagy). Many species of sharks and rays possess a placenta, and all enter the world as well-developed juveniles. Among fishes, sharks have low genetic diversity (Smith, 1986).

Rarely, some sharks not included here may be encountered. For example, the world-wide sixgill shark, *Hexanchus griseus,* and sevengill shark, *Heptranchias perlo,* are occasionally taken on the continental shelf. These may be strays from deeper water; the ocean contains other sharks with seven gill slits and both sharks and one ray species with six (all the sharks included here have five). The rare bramble shark, *Echinorhinus*

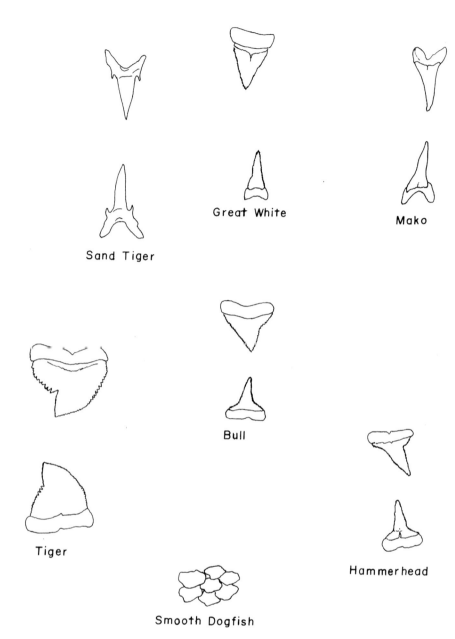

Fig. 1. Distinctive shark teeth

brucus, has recently been taken off the coast (Thompson and Russell, 1995), so more rare strays are to be expected.

Sharks are edible and quite good eating when properly prepared, and although the skin and liver have also been used, shark fisheries have generally been marginal. In recent years a number of species have been increasingly marketed.

Shark attacks are nowhere common and have been exceptionally rare in the Gulf of Mexico. While a few have occurred on the Gulf coast, most Florida attacks have been in the Atlantic. However, in 1987 there were three attacks at Port Aransas, two in one day. This occurred the year after a red tide had killed large numbers of fishes. Single attacks in South Texas happened the summer after freezes in 1962, 1983, and 1989. All involved aggressive attacks and small but damaging bites, with only the first case being fatal. A tooth from one of the Port Aransas cases was identified as a blacktip, and other evidence suggests that small sharks were involved. Since 1900 a handful of other unconfirmed cases exist. One in 1977, a year of very large shark populations on the coast (Parker and Bailey, 1979), was apparently from a shark escaping from a seine in a bay. (Baughman and Springer, 1950; Bigelow and Schroeder, 1948, 1953b; Branstetter, 1981; Branstetter and McEachran, 1983, 1986; Castro, 1983; Clark and von Schmidt, 1965; Compagno, 1984a, b, 1988; Heemstra, 1965; Rivas and McClellan, 1982; Springer, 1950a; Springer and Joy, 1989; Wahlquist, 1966)

Ginglymostomatidae

Nurse sharks are peculiar tropical sharks with two high dorsals but with the first behind the origin of the pelvics. The nostril, with a fleshy barbel, is connected with the subterminal mouth by a groove. Only one species occurs in the Atlantic. Sharks with poorly developed mouths, such as young dogfish, are often called nurses.

1. Nurse shark *Ginglymostoma cirratum* (Bonnaterre)

Brownish, the young speckled, with small eye. The nurse shark is a rarely seen tropical species, easily recognized by its mouth and barbels. It occurs around offshore reefs, sporadically straying inshore. Tropical Atlantic, in the west from North Carolina (straying northward) through the Caribbean to Brazil. (14 feet; 4 1/4 m)

Rhincodontidae

Whale sharks are large, epipelagic fish that are occasionally struck by vessels. There is only one species in the family.

2. Whale shark *Rhincodon typus* (Smith)

Head flat, square in front; gill openings very high, seven longitudinal ridges on back; brownish on back and sides with many white spots. Whale sharks are rarely sighted in the area basking or slowly swimming at the surface. This animal, the largest living fish, is a plankton feeder; its gill apparatus is modified as a sieve, but it occasionally feeds on fishes as big as small tuna. For many years the reproductive habits of this species were a mystery. A 14-1/12-inch embryo in an egg case was taken in the Gulf off northern Mexico in the early 1950s. From this, it was assumed that the species was ovigerous (egg laying); however other evidence implied that eggs and embryos might be retained in the mother and born alive (ovoviviparous). In 1996 the collection of a pregnant female whale shark off Asia, proved that the species is ovoviviparous. Circumtropical; in the western Atlantic from Massachusetts through the Caribbean to Brazil. Anonymous, 1996; Breuer, 1954; Baughman, 1955; Garrick, 1964; Hoffman et al., 1981. (45 feet; 13 3/4 m)

Odontaspididae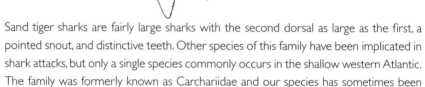

Sand tiger sharks are fairly large sharks with the second dorsal as large as the first, a pointed snout, and distinctive teeth. Other species of this family have been implicated in shark attacks, but only a single species commonly occurs in the shallow western Atlantic. The family was formerly known as Carchariidae and our species has sometimes been placed in the genus *Carcharias*.

3. Sand tiger; sand shark *Odontaspis taurus* (Rafinesque)
Teeth long and slender with sharply pointed cusps; gray-brown with darker spots on body and on fins behind pectorals. Although first reported from Texas in the 1960s, this species does not seem to be uncommon. A cool temperate species, it is more common north of Cape Hatteras. Of the larger sharks, only the sand tiger, the nurse shark, and the lemon shark have equal-sized dorsals, and in the nurse shark the first dorsal is very close to the tail. When the sand tiger is seen swimming, both dorsals may break water simultaneously. These are unusual sharks which have an oviphagous fetus. *O. noronhai*, which has the pelvic fin base under the second dorsal (anterior in *O. taurus*) has been taken in the offshore Gulf. Worldwide, except eastern Pacific, in the western North Atlantic from Nova Scotia to the northern Bahamas and Florida, and in the Gulf to Texas. Branstetter and McEachran, 1986; Gilmore et al., 1983. (10 feet; 3 m)

Alopiidae

Thresher sharks are easily recognized by their long, scythelike caudal fin, which is used to herd and stun schools of fish. In addition, threshers have a very small second dorsal set ahead of the small anal fin. (Gilmore, 1983)

4. Common thresher *Alopias vulpinus* (Bonnaterre)
Rear tip of first dorsal terminating far forward of pelvic fins; bluish, undersides sometimes mottled; first dorsal low, rounded. A cold temperate species most common off

New England, the thresher is rare in the Gulf. It is a big shark, maturing at about fourteen feet (4 1/4 m), giving birth to young four to five feet long. The bigeye thresher, A. *superciliosis* (Lowe), has been taken past the shelf edge; it differs by having a very large eye and only ten or eleven teeth on each side of the jaw versus the twenty of the common thresher. Worldwide, in the northwestern Atlantic from Newfoundland to Florida and Texas. Branstetter and McEachran, 1983; Gruber and Compagno, 1982; Gunter, 1941. (20 feet; 6 m)

Lamnidae

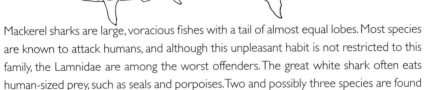

Mackerel sharks are large, voracious fishes with a tail of almost equal lobes. Most species are known to attack humans, and although this unpleasant habit is not restricted to this family, the Lamnidae are among the worst offenders. The great white shark often eats human-sized prey, such as seals and porpoises. Two and possibly three species are found in our area. (Gilmore, 1983)

1 Upper teeth broadly triangular, with serrated cusps ... great white shark, *Carcharodon carcharias*.
    Upper teeth slender, with smooth-edged cusps 2
2 Pectoral fins short, about 17 percent of total length; underside of snout white ... shortfin mako, *Isurus oxyrinchus*.
    Pectoral fins long, more than 18 percent of total length; underside of snout dusky ... longfin mako, *Isurus paucus*.

5. Great white shark *Carcharodon carcharias* (Linnaeus)
Very large girth, making it heavy for its length; much white on lower side; short caudal peduncle. Rare in the Gulf, the great white shark is usually encountered far offshore in cooler water. The largest of predaceous sharks, maturing at fifteen feet (4 1/2 m), it is a cold temperate species more abundant north of Cape Hatteras. Worldwide except near the poles. Baughman, 1950a; Gunter and Knapp, 1951. (at least 21 feet; 7 m; maximum size undetermined)

6. Shortfin mako *Isurus oxyrinchus* (Rafinesque)
Slender; often bluish dorsally. This distinctive and beautiful shark is a highly prized game fish. The longfin mako, *I. paucus*, with a larger eye and a pectoral as long as its head, has been caught off Florida and the Mississippi Delta. Worldwide, in the western Atlantic Ocean from Massachusetts and Bermuda to Argentina. Garrick, 1967a; Killam and Parsons, 1986. (12 feet; 4 m)

Carcharhinidae

Requiem sharks are the most abundant of sharks, being named for the tendency of some species to occur in large "masses" near the surface. Often called sand sharks, for want of a better name, the species are difficult to identify. The ridgeback sharks (with a ridge between the dorsals) are common pelagic species, whereas most of the others occur near the bottom, but this is a loose distinction. The oceanic whitetip, *Carcharhinus longimanus*, is common just outside the one-hundred-fathom line but rarely, if ever, strays inshore. There are at least twenty species in the western Atlantic, thirteen of which occur on the continental shelf of the northwestern Gulf. The night shark, *C. signatus*, may also occur rarely on the shelf edge. Hammerheads, although distinctive, are often considered to be in the same family. (Bigelow and Schroeder, 1948; Garrick, 1967b, 1982, 1985; Springer, 1950a)

1 Spiracles present as narrow slit, sides marked with stripes and blotches . . . tiger shark, *Galeocerdo cuvier.*

 Spiracles absent; various markings possibly on sides, but never stripes 2

2 Cusps of upper teeth as well as lower teeth smooth-edged 3

 Cusps of upper teeth serrated; those of lower teeth serrated or smooth 5

3 Second dorsal at least three-fourths as long as first, with posterior margin deeply concave; snout rounded . . . lemon shark, *Negaprion brevirostris.*

 Second dorsal less than one-half as long as first and much smaller in area, with posterior margin weakly concave or straight; snout pointed 4

4 Teeth slender, symmetrical, erect in both jaws; longest gill opening about one-half as long as dorsal base . . . finetooth shark, *Carcharhinus isodon.*

 Teeth in sides of jaw oblique, with outer edges notched; longest gill opening only one-fourth as long as base of first dorsal . . . Atlantic sharpnose shark, *Rhizoprionodon terraenovae.*

5 Origin of second dorsal over or behind midpoint of base of anal . . . smalltail shark, *Carcharhinus porosus.*

 Origin of second dorsal over origin of anal or anterior to it 6

6 Midline of back between first and second dorsals with low but distinct ridge 7

 Midline of back between dorsals smooth 10

7 Apex of first dorsal broadly rounded; tip of anal reaching nearly to origin of caudal . . . oceanic whitetip shark, *Carcharhinus longimanus.*

 Apex of first dorsal subangular; tip of anal separated from origin of caudal by distance at least as great as diameter of eye 8

8 Lower free edge of second dorsal more than twice as long as height of fin . . . silky shark, *Carcharhinus falciformis.*

 Lower free edge of second dorsal much less than twice as long as height of fin 9

9 Origin of first dorsal over pectoral axil; height of first dorsal equal to distance from eye to third gill opening . . . sandbar shark, *Carcharhinus plumbeus.*

Origin of first dorsal about over posterior, inner corner of pectoral; height of first dorsal less than distance from eye to first gill opening ... dusky shark, *Carcharhinus obscurus*.

10   Snout in front of line connecting outer ends of nostril less than one-half of distance between inner ends of nostrils ... bull shark, *Carcharhinus leucas*.

Snout in front of line connecting outer ends of nostrils two-thirds or more of distance between inner ends of nostrils 11

11   Upper teeth asymmetrical, directed backward, with outer margins notched (deeply concave) ... blacknose shark, *Carcharhinus acronotus*.

Upper teeth symmetrical 12

12   Origin of first dorsal behind vertical of rear margin of pectoral; interdorsal distance greater than height of first dorsal; edges of lower teeth smooth or slightly serrated; no notch in posterior edge of lower jaw ... spinner shark, *Carcharhinus brevipinna*.

Origin of first dorsal in front of vertical of rear margin of pectoral; horizontal diameter of eye about 20 percent of snout length; edges of lower teeth finely serrated; notch in posterior edge of lower jaw ... blacktip shark, *Carcharhinus limbatus*.

7. Tiger shark *Galeocerdo cuvier* (Peron and Lesueur)

Snout bluntly rounded; teeth strongly asymmetrical and serrated; sides spotted in young, becoming striped, eventually fading; tail with long upper lobe; grayish brown. Easily recognized by its markings, teeth, and tail, the tiger shark is often taken from Gulf jetties and piers and follows boats feeding on any trash thrown overboard. It has been implicated in a number of shark attacks. A frequent food item is seabirds. Worldwide in temperate and tropical waters; in the western Atlantic from Maine to Uruguay. Branstetter et al., 1987. (at least 18 feet; 5 1/2 m)

8. Lemon shark *Negaprion brevirostris* (Poey)

Snout bluntly rounded; central teeth symmetrical and unserrated, second dorsal nearly as high as first. This shark is a distinctive species with a slender body. The young are born in summer, when they are often caught in marsh channels. Temperate and tropical Atlantic, in the west from New Jersey through the Caribbean to Brazil. Springer, 1950b. (11 feet; 3 1/3 m)

9. Finetooth shark; blueback shark *Carcharhinus isodon* (Valenciennes)

Head triangular in front of nostrils; teeth slender, unserrated, and symmetrical; gill openings long; second dorsal much smaller than first. This is a slender shark with a cobalt blue back. Young occur in the surf zone in summer and the adults seem to stay on the inshore shelf. Atlantic Ocean, in the west from New York to at least southern Texas and Cuba. (5 feet; 1 1/2 m)

10. Atlantic sharpnose shark *Rhizoprionodon terraenovae* (Richardson)

Snout more or less pointed; teeth asymmetrical in both jaws, unserrated; origin of second dorsal over midpoint of anal base; gray with dark-edged dorsals and caudal; sides with a few small, white spots. This is one of the most common inshore species, with young appearing in the surf zone and saltier estuaries in summer. Adults are often caught far offshore at the snapper banks. It is easy to confuse with the smalltail shark, from which it is distinguished by the presence of a low interdorsal ridge, long labial furrows, and smooth teeth, which are asymmetrical in the lower jaw. Bay of Fundy to Yucatán. Branstetter, 1987a; Parsons, 1982; Springer, 1964. (3 feet; 1 m)

11. Smalltail shark *Carcharhinus porosus* (Ranzani)

Snout moderately pointed; teeth asymmetrical in upper jaw, straight in most of lower, slightly serrated; origin of second dorsal over midpoint of anal base; gray with reddish tinge. The status of this small shark is uncertain because it is easily confused with the sharpnose shark, since these are the only carcharhinid sharks with the second dorsal origin behind the anal origin. Eastern tropical Pacific; western Atlantic from the northern Gulf to Brazil. (4 feet; 1 1/4 m)

12. Silky shark *Carcharhinus falciformis* (Bibron)

Snout moderately pointed; interdorsal ridge present; free tips of second dorsal and anal very long; teeth nearly symmetrical, uppers broad. This is the common shark seen at the surface over the continental shelf. Worldwide, in the northwestern Atlantic from Maine to Brazil. Branstetter, 1987b; Garrick et al., 1964. (10 feet; 3 m)

13. Sandbar shark; brown shark *Carcharhinus plumbeus* (Nardo)

Snout broadly rounded; first dorsal large for a requiem shark, with origin over axil of pectoral; teeth in upper jaw broad, somewhat asymmetrical, those in lower jaw thin and symmetrical; body gray to brown. This is a cold temperate species more common north of Cape Hatteras. It is uncommon in the Gulf. Worldwide, in the western Atlantic Ocean from Massachusetts to Uruguay. Springer, 1960. (8 feet; 2 1/2 m)

14. Dusky shark; sand shark *Carcharhinus obscurus* (Lesueur)

Snout moderately rounded; first dorsal relatively low, with origin at corner of pectoral; upper teeth slightly asymmetrical, broad; interdorsal ridge present; bluish gray, sometimes pale, with pectorals sooty at tips. The habits of the dusky shark are not well known, although a number have been taken over the middle shelf. Atlantic Ocean, in the west from Massachusetts and Bermuda to Brazil. (11 feet; 3 1/3 m)

15. Bull shark *Carcharhinus leucas* (Valenciennes)

Snout bluntly rounded; first dorsal origin over pectoral axil; no interdorsal ridge, upper teeth broad, slightly asymmetrical, lower teeth thin, symmetrical; gray. A common species inshore, this is the only shark in low-salinity estuaries, and it even penetrates fresh water. It is known from St. Louis, Missouri (one), and from Simmesport and Saline Lake off the Red River in Louisiana, over one hundred miles from the Gulf up the Atchafalaya, although it may have come up the Mississippi. During dry spells, the river has salt wedges flowing along the bottom past Baton Rouge. Worldwide, in the western Atlantic from New York and Bermuda through the Caribbean to Brazil. Branstetter and Stiles, 1987; Caillouet et al., 1969; Gunter, 1938c; Thomerson et al., 1977. (10 feet; 3 m)

16. Blacknose shark *Carcharhinus acronotus* (Poey)

Snout moderately pointed, with black smudge on tip lost with growth; no interdorsal ridge; upper teeth broad, asymmetrical; lower teeth thin, nearly symmetrical; second dorsal origin over anal; usually cream or yellow, with second dorsal black-tipped. A poorly known species, this shark prefers coarse shell-sand habitats and is therefore more common in the northeastern and southern Gulf. North Carolina through the Caribbean to Brazil. (6 feet; 1 2/3 m)

17. Spinner shark *Carcharhinus brevipinna* (Muller and Henle)

Snout very slender and pointed; upper and lower teeth slender, nearly symmetrical; gray, adults with dorsals, pectorals, anal, and caudal black-tipped. This is apparently a common inshore species, named for its habit of leaving the water vertically in a spiral. Gulf of Mexico barely into the Caribbean. Branstetter, 1982, 1987c. (8 feet; 2 1/2 m)

18. Blacktip shark *Carcharhinus limbatus* (Valenciennes)

Snout slender, pointed; upper and lower teeth slender, nearly symmetrical; gray, adults with black-tipped dorsals, pectorals, and caudal (but not anal); black tips obscured with age. Like the spinner shark, the blacktip also spins. Worldwide in temperate and tropical waters; in the western Atlantic from Massachusetts to Brazil. Branstetter, 1982, 1987c. (8 feet; 2 1/2 m)

Sphyrnidae

The hammerhead sharks are among the most common sharks found in warm waters. The family possesses an exceptionally tall first dorsal fin, which allows sharks cruising at the surface to be recognized.

The wide snout is thought to be an aid in locating prey by smell; it may also aid in disturbing food on the bottom and in increasing maneuverability. The shape of the head can be used to distinguish most species at a glance (fig. 2). They are only superficially distinct from the carcharhinids, and are currently placed in the same family by many researchers; however, they differ enough externally to argue for separate family status. Compagno, 1988; Garrick, 1967b; Gilbert, 1967.

MOKARRAN   ZYGAENA   LEWINI   TUDES   TIBURO

Fig. 2. Hammerhead shark head shapes

1   Head spade-shaped; anterior margin of head not lobed. . . bonnethead, *Sphyrna tiburo*.

     Head hammer-shaped, anterior margin lobed 2

2   Anterior margin of head without a median notch . . . smooth hammerhead, *Sphyrna zygaena*.

     Anterior margin of head with distinct median notch 3

3   Free tip of second dorsal fin as long as height of second dorsal; cusps of teeth serrated . . .

     great hammerhead, *Sphyrna mokarran*.

     Free tip of second dorsal fin much longer than height of second dorsal; teeth not serrated

     on cusps 4

4   Center of eye well in front of mouth; posterior margin of anal weakly concave; posterior

     corner of head in front of corner of mouth; posterior margin of head straight . . . smalleye

     hammerhead, *Sphyrna tudes* (= *bigelowi*).

     Center of eye about opposite front of mouth; posterior margin of anal deeply concave,

     posterior corner of head behind corner of mouth; posterior margin of head curved . . .

     scalloped hammerhead, *Sphyrna lewini*.

19. Bonnethead; bonnetnose *Sphyrna tiburo* (Linnaeus)

Head rounded, dark spots on body; teeth smooth. Certainly one of the most common
sharks, often occurring in schools, the bonnethead usually stays close inshore and in the
saltier bays, feeding mostly on crabs. Eastern Pacific, and western Atlantic from Massachusetts through the Caribbean to Brazil. Hoese and Moore, 1958. (4 feet; 1 1/4 m)

20. Great hammerhead *Sphyrna mokarran* (Rüppell)

Deep median indentation on head; deeply falcate pelvic fin; teeth serrated. This, the
largest species of hammerhead, is sometimes known to attack humans. It is the common
large hammerhead often reported as *S. tudes*. Circumtropical, in the western Atlantic
from North Carolina through the Caribbean to Brazil. (15 feet; 4 1/2 m)

21. Scalloped hammerhead *Sphyrna lewini* (Griffith and Smith)

Median indentation on head; pelvic not falcate, second dorsal and anal with long extensions. This is the common hammerhead shark of our coast. Atlantic populations have
been reported as *S. diplana* Springer. Another species of hammerhead with a small eye,

S. tudes, has been erroneously reported from the Gulf but has not been confirmed here yet. It is distinguished from *S. lewini* by having a more rounded head, and smaller eyes, and from *S. tiburo* by having a median anterior notch and an internarial groove along the front of the head and a proportionally larger anal fin. The smooth hammerhead, *S. zygaena* (Linnaeus), is a cold temperate species which, although often reported, has not been verified for the Gulf of Mexico. Circumtropical; in the western Atlantic from Nova Scotia through the Caribbean to Uruguay. Branstetter, 1987b. (10 feet; 3 m)

Triakidae

Smooth dogfishes or smoothhounds are small sharks with the second dorsal almost as large as the first; narrow, catlike eyes; and a spiracle behind each eye. Commonly called nurses because of having small teeth and a rounded mouth, they are sometimes put in the Carcharhinidae, from which they differ in dentition and in lacking a well-developed nictitating membrane. The taxonomy of Gulf species is not clear, but two species are recorded. See fig. 2. Heemstra, 1973; Springer and Lowe, 1963.

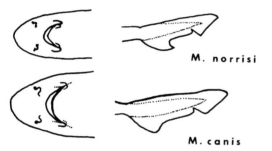

Fig. 3. Features of smooth dogfishes, genus *Mustelus*

1   Lower lobe of caudal fin sharp-pointed, directed rearward … Florida smoothhound, *Mustelus norrisi.*
    Lower lobe of caudal fin broadly rounded … smooth dogfish, *Mustelus canis.*

22. Florida smoothhound *Mustelus norrisi* Springer
Dorsal origin behind pectoral so that midpoint is nearer to pelvic origin than to pectoral axil by one eye diameter; trunk slender; tail with lower lobe sharp-pointed; probably grayish. This is a poorly known species. Florida to Texas. Briggs et al., 1964. (3 feet; 91 cm)

23. Smooth dogfish *Mustelus canis* (Mitchill)
Dorsal origin near rear corner of pectoral so that midpoint is as close to pectoral axil as to pelvic origin; trunk slender but fatter than that of Florida smoothhound; tail some-

times with lobe, but never sharp-pointed; grayish above, lighter below; dorsals with black trim; caudal with sooty spot near tip. Dogfish are commonly taken on hook and line at the snapper banks, but they also appear in trawls on the middle to outer shelf. We have not verified inshore captures, although they have been reported. This is a cold temperate species common inshore from Cape Hatteras to Cape Cod. Bermuda; Bay of Fundy to Uruguay, including Cuba and Jamaica. (5 feet; 1 1/2 m)

Squalidae

The spiny dogfishes are distinctive sharks possessing spines before their dorsal fins and lacking anal fins. Like the smooth dogfishes, they have an oval eye. On the Atlantic coast, the common spiny dogfish, *Squalus acanthias* Linnaeus, ranges from Nova Scotia to Florida but is found south of Cape Hatteras only in winter. It is the common shark used in college biology laboratories.

24. Cuban dogfish *Squalus cubensis* Howell Rivero
This is an upper slope species (60–380 meters) rarely on the outer edge of the shelf. Northern Gulf to Brazil. (2 feet; 61 cm)

Squatinidae

Angel sharks are flattened, raylike fishes, which have some characteristics linking them to rays but which seem to be as different from rays as from most sharks. Unlike in rays, their pectoral fins are not attached in front. The gill openings are ventrolateral.

25. Atlantic angel shark *Squatina dumeril* Lesueur
Broadly rounded, flattened head, with fairly well developed teeth; tapered nasal barbel; brown to dark. This peculiar shark is another cold temperate species residing in the Gulf on the outer shelf, rarely straying inshore. It has the habit of burying itself like many of the rays do. There is some question whether one or two species occur in the western Atlantic. The southern form, with a spatulate nasal barbel, is often called *S. argentina* Marini. Massachusetts to the West Indies and the southern Gulf. (5 feet; 1 1/2 m)

Pristidae

The sawfishes are sharklike rays named for their long, toothed rostral process (saw), which they use to disturb bottom animals and to slash through schools of fish. There are two tropical species in the Gulf, both entering low-salinity water and occasionally fresh water, but they have rarely been reported in recent years. There are also similar true sharks called saw sharks (Pristiophoridae), but these occur in very deep water. (Baughman, 1943a)

1 Caudal fin with a lower lobe; 16–20 rostral teeth ... largetooth sawfish, *Pristis pristis.*
Caudal fin without a lower lobe; 25–32 rostral teeth ... smalltooth sawfish, *Pristis pectinata.*

26. Largetooth sawfish *Pristis pristis* Linnaeus
Saw tapering, with relatively few large teeth. A tropical species previously not uncommon on the Texas coast during the summer but rarely seen lately. This sawfish (formerly known as *P. perotteti*) is not verified from Louisiana but is to be expected there. Tropical Atlantic, in the west from southern Florida and eastern Texas to Brazil. (18 feet; 5 1/2 m)

27. Smalltooth sawfish *Pristis pectinata* Latham
Saw tapering only slightly, with many relatively small teeth. Similar to the common sawfish, this species occurs close inshore. This is the common sawfish in the northern Gulf. Tropical Atlantic, in the west from New York and Bermuda to Brazil. (18 feet; 5 1/2 m)

Rhinobatidae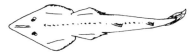

Guitarfishes are slender rays with pointed snouts and a few thorns on the median line of the back. They have small, rounded teeth used to crush small mollusks, crustaceans, and other animals they find on the bottom.

28. Atlantic guitarfish *Rhinobatos lentiginosus* (Garman)
Rostrum translucent; gray to brown, with many small light spots on back, except in northwestern Gulf, where spots are often partly or wholly lacking. This fish, apparently an inshore shelf species, is often taken by trawlers. North Carolina to Florida and throughout the Gulf. (30 inches; 76 cm)

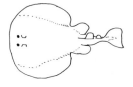

Torpedinidae

Torpedoes are flattened with a fairly large tail (for rays) extending from a more or less circular disc. Two families are unique among elasmobranchs in possessing electric organs—large, specialized muscles from each side of the anterior part of the disc rearward to nearly the end of the pectoral. These organs can be used to repel predators and perhaps to stun prey, or as recent evidence in other electric fishes suggests, to receive information on the surrounding environment by perceiving changes in the electric current. *Narcine,* formerly placed here, is now considered to be in a separate family.

29. Atlantic torpedo *Torpedo nobiliana* Bonaparte

This dark-colored, large ray is a cold temperate species known from the northern Gulf only at the shelf edge off the Mississippi Delta. It has been reported more widely, but it may have been confused with the lesser electric ray. Atlantic Ocean, in the west from Nova Scotia to Trinidad. Bigelow and Schroeder, 1965. (6 feet; 1 2/3 m)

Narcinidae

The lesser electric ray was formerly considered to belong to the same family as the Atlantic torpedo and is the only inshore electric ray.

30. Lesser electric ray *Narcine brasiliensis* (Olfers)

Large kidney-shaped electric organs on pectorals; both dorsals similar in size; varying from gray, blue, or brown to very dark, with or without dark areas outlined by spots. This is the common electric ray in the Gulf, being limited to the inshore shelf, often in the surf zone. It can deliver a sizable shock of over thirty-five volts, which could disable a sensitive person. North Carolina to Brazil. (18 inches; 46 cm)

Rajidae

Skates are small rays with slender tails and varying degrees of armament mostly in the form of small thorns and prickles. They resemble stingrays somewhat, but they have no tail spines, and they do have well-developed dorsal and caudal fins. All species are characteristic of the shelf bottom. Their egg cases, called "mermaids' purses," are commonly washed ashore. (Bigelow and Schroeder, 1958, 1965; McEachran, 1977; McEachran and Musick, 1975)

1   No large thorns on disc posterior to spiracles . . . spreadfin skate, *Raja olseni.*
    Disc with spines posterior to spiracles 2
2   Distance from origin of first dorsal to axils of pelvics as long as distance from axils of pelvics
    to front of orbits, or longer . . . rosette skate, *Raja garmani.*
    Distance from origin of first dorsal fin to axils of pelvics shorter than or hardly longer than
    distance from axils of pelvics to rear of orbits 3

3   No ocellated spots on upper surface of pectorals . . . clearnose skate, *Raja eglanteria*.
    Ocellated spots on upper surface of pectorals . . . roundel skate, *Raja texana*.

31. Spreadfin skate *Raja olseni* Bigelow and Schroeder
Thorns lacking on middle of disc; pectoral fins broadly rounded but somewhat subangular.
This is an outer shelf–upper continental slope species (30–130 fathoms) closely related
to the barndoor skate, *Raja laevis* Mitchill, of the Atlantic coast. Northern Gulf from the
Florida panhandle to northern Mexico. (20 inches; 51 cm)

32. Rosette skate *Raja garmani* Whitley
Pectorals broadly rounded, disc midline with thorns, back speckled. This continental slope
species, formerly thought distinct from Atlantic populations and known as *R. lentiginosa,*
occurs rarely on the lower shelf. New Jersey to Nicaragua. McEachran, 1977. (17 inches;
43 cm)

33. Clearnose skate *Raja eglanteria* Bosc
Rostrum translucent; no spots on back, central row of median spines on back with a few
scattered to the side. This is the common skate of the eastern seaboard; it is also common in the northeastern Gulf but rare in the western Gulf. Massachusetts to southern
Mexico. (3 feet; 91 cm)

34. Roundel skate *Raja texana* Chandler
Rostrum translucent; two ocellated spots on back, median row of spines on back. The
common inshore and middle shelf skate of the northwestern Gulf, it was named by a
parasitologist who, while studying its parasites, realized that it was unknown to science.
This skate feeds mostly on mollusks and benthic polychaete worms. Apparently restricted to the whole Gulf of Mexico. (2 feet; 61 cm)

Urolophidae

The yellow stingray is the only member of this family found in the northwestern Gulf.

35. Yellow stingray *Urolophus jamaicensis* (Cuvier)
Body rounded, almost circular; tail with caudal fin; color a reticulum of darker lines on
light background. Only recently confirmed for Texas, this fish is a rare tropical stray.
Although it has a spine, it is now placed in its own family, Urolophidae. North Carolina
and through the Caribbean to Trinidad. (width 1 foot; 30 cm)

Dasyatidae

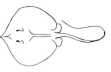

Stingrays possess on the tail one to many serrated spines, which are covered with a toxin and can inflict painful wounds that often become infected. At least one fatality is known in Texas. They are usually shy creatures and avoid humans if given the chance. Although stingrays are plentiful in the bay and Gulf surfs, swimmers or waders generally make sufficient noise to scare away any stingrays that might be in their path. Stingrays may be safely handled by carefully and firmly picking them up by the tip of the tail or by grasping them from the front with the thumb and forefinger in the spiracles, the safest way being to combine both.

Most stingrays are bottom animals, burying themselves with only their eyes and spiracles showing, but the pelagic stingray, *Dasyatis violacea* (Bonaparte), which has a very blunt snout, occurs in the open ocean. (Branstetter and McEachran, 1983)

1	Outer edges of disc broadly rounded	2
	Outer edges of disc subangular, not rounded	3
2	Snout anterior to eyes larger than distance between spiracles; no black fins on tail, only low cutaneous folds . . . Atlantic stingray, *Dasyatis sabina*.	
	Snout anterior to eyes shorter than distance between spiracles; black fins on tail . . . bluntnose stingray, *Dasyatis say*.	
3	No cutaneous fold on upper surface of tail; sides of body and tail covered with tubercles or thorns . . . roughtail stingray, *Dasyatis centroura*.	
	Upper surface of tail with low cutaneous fold; sides of body and tail without tubercles and thorns . . . southern stingray, *Dasyatis americana*.	

36. Atlantic stingray; stingaree *Dasyatis sabina* (Lesueur)

Disc broadly rounded; snout pointed; tail very slender with low brownish fold dorsally and ventrally; brown, often tan. The common inshore stingray, this species is found from nearly fresh to marine salinities. It leaves bays during the colder months but stays on the inshore shelf. Known occasionally to enter Louisiana rivers, it is perhaps more common in Texas. Chesapeake Bay to southern Mexico. Sage et al., 1972. (width 2 feet; 61 cm)

37. Bluntnose stingray *Dasyatis say* (Lesueur)

Disc broadly rounded; snout rounded; tail slender with well-developed dusky to black fold on both sides of tail; body dark, often nearly black. Large rays, often bearing young, are common inshore during the summer but are rarely found in the bays. Massachusetts to Brazil. (width 3 feet; 91 cm)

38. Roughtail stingray *Dasyatis centroura* (Mitchill)

Disc subangular; snout somewhat pointed; tail relatively thick with many thorns and prickles and only lower tail fold; body dark, with tail black. This ray is found in deeper water than most stingrays. Not much is known about it in the Gulf, but it is a cold temperate species common on the North Atlantic coast. North Atlantic, in the west from Massachusetts to Florida, and in the Gulf at least off Louisiana. (width at least 7 feet; 2 m)

39. Southern stingray *Dasyatis americana* Hildebrand and Schroeder
Disc subangular; snout somewhat pointed; tail slender, no thorns, with large lower fold but tiny upper fold, both black; disc gray or dark brown. An inshore ray over much of its range, it occurs in the northern Gulf from the saltier bays to the edges of offshore reefs. New Jersey through the Caribbean to Brazil. (width 5 feet; 1 1/2 m)

Gymnuridae

Butterfly rays are similar to stingrays but have a very short tail and a disc about twice as broad as it is long. Their habits are poorly known but are thought to be similar to those of stingrays. The spiny butterfly ray, *Gymnura altavela* (Linnaeus), possibly occurs in the area as well. It can be recognized by the presence of a tail spine and a tentacle on the spiracle.

40. Smooth butterfly ray *Gymnura micrura* (Schneider)
Disc broad, subangular; tail without spine; spiracle without tentacle; brown with dark blotches. This is a small ray that frequents the inshore shelf and saltier bays, where it prefers sandy bottoms. This habit may account for its apparent scarcity in Louisiana. Atlantic Ocean, in the west from Massachusetts to Brazil. (width 4 feet; 1 1/4 m)

Myliobatidae

Eagle rays are large, free-swimming rays with wide, pointed pectorals. The mouth is ventral and supplied with teeth modified as crushing plates for breaking shells of mollusks and crustaceans. The eagle ray has a blunt snout, no cephalic lobes, and a spine near the base of the tail.

Manta rays are giant, free-swimming rays bearing on the head large fins which, when unrolled, are used to channel larger plankton such as schools of small fishes and crustaceans into the mouth. The mantas were formerly placed in their own family, the Mobulidae. (Notarbartolo-di-sciara, 1987)

1   Teeth large, in few series; anterior divisions of pectorals forming one fleshy lobe below or in front of head or two such lobes, joined 2

Teeth tiny, in many series; anterior divisions of pectorals forming two thin, narrow finlike projections 4

2　One subrostral lobe 3

　　Two joined subrostral lobes . . . cownose ray, *Rhinoptera bonasus.*

3　Single series of teeth in each jaw; back spotted . . . spotted eagle ray, *Aetobatis narinari.*

　　Seven series of teeth in each jaw; back unspotted . . . bullnose ray, *Myliobatis freminvillei.*

4　Mouth on lower surface of head, teeth in both jaws . . . devil ray, *Mobula hypostoma.*

　　Mouth terminal, teeth in lower jaw only . . . manta, *Manta birostris.*

41. Cownose ray *Rhinoptera bonasus* (Mitchill)

Disc broad; pectorals angular; slender tail with spine at base; brown; usually seven series of teeth. Large schools of these rays are found in the saltier bays and on the inshore shelf in summer, with masses leaving at the onset of cold weather. Massachusetts to Brazil. Rogers et al., 1990. (width 3 feet; 91 cm)

42. Spotted eagle ray; duck-billed ray *Aetobatis narinari* (Euphrasen)

Disc wide, pectorals angular; snout elongated somewhat like bill of a duck; brown to black with light spots on back; tail slender. Individuals occur sporadically on the shelf during the warmer months. Worldwide in temperate and tropical waters. (width 7 feet; 2 m)

43. Bullnose ray *Myliobatis freminvillei* Lesueur

Disc wide with angular pectorals, tail long, with a spine at base of rear dorsal fin; head ducklike. This is a poorly known, moderate-sized ray, probably rarely visiting the Gulf. Specimens have been taken east of the Mississippi delta and there is an old record for Galveston. The relationship between this species and the southern eagle ray, *M. goodei* Garman, which has a smaller dorsal fin set far back from the pelvic fin, is unclear. Range uncertain, at least Massachusetts to Florida and occasionally in the northern Gulf. (3 feet; 1 m)

44. Manta; devil ray *Manta birostris* (Walbaum)

Disc wide with pointed pectorals, tail long and slender; mouth terminal; teeth in lower jaw only. Large rays often in schools may be seen almost anywhere and have been captured in Corpus Christi Bay. They often frequent the surface in clear water and sometimes jump high out of the water, smacking the water flat to produce much noise and spray. At the surface they can be seen at a distance because of their habit of curling the pectoral tip up and out of the water. Young are born at a size of four or five feet (1– 1 1/2 m), and maturity is reached at about twelve feet (3 1/2 m). Because of their large size (up to 1 1/2 tons) they are poorly represented in collections. Circumtropical, unless Pacific populations are distinct, in the western Atlantic from Massachusetts and Bermuda through the Caribbean to Brazil. Brasseaux and Hoese, 1991. (width 22 feet; 6 2/3 m)

45. Devil ray *Mobula hypostoma* (Bancroft)

A small version of the manta with cephalic fins. There is a manta-size version of this genus, *M. mobular,* from the eastern Atlantic, which unlike other devil rays has a tail spine. Observers often assume that such large rays must be mantas, which—although likely—may not always be true because schools of devil rays have been seen off Louisiana. New Jersey to Brazil. (4 feet; 1.2 m)

Bony Fishes

(Osteichthyes)

The so-called bony fishes have at least some bone in their skeletons, but they are more readily identified by having only one gill slit covered by an operculum. Actually there are usually three or four pairs of gill arches under the operculum. The sturgeons and the gars are considered the most primitive (oldest or closest to the ancestral types) of the bony fishes and the remainder are divided into a large number of orders. We have bypassed the orders for the families. Details of orders are available in many of the references.

Most bony fishes are layers (oviparous) of floating eggs, but those in a few families (Gobiidae, Blenniidae, Clinidae, Batrachoididae, Gobiesocidae) produce eggs that are demersal (adhering to the bottom) and marine catfishes (Ariidae) are mouth brooders. The male pipefishes (Syngnathidae) incubate the eggs in a pouch, and the live-bearers (Poeciliidae) give birth to living young, like the hammerhead, most requiem, and mackerel sharks. Most families have a pelagic, almost transparent larval stage, but in other families, for example the toadfishes (Batrachoididae), the juveniles hatch directly from the egg. (Bigelow, 1963; Greenwood et al., 1966; Nelson, 1994)

Acipenseridae

Sturgeons are primitive fishes with naked skin embedded with bony plates (scutes). They have small, ventral mouths, preceded by barbels, for feeding on small bottom animals, but they may feed elsewhere, and they have been caught on hook and line. Most species of sturgeon are freshwater fishes, and those occurring in salt water are anadromous. Sturgeons are not common in the Gulf of Mexico, and although some are still caught, especially in the Pearl River drainage, they have been listed as threatened. (Gilbert, 1992)

46. Atlantic sturgeon *Acipenser oxyrhynchus* Mitchill

Scutes in dorsal rows 7–13, in lateral rows 2–35; other small ossifications in skin common. Gulf populations are considered a subspecies, *A. o. desotoi* Vladykov. A freshwater sturgeon, the shovelnose, *Scaphirhynchus platorhynchus* (Rafinesque), occurs in all the larger rivers of the area and the rarer pallid sturgeon, *S. albus* (Forbes and Richardson), may rarely enter low-salinity waters in Louisiana. Species of *Scaphirhynchus* are distinguished from *Acipenser* by their lack of a spiracle. Labrador and Bermuda to Guinea (French Guiana); in the Gulf from the Suwanee River to west Lake Pontchartrain, and the vicinity of the Mississippi River mouth. Gowanloch, 1933; Vladykov, 1955. (14 feet; 4 1/4 m—but in the Gulf may be only 6 ft; 1 2/3 m).

Lepisosteidae

Gars are freshwater fishes with great tolerance for salt water. Alligator gars especially are known to enter coastal bays and the Gulf of Mexico, where they have been found with crabs, mullets, and ducks in their stomachs. Three local species may be found in salt water. A fourth species, the shortnose gar, *Lepisosteus platostomus,* is found in coastal areas of Louisiana but only in fresh water or extremely low salinities. It is recognizable by its short snout and lack of spots. Another form, which may be a hybrid, has been taken in fresh water in Louisiana. (Suttkus, 1963)

1 Snout long and slender, nearly six times interorbital width; head length 32–41 percent of total length ... longnose gar, *Lepisosteus osseus.*
   Snout short and broad, not more than three times interorbital width; head length less than 36 percent of total length 2
2 Gill rakers 59–81; row of enlarged teeth on palatines inside major tooth rows; spots, if present, largely limited to fins ... alligator gar, *Atractosteus spatula.*
   Gill rakers 15–24; no inner row of teeth; many dark spots on body and fins ... spotted gar, *Lepisosteus oculatus.*

47. Longnose gar *Lepisosteus osseus* (Linnaeus)

D. 6–9; A. 8–10; P. 10–13; Sc. 57–63; Gr. 14–31; body olive above, white below, with dark spots on median fins and body. The longnose gar seems most common in coastal waters of the northwestern Gulf near and in Lake Pontchartrain. It may be expected in salt water where it occurs close to the coast, especially in marsh channels. Atlantic coast from Canada to Florida, except in the New England region, and in the Great Lakes; south along the Mississippi drainage to the Gulf of Mexico and the northern Mexican coast. (5 feet; 1 1/2 m)

48. Alligator gar *Atractosteus spatula* (Lacepède)

D. 7–10; A. 7–10; P. 11–15; Sc. 58–62; Gr. 59–81; body olivaceous above, white below, with a few dark spots on body and median fins becoming indistinct with age. Alligator gars are common in brackish water, especially near marshes, and they even enter the Gulf of Mexico, where they are frequently seen gulping air near the surface. They are common market fish in Louisiana, but little is known of their habits in salt water. *A. spatula* is replaced to the south by the similar *A. tropicus* (Gill), and both are sometimes placed in the genus *Lepisosteus* with the other gars. Mississippi and Ohio river drainages and along the coast of the Gulf of Mexico from the Florida panhandle to northern Mexico. (9 feet; 2 3/4 m)

49. Spotted gar *Lepisosteus oculatus* (Winchell)

D. 6–9; A. 7–9; P. 9–13; Sc. 53–59; Gr. 15–24; body olivaceous, darker than in other species of gar, with profusion of dark spots on fins and sides of body and head. This species does not enter salt water as readily as the alligator gar does, and it is usually confined to low salinities. Records of *L. productus* refer to this species. It also may rarely hybridize with the longnose gar. A rare gold-colored variant is also known. On the Florida peninsula it is replaced by the Florida gar, *L. platyrhincus* DeKay, which also may enter salt water. Great Lakes, along the Mississippi River, and in the Gulf of Mexico from western Florida to Corpus Christi. (4 feet; 1 1/4 m).

Megalopidae

Tarpons, which are also known as silver kings or grande écaille, are commonly regarded as a prime inshore game fish. These are large, scaled fish with a gular plate—a hard, bony plate located at the center of the lower jaw. In tarpon, ladyfish, and bonefish the elongate, transparent larva is called a leptocephalus, also found in eels, indicating a close relationship between these otherwise dissimilar fishes. (Greenwood, 1977; Hildebrand, 1963; Lauder and Liem, 1983; Smith, 1980)

50. Tarpon *Megalops atlanticus* Valenciennes

D. 13–15; A. 22–25; Sc. 41–48. The produced last ray of the dorsal fin, the large, silver, platelike scales, and the underslung mouth make the tarpon unmistakable. Young fish frequent low-salinity waters, often in small marsh channels; both young and adults are often found upstream in South Texas. Tarpon and snook *(Centropomus undecimalis)* are similar in many of their habits and requirements and frequently occur together, except that snook are more tropical. Atlantic Ocean, in the west from Nova Scotia through the Caribbean to Brazil. (8 feet; 2 1/2 m)

Elopidae

The ladyfish, like the tarpon, possesses a gular plate and also develops from a leptocephalus larvae. These characters, among others, have led to the classification of tarpon and ladyfish together in the order Elopiformes. The two families are often combined as an expanded Elopidae. Ladyfish, also known as tenpounder, are also excellent game fish although they rarely exceed three pounds. (Thompson and Deegan, 1982)

51. Ladyfish; tenpounder; skipjack *Elops saurus* Linnaeus

D. 21–25; A. 14–17; Sc. 103–120. This smaller, finer-scaled relative of the tarpon is also a noted game fish. The common name tenpounder is derived from this small fish's fighting ability, not its actual weight. Leptocephali of *E. saurus* are found during most of the year, but their greatest abundance occurs in the late spring and early summer. Massachusetts and Bermuda through the Caribbean to Brazil. Herke, 1969. (3 feet; 91 cm)

Albulidae

Bonefish are silvery bottom fish with a subterminal mouth and a sloping forehead. They differ from the elopiform fishes by lacking the gular plate, but they also have a leptocephalus larva. (Hildebrand, 1963; Thompson and Deegan 1982)

52. Bonefish *Albula vulpes* (Linnaeus)

D. 17–18; A. 8–9; Sc. 65–71. Bonefish are highly regarded sport fish in south Florida and throughout the tropical Atlantic. However, they are a rare visitor to the coast of South Texas, where larvae and young fish up to about eighteen inches (46 cm) long have been reported. Leptocephali have also been collected in Louisiana and juveniles have been taken from the Florida panhandle. Circumtropical; in the western Atlantic from Massachusetts and Bermuda through the Caribbean to Brazil. Hoese, 1965; Leary, 1957. (3 feet; 91 cm)

Anguillidae

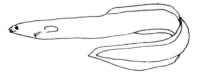

The American eel is the only representative of this family in the western Atlantic. American eels in New England and also their close relatives in Europe and Asia are important food fishes. This and a few other eels are known to have poisonous blood serum, but the toxin is destroyed by cooking. (Halstead, 1967)

53. American eel; congo *Anguilla rostrata* (Lesueur)

This species is easily distinguished from other local eels by the presence of small, embedded scales in the skin. The edges of the tongue are free. Pectoral fins are well developed, and the dorsal, anal, and caudal fins are present and confluent. The American eel spawns in the Sargasso Sea, and the leptocephalus larvae then swim and drift thousands of miles before they ascend freshwater streams, where they grow to maturity. Large eels are often caught in the bays during fall through spring. Greenland to the Guianas. Smith, 1989a. (3 feet; 91 cm)

Moringuidae

Spaghetti eels are a small family of tropical eels. In addition to the ridged eel, the spaghetti eel, *Moringua edwardsi,* has been taken from the Flower Gardens. It can be distinguished by an extended lower jaw, much like the freshwater eel's, and it is unusual because some individuals have lobed caudal fins.

   1   Lower jaw not extending beyond upper jaw . . . ridged eel, *Neoconger mucronatus.*
       Lower jaw extending beyond upper jaw . . . spaghetti eel, *Moringua edwardsi.*

54. Ridged eel *Neoconger mucronatus* Girard

Gill opening low on side; dorsal origin over or behind anus. This eel is seldom seen because of its nocturnal habits. It is apparently common on the middle and inner shelf, with small specimens seen inshore. Off the Mississippi Delta to southern Texas, Cuba, and Colombia. Smith and Castle, 1972. (2 feet; 61 cm)

Muraenidae

Moray eels have the worst reputation of all the eels because of the vicious nature ascribed to the larger members of the family. The less well known smaller species are important members of the continental shelf fauna of the area. They are just as feisty as their larger relatives and should be handled with the same care. Also, two species of the tropical *Enchelycore,* distinguished by arched jaws that allow the teeth to be seen even when the mouth is closed, have been found at the Flower Gardens reefs, and other species are known from off west Florida. (Ginsburg, 1951a; Rezak et al., 1985)

   1   Tail dark, spots lessening posteriorly . . . blacktail moray, *Gymnothorax kolpos.*
       Tail light, spots continuous 2
   2   Teeth entire; two or three fangs may be on the palate; reticulated brown on lighter back-

ground 4

Teeth serrated; no fangs on palate; color solid or with white spots on darker background 3

3   Dorsal fin margined with continuous black; no black lines over branchiostegal region . . . blackedge moray, *Gymnothorax nigromarginatus.*

Dorsal fin margined with white-edged black spots; black lines on branchiostegal region . . . honeycomb moray, *Gymnothorax saxicola.*

4   Corners of mouth purple in adults; background color uniform . . . purplemouth moray, *Gymnothorax vicinus.*

Corners of mouth not purple in adults, lower jaw pale; background color well marked, often separating reticulations into spots . . . spotted moray, *Gymnothorax moringa.*

55. Blacktail moray *Gymnothorax kolpos* Böhlke and Böhlke

This is a little-known outer shelf species, easily identified by small ocellated spots anteriorly, becoming fewer and larger posteriorly, the tail otherwise black. These are the dark morays we described as large *O. ocellatus* in the first edition. The young of this species have not been recognized. North Carolina to Florida and throughout the Gulf. Böhlke and Böhlke, 1980. (2 1/2 feet; 79 cm)

56. Blackedge moray *Gymnothorax nigromarginatus* (Girard)

This is the common moray caught by shrimpers in the northwestern Gulf. It often lives in shells of large snails offshore and in jetties inshore. Alabama west to Yucatán. (2 feet; 61 cm).

57. Honeycomb moray *Gymnothorax saxicola* Jordan and Davis

The honeycomb moray is common over much of the middle shelf eastward from Mobile Bay, where it replaces the blackedge moray. Color differences illustrated as well as range are useful in distinguishing the two species. Both are replaced further south by *G. ocellatus,* a name formerly applied to all three forms. Northern Gulf and North Carolina to Brazil. (2 feet; 61 cm)

58. Purplemouth moray *Gymnothorax vicinus* (Castlenau)

This species is generally unpatterned, although a spotted race is known from elsewhere in its range. It is a tropical reef species as yet known in the area only from the 7 1/2 Fathom Reef off South Texas. Sometimes put in the genus *Lycodontis.* Atlantic Ocean, in the west from Bermuda, North Carolina, and the Bahamas through the Caribbean to Brazil. (2 feet; 61 cm)

59. Spotted moray *Gymnothorax moringa* (Cuvier)

This moray is another tropical species; a common moray on the offshore reefs. It is characterized by a brown or blackish speckled pattern on a white to yellow background.

Like the purplemouth moray, this species is sometimes placed in the genus *Lycodontis*. North Carolina to Brazil. (3 feet; 91 cm)

Nettastomatidae

The duckbill eels are silvery with very slender bodies and long jaws supplied with canines above and below, the most conspicuous being the vomerine fangs in the upper jaw. (Lane and Stewart, 1968; Smith, 1989e)

1   Two lateral rows of vomerine teeth 2
    No lateral rows of vomerine teeth ... freckled pike conger, *Hoplunnis macrurus*.
2   Lateral vomerine teeth movable and concealed by flesh of mouth; five or six branchiostegals
    ... blacktail pike-conger, *Hoplunnis diomedianus*.
    Lateral vomerine teeth fixed and not concealed; seven branchiostegals ... spotted pike-
    conger, *Hoplunnis tenuis*.

60. Freckled pike-conger, silver conger *Hoplunnis macrurus* Ginsburg
The silver conger is distinguished by its large palatal teeth, lizardlike head, and bright, silvery sides. It is the most abundant eel in shrimp trawls in the inshore Gulf. Two other species, *H. tenuis* Ginsburg and *H. diomedianus* Goode and Bean, are predominantly northeastern Gulf species and are rare west of the Mississippi River. Both of these are deepwater species which may occur at the edge of the shelf. Northern Gulf to northern Brazil, but absent in Florida. (20 inches; 51 cm)

Congridae

Although conger eels are among the most common of fishes, most coastal residents have never seen one. Less spectacular than the morays, these eels are most apt to be encountered at night. The life histories of all species are poorly known at best. As with the ophichthids, few are known by common names other than "conger eel." In addition to the species described below, the conger eel, *Conger oceanicus* (Mitchill), has been rarely found in deep waters near the Mississippi Delta and the bandtooth conger, *Ariosoma balearicum* (Delaroche) (= *A. impressa*) has been reported from shelf waters off Alabama and Yucatán, and others are likely. The former distinctively has its outer row of teeth with a cutting edge, and the latter has jaw teeth in bands. (Kanazawa, 1958; Smith, 1989c)

1   Snout projecting well past lower jaw 2
    Snout projecting only slightly; jaws subequal 3

2   Body depth under 4 percent of length; tail over 70 percent of length; palatal teeth in wedge-shaped patch, the posteriormost teeth large; supraorbital pore present . . . whiptail conger, *Rhynchoconger gracilior.*
    Body depth over 4.5 percent of length; tail less than 70 percent of length; palatal teeth in oblong patch; all teeth of similar size; no supraorbital pore present between anterior and posterior nostrils . . . yellow conger, *Rhynchoconger flava.*
3   Upper end of gill opening as high as upper end of pectoral, dorsal origin behind pectoral origin and near posterior end of pectoral fin . . . margintail conger, *Paraconger caudilimbatus.*
    Upper end of gill opening only as high as center of pectoral fin base 4
4   Tail length less than 60 percent of total length; posterior nostril below middle of eye; dorsal and anal rays unsegmented . . . bandtooth conger, *Ariosoma balearicum.*
    Tail length more than 60 percent of total length; posterior nostril at or above middle of eye; dorsal and anal rays segmented 5
5   Dorsal origin over pectoral base; flange present on lower but not upper lip; outer teeth in jaws not forming a cutting edge . . . threadtail conger, *Uroconger syringinus.*
    Dorsal origin behind pectoral fin base, normally over tip of depressed fin; flange present on both lips, that on upper lip well developed; outermost teeth in jaws forming a cutting edge . . . conger eel, *Conger oceanicus* (Mitchell).

61. Yellow conger *Rhynchoconger flava* (Goode and Bean)
A greenish eel with a long snout, it is very abundant on the middle shelf west of Mobile Bay. Tail lengths (see species key) vary from very short and blunt to extremely long and tapering due to the tail healing well enough to disguise damage. Also, the shape of the tooth patch is variable. *Congrina macrosoma* (Ginsburg, 1951a) from off the Isles Dernieres is a stubby version. The whiptail conger *Rhynchoconger gracilior* (Ginsburg) is similar to the yellow conger, occurring on the edge of the shelf onto the slope, especially in the northeastern Gulf. Both species were formerly placed in *Congrina* or *Hildebrandia*. Northern Gulf to Trinidad. (3 feet; 91 cm)

62. Margintail conger *Paraconger caudilimbatus* (Poey)
Gill opening extending to upper pectoral base; dorsal origin after pectoral base. Another poorly known but distinctive eel, this conger has golden hues on its body and is widespread on the middle shelf of the Gulf. North Carolina to Guiana. Kanazawa, 1961. (1 foot; 30 cm)

63. Threadtail conger *Uroconger syringinus* Ginsburg
Gill opening extending to lower pectoral base; dorsal origin reaches pectoral base. This is an offshore shelf—slope species. East coast of Florida and northern Gulf to Suriname, rare in the Bahamas. (1 foot; 30 cm)

Ophichthidae

The snake and worm eels are common in many habitats, where they burrow tail-first into the sediments. The snake eels are characterized by a hard, pointed, finless tail; the worm eels, on the other hand, possess a caudal fin. The worm eels were formerly considered to be in a separate family (Echelidae). The tusky eel, *Aplatophis chauliodus* Böhlke, is known from deep water off Texas. Several species of tropical ophichthids completely lack pectoral fins. Of these (see following key), the indifferent eel, *Ethadophis akkistikos,* is known from a few specimens taken off Texas and the horsehair eel, *Gordiichthys irretitus* Jordan and Davis, is known in the northeastern Gulf and may range to the west; however, identifications of any eels without pectoral fins should be confirmed in McCosker et al. 1989. (Ginsburg, 1951a; Leiby, 1981; Leiby and Yerger, 1980; McCosker, 1973)

1　Caudal fin rays conspicuous and continuous with dorsal and anal fins; gill opening constricted 2

　　Caudal fin rays lacking, with tip of tail a hard or fleshy finless point; gill opening not constricted 3

2　Origin of dorsal fin in front of anus; palatine (vomerine) teeth numerous ... speckled worm eel, *Myrophis punctatus.*

　　Origin of dorsal fin above or behind anus; at most, only one or two palatine teeth ... key worm eel, *Ahlia egmontis.*

3　Dorsal origin behind gill opening; tail longer than body; pectoral fin well developed 4

　　Dorsal origin ahead of gill opening; tail shorter than body; pectoral fins not well developed 8

4　Anterior teeth of both jaws are long fanglike canines extending far outside mouth when it is closed; lower jaw extending beyond snout ... tusky eel, *Aplatophis chauliodus.*

　　Anterior teeth in jaws not fanglike or extending beyond tip of snout 5

5　Jaws subequal; eye over middle of upper jaw; teeth not fanglike 6

　　Jaws about equal; eye anterior to middle of upper jaw; some teeth long and fanglike 7

6　Tail longer than body (about 55 percent of total length); dorsal origin over or before end of pectoral ... snake eel, *Ophichthus gomesi.*

　　Tail equal to or shorter than body; origin of dorsal behind end of pectoral; dark bands on body ... king shrimp eel, *Ophichthus rex.*

7　Largest spots same size as or larger than snout ... spotted spoon-nose eel, *Echiophis intertinctus.*

　　Largest spots smaller than snout length, in about six rows ... stippled spoon-nose eel, *Echiophis punctifer.*

8　Pectoral fins present but appearing as small flaps of skin 9

　　Pectoral fins absent 10

9　Pectoral fin base 13–32 percent of gill opening; small spots above each lateral line pore ... whip eel, *Bascanichthys scuticaris.*

Pectoral fin base greater than 25 percent of gill opening; no spots on lateral line ... sooty eel, *Bascanichthys bascanium.*

10 Underside of snout not grooved, intermaxillary teeth inconspicuous . . . indifferent eel, *Ethadophis akkistikos.*

Underside of snout grooved; intermaxillary teeth protruding ... horsehair eel, *Gordiichthys irretitus.*

64. Speckled worm eel; white eel *Myrophis punctatus* Lütken
This is one of the more common eels found on mud bottoms inshore and in the bays, even occasionally coming into fresh water. Only the juveniles are found inshore, with the strange leptocephalus larvae that probably come from offshore spawning areas appearing on the coast from December through May. North Carolina to Brazil. (2 feet; 61 cm)

65. Key worm eel *Ahlia egmontis* (Jordan)
This tropical worm eel is so far known in this area only from 7 1/2 Fathom Reef. Florida through the Caribbean to Brazil. (16 inches; 41 cm)

66. Shrimp eel *Ophichthus gomesi* (Castelnau)
The shrimp eel is a common inshore eel usually found in muddy habitats in the shallow Gulf of Mexico and the high-salinity bays. Another species reported, the palespotted eel (plate 66b), *Ophichthus puncticeps* (Kaup), formerly known as *O. ocellatus,* derives its name from a series of large, pale spots found along its tan or gray side. We have not verified the palespotted eel from the northwestern Gulf, but it is not uncommon in the northeastern Gulf to North Carolina. Massachusetts and Bermuda through the Caribbean to Brazil. Leiby, 1979. (2 feet; 61 cm)

67. King snake eel *Ophichthus rex* Böhlke and Caruso
This unusually large eel has 14–15 dark bands, more prominent anteriorly. It has been fished commercially in Florida. Böhlke and Caruso, 1980; Burgess et al., 1989. (6 feet; 1 2/3 m, probably larger)

68. Stippled spoon-nose eel *Echiophis punctifer* (Kaup)
This is a common snake eel in the northwestern Gulf, replaced in the northeastern Gulf to North Carolina by the spotted spoon-nose eel, *Echiophis intertinctus* (Richardson). Their habits are not well known, but they occur on the inshore to middle shelf and may occasionally be found in the saltier bays. Large individuals are caught from the Galveston and Port Aransas jetties during the fall months. The appellation "spoon-nose" comes from the unusually flattened skull found in large individuals. All three species were formerly placed in the genus *Mystriophis*. *E. mordax* is a synonym. Mississippi to Mexico through the Caribbean to Brazil (4 feet; 1 1/4 m)

69. Sooty eel *Bascanichthys bascanium* (Jordan)

This slender eel is common in the bays and shallow Gulf where hard-packed fine sand occurs. The whip eel, *Bascanichthys scuticaris*, replaces it in the northeastern Gulf. North Carolina to Florida, west Florida to Texas. Leiby, 1981; Leiby and Yerger, 1980. (2 feet; 61 cm)

Synaphobranchidae

The so-called cutthroat eels are poorly known fishes that differ from the conger eels by having a row of canines on the upper jaw. Similar also to the pike-congers, they differ from the latter by having jaws more typical of an eel and no canines in the lower jaw. (Ginsburg, 1951a; Robins and Robins, 1970, 1989)

70. Shortbelly eel *Dysomma anguillare* Barnard

Tail much longer than body; jaws long, with lower jaw about 40 percent of head length; tongue adnate; three median canines on palate. Southern Texas to Campeche. (1 foot; 30 cm)

Clupeidae

The herrings are schooling fishes occurring in masses of seemingly innumerable individuals that move together as if coordinated by some unseen force. They are important as food for many of the larger species of fish, including important game fish and commercial species. In the Gulf of Mexico menhaden support a sizable commercial fishery. The North Atlantic herring fishery is also well known, and other species of clupeids are exploited in other parts of the world.

A good introduction to those tropical species which are primarily known only from offshore waters may be found in Hildebrand et al. (1963), Berry (1964), and Whitehead (1985). *Harengula* was revised by Rivas (1950) and Whitehead (1973), *Dorosoma* by Miller (1960), *Opisthonema* by Berry and Barrett (1963), *Etrumeus* by Whitehead (1963), and *Brevoortia* by Dahlberg (1970). (Whitehead, 1985)

1 Body rounded, abdomen with ordinary scales 2
   Body compressed, abdomen with keel of modified scales 3
2 Pelvic fins much smaller than pectorals, inserted behind base of dorsal . . . round herring, *Etrumeus teres*.
   Pelvic fins only slightly smaller than pectoral fins, inserted under base of dorsal . . . dwarf herring, *Jenkinsia lamprotaenia*.
3 Back in front of dorsal fin completely scaled; fewer than 150 gill rakers 4

Back in front of dorsal fin with unscaled median strip; more than 150 gill rakers 15
4   Vertical edge of shoulder girdle under opercle with two lobes 5
   Vertical edge of shoulder girdle under opercle smooth, not lobed 10

Fig. 4. Shoulder girdle of *Opisthonema, Sardinella,*
and *Harengula,* showing projecting lobes

5   Last ray of dorsal fin extended, with length about twice dorsal height; 20–25 anal rays . . .
   Atlantic thread herring, *Opisthonema oglinum.*
   Last ray of dorsal same length as rest; 15–20 anal rays 6
6   Last two anal rays enlarged, almost finletlike 7
   Last two anal rays normal 8
7   Anterior gill rakers on lower limbs of second and third arches more or less flat . . . Spanish
   sardine, *Sardinella aurita.*
   Anterior gill rakers on lower limbs of second and third arches curled upwards . . . orangespot
   sardine, *Sardinella brasiliensis.*
8   Tooth plates on tongue and floor of mouth narrow, their width going about 10 times into
   combined length; lower limb gill rakers 27–31; scales loosely attached, usually lost; tips of
   anterior dorsal fin rays dark . . . redear sardine, *Harengula humeralis.*
   Tooth plates on tongue and floor of mouth broad, their width going 3–5 times into com-
   bined length 9
9   Lower limb gill rakers 28–34 (30–32); 40–43 scale rows . . . false pilchard, *Harengula clupeola*
   (Cuvier)
   Lower limb gill rakers 30–40 (32–39); 34–41 scale rows . . . scaled sardine, *Harengula jaguana.*
10 Median row of scales in front of dorsal normal; eight or nine pelvic rays 11
   Median row of scales in front of dorsal enlarged; seven pelvic rays 12
11 Teeth usually lacking in adults; body deep, 25–36 percent of standard length; lower margin of
   upper jaw at a 45-degree angle; gill rakers on lower limb more than 40 . . . Alabama shad,
   Alosa alabamae.
   Teeth always present in lower jaw; body slender, 24–28 percent of standard length; lower
   margin of upper jaw nearly vertical except at tip; gill rakers on lower limb fewer than 30 . . .
   skipjack herring, *Alosa chrysochloris.*
12 Scale rows 36–50; preopercle striated; inner rays of ventral fins shorter than outer rays;
   shoulder spot in adults usually followed by smaller spots 13
   Scale rows 60–75; preopercle smooth; inner and outer rays of ventral fins about equal,
   middle rays longest; shoulder spot single 14
13 More than half the greatest depth below a line from lower margin of eye to middle of caudal
   base; pectoral rays usually 15 or 16; lateral line scales 42–48; Gulf of Mexico distribution . . .
   gulf menhaden, *Brevoortia patronus.*

About half of the greatest depth below a line from lower margin of eye to middle of caudal base; pectoral fin rays 16–18; lateral line scales 45–52; Atlantic Coast distribution ... Atlantic menhaden, *Brevoortia tyrannus*.

14　Ventral scutes 27–29, rarely 30; depressed pectoral fin fails to reach pelvic fin by 1–2 scales ... finescale menhaden, *Brevoortia gunteri*.

　　Ventral scutes 30–32; depressed pectoral fin fails to reach pelvic fin by 3–5 scales ... yellowfin menhaden, *Brevoortia smithi*.

15　Mouth terminal; fewer than 50 scale rows; last dorsal ray twice height of dorsal fin; anal rays 27 or fewer ... threadfin shad, *Dorosoma petenense*.

　　Mouth subterminal or inferior; more than 50 scale rows; last dorsal ray less than 1.5 times height of dorsal fin; more than 25 anal rays ... gizzard shad, *Dorosoma cepedianum*.

71. Round herring (red-eye round herring) *Etrumeus teres* (DeKay)

D. 16–20; A. 10–12; P. 14–16; Sc. 48–55; Gr. 14 + 32–38. The round herring is a poorly known species occurring over much of the shelf. It has been considered to be in a separate family, the Dussumieridae. The name *E. sadina* Mitchill is often used for Atlantic populations south of Florida. Bay of Fundy to the Guianas, also in the eastern Pacific, Hawaii, southern Australia, and Japan. Fore, 1971; Houde, 1977a. (6 1/2 inches; 17 cm)

72. Dwarf herring *Jenkinsia lamprotaenia* (Gosse)

D. 9–13; A. 12–15; P. 12–15 (13); Sc. 33–37; Gr. 19–24 on lower limb; scales usually lost in preservation, greenish above with distinct silver lateral band. Dwarf herring occur in large schools, probably numbering in the millions, chiefly inshore throughout the tropical western Atlantic; occurrence in the northwestern Gulf needs confirmation. Bermuda, Florida, and the Bahamas through the Caribbean to southeastern Brazil. Bullis and Thompson, 1965. (2 inches; 5 cm)

73. Atlantic thread herring; hairyback *Opisthonema oglinum* (Lesueur)

D. 17–21; A. 21–25; P. 15–17; Gr. 40–100+; body silvery, greenish on back, with dark humeral spot; some Gulf specimens showing additional spots, usually with row of less distinct spots behind humeral spot but sometimes with short row of spots along base of dorsal fin and mid-dorsal row after dorsal fin; dorsal and caudal fins yellow. The fish is fairly common in saltier waters and possibly represents an unexploited fishery. Large schools occur, although the thread herring is often taken singly inshore. Gulf of Maine and Bermuda to southeast Brazil. Houde, 1977b. (10 inches; 25 cm)

74. Spanish sardine *Sardinella aurita* Valenciennes

D. 17–19; A. 16–18; P. 15–16; Sc. 41–46; lower limb Gr. 70–100 in adults, 55–85 in younger fish; body fairly elongate, with no shoulder spot. The Spanish sardine is reported from Galveston Bay and Caminada Pass and is not rare in the northeastern Gulf; however, it is primarily a tropical species. The name *S. anchovia* Valenciennes also refers to this species. Both it and other species of *Sardinella* may be confused with the deeper-bodied scaled sardine. The orangespot sardine (Brazilian sardinella), *Sardinella brasiliensis* (Steindachner), which may not be a separate species, is known in the northwestern Gulf only from offshore waters, although it occurs inshore further south. Atlantic Ocean, in the west from Massachusetts to Argentina. (6 inches; 15 cm)

75. Scaled sardine *Harengula jaguana* Poey
D. 17–20; A. 16–18; P. 13–17; Sc. 39–43; Gr. 34–40; relatively deep-bodied, with silvery sides, greenish above; often with a dark humeral spot. This is the most common inshore clupeid on the continental shelf, except where it is replaced inshore off Louisiana by the menhaden. It sometimes enters high-salinity estuarine areas. Previously known as *H. pensacolae* Goode and Bean. Two similar species of *Harengula*—*H. humeralis* (Cuvier), the redear sardine, and *H. clupeola* (Cuvier), the false pilchard—are also known from offshore waters as juveniles and larvae. East coast of Florida (rarely north to New Jersey) through the Caribbean to southeastern Brazil. Houde, 1977c; Whitehead et al., 1988. (6 inches; 15 cm)

76. Alabama shad *Alosa alabamae* Jordan and Evermann
D. 16–20; A. 19–22; P. 16–17; Sc. 55–60; Gr. 42–48. The Alabama shad is an anadromous species, found inland in much of the Mississippi embayment. On the coast it is rare west of the Mississippi River and not known west of Grand Isle or east of Choctawhatchee Bay in the Florida panhandle. (20 inches; 51 cm)

77. Skipjack herring *Alosa chrysochloris* (Rafinesque)
D. 16–21; A. 18–21; P. 16–17; Sc. 51–60; Gr. 20–24 on lower limb. This is a poorly known anadromous fish, fair numbers of which are occasionally found in low-salinity waters in western Louisiana. It is sometimes placed in the genus *Pomolobus*. Also in the Mississippi embayment, it has been caught in salt water from the Apalachicola River to Corpus Christi Bay. (18 inches; 46 cm)

78. Gulf menhaden *Brevoortia patronus* Goode
D. 17–21; A. 20–23; P. 14–17; Sc. 36–50; Gr. 40–150; body silvery, greenish on back, with dark humeral spot and usually with series of smaller spots behind humeral one. This is the commercial "pogy," with the center of its abundance off western Louisiana. Juveniles are found in marshes of very low salinity, and the adults are only rarely taken far offshore. The gulf menhaden is closely related to and resembles the Atlantic menhaden, *Brevoortia tyrannus* Latrobe, which occurs on the Atlantic Coast from Nova Scotia to the Indian River of Florida. The gulf menhaden occurs throughout the northern Gulf of Mexico, from the Caloosahatchee River, Florida, to Yucatán. Christmas et al., 1982; Simoneaux, 1979; Shaw et al., 1985a, b; Vaughan, 1987; Warlen, 1988. (10 inches; 25 cm)

79. Finescale menhaden *Brevoortia gunteri* Hildebrand

D. 17–20; A. 20–25; P. 15–16; Sc. 60–75; Gr. 97–150. In general appearance *B. gunteri* is like *B. patronus*, except that *B. gunteri* is much more silvery and it never has more than one spot on its sides. Although it is known from the entire area, this fish is more common off southern Texas. The closely related yellowfin menhaden, *B. smithi* Hildebrand, occurs as far west as the Chandeleurs and replaces *B. gunteri* in the eastern Gulf. They differ by a number of overlapping characteristics, making identification difficult. Chandeleur Islands west and south to Yucatán. Christmas and Gunter, 1960. (10 inches; 25 cm)

80. Yellowfin menhaden (yellowfin shad) *Brevoortia smithi* Hildebrand

D. 18–20; A. 22–23; P. 16–17; Sc. 60–70 (too irregular to count easily); lower limb Gr. 121–149 in adults. Sides silvery, back bluish green; large black spot at shoulder not followed by additional spots; fins golden yellow, margin of caudal paler than rest of fin. Intergrades with *B. gunteri* through north-central and eastern Gulf. Reports from Texas (Nelson, 1992) probably refer to *B. gunteri*. Beaufort, N.C., to the Chandeleur Islands off Louisiana. (13 1/4 inches; 33 cm)

81. Threadfin shad *Dorosoma petenense* (Gunther)

D. 11–14; A. 17–27; P. 12–17; Sc. 41–48; Gr. 300+. The threadfin shad is a freshwater fish known to enter the bays, especially in the summer and fall. Throughout the central United States and Gulf drainages, south to Belize. (7 inches; 18 cm)

82. Gizzard shad *Dorosoma cepedianum* (Lesueur)

D. 10–13; A. 25–36; P. 14–17; Sc. 52–70; Gr. 300+. This is another freshwater fish, but one common in low-salinity bays. Atlantic drainages of North America south to central Mexico. (12 inches; 30 cm)

Engraulidae

The anchovies are the most abundant of the schooling, pelagic fishes. Although most of the local species are not large enough to be of commercial importance, they serve as food for many of the larger fishes. Only four species of anchovies have been confirmed from the northwestern Gulf of Mexico, but other tropical species should be expected offshore during the summer. Although individuals of different species are occasionally found together, the schools are usually limited to distinct areas. (Daly, 1970; Hildebrand, 1964a; Nelson, 1986; Whitehead et al., 1988)

1	Posterior part of maxilla square or rounded, not reaching mandible 2
	Posterior part of maxilla pointed, reaching beyond mandible (often to opercular margin) 3

2   Head short, less than 25 percent of standard length ... flat anchovy, *Anchoviella perfasciata*.
    Head long, greater than 25 percent of standard length ... silver anchovy, *Engraulis eurystole*.
3   Anal fin origin under anterior half of origin of dorsal fin, snout short, less than 4.5 percent of
    standard length 4
    Anal fin origin under or behind midpoint of dorsal fin (usually behind end of dorsal fin in
    adults), snout long, more than 4.5 percent of standard length 5
4   Anal fin rays 25–30; body deep, greater than 19 percent of standard length; anus just ante-
    rior to anal fin origin ... bay anchovy, *Anchoa mitchilli*.
    Anal fin rays 24 or less; body slender, less than 18 percent of standard length, anus well in
    advance of anal fin origin ... Cuban anchovy, *Anchoa cubana*.
5   Snout long, more than 6.5 percent of standard length, pseudobranch longer than eye diam-
    eter ... dusky anchovy, *Anchoa lyolepis*.*
    Snout moderate, less than 6.5 percent of standard length; pseudobranch short, not reaching
    onto inner face of operculum .... striped anchovy, *Anchoa hepsetus*.

83. Flat anchovy *Anchoviella perfasciata* (Poey)

D. 12–15; A. 15–18; P. 14–16; Sc. about 40–44; Gr. 19–23 + 24–28; sides with distinct silvery lateral band, nearly as broad as eye. The status of this species in the western Gulf is not known. It has been reported occasionally in the northeastern Gulf; however, Hastings (1977) has referred some northeastern Gulf collections to *Engraulis eurystole*, a practice followed by Boschung (1992) for Alabama collections. *E. eurystole* closely resembles *A. perfasciata* except that in the former species the dorsal fin is entirely in front of the anal fin base (with a gap) and the eye is smaller. As indicated by its occurrence else-where, the flat anchovy should be expected over much of the continental shelf. It is generally found inshore but is not known to enter brackish water. North Carolina to Florida, West Indies, northeastern and southern Gulf of Mexico. Hastings, 1977; Guillory et al., 1985 (4 inches; 10 cm)

84. Bay anchovy *Anchoa mitchilli* (Valenciennes)

D. 14–16; A. 24–30; P. 11–12; Sc. 38–40; Gr. 15–19 + 21–23; sides with silvery lateral band scarcely as wide as pupil of eye. This is an extremely common fish, restricted to the bays, close inshore areas, and coastal fresh water. Maine to Florida and throughout the Gulf of Mexico, but rare in the Florida Keys and Yucatán. Robinette, 1983. (4 inches; 10 cm)

---

*   Considerable confusion exists in the literature concerning the exact number and names of anchovies with long snouts. Daly (1970) referred all Gulf specimens to *A. nasuta*, while noting that *A. lyolepis* also occurred off Miami. Whitehead (1973) synonymized the forms (as *lyolepis*) but Robins et al. (1980) repeated Daly's contention of two distinct sympatric forms. Nelson (1986) considered *nasuta* to be a South American form but notes that North American *lyolepis* more closely resemble *nasuta* than do southern *lyolepis*. The possibility exists then that one of the two southern forms may co-occur with the northern form or that there may be an undescribed species of anchovy from Florida and the eastern Gulf. The longnose anchovy, *A. nasuta*, should be distinguishable from the dusky anchovy by its higher gill raker count, typically more than 24 in *A. nasuta* and 23 or fewer in *A. lyolepis*.

85. Cuban anchovy *Anchoa cubana* (Poey)
D. 14–16; A. 20–24; Sc. 40–43; Gr. 17–23 + 23–33. Anus located well in advance of anal fin origin, about halfway between bases of ventral fins and anal fin origin. This is a slender anchovy poorly known from scattered specimens from Louisiana. North Carolina through the Caribbean to southern Brazil. (3 inches; 7 cm)

86. Striped anchovy *Anchoa hepsetus* (Linnaeus)
D. 13–17; A. 18–24; P. 13–17; Sc. 37–43; Gr. 15–20 + 18–24; sides with silvery stripe about 75 percent as wide as eye. This common species is usually found farther offshore than the bay anchovy. These are fish of saltier, clearer waters and may be found from the beach to the middle shelf. Nova Scotia through the Caribbean to Uruguay. Robinette, 1983. (5 1/4 inches; 14 cm)

87. Dusky anchovy *Anchoa lyolepis* Evermann and Marsh
D. 12–15; A. 19–23; P. 12–14; Sc. 40–44; Gr. 18–19 + 21–27. A poorly known species, this anchovy occurs in schools over the continental shelf, with occasional individuals straying inshore. Its distribution may at times overlap that of other anchovies, but it is usually found in deeper water. Large schools appear reddish on the surface when seen from a distance; the explanation for this phenomenon is not clear. The taxonomy of this species has been confused, although Whitehead et al. (1988) consider all *A. nasuta* records as this species. Based on the conclusions of Daly (1970), the species was included in our 1977 edition and in other works on Gulf fishes under the name *A. nasuta* Hildebrand and Carvalho, a species which, if different, would not occur in the Gulf (but see footnote in key) and from which *A. lyolepis* can be distinguished by the higher number of gill rakers in *nasuta*. North Carolina (rarely New York) to southern Brazil. Nelson, 1986. (2 1/2 inches; 6 cm)

Synodontidae

The lizardfishes (also known as cigarfishes) are a family of mostly small, benthic, carnivorous fishes. All are elongate and possess a fleshy adipose fin. They are occasionally caught on hook and line, and they show up regularly in shrimp trawls; however, they are of no commercial value. In some parts of the southern United States they are mistakenly believed to be poisonous. A large lizardfish might inflict a painful bite, but none of them are known to possess any toxin or venom. One species, *Saurida normani,* is known from the northeastern but not the northwestern Gulf. (Anderson et al., 1966a, b)

1   Ventral rays eight, with inner rays much longer than outer rays; single band of teeth on each side of palate 2
     Ventral rays nine, with inner rays about as long as outer ones; double row of teeth on each

side of palate 6

2   Anterior profile rounded; anal fin origin about midway between base of caudal fin and insertion of pectoral fin, anal fin closer to origin of ventral fins than to base of caudal; anal fin base more than 23 percent of standard length; anal rays 14–16 ... snakefish, *Trachinocephalus myops*.

Anterior profile pointed, anal fin origin much nearer to base of caudal fin than to insertion of pectoral fins; anal fin origin closer to caudal base than to origin of ventrals; anal fin base only 18 percent of standard length; anal rays 8–13, rarely 14 3

3   Scales in lateral line more than 52 (usually 54–65) 4

Scales in lateral line fewer than 52 (usually 43–50) 5

4   Anal rays usually 10–13; anterior rays of dorsal fin reaching past tips of posterior rays when fin is depressed ... inshore lizardfish, *Synodus foetens*.

Anal rays usually 8–10; anterior rays of depressed dorsal fin not reaching past posterior rays ... red lizardfish, *Synodus synodus*.

5   Dorsal fin with anterior rays not extending beyond tips of posterior rays when fin is depressed; lower jaw rounded and without fleshy knob at tip; black patch on shoulder girdle under gill cover ... sand diver, *Synodus intermedius*.

Dorsal fin with anterior rays extending to and usually beyond tips of posterior rays when fin is depressed; lower jaw ending in fleshy knob; no black patch on shoulder girdle under gill cover ... offshore lizardfish, *Synodus poeyi*.

6   Lower jaw shorter than upper ... shortjaw lizardfish, *Saurida normani*.

Lower jaw longer than upper 7

7   Scales in lateral line 40–50 ... largescale lizardfish, *Saurida brasiliensis*.

Scales in lateral line 51–60 ... smallscale lizardfish, *Saurida caribbaea*.

88. Snakefish *Trachinocephalus myops* (Forster)

D. 11–13; A. 14–16; P. 11–13; Sc. 53–59; anterior profile rounded; dark spot at the upper corner of gill opening. The snakefish is a tropical species, usually found on coarse bottoms from twenty to over two hundred fathoms. Circumtropical, except absent from the eastern Pacific; in the western Atlantic from Massachusetts and Bermuda through the Caribbean to Brazil. (7 inches; 18 cm)

89. Inshore lizardfish *Synodus foetens* (Linnaeus)

D. 10–13; A. 10–14; P. 12–15; Sc. 56–65; adults brownish with greenish tint on back; small fish with distinctive spots along back (generally true for all lizardfishes; for key to juveniles of this family, see Gibbs, 1959). Regularly occurring inshore and in the bays, this is the only lizardfish that commonly enters brackish water; however, the larger individuals occur farther offshore in depths out to one hundred fathoms. The scientific name *foetens* refers to the fetid smell the fish rapidly develops when left out in the sun. Massachusetts and Bermuda through the Caribbean to southeastern Brazil. (16 inches; 41 cm)

90. Red lizardfish; rockspear *Synodus synodus* (Linnaeus)

D. 12–14; A. 8–10; P. 11–12; Sc. 54–59. This bright red tropical species is known here only from an offshore reef, and it is probably limited to such habitats. Tropical Atlantic, in the west from the northern Gulf, the Bahamas, through the Caribbean to Uruguay. (6 inches; 15 cm)

91. Sand diver *Synodus intermedius* (Spix)

D. 11–13; A. 10–12; P. 11–13; Sc. 42–52. The large dark spot on the shoulder, partly covered by the opercle, makes this species the synodontid with the most distinctive color pattern. This species is most common in waters twenty to sixty fathoms deep; however, it has been collected at depths between eight and 175 fathoms. North Carolina and Bermuda through the Caribbean to northeastern Brazil. (18 inches; 46 cm)

92. Offshore lizardfish *Synodus poeyi* Jordan

D. 11–12; A. 9–12; P. 10–12; Sc. 43–48. A dark, fleshy knob at the tip of the lower jaw distinguishes this fish. It is an offshore species usually found between fifteen and 175 fathoms. North Carolina to Suriname. (6 inches; 15 cm)

93. Largescale lizardfish *Saurida brasiliensis* Norman

D. 9–12; A. 10–13; P. 11–13; Sc. 43–49; usually three and sometimes four complete rows of scales between dorsal fin and lateral line. Generally found between ten and 125 fathoms, this species is not rare in the middle shelf region. North Carolina to Guianas and Africa. (6 inches; 15 cm)

94. Smallscale lizardfish *Saurida caribbaea* Breder

D. 10–12; A. 11–12; P. 12–13; Sc. 54–60; always four complete rows of scales between dorsal fin and lateral line. Found in three to 250 fathoms, this species has been reported only once from the western Gulf of Mexico. North Carolina to Brazil. Bullis and Thompson, 1965. (3 inches; 8 cm)

Ictaluridae

Although several freshwater catfishes occur in the coastal plain, only a single species, the blue catfish, regularly enters salt water. Channel catfish, *Ictalurus punctatus* (Rafinesque), which usually has spots, is an important commercial and sport fish, but it penetrates only into very low salinities. The white catfish, *I. catus* (Linnaeus), which is distributed in the Gulf east of the range of the blue catfish and on the Atlantic Coast, also enters low salinities. (Perry, 1969)

95. Blue catfish *Ictalurus furcatus* (Lesueur)

D. I, 5–6; A. 32–35. Eight barbels easily separate the blue catfish from the saltwater catfishes. The long anal fin of the blue catfish, with usually three to eight more rays, and the absence of spots on the body distinguish it from the channel catfish. Color is variable but often light to slate blue. A common fish in low salinities, normally entering open bay waters in winter, it is caught on trotlines and set lines over much of the Louisiana coast and in some areas of Texas. Mississippi Valley west to Mexico; Gulf Coast from at least Mobile Bay to the central Mexican coast. (18 inches; 46 cm—larger in fresh water)

Ariidae

The sea catfishes have two representatives in the northwestern Gulf of Mexico. Both species resemble "typical" catfishes, with naked skin and large, serrated spines on the dorsal and pectoral fins. Both species also have the oral incubation habit in which the males carry the fertilized eggs in their mouths. Catfishes may be safely handled by firmly grasping the body from the front with the whole hand so that the fingers push against the backs of the erect pectoral spines and the front of the erect dorsal spine. Most people prefer to use pliers. Gudger, 1916.

I Barbels on both jaws rounded, six in number; dorsal and pectoral fins without elongated first rays ... hardhead catfish, *Arius felis*.

Barbels on both jaws flattened, four in number; dorsal and pectoral fins with elongated first rays ... gafftopsail catfish, *Bagre marinus*.

96. Hardhead catfish; tourist trout; TR *Arius felis* (Linnaeus)

D. I, 7; A. 16; sides blue or gray; venter white; barbels relatively short. The hardhead is quite abundant in the bays and the shallow Gulf. Although edible, it is generally considered to be a pest by most fishermen and is rarely eaten. Hardheads are known for their diverse food habits, and their young have been observed scraping the sides of other fish, presumably feeding on the mucous, scales, and ectoparasites. There is evidence that these fish possess a crude sonar. The spines are covered with a layer of venomous tissue that can inflict considerable pain, which is lessened with bleeding. Massachusetts to southern Mexico. Halstead, 1978; Hoese, 1966a; Tavolga, 1971; Ward, 1957. (2 feet; 61 cm)

97. Gafftopsail catfish; gafftop *Bagre marinus* (Mitchill)

D. I, 7; A. 23; sides light blue; venter white; barbels and first rays of pectoral and dorsal fins elongate. Common in the bays and shallow Gulf, larger individuals are good food fish. Massachusetts to Panama. (2 feet; 61 cm)

Batrachoididae

The toadfishes are primarily benthic fishes, spending most of their time near or even buried in the bottom. They attach their eggs to hard substrates and have no free-swimming larval stages. Some members of the family are highly venomous; however, of the local species only the midshipman has venom, and even it has no serious effects on large organisms like humans. On the other hand, large toadfishes can inflict painful bites with their powerful jaws, but their blunt teeth usually do not break the skin.

1 Dorsal spines three; opercle with two strong, diverging spines 2

   Dorsal spines two; opercle very small but with single spine; sides of body and venter lined with buttonlike photophores ... Atlantic midshipman, *Porichthys plectodon.*

2 Background color light, overlaid with brown spots as large as pupil of eye and covering head, body, and fins; pectoral fins with brown spots on light background . . . leopard toadfish, *Opsanus pardus.*

   Background color dark, overlaid with lighter crossbars or by a mottled pattern, but not as above; pectoral fins with barred pattern 3

3 Pectoral rays 18–19; dorsal rays 24–25; pectoral fin with light crossbars, each composed of a row of definite light spots ... gulf toadfish, *Opsanus beta.*

   Pectoral rays 19–20; dorsal rays 25–26; pectoral fin crossbars uniformly pale, not composed of rows of spots ... oyster toadfish, *Opsanus tau.*

98. Atlantic midshipman *Porichthys plectodon* Jordan and Gilbert

D. II + 34–36; A. III, 30–37; P. 15–20; sides and ventral surface of body covered with regularly arranged rows of photophores; body light tan to golden on sides, often with large or small brown blotches. Fishes living in areas with predominantly light sediments show a lighter pattern than most midshipmen from the northwestern Gulf of Mexico. The opercle is small but ends in a sharp spine, by which the fish's venom may be injected. Members of the genus *Porichthys* are the only North American shore fishes that possess photophores, and the common name and a former generic name, *Nautopaedium,* refer to the rows of photophores, which resemble the buttons on a nineteenth-century naval midshipman's uniform. The Atlantic midshipman was formerly known as *P. porossisimus* (Valenciennes). Virginia to Brazil. Gilbert and Kelso, 1971; Lane, 1967. (8 inches; 20 cm)

99. Leopard toadfish *Opsanus pardus* (Goode and Bean)

D. III + 23–26; A. III, 20–23; P. 20–21; body with light background covered by darker spots. This species is found offshore on reefs and other rocky areas. Similar-appearing specimens from the southeastern Atlantic Coast (Dahlberg, 1975; Gilligan, 1989) apparently belong to an undescribed species. Gulf of Mexico and possibly throughout the Caribbean. Causey, 1969; Moseley, 1966a. (1 foot; 30 cm)

100. Gulf toadfish; oyster dog (dogfish; mudfish) *Opsanus beta* (Goode and Bean)

D. III + 23–26; A. III, 19–23; P. 18–19; body dark, with irregular light blotches or cross-bars; crossbars on pectoral fins composed of a series of round light spots. Gulf toadfish are common in the bays, on oyster reefs, and around jetties. Small individuals sometimes enter sunken cans or jars and subsequently grow to fill them and become trapped while feeding on other animals also seeking shelter in the containers. This species is replaced on the Atlantic Coast north of Cape Sable, Florida, by the closely related species, *O. tau* (Linnaeus), which can be distinguished by its higher fin ray counts (see key) and lack of spots in the pectoral fin crossbars. Cape Sable, Florida, through the Gulf of Mexico to Yucatán, and in the West Indies. (15 inches; 38 cm)

Antennariidae

The frogfishes are rather grotesque creatures characterized by having the first two dorsal spines detached and modified into a movable "fishing rod," the illicium, which is complete with "lure," the esca. The batfishes (Ogcocephalidae) share this trait, but their illicium is more concealed. In both families the shape of the lure differs among species and is used as an important taxonomic distinction. Frogfishes have distensible stomachs, which allow them to eat fish longer than themselves. (Schultz, 1957; Pietsch and Grobecker, 1987)

1 Two fleshy cirri on dorsal midline before first modified dorsal spine ... sargassumfish, *Histrio histrio*.

No cirri on snout in front of first modified dorsal spine 2

2 Lure at end of illicium singular, either unexpanded or bulbous 3

Lure at end of illicium forked (bifid) or with multiple ends; dorsal rays 11–12; anal rays 6–7 ... striated frogfish, *Antennarius striatus*.

3 End of illicium bulbous; dorsal rays 13; anal rays 8 ... singlespot frogfish, *Antennarius radiosus*.

End of illicium flat, unexpanded; dorsal rays 12; anal rays 6 or 7 ... longlure frogfish *Antennarius multiocellatus*.

101. Sargassumfish *Histrio histrio* (Linnaeus)

D. I + I + 12 (incl. illicium); A. 6; numerous cirri about mouth and head, with two on the dorsal midline before illicium being characteristic of the species. The coloration of this fish closely resembles that of the *Sargassum* weed in which the fish usually lives, but is quite variable when the fish is found elsewhere. In general the body is tan, variously mottled, streaked, and spotted with cream, yellow, and darker brown. The fish is found in all warm seas, wherever *Sargassum* is found. *H. gibba* is a synonym. (6 inches; 15 cm)

102. Striated frogfish *Antennarius striatus* (Shaw and Nodder)

D. I + I + I + 11–12; A. 6–7; illicium bifid, Y-shaped; body either plain or pale purple with dark brown stripes and spots and with spots on fins; however, spots are never ocellated. Previously known as the split-lure frogfish, *Antennarius* (or *Phrynelox*) *scaber* (Cuvier). A plain color phase has been described as a separate species, *P. nuttingi* (Garman). The striated frogfish is not as common here as the singlespot frogfish, and it occurs farther offshore. New Jersey and Bermuda through the Caribbean to southern Brazil, also eastern Atlantic and Indo-Pacific. (5 inches; 13 cm)

103. Singlespot frogfish *Antennarius radiosus* Garman

D. I + I + I + 13; A. 8; illicium bulbous; body dark brown or gray with single large, ocellated spot at base of soft dorsal fin. This species is common on the middle shelf off most of the coastline. It was formerly included in the genus *Phrynelox*. Bermuda and New York south through the Gulf to northern Venezuela. (3 inches; 8 cm)

104. Longlure frogfish *Antennarius multiocellatus* (Valenciennes)

D. I + I + I + 12; A. 6–7; illicium long and slender; body color variable, tan, red, yellow, or orange, often matching coral or sponge-encrusted substrates upon which the fish lives. Characteristic ocellated spots occur at the base of the posterior soft dorsal and along the middle of the anal base, and three (rarely 4) form a narrow triangle on the caudal fin. Less developed ocellations appear on the sides of the body beneath, above, and behind the pectoral fins. The spots distinguish this species from the ocellated frogfish, *A. ocellatus* (Bloch and Schneider), which has three darkly pigmented ocelli on each side—one at the dorsal base, one on the mid-body, and one on the caudal fin. Further, the ocellated frogfish has eight anal rays and an illicium with numerous short filaments; and, while it occurs in the eastern Gulf, it has not been reported from Texas or Louisiana. The longlure frogfish has only recently been reported from the Gulf of Mexico by Dennis and Bright (1988b). Bermuda and the northern Gulf through the Caribbean to Venezuela. (1 foot; 30 cm)

Ogcocephalidae

The grotesque flattened batfishes cause considerable wonder the first time a representative is seen. They are fairly common inhabitants of the shelf and deeper areas and occur regularly in shrimp trawls. They frequent the bottom, using a downward-projecting "bait" (known as the esca), located between the mouth and the tip of the rostrum, to attract food out of the bottom. As in the related frogfishes, the shape of this bait can be used to separate genera and species. Batfishes, together with practically all other ugly fishes, are colloquially called "dogfish."

Due to the confusion in application of names, exact ranges are uncertain. Besides the species below, all of which occur commonly off Louisiana, Texas, and at least part of Mexico, three additional species are known in the Gulf:

(1) the tricorn batfish, *Zalieutes mcgintyi* Fowler, primarily a slope species, with two longitudinal rows of bucklers on the underside and three-pointed rostrum;

(2) the roughback batfish, *Ogcocephalus parvus* Longley and Hildebrand, with 10–11 pectoral rays, wide bands on the outer part of the pectorals, a short rostrum, and a triangular body; known from North Carolina to the shelf of the northeastern Gulf, to Alabama and Yucatán; and

(3) the longnose batfish, *Ogcocephalus corniger* Bradbury, with a long rostrum, a triangular body, and pectorals with an outer band, common on the shelf of the northeastern Gulf but to the west known only from reefs off Galveston and Mexico. (Bradbury, 1967, 1980)

1   Dorsal fin usually with four rays; dorsal body outline triangular; eyes lateral 2
    Dorsal fin with 5–7 rays; dorsal body outline rounded; eyes partly dorsal 3
2   Pectoral rays 10–11; pectoral fin with a few small spots not in reticulated pattern; tips without fleshy pads on ventral side ... slantbrow batfish, *Ogcocephalus declivirostris*.
    Pectoral with 12–13 rays; pectoral fin and shoulder with numerous brown spots forming reticulated pattern; tips with fleshy pads on ventral surface ... spotted batfish, *Ogcocephalus pantostictus*.
3   Vomer and palatines with teeth; two and one-half gill arches; disc circular; esca not lobed ... pancake batfish, *Halieutichthys aculeatus*.
    Vomer and palatines toothless; two gill arches; disc oval to subtriangular; esca lobed ... offshore batfish, *Dibranchus atlanticus*.

105. Slantbrow batfish *Ogcocephalus declivirostris* Bradbury

D. 4; A. 4; P. (10)–11; head narrowly triangular but body behind pectorals relatively thick; pectorals and body not spotted; back very rough; rostrum short and not upturned. This is perhaps the most common middle shelf batfish from Louisiana to northern Mexico. In the past it has been confused with *O. parvus* because of its pectoral ray counts. Florida panhandle to South Texas. (6 inches; 15 cm)

106. Spotted batfish *Ogcocephalus pantostictus* Bradbury

D. 4; A. 4; P. 12–13; head broadly triangular, with body behind pectorals relatively thin; body and pectorals spotted, often with reticulations on fin; rostrum short and upturned. This seems to be the common inshore species from Louisiana to Mexico. It has been reported as *O. vespertilio, radiatus,* and *cubifrons*. Florida panhandle to northern Mexico. (1 foot; 30 cm)

107. Pancake batfish *Halieutichthys aculeatus* (Mitchill)

D. I, 4–5; A. 4; P. 16–18; head rounded, no rostrum, pectorals and caudal banded; body very flat; brown. This is a common species on the middle shelf, but its young may be taken inshore. North Carolina to Venezuela and throughout the Gulf. (4 inches; 10 cm)

108. Offshore batfish *Dibranchus atlanticus* Peters

D. 6–7; A. 4; P. 13–15; head oval to subtriangular; tail long. This continental slope species rarely occurs on the shelf. Atlantic Ocean, in the west from Rhode Island to northern Brazil. (6 inches; 15 cm)

Bregmacerotidae

The codlets are small, midwater fishes related to the cod family. Although four species have been reported in the northwestern Gulf of Mexico, three are known only from larvae or small juveniles collected from offshore waters. All four species closely resemble one another as adults, differing primarily in meristics as noted in the key, and may occur together in the same collections. Ditty et al., 1988; Fahay and Markle, 1984; Houde 1981; Milliken and Houde, 1984; Saksena and Richards, 1986.

<table>
<tr><td>1</td><td>Second dorsal fin rays 57 or more, anal fin rays 58 or more ... MacClelland's codlet, Bregmaceros macclellandi.</td></tr>
<tr><td></td><td>Second dorsal fin rays 56 or fewer, anal rays 57 or fewer .... 2</td></tr>
<tr><td>2</td><td>Second dorsal fin rays 47–56, anal fin rays 49–58 ... antenna codlet, Bregmaceros atlanticus.</td></tr>
<tr><td></td><td>Second dorsal usually with fewer than 47 rays, anal usually with fewer than 49 rays .... 3</td></tr>
<tr><td>3</td><td>Second dorsal fin rays 45–48, anal fin rays 45–49; larvae and juveniles plain, without distinctive dark coloration ... Bregmaceros cantori.</td></tr>
<tr><td></td><td>Second dorsal fin rays 40–44, anal fin rays 41–46; larvae and juveniles possess distinctive dark pigmentation at tip of lower jaw and between the two dorsal fins ... stellate codlet, Bregmaceros houdei.</td></tr>
</table>

109. Antenna codlet *Bregmaceros atlanticus* Goode and Bean

D. I + 47–56; A. 49–59; Sc. 65; dorsal and anal fins with centermost rays depressed. The greatly elongate ventral fins and single free dorsal ray give this fish its common name and make it rather distinctive. Common on the middle shelf in the northwestern Gulf, it is seldom caught except in plankton nets because of its small size and habit of migrating off the bottom at night. This codlet and other similar species are widespread in the Gulf. Atlantic Ocean, in the west from New Jersey to Guayana. Dawson, 1968. (2 1/2 inches; 61 cm).

Steindachneridae

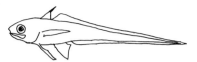

The luminous hake is the only member of this family, which has often been combined with other families of codlike fishes: Gadidae, Merlucciidae, or Macrouridae. It is an oddly shaped species, most common in deeper waters but regularly occurring over certain very muddy regions of the shelf.

110. Luminous hake *Steindachneria argentea* Goode and Bean

D. VIII + 123+; A. 10 + 113; Sc. very small and numerous; head large, with gradually tapering body and tail (often damaged) ending in filament; body silvery, with striated light organ on ventral half of body and sides of head; eye large. A continental slope species, it is common on the steep outer and middle shelf off the Mississippi River mouth, where it was first discovered nearly a century ago. Its range outside the Gulf of Mexico is uncertain, although it has recently been reported from as far south as Guyana off the Orinoco by Cervigon (1991). Marshall and Cohen, 1973. (1 foot; 30 cm)

Phycidae

The hakes are closely related to the codfishes, family Gadidae, in which they have been commonly included. The Merlucciidae, Moridae, and Macrouridae are other families of codlike fish sometimes also included in the Gadidae. These other groups typically occur even farther offshore in deeper, colder water. One morid, *Physiculus fulvus* Bean, with six or seven ventral rays, a well-developed chin barbel, and villiform teeth, as well as the macrourid *Nezumia bairdi*, with a very elongate anal fin, low second dorsal, and no caudal, have been reported from inside one hundred fathoms, although these latter species usually occur well outside this depth. (Chittenden and Moore, 1977; Cohen, 1973; Svetovidov, 1948)

1   Dorsal rays 62–68; anal rays 55–59; pelvic rays extend well beyond anal origin ... Gulf hake, *Urophycis cirrata*.
    Dorsal rays 40–59; anal rays 42–53; pelvic rays not reaching anal origin 2
2   Dorsal rays usually 48; anal rays usually 45; length of mandibular barbel less than one-half eye diameter ... spotted hake, *Urophycis regia*.
    Dorsal rays normally 57; anal rays normally 50; mandibular barbel more than one-half eye ... southern hake, *Urophycis floridana*.

111. Gulf hake *Urophycis cirrata* (Goode and Bean)

D. 10 + 66; A. 57; Sc. 93; Gr. 2 + 12; first dorsal fin without elongate rays; ventral fins very long, reaching beyond origin of anal fin; body light silvery, tan on back, spotted below. The gulf hake occurs in the northern Gulf usually deeper than one hundred fathoms, but young are found inshore into the middle shelf. Florida and northern Gulf at least to the Orinoco. (22 inches; 57 cm)

112. Spotted hake *Urophycis regia* (Walbaum)
D. 8–9 + 46–51; A. 43–49; P. 16; Sc. 89–97; Gr. 3 + 12; brown, darker above; first dorsal fin black with white border and base; lateral line darker than rest of body, with row of pale spots along it; face with two rows of dark spots sometimes fusing into facial bars. Because of confusion with the southern hake, the spotted hake's range is uncertain. Massachusetts to Florida and the northeastern Gulf. (16 inches; 41 cm)

113. Southern hake *Urophycis floridana* (Bean and Dresel)
D. 12–13 + 55–59; A. 40–49; Sc. 110–112; Gr. 2 + 11; back brown and belly silvery; lateral line dark with row of pale spots, first dorsal black, without white margin; other vertical fins brown with darker margins. Although this is normally an offshore species, southern hake young move into shallow water and saltier bays during the winter months. North Carolina to Florida, across the northern Gulf to Mexico, possibly Venezuela. (14 inches; 35 cm)

Ophidiidae

The cusk-eels and closely allied brotulids that lay eggs are now generally considered to belong to the same family (Ophidiidae), while live-bearing species belong to the Bythitidae. All are curious, elongate fishes possessing filamentous ventral fins. Most are highly nocturnal, remaining hidden in crevices or in burrows in the mud during the daylight hours. Primarily deep-water fishes, at least five cusk-eels and two brotulids are found in the shallow northwestern Gulf.

The specific names and generic affinities of the commoner species of cusk-eels are still in a state of flux pending completion of a major revision of the group. (Cohen and Nielsen, 1978; Fahay, 1992; Retzer, 1991)

1 Ventral fins inserted well forward near anterior tip of lower jaws (Ophidiidae of authors) 2
   Ventral fins inserted below shoulder girdle (Brotulidae of authors) 6
2 Snout with a decurved spine (hook) at tip; head scaly on top 3
   Snout without a decurved spine; head scaleless; scales of body rudimentary 4
3 Dorsal and anal fins edged in black ... blackedge cusk-eel, *Lepophidium brevibarbe*.
   Dorsal and anal fins with large, dark spots along margin ... mottled cusk-eel, *Lepophidium jeannae*.
4 Sides of body variously mottled, striped, or blotched 5
   Sides of body plain ... bank cusk-eel, *Ophidion holbrooki*.

5   Sides of body with three or four longitudinal stripes . . . crested cusk-eel, *Ophidion welshi*.

Sides of body spotted . . . blotched cusk-eel, *Ophidion grayi*.

6   Lower jaw and snout with barbels . . . bearded brotula, *Brotula barbata*.

Lower jaw and snout without barbels . . . deepwater brotula *Neobythites gillii*.

114. Blackedge cusk-eel *Lepophidium brevibarbe* (Cuvier)

This fish is the most common cusk-eel in the northwestern Gulf, widely distributed across the shelf. When brought up in a shrimper's net, this cusk-eel's pale silver-blue body takes on an iridescent sheen, which lasts only as long as the fish remains alive. In recent years this species has been known as *Lepophidium graellsi*. Earlier literature referred to it as *L. brevibarbe* (Cuvier) but used the common name short-bearded cusk-eel. Northern Gulf of Mexico to Brazil. Robins, 1986. (8 inches; 20 cm)

115. Mottled cusk-eel *Lepophidium jeannae* Fowler

Brown speckled, with interrupted black trim on dorsal. Common in the eastern Gulf, it occurs as far west as eastern Mississippi, rarely to Texas. Georgia to Florida and off Yucatán. (8 inches; 20 cm)

116. Bank cusk-eel *Ophidion holbrooki* (Putnam)

This plain-sided cusk-eel with dark-edged fins is uncommon in the northwestern Gulf, although there have been several reports from Texas in the bays and on 7 1/2 Fathom Reef and from off eastern Louisiana. It is more common in the northeastern Gulf. Several newly described species similar to *0. holbrooki* are known in the Atlantic and may be present in the northern Gulf as well. Georgia, possibly North Carolina and northern Gulf to Venezuela. Causey, 1969; Nichols and Breder, 1922. (8 inches; 20 cm)

117. Crested cusk-eel *Ophidion welshi* (Nichols and Breder)

The second most abundant cusk-eel from the shrimp grounds, this species is distinguished from the related *O. grayi* by the possession of complete stripes instead of blotches on its sides. Large males (over six inches) are distinguished by a swollen nape or crest. This species was originally described as *Otophidium welshi*. A similar cusk-eel, *Ophidion marginatum* (DeKay)—formerly placed in the genus *Rissola*—has also been reported from the northwestern Gulf of Mexico. We have been unable to verify its presence. South Carolina and possibly New Jersey, and throughout the Gulf. (8 inches; 20 cm)

118. Blotched cusk-eel *Ophidion grayi* (Fowler)

Large brown spots, especially posteriorly. This rare fish is recorded rarely from Texas waters but is more common off eastern Louisiana. It is the only spotted cusk-eel in the northwestern Gulf. *Otophodium omostigmum* (Jordan and Gilbert), the polka dot cusk-eel—the other spotted one found in the eastern Gulf—has a prominent humeral spot. North Carolina to Yucatán and Florida to Mexico. (8 inches; 20 cm)

119. Bearded brotula *Brotula barbata* (Bloch and Schneider)

The body of the bearded brotula is brownish red, and the small fish are covered with many dark spots. On the cheeks are distinctive stripes, which are lost with growth. This is a fairly common fish on the rocky areas of our coast. Small fish are found over muddy bottoms in the shallow Gulf, while slightly larger fish are found near jetties, where their identity perplexes anglers. Large fish, which are good eating, have been caught on the offshore banks. Bermuda and Florida to Jamaica and throughout the Gulf. (3 feet; 91 cm)

120. Deepwater brotula *Neobythites gillii* Goode and Bean

Body compressed, its depth about 21.5 percent of total length; head longer than body depth and 22 percent of total length; interorbital space convex, equal to diameter of eye, 27.3 percent of head length; scales on body in 88 vertical, 7 horizontal rows above and 16–17 rows below lateral line (on diagonal from origin of dorsal fin to vent); yellow or tan with irregular dark blotches on dorsum, the two largest blotches extending onto dorsal fin (these may be the only apparent marks). Recorded from fifty-three fathoms to eighty-five fathoms off Port Aransas and seventy-five fathoms off Grand Isle, this species is not usually considered a part of the shelf fauna. Northern Gulf to Brazil. (6 inches; 15 cm)

Bythitidae

A single species of live-bearing brotula, the gold brotula, occurs in the shallow north-western Gulf of Mexico, although additional species may be found in very deep (abyssal) habitats and in the southern Gulf. The key brotula, *Ogilbia cayorum* Evermann and Kendall, has been reported from the Florida panhandle. This family was formerly included in the Brotulidae or Ophidiidae.

121. Gold brotula *Gunterichthys longipenis* Dawson

D. 64–68; A. 45–50; P. 18–21; caudal fin distinct, no scales on top of the head; maxillary with horizontal expansion; males with single pair of genital claspers. This distinctive pink or gold little fish has been reported before under a variety of names—from 7 1/2 Fathom Reef as *Ogilbia* sp. and from areas near Port Aransas both by that name and as *Dinematichthys* sp. It was described as a species only in 1966. Because this and related species bear live young rather than laying eggs, Cohen and Nielsen (1978) placed this species in the family Bythitidae (viviparous brotulas). Southern Texas to Mississippi. Lindemann, 1986. (3 inches, 8cm)

Carapidae

Pearlfishes are long, slender animals with no ventral fins. They are designed to live inside other animals such as mollusks and sea cucumbers in a close symbiotic relationship. Some are parasites for at least part of their life. Pearlfish possess a highly distinctive larval form known as a vexillifer; these young have been collected off Texas and Louisiana, but adults are not known from shallow water in our area. In addition, at least one deep-water species, the chain pearlfish, *Echiodon dawsoni* Williams and Shipp, is known from depths greater than two hundred feet (63–180 m) off the west coast of Florida. Its habitat is uncertain, but this species appears to be associated with polychaete tubes. (Gonovi et al., 1989; Markle and Onley, 1980, 1990; Onley and Markle, 1979; Williams and Shipp, 1982)

1   Anus well posterior to vertical through pectoral fin base; 25–29 precaudal vertebra; dorsal fin origin over vertebra 8 or 9 ... chain pearlfish, *Echiodon dawsoni*.

    Anus below or anterior to vertical through pectoral fin base; 18 precaudal vertebrae; dorsal fin origin over vertebrae 11 or 12 ... pearlfish, *Carapus bermudensis*.

122. Pearlfish *Carapus bermudensis* (Jones)

A very elongate, tapering, transparent fish that lives inside tropical sea cucumbers. The relationship seems to range from parasitism to commensalism. This species is found elsewhere throughout the tropical western Atlantic, but it is not known in the western Gulf. Bermuda, Bahamas, southern Florida through the Caribbean to Venezuela; in the Gulf from Florida to Mississippi. Dawson, 1971b; Haburay et al., 1974; Smith et al., 1981. (7 inches; 18 cm)

Mugilidae

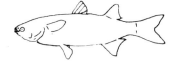

The mullets are a large family of relatively similar fishes. Most are elongate, and many have adipose eyelids. Most also show some affinity for or tolerance of fresh water. In many parts of the world mullets regularly enter fresh water and may spend considerable parts of their lifetimes in inland lakes or rivers. Some genera are found almost exclusively in fresh water. Mullets are raised for food in Africa, the Middle East, and much of the Orient and are marketed east, but not west, of the Mississippi Delta. (Moore, 1974; Thomson, 1978)

1   Adipose eyelid present; scales cycloid 2

    Adipose eyelid not present; scales ctenoid ... mountain mullet, *Agonostomus monticola*.

2   Anal soft rays usually 9; lateral line scales 38; soft dorsal and anal fins scaled; sides without

stripes at all sizes; in live specimens opercle with distinct bright gold spot; gold pigment in iris restricted to narrow region about vertical axis of eye ... white mullet, *Mugil curema*.
Anal soft rays usually 8 (rarely 9 or 7) 3

3   Second dorsal with 8 rays; lateral line scales usually 41 (38–42); soft dorsal and anal with few if any scales; large specimens with stripes on sides of body; live specimens without distinct bright gold spot on opercle; gold pigment in iris of eye not confined but covering most of iris ... striped mullet, *Mugil cephalus*.
Second dorsal with 7 rays; lateral line scales less than 40 (30–36); soft dorsal and anal densely scaled; no stripes on sides ... fantail mullet, *Mugil gyrans*.

123. Mountain mullet; freshwater mullet *Agonostomus monticola* (Bancroft)
D. IV + I, 8; A III, 9; Sc. 40–42. This species lacks the adipose eyelid found in other mullets in our area. Only a few scattered reports of juveniles exist from Texas and Louisiana; however, mountain mullet are common in fresh water and bays of the West Indies and eastern Mexico. Another species of mullet, the Bobo mullet, *Joturus pilchardi* Poey, is also known from fresh waters of eastern Mexico and the West Indies and is shown by Thomson (1978) as occurring in Texas. It is distinguished by its inferior mouth, lack of an adipose eyelid, and 11 anal rays. Mexico and Florida to Columbia and the tropical eastern Pacific. Schlicht, 1959; Suttkus, 1956b. (1 foot; 30 cm)

124. White mullet *Mugil curema* Valenciennes
D. IV + I, 8; A. III, 9; Sc. 33–39; bases of soft dorsal and anal fins scaled; body silvery, with blue or olive on back but without distinct longitudinal stripes on sides; small dark spot at base of pectoral; opercle with gold spot; gold pigment in iris of eye confined to narrow, almost vertical region. This species is absent from the northwestern Gulf during most of the cooler months of the year. It is generally found in saltier water than is *M. cephalus*, and in such habitats it may be more abundant. *Mugil curema* spawns offshore during the spring, reaching sexual maturity at a smaller size than does *M. cephalus*. Juveniles of this species, as well as those of *M. cephalus*, were once placed as separate species in the genus *Querimanna*, because at small sizes the anal spine and ray counts differ from those of adults. The name "querimanna" has been retained for the oceanic prejuvenile stage. In both species the young possess just two anal spines but have one more "ray," making the total number of elements the same in young as in adult fish. White mullet are the preferred bait for sailfish off southern Texas but otherwise have little value. Eastern Pacific and Atlantic, in the western Atlantic from Massachusetts through the Caribbean to Brazil. (2 feet; 61 cm)

125. Striped mullet *Mugil cephalus* Linnaeus
D. IV + I, 8; A. III, 8 (rarely 7); Sc. 38–42; body silvery; back blue; sides with dark longitudinal stripes; large blue spot at base of pectoral; pigment in iris more dispersed and more brownish than that of *M. curema*. Fish below about six inches (150 mm) lack stripes, but

they are readily told from *M. curema* by the coloration of their iris and opercle, their scaleless dorsal and anal fins, and their higher lateral line scale count. (The scales of *curema* are also different enough in appearance and texture that the species can be separated by touch.) One of our most abundant fish, striped mullet are found in large schools in practically all environments from fresh to hypersaline water. Mullet are known from many rivers in Texas and Louisiana; from as far inland as Lake Texoma and the Colorado River near Austin, Texas, two hundred miles inland; and from hypersaline Baffin Bay, where salinities often reach above 15 parts per thousand.

This species is a fall spawner. Large schools of striped mullet leave the bays during the autumn months, with smaller schools returning over about a six-month period. Striped mullet are regarded as an excellent food fish in Florida, but in the muddier western Gulf they may take on an oilier taste and are not generally eaten. However, they are quite edible. One highly variable species, to which numerous names have been applied, apparently exists in all tropical and temperate waters around the world. In the western Atlantic from Nova Scotia and Bermuda to Brazil, although it appears to be absent from most of the tropical Atlantic. Bishop and Miglarese 1978; Gilbert 1993; Hoese, 1985. (30 inches; 76 cm)

126. Fantail mullet *Mugil gyrans* (Jordan and Gilbert)

D. IV + I, 7; A. III, 8 (rarely 7); Sc. 30–36. Dusky olive above, silvery below; anal and ventral fins yellowish, other fins pale with brown spots, caudal with dusky margin; dark blotch at base of pectoral. This species may have been confused with other species present in the northwestern Gulf; we have not confirmed its occurrence. The name *M. trichodon* Poey has also been applied to this species. Circumtropical, in the western Atlantic from Bermuda, Florida, and the northern Gulf through the Caribbean to northeast Brazil. Thomson, 1978. (12 inches; 30 cm)

Exocoetidae

The exocoetids include the flyingfishes and the halfbeaks. The latter have often been placed in a separate family, Hemiramphidae, but Greenwood et al. (1966) considered the two groups too closely related to warrant separation. The flyingfishes are best characterized by their elongate pectoral fins, which enable them to glide for considerable distances. The nonflying halfbeaks frequently jump from the water or skip over the surface, and some halfbeaks possess relatively long pectorals, which aid them in their extended leaps. There are flyingfishes with shorter pectorals (approaching the condition usually seen in halfbeaks) and halfbeaks that lack the elongate lower jaw generally characteristic of the group. The presence of such intermediate types makes separation into two families difficult. Ecologically, however, there are two groups: those which are basically offshore species living more than two hundred miles from land; and inshore species living less than two hundred miles from land and entering the bays. Here, too, the division is not absolute, since several offshore species occasionally venture into inshore waters. For example, the bandwing flying fish *Cypselurus exsiliens* (Linnaeus) occurs rarely offshore. Generally, few flyingfishes come very close to shore, but there are more oceanic species that may rarely occur inshore. (Breder, 1938; Bruun, 1935; Miller, 1945; Staiger, 1965)

1　Lower jaw elongate, much longer than upper jaw 2

　　Lower jaw not elongate, scarcely if at all longer than upper jaw 5

2　Pectoral fins very short, less than one-half length of lower jaw 3

　　Pectoral fins long, more than one-half length of lower jaw ... flying halfbeak, *Euleptorhamphus velox.*

3　Dorsal fin inserted above anal fin origin, upper lobe of caudal about as long as lower lobe; snout with scales ... American halfbeak, *Hyporhamphus meeki.*

　　Dorsal inserted well before anal fin origin, lower lobe of caudal much longer than upper lobe; snout without scales 4

4　Pectoral fin short, barely reaching anterior nostril when folded forward; upper lobe of caudal fin in adults orange ... ballyhoo, *Hemiramphus brasiliensis.*

　　Pectoral fin long, reaching beyond nostril when folded forward; upper lobe of caudal fin in adults blueish with red tip ... balao, *Hemirhamphus balao.*

5　Pectorals short, scarcely reaching insertion of ventral fins ... smallwing flyingfish, *Oxyporhamphus micropterus.*

　　Pectorals long, reaching well beyond origin of dorsal fin 6

6　Pectorals reaching well beyond end of dorsal fin; ventral fins long, reaching past anal origin, or else very short, reaching no more than halfway to anal origin 7

　　Pectorals reaching only to middle of dorsal base; ventral fins moderate, reaching no farther than anal origin ... sailfin flyingfish, *Parexocoetus brachypterus.*

7　Ventral fins short, inserted nearer to snout than to caudal base and failing to reach anal origin by their own length ... oceanic two-wing flyingfish, *Exocoetus obtusirostris.*

　　Ventral fins long, inserted nearer to caudal base than to snout and reaching well beyond anal origin 8

8　Origin of dorsal fin over origin of anal fin; anal rays equal to or greater than dorsal rays in number ... blackwing flyingfish, *Hirundichthys rondeleti.*

　　Origin of dorsal fin anterior to origin of anal fin; anal rays fewer than number of dorsal rays 9

9　First and second rays of pectoral fin simple, unbranched; third pectoral ray bifurcate ... bluntnose flyingfish, *Prognichthys gibbifrons.*

　　First ray of pectoral simple, second bifurcate 10

10　Dorsal with prominent dark spot covering all, most of, or just upper area of fin ... margined flyingfish, *Cypselurus cyanopterus.*

　　Dorsal without spot 11

11   Pectorals grayish, with light outer margin narrower than diameter of pupil and with incon-
      spicuous light crossband ... Atlantic flyingfish, *Cypselurus melanurus.*
      Pectorals nearly black, with broad, light outer margin wider than diameter of eye and with
      prominent light crossband .... spotfin flyingfish, *Cypselurus furcatus.*

127. Flying halfbeak *Euleptorhamphus velox* Poey

D. 22; A. 21; pectorals long, greater than one-half length of lower jaw. This halfbeak is an offshore species capable of short flights. Atlantic Ocean, in the west from Massachusetts and Bermuda to Brazil. (2 feet; 61 cm)

128. American halfbeak *Hyporhamphus meeki* Banford and Collette

D. 14–16; A. 15–17; P. 11–12; Gr. 33–39 on first arch. Body silvery, greenish above; tip of jaw red. This is the most common inshore halfbeak in the northwestern Gulf, and it commonly enters the bays. Until 1993 the name *Hyporhamphus unifasciatus* (Ranzani) was applied to this species on the Atlantic and Gulf coasts as well as south through the Caribbean to Argentina. However, Banford and Collette (1993) have shown that there are two species involved: *Hyporhamphus unifasciatus,* which occurs from the tip of Florida south, and a new species, *H. meeki,* which is found on the eastern and Gulf coasts of the United States and off northern Yucatán. *H. unifasciatus* can be distinguished by its lower pectoral ray count (10–11 vs. 11–12 in *H. meeki*) and first and second arch gill raker counts (26–29 and 19–25 respectively in *H. unifasciatus* vs. 33–39 and 28–32 in *H. meeki*). New Brunswick to Miami and throughout the Gulf. Banford and Collette, 1993. (8 inches; 20 cm)

129. Ballyhoo *Hemiramphus brasiliensis* (Linnaeus)

D. 12–15; A. 11–15; body silvery, greenish on back; upper lobe of caudal fin and dorsal fin orange; tip of lower jaw orange. Atlantic Ocean, in the west from New England through the Caribbean to Rio de Janeiro, Brazil. (15 inches; 38 cm)

130. Balao *Hemirhamphus balao* Lesueur

D. 12–15 (13–14); A. 10–13 (11–12); body silvery, back bluish; upper lobe of caudal fin bluish with red tip; tip of lower jaw orange. Occurs throughout the tropical Atlantic, but only recently reported from the Flower Garden banks (Dennis and Bright 1988a), al-though Springer and Bullis (1956) had reported one specimen from oceanic waters off Louisiana. South Carolina and northern Gulf to Venezuela. (16 inches, 40 cm)

131. Smallwing flyingfish *Oxyporhamphus micropterus* (Valenciennes)

D. 13–15; A. 14–15; Sc. 51–53; mandible produced as in halfbeaks in small individuals up to two inches (50 mm) standard length. The similarity of this fish to the halfbeaks has, in the past, led to its inclusion in a third, separate family, the Oxyporhamphidae. Circumtropical, in the western Atlantic in offshore waters from North Carolina to Brazil.

132. Sailfin flyingfish *Parexocoetus brachypterus* (Richardson)

D. 11–12; A. 12–13; Sc. 39–42; pectoral fin intermediate in length, only reaching middle of dorsal base. Breder (1938) differentiates two subspecies on the basis of the relative length of the ventral fins and of jaw proportions. Both forms occur from Cape Cod to Brazil in offshore waters, usually more than four hundred miles from land. (6 inches; 15 cm)

133. Oceanic two-wing flyingfish *Exocoetus obtusirostris* Günther

D. 12–14; A. 12–14; Sc. 38–42; juveniles of this species, less than 1 5/8 inches (40 mm) in standard length, are quite high-bodied, with depth about 25–30 percent of standard length, decreasing to 20–23 percent in adults. As the common name implies, this species is usually found farther offshore than most of the other species. In offshore waters from about 40° N (New Jersey) to Brazil. (6 inches; 15 cm)

134. Blackwing flyingfish *Hirundichthys rondeleti* (Valenciennes)

D. 11–12; A. 12–13; Sc. 42–49. The blackwing is the common inshore flyingfish of the northwestern Gulf, its young occurring even in the bays. The most noteworthy characteristic of the species is the black coloration of the pectorals and ventrals. The fourwing flyingfish, *Hirundichthys affinis,* with a clear dorsal fin, also rarely occurs offshore. Worldwide, possibly antitropical; Atlantic Ocean, in the west from Massachusetts and Bermuda to Brazil. (10 inches; 25 cm)

135. Bluntnose flyingfish *Prognichthys gibbifrons* (Valenciennes)

D. 12; A. 9–10; Sc. 33; ventrals very long, reaching past caudal origin. This is another offshore species. Atlantic Ocean, in the west from Massachusetts to Brazil. (8 inches; 20 cm)

136. Margined flyingfish *Cypselurus cyanopterus* (Valenciennes)

D. 11–14; A. 8–11; Sc. 50–53; prominent dark spot on upper part of dorsal fin, most apparent in specimens over 4 3/4 inches (120 mm) in standard length (below this size spot may cover entire dorsal fin); pectoral fins evenly pigmented, not banded; body silvery, darker on back, with no banding apparent even in juveniles. This is essentially a coastal species, rarely occurring more than four hundred miles offshore, but not venturing into the nearshore areas either. Tropical Atlantic, in the west from New Jersey to southern Brazil. (12 inches; 30 cm)

137. Spotfin flyingfish *Cypselurus furcatus* (Mitchill)

D. 11–15; A. 8–12; Sc. 47–50; adults pale silvery on venter, darker dorsally, with dorsal fin only sparsely pigmented; juveniles with six dark bands on body which disappear with age; pectoral fins with clear V-shaped area between dark blotches. Atlantic Ocean, in the west from New Jersey and Bermuda to Brazil. (12 inches; 30 cm)

138. Atlantic flyingfish *Cypselurus melanurus* (Valenciennes)

D. 10–15; A. 8–12; Sc. 46–52; adults darker dorsally, silver ventrally; pectorals with a pale, narrow band along posterior border; juveniles with body banded as in *C. furcatus* and pectorals with two large spots along first ray and a third spot at base of fin. Formerly called *C. heterurus.* Atlantic Ocean, in the west from Nova Scotia to Brazil. (16 inches; 41 cm)

Belonidae

The needlefishes are elongate fishes with both jaws extended into a beak. The jaws are well supplied with teeth, indicating the carnivorous habits of all the species. (Berry and Rivas, 1962; Collette and Berry, 1965)

1　Dorsal rays 12–17 2
　　Dorsal rays 21–26 3
2　Gill rakers present; caudal peduncle compressed dorsoventrally . . . keeltail needlefish, *Platybelone argalus.*
　　Gill rakers absent; caudal peduncle not compressed . . . Atlantic needlefish, *Strongylura marina.*
3　Anal rays 25–28; head and body compressed laterally . . . flat needlefish, *Ablennes hians.*
　　Anal rays 18–22; body not strongly compressed laterally . . . houndfish, *Tylosurus crocodilus.*

139. Keeltail needlefish *Platybelone argalus* (Lesueur)

D. 12–15, A. 17–19; P. 11; Gr. (only in this species among the belonids) 1–5 + 1–9; lower jaw projecting beyond upper jaw by about one-fourth of its length (when both jaws unbroken). This is primarily an offshore, tropical species although it has been collected from the lower Laguna Madre. The name *Strongylura* (or *Belone*) *longleyi* refers to this species (Berry and Rivas, 1962). Circumtropical; in the western Atlantic from Virginia and Bermuda through the Caribbean to Trinidad. Pezold and Edwards, 1983. (15 inches; 38 cm)

140. Atlantic needlefish; needlegar; saltwater gar *Strongylura marina* (Walbaum)

D. 14–17; A. 16–20; P. usually 11 in both, but sometimes 10 or 12 in one or both; both jaws approximately equal in length; no gill rakers. This species is quite common in the inshore Gulf and bays during the spring and summer, and it even ascends far up rivers. *S. timucu* is generally regarded as a synonym, and reports of *S. notata* from Texas are probably based on *S. marina. S. notata* differs from *S. marina* in possessing 13–15 dorsal rays and 13–16 anal rays. Massachusetts to southern Brazil, including Cuba and Jamaica. (2 feet; 61 cm)

141. Flat needlefish *Ablennes hians* (Valenciennes)

D. 23–26; A. 25–28, P. usually 14 in both, rarely 15 in both; no gill rakers; jaws about equal; body strongly compressed, not rounded or square in cross section; sides silvery; back green. Usually found offshore, this species is considered rare but has been located in large concentrations near schools of spawning red drum. Probably circumtropical; in the western Atlantic from Massachusetts and Bermuda through the Caribbean to southern Brazil. (3 feet; 91 cm)

142. Houndfish *Tylosurus crocodilus* (Peron and Lesueur)

D. 22–24; A. 18–22, P. 14 in both, no gill rakers; jaws approximately equal; body somewhat compressed laterally but not as noticeably as in flat needlefish; sides silvery; back green. This fish is primarily found in offshore waters, but it ventures inshore occasionally. *Tylosurus* (or *Strongylura*) *raphidoma* (Ranzani) refers to this species. Circumtropical, in the western Atlantic from Massachusetts through the Caribbean to eastern Brazil. (2 feet; 61 cm)

Fundulidae

The killifishes, which were formerly included in the family Cyprinodontidae, are shore or inland fishes which venture or are driven into open bay waters only under extreme conditions such as low temperatures. All tolerate a wide range of salinities, so the same species can be found inhabiting freshwater marshes in Louisiana as well as the hypersaline Laguna Madre of Texas. Most also invade coastal fresh water. They normally lack brilliant colors; however, males develop iridescent blues during the breeding season. In coastal fresh water, about four additional species may be expected, but these are absent from marine or brackish waters. Keys including these forms are given by Eddy and Underhill (1978), Blair et al. (1968), Rosen (1973), and Douglas (1974). (Forman, 1968; Kilby, 1955; Simpson and Gunter, 1956)

1.   Dorsal fin origin closer to caudal base than to preopercle 2
      Dorsal fin origin closer to preopercle than to caudal base 5
2.   Snout length more than twice eye diameter; body with about 15 dark vertical bars, the last with dark spot dorsally ... striped killifish, *Fundulus majalis.*
      Snout length less than twice eye diameter; body sometimes with bars but never with dark spot on last 3
3.   Dorsal fin origin posterior to anal fin origin; fewer than 15 scale rows in front of ventral fin origin; large black spots on body in two irregular rows ... saltmarsh topminnow, *Fundulus jenkinsi.*
      Dorsal fin origin anterior to or over anal fin origin; more than 15 scale rows in front of ventral fins 4

4   Males with only faint (fuzzy) vertical stripes at best; females without markings; distance between eyes one-third of head length … gulf killifish, *Fundulus grandis*.
Males with 12–14 distinct vertical bars; females with spots; distance between eyes about one-half of head length; upper jaw length less than one-third of head length … bayou killifish, *Fundulus pulvereus*.

5   Body with vertical bars; 9–10 dorsal rays … diamond killifish, *Adinia xenica*.
Body with no large markings; 10–12 dorsal rays … rainwater killifish, *Lucania parva*.

143. Striped killifish *Fundulus majalis* (Walbaum)

D. 11–13; A. 10; Sc. 33. This is a fairly large killifish not usually found in very low salinities. The long snout and the spot on the caudal peduncle distinctively mark the species. While Gulf populations are usually recognized as the longnose killifish, *Fundulus similis* (Baird and Girard) (Plate 143b), the evidence seems to us persuasive they are identical. Gulf populations tend to have more vertical stripes while those in the Atlantic (Plate 143a), especially the females, possess horizontal ones. Maine through Florida and the northern Gulf to Tampico. Relyea, 1983. (6 inches; 15 cm)

144. Saltmarsh topminnow *Fundulus jenkinsi* (Evermann)

D. 8–9; A. 11–13; Sc. 33; adults vertically striped. This rare species is restricted to coastal streams and adjacent bay shores on the western side of Galveston Bay and from Vermilion Bay to the Florida panhandle. Usually found in low salinities, it has been taken from the Chandeleur Islands. Its absence from East Texas and western Louisiana has not been explained, and while there are no new reports for Texas, the species has been taken in some numbers recently in Louisiana. Galveston Bay to Pensacola Bay. Gilbert, 1992. (2 inches; 5 cm)

145. Gulf killifish *Fundulus grandis* Baird and Girard

D. 11; A. 10–11; Sc. 35–38. The gulf killifish is a large, widespread shore fish occasionally used as bait. In low salinities in East Texas and Louisiana, where *F. similis* is absent, a form of *F. grandis* with dark stripes similar to those of *F. similis* is found. This form, originally described as the nominal species *F. pallidus* Evermann, is readily separable from *F. similis* by its short snout and lack of a spot on the caudal peduncle. *F. similis* from areas where *F. grandis* is absent may also lack the spots. *F. grandis* frequently has stripes when young, but except in the above case these stripes usually fade with growth, unlike the stripes in *F. similis* and *F. pulvereus*. This species goes under a variety of common names. Bait dealers refer to most cyprinodontid fishes as "chubs" or just "(mud) minnows," and *F. grandis* is sometimes sold in Louisiana as "cockahoe minnow" and mistakenly as "finger mullet" in Texas. This species is closely related, if not identical, to the Atlantic mummichog, *F. heteroclitus* Linnaeus, although the relationships are not as close as those between Atlantic and Gulf populations of *F. majalis/similis*. Cuba, eastern Mexico, throughout the Gulf of Mexico, and on Atlantic coast of Florida. (6 inches; 15 cm)

146. Bayou killifish *Fundulus pulvereus* (Evermann)

D. 9; A. 11; Sc. 33. This is a small, usually uncommon, but beautiful fish with great color differences between the sexes. Males in breeding colors are the most attractive members of the family. As its name implies, the bayou killifish commonly inhabits marshes and inlets at least from the upper Laguna Madre to Alabama, where it intergrades with the marsh killifish, *Fundulus confluentus* Goode and Bean, which ranges through Florida to Virginia. As with other pairs of killifish species, some biologists think these two forms belong to the same species, but the latter has a spot on the dorsal. (3 inches; 8 cm)

147. Diamond killifish *Adinia xenica* (Jordan and Gilbert)

D. 9–10; A. 11–12; Sc. 25. This poorly known fish, sometimes found singly with other killifish or in small schools, seems to prefer bay margins and marshes. Florida panhandle to South Texas. Greeley, 1984. (2 inches; 5 cm)

148. Rainwater killifish *Lucania parva* (Baird and Girard)

D. 10–12; A. 10–11; Sc. 26. This killifish is generally limited to vegetated areas such as turtlegrass flats and algal communities. It also occurs in vegetated areas in coastal fresh water. Breeding males of this species possess a reddish orange anal fin tinged with black and a bright yellow caudal fin. Massachusetts to Tampico. Duggins, 1980. (2 inches; 5 cm)

Cyprinodontidae

Pupfishes were previously placed in the same family as the closely related killifishes. The coastal ancestral species seems to have given rise to a number of species in alkaline fresh water. The goldspotted topminnow, *Floridichthys carpio,* is common on the Florida peninsula and is sometimes confused with *Cyprinodon.*

149. Sheepshead minnow *Cyprinodon variegatus* Lacepède

D. 11; A. 10; Sc. 26. Perhaps the most common shore fish and the most pugnacious, the sheepshead minnow is found along bay margins, in marsh ponds, and in a variety of extreme (hot and salty) habitats in which no other fish are found. This species has the greatest salinity tolerance of any known fish. Maine through the Caribbean to Venezuela. (3 inches; 8 cm)

Poeciliidae

The livebearers are a freshwater family with three species that enter salt water in our area. Recent revision has also included in the family certain oviparous tropical forms, none of which occur here. All are quite tolerant of salt water and are common in coastal marshes. All local species of this family bear live young. The males are easily recognized since they are much smaller than the females and possess an elongated anal fin, which is specialized as an intromittent organ for sperm transfer. The common guppy of home aquaria belongs to this family. (Rosen, 1973)

1   Dorsal fin originating anterior to anal fin; more than ten dorsal rays . . . sailfin molly, *Poecilia latipinna.*

     Dorsal fin originating posterior to anal fin; fewer than ten dorsal rays 2

2   Sides without bands or bars, no spots on median fins . . . mosquitofish, *Gambusia affinis.*

     Sides with dark bands and bars; black spots on some median fins . . . least killifish, *Heterandria formosa.*

150. Sailfin molly *Poecilia latipinna* (Lesueur)

D. 13–16; A. 8; Sc. 26. A common resident of Texas and Louisiana coastal marshes, the occasionally black wild individuals of this and closely related species are the same as the black molly of tropical fish aquaria. Another molly, the Amazon molly, *P. formosa,* occurs in southern Texas and has been introduced into the Nueces River but is not yet known from salt water. The latter species has fewer than 13 dorsal rays and a definite diamond-shaped pattern on the sides, while the sailfin molly has 13–16 dorsal rays and a spotted pattern. North Carolina to Campeche and rarely in the Bahamas (where it may be introduced). Darnell and Abramoff, 1968; Hubbs, 1964. (3 inches; 8 cm)

151. Mosquitofish *Gambusia affinis* (Baird and Girard)

D. 7–9; A. 8–10; Sc. 29–32; females look a little like the rainwater killifish, *Lucania parva.* Like the sailfin molly, this fish is common in low-salinity marshes; however, it is generally found in fresher water than the molly. This small species has been widely introduced as a mosquito control agent. Recent work has again concluded that populations east of Mobile are a different species, *Gambusia holbrooki* Girard. New Jersey to central Mexico. Brown-Peterson and Peterson, 1990; Wooten et al., 1988. (2 inches; 5 cm)

152. Least killifish *Heterandria formosa* Agassiz

D. 7; A. 6–9; Sc. 25–30; brownish with lateral dark strip and faint vertical bars, with spot on dorsal fin. The smallest of American marine vertebrates, this is a very common fish in coastal freshwater vegetation and is sometimes found in brackish water. Its range, formerly thought to end in the west near the Vermilion River, is now known to extend to the Texas border, and populations are also known in several locations in southwestern Louisiana marshes. Whether this is a recent expansion of the species' range westward or an artifact due to lack of collecting is not known. Coastal plain from North Carolina to Florida, west to the Sabine drainage. Hanks and McCoid, 1988. (1 inch; 3 cm)

Atherinidae

Silversides are small fishes found in relatively shallow water along bay margins. There are two estuarine and marine species in our area and two freshwater species, which may occasionally be found in very low salinities. Members of this family are famous for their interest in surface objects, butting into and jumping over twigs, string, and other floating things. (Gunter, 1953; Middaugh et al., 1986)

1   Scales rough to the touch, with serrated edges; bases of dorsal and anal fins covered with deciduous scales, two rows of spots along dorsum ... rough silverside, *Membras martinica*. Scales smooth; bases of dorsal and anal fins scaleless; no definite rows of spots along dorsum, but dorsal scales outlined in black 2

2   Second dorsal fin with mode of 8 (7–9) rays ... Texas silverside, *Menidia clarkhubbsi*. Second dorsal fin with mode of 9 (7–10) rays 3

3   Margin of anal fin slightly concave; swimbladder beyond anal origin appears long, transparent, and with a pointed tip in fresh or freshly preserved specimens; typically 4 or 5 anal rays in front of posterior tip of swimbladder; number of lateral line scales with canals usually 14 or fewer ... inland silverside, *Menidia beryllina*.
Margin of anal fin straight; swimbladder beyond anal origin appears short, opaque, and blunt in fresh or freshly preserved specimens; typically fewer than 4 anal rays in front of posterior tip of swimbladder; number of lateral line scales with canals usually 15 or more ... tidewater silverside, *Menidia peninsulae*.

153. Rough silverside *Membras martinica* Valenciennes
D. V + I, 7; A. I, 14–21; Sc. 46–48; scales rough to the touch; caudal fin with dusky posterior margin; lateral silver stripe wider than the eye. Reports of *Membras vagrans* refer to this species, which is generally found in the deeper, more saline portions of bays and out into the Gulf as far as fifteen miles offshore. New York to southern Mexico. (3 1/2 inches; 9 cm)

154. Texas silverside, Amazon silverside *Menidia clarkhubbsi* Echelle and Mosier
D. IV–VI (V) + I, 8 (rarely 7 or 9); A. I, 16–18 (17); Sc. 38–40; this all-female (gynogenetic) species is known only from two locations on the Texas coast, both of which have been subject to frequent disturbance since the description of the species in 1982. This and the difficulty in correctly identifying members of the species make its recognition problematic. While the number of second dorsal rays and the long and opaque appearance of the swimbladder (contrast with *M. beryllina* and *M. peninsulae* in the foregoing key) in fresh or freshly preserved specimens provide a means of identifying most specimens in hand, the species can only be identified with certainty using electrophoretic means.

Ponds adjacent to Galveston and Aransas Bays, Texas. Echelle and Mosier, 1982. (2 inches, 5 cm)

155. Inland silverside *Menidia beryllina* (Cope)

D. V + I, 10 (rarely 9 or 11); A. I, 15–18; Sc. 38–40; scales quite smooth, offering no resistance to the thumb when it is run along the sides of the body; caudal fin usually plain and without dusky margin; silvery lateral stripe narrower than pupil of eye. This species is generally limited to the shorelines, in very low salinities. In the lower Atchafalaya River it intergrades with the freshwater subspecies, *Menidia b. audens*. Massachusetts to Vera Cruz, Mexico. Chernoff et al., 1981; Johnson, 1975. (3 inches; 8 cm)

156. Tidewater silverside *Menidia peninsulae* (Goode and Bean)

D. IV–VI (V) + 7–12 (8–9); A. I, 13–19 (15–16); P. 11–14 (12–13); Sc. 34–43 (36–38). The tidewater silverside is a deeper-bodied fish and is typically found in higher salinities than *M. beryllina,* with which it was confused prior to 1975. This species shows the same salinity relationship to *M. beryllina* as does *M. menidia* on the East Coast; however, *M. menidia* is easily distinguished by its much higher (23 and above) anal fin ray count. The actual extension of the swimbladder over the anal fin varies with salinity (Edwards et al., 1978); Echelle and Mosier (1982) were nevertheless able to use this character, as noted in the key, to separate individuals of the two species collected from the same habitat. It has been suggested that silverside populations may be highly variable species flocks, or some similar nontypical species distinction, with *peninsulae* types predominating near the ocean and *audens* types in fresh water, but Johnson (1975) found sufficient genetic differentiation to regard *M. beryllina* and *M. peninsulae* as separate species. Northeastern Florida to Vera Cruz, rare in Louisiana. (3 inches; 8 cm)

Holocentridae

Squirrelfishes are a tropical family represented in the Gulf of Mexico by several species so far found only on the offshore reefs. In all local species except *Myripristis jacobus,* the swimbladder is connected to the skull so that it serves as a sound amplifier. Many species of squirrelfishes use sound as part of their courtship behavior. Squirrelfishes are all good to eat, although they may be rather small. Additional tropical species may occur rarely on some offshore reefs. Although scientific names have been uniformly applied, the common names of three squirrelfishes have been variously intermixed in the literature. Woods (1955) avoided using common names entirely. However, in Böhlke and Chaplin (1968), and Randall (1968), the common name squirrelfish is used for *H. rufus,* longjaw squirrelfish is applied to *H. adscensionis,* and longspine squirrelfish to *H.* (or *Flammeo*) *marianus.* Bailey et al. (1970), Woods and Sonada (1973), Robins et al. (1980, 1986,

1991), Manooch (1984), Shipp (1986), and Humann (1994) all apply the common names as we do here. (Bright and Cashman, 1974; Woods, 1955; Woods and Sonoda, 1973)

1   Third anal spine exceedingly long, reaching past base of caudal fin . . . longjaw squirrelfish, *Holocentrus marianus.*

     Third anal spine not reaching to base of caudal fin 2

2   Strong preopercular spine present 3

     No preopercular spine present 6

3   Gill rakers on lower limb of first arch 14–17; upper lobe of caudal fin noticeably longer than lower 4

     Gill rakers on lower limb of first arch 11–13; upper and lower lobes of caudal fin about equal in length 5

4   Length of upper jaw 12–14 percent of standard length; pored lateral line scales 50–55 to base of caudal fin; interspinous membrane of dorsal fin white-edged . . . longspine squirrelfish, *Holocentrus rufus.*

     Length of upper jaw 14–16 percent of standard length; pored lateral line scales 45–50; interspinous membrane of dorsal fin orange . . . squirrelfish, *Holocentrus adscensionis.*

5   Axil of pectoral black; anal rays nine . . . dusky squirrelfish, *Holocentrus vexillarius.*

     Axil of pectoral pale; anal rays eight . . . saddle squirrelfish, *Holocentrus poco.*

6   Prominent bar crossing body just behind head . . . blackbar soldierfish, *Myripristis jacobus.*

     No such bar; body uniformly colored . . . cardinal soldierfish, *Plectrypops retrospinus.*

157. Longjaw squirrelfish *Holocentrus marianus* Cuvier

D. XI, 12–13; A. 8–9; P. 12; Sc. 46–47; Gr. 6–7 + 13. Head pointed, lower jaw projecting beyond upper jaw; opercular spines short; third anal spine exceedingly long, reaching well beyond base of caudal fin. Body reddish with yellow-gold stripes, membrane of spinous dorsal orange, with white near the tips and a white longitudinal band between middle and base of membrane. Sometimes placed in the genus *Flammeo* Jordan and Evermann. North Carolina, Bahamas to Trinidad and Colombia. Dennis and Bright, 1988a. (8 inches, 40cm).

158. Longspine squirrelfish *Holocentrus rufus* (Walbaum)

D. XI, 14–16; A. IV, 9–11; P. 15–17; Sc. 50–57; maxillary not reaching to center of eye; body reddish with longitudinal yellow or white stripes; interspinous membranes of dorsal fin with white spot at upper margin and with long second dorsal. This squirrelfish is known in the area only from offshore reefs. Florida and the northern Gulf through the Caribbean to Venezuela. (12 inches; 30 cm)

159. Squirrelfish *Holocentrus adscensionis* (Osbeck)

D. XI, 14–16; A IV, 10; P. 15–17; Sc. 46–51; maxillary reaching to or beyond midpoint of eye; coloration like that of *H. rufus* except dorsal fin membranes without white spots, either uninterrupted orange or with orange spots near edge. This is the most common local squirrelfish. The spelling of the scientific name has recently been emended from *ascensionsis* to conform with the original spelling. New York through the Caribbean to Rio de Janeiro, Brazil. (2 feet; 61 cm)

160. Dusky squirrelfish *Holocentrus vexillarius* (Poey)

D. XI, 13; A. IV, 9; P. 15; Sc. 40–44; body reddish with lighter longitudinal stripes; dorsal fin red with white along membranes next to spines; other fins reddish. This small squirrelfish is sometimes placed in the genus *Adioryx*. It is found off Florida and rarely on reefs in the northwestern Gulf. Bermuda, Florida, and the northern Gulf through the Caribbean to Venezuela. (6 inches; 15 cm)

161. Saddle squirrelfish *Holocentrus poco* (Woods)

D. XI, 13; A. IV, 8; P. 14, Sc. 37–40; sides red, often with dark blotch or saddle at base of soft dorsal and another on caudal peduncle. This rare squirrelfish is known only from the Bahamas, Grand Cayman Island, and the West Flower Garden bank, but presumably it must occur elsewhere. Bright and Cashman, 1974; Woods, 1965. (5 inches; 13 cm)

162. Blackbar soldierfish *Myripristis jacobus* Cuvier

D. X + 1, 14; A. IV, 13; P. 15; Sc. 34–36; no large spines on head; reddish brown on back; body silvery with distinct dark (reddish brown to black) bar behind opercular opening; spinous dorsal with blue blotches; soft dorsal red anteriorly and blue posteriorly, ventral and anal fins blue; caudal red with blue margin. This fish is not rare on offshore reefs. Tropical Atlantic, in the west from the Bahamas, North Carolina, and the northern Gulf through the Caribbean to northeastern Brazil; also Cape Verde and Ascension islands. (8 inches; 20 cm)

163. Cardinal soldierfish *Plectrypops retrospinus* (Guichenot)

D. XII, 14; A. IV, 11; P. 16–17; Sc. 32–35; body uniformly red; lobes of caudal rounded; strong forward-pointing spines beneath eye. The cardinal soldierfish is an elusive and deeper-dwelling squirrelfish known in our area only from the West Flower Garden bank. Bermuda, the Bahamas, Florida, northern Gulf through the Caribbean to Venezuela. Bright and Cashman, 1974. (5 inches; 13 cm)

Aulostomidae

The trumpetfishes are an oddly shaped family of tropical reef fishes related to the pipefishes, seahorses, and cornetfishes. The common name is derived from the trumpet-like shape the fish acquire when they open their mouths.

164. Trumpetfish *Aulostomus maculatus* Valenciennes

D. IX–XII + 24–28; A. 25–28; dorsal spines supporting separate fins or finlets; brownish, with scattered spots and streaks. This fish often aligns itself with gorgonians (whip corals) or other vertical features in the water and is consequently hard to detect. Throughout the tropical Atlantic; in the northwestern Gulf it has so far been reported only from offshore reefs. Lochmann and Alevizon, 1989. (30 inches; 76 cm)

Fistulariidae

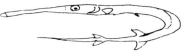

Cornetfishes, like trumpetfishes, are long and slender with small mouths, but they have a longer beak and a long filament extending from the caudal fin. The bluespotted cornetfish is the only reported representative of this small tropical family that occurs in our area, but the red cornetfish in all likelihood will be found rarely. Burgess, 1976; Fritzsche, 1976.

1   Blue spots from head to dorsal fin; no bony plates on midline of caudal peduncle ... bluespotted cornetfish, *Fistularia tabacaria*.

No blue spots on head; bony plates on midline of flattened caudal peduncle ... red cornetfish, *Fistularia petimba*.

165. Bluespotted cornetfish *Fistularia tabacaria* Linnaeus

D. and A. 14–16; body very long and slender with produced median section of caudal fin and elongate snout. The cornetfish has large blue spots but lacks the separate dorsal spines found in the similar trumpetfish. This species is commonly found in vegetated areas while *Aulostomus* is more of a reef dweller. There have been several reports of bluespotted cornetfish offshore, although it is probably not common. Tropical Atlantic, in the west from Nova Scotia and Bermuda through the Caribbean to Brazil (6 feet, 1.8 m)

166. Red cornetfish *Fistularia petimba* Lacepède

D. 14–16; A. 14–15. Red-orange brown with bands. It has been taken at least once on the shell reefs east of the delta but is more at home on tropical reefs. Indo-Pacific east to Hawaii and tropical Atlantic, in the west from Florida and the northern Gulf through the Caribbean to Venezuela, probably as a stray to the northeastern Gulf. (5 feet; 1.5m)

Syngnathidae

The pipefishes and seahorses are among the most curious and interesting of marine fishes. Their armored bodies and odd shapes make them attractive aquarium fish. One interesting biological characteristic of the family is that the males carry the fertilized eggs in a special brood pouch (Azzarello, 1991). The location and size of this pouch is important in determining species. Syngnathids are commonly found in vegetated areas, and they closely resemble the vegetation in which they live. One peculiar and distinctive member of this family, the pipehorse, *Acentronura dendritica,* has been taken off the Mississippi coast. It looks like a pipefish but has a prehensile tail like a seahorse. The bull pipefish, *Syngnathus springeri,* and three species of *Cosmocampus* have been taken commonly from the northeastern Gulf, and there is one record of the whitenose pipefish, *Cosmocampus albirostris,* from Texas. (Azzarello, 1991; Dawson, 1972, 1982b; Ginsburg, 1937; Herald, 1942, 1965; Vari, 1982)

1 Head and body continuous, in straight line; tail not prehensile; caudal fin present 2
   Head and body at about right angle; tail prehensile; caudal fin absent 11
2 Median trunk ridge terminated above anus; lateral tail ridge beginning just posterior to it, swinging upward posteriorly (fig. 5B) 4
   Median trunk ridge deflected ventrally at anus and continuous with inferior trunk ridge (fig. 5A) 3
3 With supraopercular and lateral snout ridges ... *Cosmoscampus* spp.
   Without supraopercular and lateral snout ridges 5

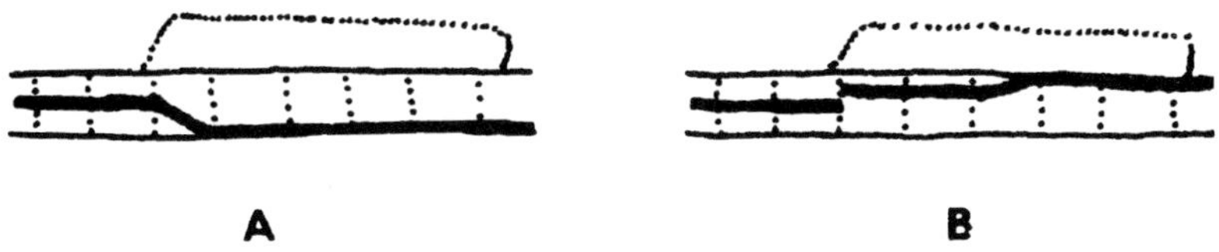

A   **B**

Fig. 5. Lateral ridges in syngnathid fishes

4 Snout long, more than half head length ... opossum pipefish, *Microphis brachyurus.*
   Snout short, less than half head length ... fringed pipefish, *Anarchopterus criniger.*
5 Trunk rings 23, rarely 24 ... bull pipefish, *Syngnathus springeri.*
   Trunk rings 15–21 6
6 Dorsal fin short, with 21–25 rays, beginning approximately over anal fin ... shortfin pipefish, *Cosmocampus elucens.*
   Dorsal fin long, with 27 or more rays, usually beginning in advance of anal fin 7
7 Snout short, 40–50 percent of head length; dorsal fin 88–116 percent of head length 8
   Snout long, 49–66 percent of head length; dorsal fin 53–100 percent of head length 9
8 Dorsal rays 33 or more; tail rings 34–40; dorsal fin covering 4–6 trunk rings and 4–5 tail rings ... Texas pipefish, *Syngnathus affinis.*
   Dorsal rays fewer than 35; tail rings 30–34; dorsal fin covering 2–4 trunk rings and 4–6 tail rings ... Gulf pipefish, *Syngnathus scovelli.*
9 Trunk rings 19–21, usually 20; dorsal rays 32–40 ... chain pipefish, *Syngnathus louisianae.*

Trunk rings 16–18, rarely 19; dorsal rays 27–33 10

10 Tail rings 35–40; preorbital broad ... dusky pipefish, *Syngnathus floridae.*

 Tail rings 33–34; preorbital narrow ... sargassum pipefish, *Syngnathus pelagicus.*

11 Dorsal rays 10–14; pectoral rays 10–12 ... dwarf seahorse, *Hippocampus zosterae.*

 Dorsal rays 16–21; pectoral rays 13 or more 12

12 Body usually spotted; snout length usually less than postorbital length ... longsnout seahorse, *Hippocampus reidi.*

 Body usually with fine lines or blotches, not spotted; snout length usually less than postorbital length except in very large males (greater than 5 inches; 12.75 cm) where body depth is greater than 20 percent of total length ... lined seahorse, *Hippocampus erectus.*

167. Opossum pipefish *Microphis brachyurus* (Bleeker)

D. 40–47; trunk rings 21; tail rings 20–26. The spiny projections on the rings and the location of the brood pouch (on males) under the belly make this species distinctive. This species has been reported from the Rio Grande. Elsewhere, it may be found in many habitats, including *Spartina* marshes or in *Sargassum.* Formerly known as *Oostethus lineatus.* New Jersey to southeast Brazil. Dawson, 1970, 1984; Gilmore, 1977; Pezold and Edwards, 1983. (3 1/2 inches; 9 cm)

168. Fringed pipefish *Anarchopterus criniger* (Bean and Dressel)

D. 16–18; trunk rings 14–16; tail rings 37–39. The pattern of body ridges and the lack of an anal fin are the best traits for distinguishing this species. An early report from Cameron, Louisiana, is probably erroneous, because this is another grassflat species not otherwise known west of the Mississippi River. It occurs in grass beds in the Chandeleur Islands. Most older literature refers the species to the genus *Micrognathus.* North Carolina, Bahamas, Florida, and Yucatán but not in western Gulf. Powell and Strawn, 1963. (3 inches; 8 cm)

169. Texas pipefish *Syngnathus affinis* Günther

D. 36–39; trunk rings 18–19; tail rings 33–36. The best characteristics for distinguishing this species are the number of trunk rings (usually 19), the position of the dorsal fin (covering 4–6 trunk rings and 4–6 tail rings) and the moderate snout length (44–59 percent of head length). There is often a banded pattern on the sides but never a reticulated pattern. This species is quite similar to and has sometimes been regarded as a subspecies of the northern pipefish, *S. fuscus,* which occurs along the Atlantic Coast of the United States southward to northern Florida. Range uncertain, perhaps Louisiana to Laguna de Terminos, Tampico, Mexico. Dawson, 1982b. (6 inches; 15 cm)

170. Gulf pipefish *Syngnathus scovelli* (Evermann and Kendall)

D. 27–36; trunk rings 15–17; tail rings 30–34. This pipefish is distinguished by its short snout (40–45 percent of head length) and its dorsal fin covering 2–4 trunk rings and

3–5 tail rings (usually 3 and 5 respectively). The dorsal fin is usually banded in females of this species. In males, the brood pouch covers 10–13 tail rings. This is a common pipefish in many areas, and populations have been reported from fresh waters in both Louisiana (at Lake St. John about 150 miles inland) and Texas (Lake Texana, 50 miles inland). It is also found in fresh water in most of peninsular Florida. Georgia and northern Gulf to southeast Brazil. Viola, 1992; Whatley, 1962. (6 inches; 15 cm)

171. Chain pipefish *Syngnathus louisianae* Günther

D. 33–36; trunk rings 19–21; tail rings 34–37. The very long snout (53–65 percent of head length), the position of the dorsal fin (covering 2 1/2–3 1/4 trunk rings and 4–6 tail rings, usually 3 and 4, respectively), and a chainlike pattern of bands and reticulations on the sides identify this species. Females are always flat-bellied (in the other species of *Syngnathus* they are V-bellied). This is the most common pipefish of the area, especially in the bays. Individuals occasionally turn up offshore. New Jersey to Florida and the whole Gulf. (10 inches; 25 cm)

172. Dusky pipefish *Syngnathus floridae* (Jordan and Gilbert)

D. 29–33; trunk rings 17–18; tail rings 35–40. This dusky-sided fish is best distinguished by its moderate snout (48–66 percent of head length) and high number of tail rings. Although the snout length commonly overlaps that found in *S. louisianae*, *S. floridae* is usually a stouter-bodied fish. The subspecies in our area is *S. f. floridae*. Generally not as common as the chain and Gulf pipefishes, it is seasonally abundant (during the summer) in high-salinity grass flats. Bermuda, the Bahamas, and Chesapeake Bay to Panama. (8 inches; 20 cm)

173. Sargassum pipefish *Syngnathus pelagicus* Linnaeus

D. 28–31; trunk rings 16–18; tail rings 30–34. Böhlke and Chaplin (1968) remark that this species is usually distinctively marked with narrow vertical white lines margined with black, which occasionally take the form of ocellated spots common to most other animals that live in or around *Sargassum*. The specimens we have examined lacked this coloration. Very similar to *S. floridae*, this species is known only from far offshore, where it inhabits the floating *Sargassum*. Since other species of pipefish, notably *S. louisianae* juveniles, also occur in the *Sargassum* community, any identification of *S. pelagicus* from inshore waters should be carefully checked. Worldwide in *Sargassum*. (6 inches; 15 cm)

174. Dwarf seahorse *Hippocampus zosterae* Jordan and Gilbert

D. 10–13 (usually 11, rarely 13); A. 4; trunk rings 9–11 (10); tail rings 28–34. This is the common small seahorse limited to high-salinity grass flats. Western Gulf populations have been reported as *H. regulus*. Individuals range from green to nearly black in color. Bermuda, Bahamas, northeast Florida, and the whole Gulf. Strawn, 1958. (1 1/2 inches; 3 cm)

175. Lined seahorse *Hippocampus erectus* Perry

D. 16–21; A. 3–4; trunk rings 11; tail rings 33–38; body usually dark but gold individuals are known; body variously lined or covered with blotches but not with distinct spots. Some lined seahorses have filaments spread over their bodies, giving them the appearance of plants. This species is the common larger seahorse of the bays and shallow Gulf of Mexico. It was previously reported as *H. hudsonius.* Nova Scotia through the Caribbean to Uruguay. Matlock, 1992b. (7 inches; 17 cm)

176. Longsnout seahorse *Hippocampus reidi* Ginsburg

D. 16–19; A. 4; trunk rings 11; tail rings 33–37; color variable, may be bicolored. Body with distinct black punctulations. Snout length usually greater than postorbital length (41–49 percent of head length). *H. reidi* has been reported as *H. obtusus* Ginsburg both in Louisiana and Texas. Vari (1982) refers *H. obtusus* to *H. reidi* and notes that the adults of this species also lack tubercles. Robins et al. (1980) state that *H. obtusus* refers to the pelagic juvenile of *H. reidi.* Bermuda, Bahamas, and North Carolina through the Caribbean to southern Brazil; status in Gulf unclear. (6 3/4 inches; 17.5 cm)

Centropomidae

Snooks are popular tropical game and food fishes with an extended, pikelike lower jaw. Two species of the genus *Centropomus* occur in the northwestern Gulf of Mexico. In addition, there are two other tropical species in the southern Gulf. One, the tarpon snook *(C. pectinatus),* has also been taken on the Florida panhandle. It has fewer than seventy scale rows and seven anal rays. (Greenfield, 1975; Rivas, 1962, 1986)

1   Lateral line black; body slender, depth less than head length; lower arch gill rakers 7–9 . . . common snook, *Centropomus undecimalis.*
    Lateral line dark, not black; body fat, depth about equal to head length; lower arch gill rakers 10–13 (other snooks have more than 13) . . . fat snook, *Centropomus parallelus.*

177. Common snook; robalo; saltwater pike *Centropomus undecimalis* (Bloch)

D. VIII + 1, 10; A. III, 6; Sc. 69–80; Gr. 7–10 on lower limb; body silvery, countershaded tan to olive brown above; lateral line black. The distinct lateral line, together with the high, divided dorsal fin, the sloping forehead, and the large mouth, make the common snook unmistakable. It regularly frequents fresh water or brackish areas near the mouths of rivers or mangroves or salt marshes. Young are usually caught in the bays and the adults in the Gulf. This species is extremely sensitive to cold (Böhlke and Chaplin, 1968), not tolerating temperatures much below 60°F (15°C). The similarity of the favorite habitats of common snook and tarpon supports hypotheses of habitat destruction or environmental change as a common cause for the disappearance of both species in recent years. Baughman's report (1943a) on this species indicates that its distribution has moved southward since the early twentieth century. However, more have been caught recently in Texas, and even a few in Louisiana. Other hypotheses were suggested by Matlock (1987).

This fish reaches a weight of fifty pounds (23 kg), ten pounds (4.5 kg) being the usual limit. In areas where it is more abundant, it is a highly prized game and food fish. North Carolina and northern Gulf through the Caribbean to Rio de Janeiro, Brazil. In the Gulf from about Galveston and Tampa south but rarely in between. Baughman, 1943a; Pezold and Edwards, 1983; Marshall, 1958; Moore, 1976; Matlock, 1987. (4 1/2 feet; 1.4 m)

178. Fat snook *Centropomus parallelus* Poey
D. VIII + I, 10; A. III, 6; Sc. 80–90; Gr. 10–13. More tropical than the common snook, this species has recently been found in South Texas but is rare there. South Texas and southern Florida through the Caribbean to southeastern Brazil. Martin and King, 1991. (1 1/2 feet; 70 cm)

Moronidae

The moronids are a small group of freshwater or anadromous fishes formerly aligned with the serranids or percichthyids. Of those on our coast, only one species is normally in salt water, but the yellow bass, *Morone mississippiensis*, with its interrupted horizontal stripes, often enters low salinities in Louisiana and East Texas.

179. Striped bass *Morone saxatilis* (Walbaum)
D. IX + I, 12; A. III, 11; Sc. 57–67. A slender species with about seven uninterrupted horizontal dark stripes on a silver background, striped bass (formerly placed in the genus *Roccus*) are anadromous fish with some landlocked populations, native in the Gulf from streams entering Lake Pontchartrain east to the Florida panhandle. Widespread introductions into most southern and some western states have increased its range and abundance, in our area since 1965, and individuals have been caught in salt water in Louisiana and Texas, usually in relatively clear water. The future of this range extension without continual stocking is still uncertain, but more unlikely. Currently striped bass can be expected almost anywhere. There is no evidence that there was ever a commercial fishery in Texas or that its native range was west of the Mississippi River, as has been reported in the popular press in Texas. New Brunswick to northeast Florida and across the Gulf to somewhere along the Texas coast; Gulf native range Apalachicola to Lake Pontchartrain drainages. Benefield et al., 1977; Horst, 1976; Perry and Williams, 1985; Ward et al., 1995. (1 foot; 30cm—but on the Atlantic Coast up to 4 feet; 1 1/4 m)

Acropomatidae

The temperate ocean basses, family Acropomatidae, are represented locally by only one genus, with one or two species occurring regularly near the continental shelf margin. Fishes in this family were formerly assigned to other families such as the Serranidae, Centropomidae, Apogonidae, or Percichthyidae. The latter family comprised an assortment of marine and anadromous fishes with divided dorsal fins, which most ichthyologists agreed was a catchall category for generalized forms that did not fit well into other families. The Percichthyidae have recently been split into several families. After removal of the Moronidae, the only other former percichthyids known from the northwestern Gulf are in a genus that in our first edition was included in the cardinalfish family (Apogonidae). (Johnson, 1994; Roberts, 1993)

180. Blackmouth bass *Synagrops bellus* (Goode and Bean)
D. IX + I, 9; A. IV, 7; Gr. on lower limb 14. A dark-bodied fish with darker-shaped markings on sides and with yellow-orange eyes. This is a deeper-water species typically found in seventy-five to over one hundred fathoms. A second species of this genus, *S. spinosus* Schultz, with serrations on the second spines of the dorsal and anal fins, is also known in the northern Gulf in one hundred to two hundred fathoms, and may occur on the shelf as well. Known from both sides of the Atlantic, in the west from North Carolina to Venezuela. Garzón and Acero, 1986; Hoese, 1958a. (3 inches; 8 cm)

Serranidae

The serranids or sea basses comprise a family of generally unspecialized spiny-rayed fishes, the limits of which are not well understood. Some genera that were previously considered serranids are now placed in separate families such as the Moronidae and Grammatidae. Conversely, soapfishes (the common name is derived from the soapy mucus produced by the skin of these fishes) that were previously afforded their own family (Grammistidae) are now included in the Serranidae. Certain deep-sea and extralimital forms appear to bridge the gap between sea basses and other families, as understood here, and are, at best, confusing. Fortunately, these transitory forms are not present in the shallow northwestern Gulf of Mexico.

Serranids are typically bottom-dwelling fish, although a few, such as the Creole fish, are pelagic. Most live near rocky areas, reefs, or man-made habitats such as oil platforms, jetties, and pilings. A few are even found over open bottoms.

Fourteen genera and forty-one species of serranids have been reported from this general area, but only a dozen species are commonly encountered in trawls or by hook-

and-line anglers. The common species range in size from the tiny *Serraniculus pumilio,* which rarely attains a length of one and one-half inches (40 mm), to the giant groupers, which may weigh over half a ton. These larger fish are among the most important sport and commercial fishes. In addition to the shelf-dwelling species covered here, several deeper-dwelling slope groupers turn up in commercial catches. According to Bullock and Smith (1991), specimens of the misty grouper, *Epinephelus mystacinus,* taken in eighty to three hundred fathoms from off Texas and Louisiana appear in Florida commercial landings. This species is distinguished by its color pattern, which consists of eight to nine dark vertical bars on a light chocolate brown background, more obvious in juveniles than in adults. A black maxillary "mustache" is also prominent.

One interesting aspect of the biology of serranids is that many species are hermaphroditic; that is, the same individual may be both male and female. Most groupers, as well as the species of *Centropristis,* begin life as females and transform into males as they reach a certain age or size. Other genera, such as *Serranus* and *Hypoplectrus,* possess functional ovaries and testes at the same time and are capable of self-fertilization. (Baughman, 1943b; Bullock and Godcharles, 1982; Bullock and Smith, 1991; Cervigon, 1966; Courtenay, 1967; Heemstra, 1993; Johnson and Keener, 1984; Polovina and Ralston, 1987; Robins and Stark, 1961; Smith, 1964, 1965, 1971)

1   Dorsal spines 8–11 2
    Dorsal spines 2–4 41
2   Dorsal spines 8 or 9 3
    Dorsal spines 10 or 11 9
3   Spinous dorsal continuous 4
    Spinous dorsal interrupted by scaled-over area, with one or two free spines usually protruding 8
4   Dorsal spines 8 5
    Dorsal spines 9 6
5   Opercle without prominent, knifelike spine; pectoral fin symmetrical . . . yellowtail bass, *Bathyanthias mexicanus.*
    Opercle with a prominent, knifelike spine; pectoral fin with upper rays longest ... Spanish flag, *Gonioplectrus hispanus.*
6   Caudal forked; head short, less than 35 percent of standard length; body red without obvious markings except series of white spots beneath dorsal fin base ... Creole fish, *Paranthias furcifer.*
    Caudal fin truncate; head more than 35 percent of standard length; body variously colored 7
7   Anal rays 8; pectoral rays 16; body variously spotted, usually with three or four black or white spots below dorsal fin base ... graysby, *Epinephelus cruentatus.*
    Anal rays 9; pectoral rays 17–19; body variously colored, often with numerous black-rimmed

blue spots on head; two dark spots on tip of lower jaw and a second pair of spots on top of caudal peduncle ... coney, *Epinephelus fulvus.*

8   Dorsal spines 8 (VI + I + I); sides with five dark bands and alternating red and orange bands ... peppermint bass, *Liopropoma rubre.*

       Dorsal spines 9 (VI + I + I + I); sides with single wide, dark band ... wrasse bass, *Liopropoma eukrines.*

9   Dorsal spines 10; inner teeth of jaws not depressible or hinged 10

       Dorsal spines 10 or 11; inner teeth of jaws depressible or hinged 24

10   Gill rakers long and slender 11

       Gill rakers short 14

11   Anal with 7 rays; maxilla and frontal bones scaled ... roughtongue bass, *Holanthias martinicensis.*

       Anal rays 8 or 9; maxilla and frontal bones naked 12

12   Postero-ventral edge of maxilla with an anteriorly directed hook; membranes of spinous dorsal never filamentous ... streamer bass, *Hemanthias aureorubens.*

       Postero-ventral edge of maxilla without a hook; adults often with filamentous dorsal spines 13

13   Lateral line scales 43–53; gill rakers about 30 on lower limb of first arch ... red barbier, *Hemanthias vivanus.*

       Lateral line scales 54–64; gill rakers about 26 on lower limb of first arch ... longtail bass, *Hemanthias leptus.*

14   Horizontal margin of preopercle without forward-pointing serrations; body long and slender, less than 45 (typically less than 40) percent of standard length 15

       Horizontal margin of preopercle with several forward-pointing serrations on free portion; body short and deep, depth greater than 40 (usually near 45 percent of standard length) ... hamlets, *Hypoplectrus* spp.

15   Caudal fin truncate or lunate 16

       Caudal fin rounded or with three distinct lobes 21

16   Preopercle with numerous strong, diverging spines at its angle... 17

       Preopercle simply and finely serrated 18

17   Preopercle with two clusters of spines at its angle ... sand perch, *Diplectrum formosum.*

       Preopercle with a single cluster of divergent spines ... dwarf sand perch, *Diplectrum bivittatum.*

18   Black lanceolate mark on inner surface of opercle; top of head scaled forward to posterior edge of interorbital; scales on body often deciduous ... blackear bass, *Serranus atrobranchus.*

       No black lanceolate mark inside of opercle; top of head naked; scales ctenoid, not deciduous 19

19   Dorsal soft rays 13; caudal, soft dorsal, pectoral, and anal fins spotted; belly white or silver, sharply defined against adjacent pattern ... belted sandfish, *Serranus subligarius.*

       Dorsal soft rays 12 or fewer 20

20   Pectoral rays 16 ... tattler, *Serranus phoebe.*

       Pectoral rays 13 ... orangeback bass, *Serranus annularis.*

21 Branchiostegal rays 6; caudal rounded in fish of all sizes . . . pygmy sea bass, *Serraniculus pumilio.*

Branchiostegal rays 7; caudal fin rounded in young but with elongated tips and central rays in adults 22

22 Median fins dark; gill rakers on first arch usually more than 21 . . . Gulf black sea bass, *Centropristis striata.*

Median fins light, may have dark markings; gill rakers on first arch usually 21 or fewer, most commonly 19 or 20 23

23 Dorsal spines with dermal flaps which often project well beyond ends of spines; about seven broad, diffuse brown bars on sides of body; dark spot at base of last three dorsal spines . . . rock sea bass, *Centropristis philadelphica.*

Dorsal spines with dermal flaps scarcely reaching end of spine; sides with three horizontal rows of seven quadrate black blotches; middle caudal ray and dorsal spines with jet black spots . . . bank sea bass, *Centropristis ocyura.*

24 Anal rays 7–9 (rarely 10), usually 9; at least a few canines present, most noticeable on anterior jaw; lateral crests of skull (not visible externally) diverging 25

Anal rays 10–14; no canines present; lateral crests parallel 35

25 Dorsal soft rays 13–15; pelvic inserted under or in advance of upper end of pectoral base, pelvic fin longer than pectoral 26

Dorsal soft rays 15–20, usually 16 or 17 (19 in *E. inermis*); pelvic fins inserted under or behind lower end of pectoral fin base; pelvic fins shorter than pectorals 29

26 Dorsal spines 10 . . . Warsaw grouper, *Epinephelus nigritus.*

Dorsal spines 11 27

27 Body brownish with eight or nine vertical dark bars (last two may be fused into single wide band on caudal peduncle . . . misty grouper, *Epinephelus mystacinus.*

Body without dark vertical bars 28

28 Posterior nostril as large as anterior nostril; margin of spinous dorsal yellow in life, lighter in preserved specimens; saddle-shaped dorsal blotch on caudal peduncle of young not extending ventrally to lateral line or anteriorly to end of dorsal fin . . . yellowedge grouper, *Epinephelus flavolimbatus.*

Posterior nostril three to five times larger than anterior nostril; margin of spinous dorsal dusky in living and preserved specimens; saddle-shaped dorsal blotch on caudal peduncle of small fish extending ventrally to lateral line and anteriorly to end of dorsal fin . . . snowy grouper, *Epinephelus niveatus.*

29 Dorsal soft rays usually 16 or 17 (15–18) 30

Dorsal soft rays usually 19, rarely 20 . . . marbled grouper, *Epinephelus inermis.*

30 Gill rakers 13–15, usually 14, on lower limb of first arch . . . jewfish, *Epinephelus itajara.*

Gill rakers 15–19, usually 16–18, on lower limb of first arch 31

31 Anal rays 9 or 10; posterior margin of caudal fin straight or concave 32

Anal rays 7–9, usually 8; posterior margin of caudal fin convex 33

32 Pectoral rays 18; gill rakers 17–18 on lower limb of first arch; no black specks about eye;

head, fins, and sides of body with many white speckles; dark, saddle-shaped blotch on caudal peduncle ... speckled hind, *Epinephelus drummondhayi*.

Pectoral rays 16–18, usually 17; gill rakers 15–16 on lower limb of first arch; black spots about eye; white spots, if any, only on sides of body; no saddle-shaped blotch on caudal peduncle ... red grouper *Epinephelus morio*.

33 Gill rakers 16–19, usually 17, on lower limb of first arch; head and body with numerous dark spots on lighter background 34

Gill rakers 15–17, usually 16, on lower limb of first arch; head and body without numerous spots (a few scattered spots), but dark barring on sides always present; dorsal rays 16–18, usually 17; saddle-shaped blotch on dorsal surface of caudal peduncle ... Nassau grouper, *Epinephelus striatus*.

34 Dorsal rays 16–18, usually 17; dark, saddle-shaped blotch on dorsal surface of caudal peduncle and three dark blotches along base of dorsal fin ... rock hind, *Epinephelus adscensionis*.

Dorsal rays 15 or 16; no dark, saddle-shaped blotch on caudal peduncle; no dark blotches along base of dorsal fin ... red hind, *Epinephelus guttatus*.

35 Preopercle angulate; upper and lower limbs meeting at an angle slightly greater than 90 degrees 36

Preopercle gently rounded, upper and lower limbs meeting at a broadly obtuse angle 39

36 Total gill rakers on first arch 45 to 54 ... comb grouper, *Mycteroperca acutirostris*.

Total gill rakers on first arch fewer than 40 37

37 Dorsal, anal, and caudal fins without produced rays; predominantly gray with vermiculations ... gag, *Mycteroperca microlepis*.

Dorsal, anal, and caudal fins with some produced rays; brown or gray with large blotches or spots 38

38 Body reddish brown, occasionally broken into brown spots separated by paler yellow reticulations; exserted midcaudal rays of uniform length; total gill rakers 23–27 on first arch ... yellowmouth grouper, *Mycteroperca interstitialis*.

Body and fins light grayish brown with small red-brown spots; exserted midcaudal rays irregular, noticeably shorter than outer rays; total gill rakers 26–31 ... scamp, *Mycteroperca phenax*.

39 Developed gill rakers on lower limb of first arch 4–8; dorsum dark with about 9 to 11 upwardly oblique pale stripes usually evident ... tiger grouper, *Mycteroperca tigris*.

Developed gill rakers on lower limb of first arch 11–16; color pattern variable, but generally without upwardly oblique lines 40

40 Distal one-third of pectoral bright yellow in life, sharply delineated from rest of fin and lighter in preserved specimens; large individuals with light spots on lower part of body and head; gill rakers short, about 8 on lower limb of first arch; caudal lunate ... yellowfin grouper, *Mycteroperca venenosa*.

Pectoral with very narrow orange margin about one-fifth length of fin, gradually shading into basal color, which is dark and lacks distinct spots; sides of head and lower part of body with brassy yellow spots; gill rakers slender, about 10 on lower limb of first arch … black grouper, *Mycteroperca bonaci*.

41 Dorsal spines II; color pattern consisting of scattered but distinct, pale spots on somewhat darker background … whitespotted soapfish, *Rypticus maculatus*.
Dorsal spines III; pattern with large pale spots or blotches or small dark spots, but not as above 42

42 Body covered with dark, sometimes ocellated spots on pale background … spotted soapfish, *Rypticus subbifrenatus*.
Body with large, diffuse pale spots or blotches … greater soapfish, *Rypticus saponaceus*.

181. Yellowtail bass *Bathyanthias mexicanus* (Schultz)

D.VIII, 14; A. III, 8; Gr. 21–23; in life, reddish with more or less regular rows of yellow spots on sides (about one spot on each scale) and yellow margins to dorsal and anal interspinous membranes; caudal fin yellow. Altogether, this fish bears an amazing resemblance to the wrasse *Decodon puellaris*. Preserved specimens are straw-colored without markings except for traces of dark on the outer margins of the pectoral fins. This species was described (as *Pikea mexicana*) in 1958 from specimens taken off the Texas coast, where it apparently is not uncommon. Recent collections indicate that it does not usually occur inside fifty fathoms. Northern Gulf to Suriname. Schultz, 1958. (6 inches; 15 cm)

182. Spanish flag *Gonioplectrus hispanus* (Cuvier)

D.VIII, 13; A. III, 7; background rose with yellow-orange spots; striped on head, resembling Spanish flag; dark spot at base of anal fin, extending onto fin; large, knifelike opercular spine. This species, recorded only once from the snapper banks off Port Aransas, also occurs off the Florida panhandle. North Carolina and northern Gulf to southern Brazil. Briggs et al., 1964. (12 inches; 30 cm)

183. Creole fish *Paranthias furcifer* (Valenciennes)

D. IX, 18–19; A. III, 9–10; Gr. 35–40; caudal fin deeply forked; general color of head and body red with darker countershading above; pale red to pink on lower sides and belly; lower parts of head yellow with grooves around mouth lined with red; dorsal fin dark red with orange or red spot behind each spine; anal and caudal fins also red. The Creole fish differs from most other serranids in being essentially a midwater fish, as evidenced by its fusiform body and terminal mouth. North Carolina and Bermuda through the Caribbean to southern Brazil, but absent from western Caribbean; also reported from West Africa. (14 inches; 36 cm)

184. Peppermint bass (Swissguard basslet) *Liopropoma rubre* Poey

D.VI + I + I, 12; A. III, 8; Sc. 48–49; Gr. 16–18 (17); sides of head, body, and caudal fin with alternating pink, orange, and reddish brown or black stripes (five or six each); soft dorsal and anal each with dark spot; caudal fin with two spots, sometimes coalesced, near posterior border. This secretive little basslet, usually found in 10 to 140 feet, is known from fairly deep waters off Texas and Louisiana. Northern Gulf and Bahamas through the Caribbean to Venezuela. Bright and Cashman, 1974. (3 1/2 inches; 9 cm)

185. Wrasse bass *Liopropoma eukrines* (Starck and Courtenay)

D. VI + I + I + I, 12; A. III, 8; Sc. 44; Gr. 14–17; body with dark brown band from snout through eye, expanding rearward to cover most of caudal; this band with yellow on either side bordered by red; tip of lower jaw also brown. In our area this species is known from the West Flower Gardens Reef and from reefs off Louisiana. North Carolina to Florida and across the northern Gulf. Bright and Cashman, 1974; Starck and Courtenay, 1962. (2 inches; 5 cm)

186. Roughtongue bass *Holanthias martinicensis* (Guichenot)

D. X, 13–16 (15); A. III, 7; Sc. 35–41; Gr, 34–41 on first arch; oval patch of teeth on tongue; vomerine tooth patch with well-defined posterior extension. Color reddish gold with freckles on back; brown saddle on back from dorsal fin base to lateral midline. Generally in depths of 100 to 200 meters. Dennis and Bright (1988b) found schools of this small pelagic bass common around deep reef habitats in 33–77 fathoms (60–140 m) off the Flower Gardens reefs. Bermuda and North Carolina through the Caribbean to Brazil. Anderson and Heemstra, 1980. (5 inches; 13 cm)

187. Streamer bass *Hemanthias aureorubens* (Longley)

D. X, 15; A. III, 16–17; Sc. 44–48; Gr. 28–29 on lower limb of first arch. Preopercle finely serrate, caudal lobes long and filamentous; color pinkish, scales with yellow margins, belly silvery; dorsal and caudal fins yellow, pectorals pink, other fins pale. Originally described as *Pronotogramus aureorubens* Longley. Generally in depths of 50–166 fathoms (100–300 meters), this species in the northwestern Gulf is known only from the stomach contents of larger predators (Nelson, 1988). North Carolina and northern Gulf to Suriname. Cervigon, 1966, 1991; Strusaker, 1969. (6 inches; 15 cm)

188. Longtail bass *Hemanthias leptus* (Ginsburg)

D. X, 14; A. III, 8; Sc. 78; Gr. 10 + 26; eye large, subequal to snout length; caudal fin deeply lunate with filamentous lobes; third dorsal spine not elongated In young, becoming so in adults; golden above, silvery below; fins yellow; adults with ocellated spot near ventral base of caudal fin. Originally described as *Anthiasicus leptus,* this species occurs near the edge of the continental shelf, where it has been caught by anglers and in trawls. South Carolina and northern Gulf through the Caribbean to Suriname. Briggs et al., 1964; Ginsburg, 1952a, 1954. (12 inches; 30 cm)

189. Red barbier *Hemanthias vivanus* (Jordan and Swain)

D. X, 14–15; A. III, 7–8; Sc. 53; Gr. 14 + 30; eye larger than snout; third dorsal spine elongated in moderate to large-sized specimens; general body color carmine, deepest on back and shading into violet on sides, freckled with olive; bright gold stripe from eye to upper base of pectoral fin; another gold stripe from tip of snout running under eye to middle of pectoral fin base. Like *H. leptus*, this attractive fish is another rare offshore form. North Carolina to northern Brazil. Walls, 1973. (12 inches; 30 cm)

190. Hamlets *Hypoplectrus* spp.

D. X, 13–16; A. III, 7; P. 13–15; Gr. 17–20 (18–19) total on first arch; color patterns variable, but distinctive for different species/morphs. The genus *Hypoplectrus* consists of a group of morphometrically identical forms, distinguished primarily by coloration. These forms have variously been regarded as distinct species (Barlow, 1975; Domeier, 1994; Randall, 1968; Thresher, 1978); as subspecies of *H. unicolor* (Jordan and Evermann, 1896); as members of a "multispecies" (Fischer, 1979); or color morphs of a single polymorphic species (Graves and Rosenblatt, 1980). Despite intensive investigations on offshore banks and reefs in recent decades, there are only two old records of hamlets off Texas and Louisiana, one of which is erroneous.

The yellowtail hamlet, *Hypoplectrus chlorurus* (Valenciennes) (pl. 190a), possesses a dark body (blue, black, or brown) with a bright yellow tail. Its occurrence in the western Gulf is based on a single specimen from "near Corpus Christi" (Woods, 1942). Upon examination, however, this turned out to be a juvenile of *Epinephelus nigritus*. The butter hamlet, *Hypoplectrus unicolor* (Walbaum) (pl. 190), has also been reported from Port Aransas (Gunter and Knapp, 1951). Because this name has taxonomic priority, this usage could refer to any of the other forms as well. We have not been able to locate these specimens to confirm which (if any) of the nominal forms of the genus these represent. The barred hamlet, *Hypoplectrus puella* Poey (pl. 190c), occurs in the eastern Gulf (Bullock and Smith, 1991) and *H. chlororus, H. puella,* and *H. unicolor* are known from the Gulf of Campeche (Schaldach, n.d.) and so might be expected off southern Texas as well.

Florida, eastern and southern Gulf, through the West Indies, Venezuela, and possibly Texas. Woods, 1942; Gunter and Knapp, 1951; Randall, 1968. (5 inches; 13 cm)

191. Sand perch *Diplectrum formosum* (Linnaeus)

D. X, 12; A. III, 7; two prominent groups of spines on margin of preopercle, one at the angle and one above; body with blackish bands alternating with blue and orange stripes. A small fish common over coarse sand bottoms, it is more common off the eastern coast of the United States, off the northeastern Gulf, and in the Caribbean than in the northwestern Gulf of Mexico. Virginia through the Caribbean to Uruguay. Bortone, 1977; Darcy, 1985c. (12 inches; 30 cm)

192. Dwarf sand perch *Diplectrum bivittatum* (Valenciennes)

D. X, 12; A. III, 7; like *D. formosum* but with only a single prominent group of spines at angle of preopercle; caudal fin slightly forked; upper half of body greenish with two lateral stripes or irregular series of double bars; cheek with oblique blue lines; two blue-edged spots at upper edge of caudal base. A smaller species than *D. formosum*, the dwarf sand perch frequents areas where it is often caught by shrimpers. The local subspecies has sometimes been considered a separate species (*D. arcuarium* Ginsburg). It is replaced to the south by *D. radiale* (Quoy and Gaimard). North Carolina through the Caribbean (not Bahamas) to northern Brazil. Bortone, 1977; Ginsburg, 1948. (6 inches; 15 cm)

193. Blackear bass *Serranus atrobranchus* (Cuvier)

D. X, 12; A. III, 7; P. 15; black lanceolate to ovate mark on inner surface of operculum, commonly visible through operculum. This species was reported in earlier literature as *Paracentropristes pomospilus* Ginsburg, but Robins and Starck (1961) recognized that the Gulf of Mexico fish represented a northern, disjunct population of *Prionodes atrobranchus* and subsequently included *Prionodes* in the genus *Serranus*. This small bass occurs between six and fifty fathoms in the northern Gulf of Mexico. Northern Gulf through the Caribbean to Brazil. Hildebrand, 1954. (6 inches; 15 cm)

194. Belted sandfish; belted sand bass *Serranus subligarius* (Cope)

D. X, 11–14; A. III, 6–7; P. 14–17; body brown; caudal and pectoral fins with alternating dark and light bands; belly white to silver, sharply delineated from background color; soft dorsal with large black spot anteriorly. This small serranid is one of the commonest fishes near the southern Texas and northern Florida jetties. It has previously been placed in the genera *Serranellus* and (incorrectly) *Dules*. North Carolina, around southern Florida to south Mexico. Hastings and Bortone, 1980; Hastings and Petersen, 1986. (4 inches; 10 cm)

195. Orangeback bass *Serranus annularis* Günther

D. X, 1–12 (12); A. III, 7 (rarely 6); P. 13–14 (13); Sc. 43–50; Gr 15–18. Dorsum and top of head orange, becoming yellow posteriorly and ventrally; dorsal color pattern includes a series of inverted V's, the first represented by two characteristic yellow squares (white in preserved specimens) behind the eye; the next three marks are darkened and joined to form a dorsolateral blotch, the last two V's occurring beneath the soft dorsal. The small bass is abundant in the algal-sponge zone (33–55 fathoms; 60–100 m) off Texas and on the middle Florida shelf. North Carolina, Bermuda, and the northern Gulf through the Caribbean to Brazil. Bright and Rezak, 1976; Dennis and Bright, 1988b; Miller and Richards, 1979; Robins and Starck, 1961. (3.5 inches; 6.5 cm)

196. Tattler *Serranus phoebe* Poey

D. X, 12; A. III, 7; P. 16; color distinctive, but varying with age; juveniles characterized by dark diagonal band from second to sixth dorsal spines continuing across body to belly; in adults, diagonal band is obscure and silvery bar extends upward from anus just anterior to where dark bar was; intermediate forms exhibit both dark bar and silvery bar. Scattered specimens have been taken from most Gulf states; however, the tattler is probably more common than these collections indicate. Bermuda, South Carolina, and Florida through the Caribbean to Guyana. Moore, 1975b; Moseley, 1966a. (8 inches; 20 cm)

197. Pygmy sea bass *Serraniculus pumilio* Ginsburg

D. X, 10–11; A. III, 7; P. 14–15; Gr. 8–11, of which 3–5 occur on lower limb; four diffuse and irregular major crossbands on sides of body, sometimes barely distinguishable from background; yellowish spot behind last band on caudal peduncle, sometimes with second spot above first; ventral and anal fins black; other fins clear. This fish is the smallest American serranid, quite abundant around rough bottoms in eight to thirty-five fathoms. Its small size and secretive nature make it difficult to collect or observe. North Carolina to Guyana. Hastings, 1973. (2 inches; 5 cm)

198. Gulf black sea bass *Centropristis striata* (Linnaeus)

D. X, 11; A. III, 7; P. 16–18 (17–18); Gr. 21–26 (23); preserved specimens generally dark, including median fins and belly; in small fish, series of longitudinal lines possibly apparent as well as dark spot at bases of last dorsal spines; others possibly showing pattern of seven vertical bands similar to that in *C. philadelphica,* which has light-colored belly and fins. The subspecies *C. striata melana* Ginsburg occurs commonly in the eastern Gulf of Mexico and may stray into our area, but we have not been able to verify its presence in the western Gulf. Another subspecies, *C. s. striata,* occurs on the Atlantic Coast from Maine to Florida. These subspecies are listed as distinct species by Bailey et al. (1970) but are treated as conspecifics by Robins et al. (1980, 1991). Miller, 1959. (11 inches; 28 cm in the Gulf of Mexico—18 inches; 46 cm in the Atlantic)

199. Rock sea bass *Centropristis philadelphica* (Linnaeus)

D. X, 11; A. III, 7; P. 15–20 (18); Gr. 17–22 (19–21); preserved specimens with several distinct vertical bars and large dark spot at base of last three dorsal spines; in life, fins olivaceous above, whitish below, with bright blue and orange stripes and markings on head and fins; anal fin of males nearly twice as long, in proportion to body size, as that of females. In this as well as other species of *Centropristis,* the younger adults are predominantly female and transform into males as they get older and grow larger. The rock sea bass is very common in the shallow northwestern Gulf of Mexico, especially between ten and fifty fathoms. Despite its common name, it is an unusual sea bass in that it occurs more frequently over sandy or muddy bottoms. It has rarely been taken in bays. Carolinas around Florida and throughout the Gulf of Mexico. Hildebrand, 1954; Miller, 1959; Russ et al., 1989. (8 inches; 20 cm)

200. Bank sea bass; rock squirrel *Centropristis ocyura* (Jordan and Evermann)
D. X, 11; A. III, 7; P. 16–18 (17); Gr. 19–21. Preserved specimens have three longitudinal rows of rectangular black blotches, with blotches in center being most distinct; in small fish, these blotches possibly fused into seven black bars. Dorsal spines with three or four inky black spots, evenly spaced, with similar inky spots at pectoral fin base and on opercle; outer rays of caudal fin pale; in life, head and fins and forward position of body with numerous blue and yellow stripes and spots. This fish generally occurs in deeper water than *C. philadelphica* and shows a more pronounced preference for hard (rocky) bottoms. It appears to be most common in the northern and eastern parts of its range, where it is more abundant than *C. philadelphica*. *C. springeri* Ginsburg is regarded as a synonym. North Carolina to Florida and throughout the Gulf of Mexico. Miller, 1959. (12 inches; 30 cm)

201. Graysby *Epinephelus (Cephalopholis) cruentatus* (Lacepède)
D IX, 14; A. III, 8; P. 16; Sc. 65–79; light gray or brown with numerous dark orange-brown spots over head, body, and all fins; three or four dark spots below dorsal fin (becoming white if fish exhibits dark color pattern). This is one of the most common serranids around Caribbean reefs, and it is also common on the offshore reefs in the northwestern Gulf. This species was formerly assigned to the genus *Petrometopon*. Bermuda, North Carolina, and the northern Gulf through the Caribbean to southern Brazil. Briggs, 1964; Smith, 1971. (12 inches; 30 cm)

202. Coney *Epinephelus (Cephalopholis) fulvus* (Linnaeus)
D. IX, 15 (rarely 14 or 16); A. III, 9; P. 18; Sc. 80–94; Gr. 23–27; a pair of black spots at tip of lower jaw and a second pair on top of caudal peduncle. Having the head, upper body, and sides with small blue spots surrounded by black against a reddish brown background is the commonest color pattern exhibited by this species; however, the background can be white, yellow, red, or bicolored—white below and brown above. In the northwestern Gulf this species has recently been found on several offshore reefs. Elsewhere it is a common serranid on tropical reefs. Bermuda and South Carolina through the Caribbean to Brazil. Cordova, 1986; Dennis and Bright, 1988a; Smith, 1971. (14 inches; 37 cm—usually less than 6 inches; 15 cm)

203. Warsaw grouper; black jewfish *Epinephelus nigritus* (Holbrook)
D. X, 13–15 (14); A. III, 9; P. 18–19 (18); Sc. 85–99. This species differs from most others of *Epinephelus* in possessing ten instead of eleven dorsal spines. This character and differences in skull morphology have sometimes led to the placing of this species in the separate genus *Garrupa*. Small Warsaw groupers are common about the jetties and

offshore oil platforms, and fish up to forty pounds (18 kg) are not unusual in these waters. Apparently a cool-water, deeper-living species, moving close to shore in winter. Very small juveniles, often in grass flats and other inshore habitats, differ by having yellow or transparent caudal and ventral fins. Massachusetts to Texas, rare records in the West Indies and Brazil. (5 feet; 1 1/2 m)

204. Yellowedge grouper *Epinephelus flavolimbatus* Poey
D. XI, 13–15 (13–14); A. III, 9; P. 18; Sc. 80–99; round white spots on body; dark, saddlelike blotch on dorsal surface of caudal peduncle (becoming obscure with age). In the northwestern Gulf of Mexico, it occurs on the middle and outer shelf. North Carolina and northern Gulf through the Caribbean to southern Brazil. Jones et al., 1989. (12 inches; 30 cm)

205. Snowy grouper *Epinephelus niveatus* (Valenciennes)
D XI, 13–14; A. III, 9; P. 18; Sc. 95–104; small individuals with pearly white spots on brown background; distinguished from yellowedge grouper by larger size of saddlelike blotch on caudal peduncle, posterior nostril much larger than anterior nostril, and margin of spinous dorsal not edged with yellow in live fish and remaining dusky to its margin in preserved fish. Small juveniles rarely occur on offshore oil rigs, while the adults may be encountered in deeper water off the edge of the continental shelf. Massachusetts through the Caribbean to Brazil, with a closely related (same?) species in the eastern Pacific from Baja California to Panama. (36 inches; 90 cm. Inshore usually 12 inches; 30 cm)

206. Marbled grouper *Epinephelus (Dermatolepis) inermis* (Valenciennes)
D. XI, 19; A. III, 9; P. 18–19; Sc. 85–99; pectoral fin elongate (29–35 percent of standard length); usually dark brown to black with large white blotches and white line through eye; particularly conspicuous white spot at base of maxilla. This is the deepest-bodied grouper; the marbled pattern of this species, most obvious in juveniles, is unmistakable and is responsible for the common name. Common throughout the West Indies, in the northwestern Gulf this species occurs on offshore reefs and around oil platforms. North Carolina and northern Gulf through the Caribbean to southern Brazil. (3 feet; 90 cm)

207. Jewfish; spotted jewfish *Epinephelus itajara* (Lichtenstein)
D. XI, 15–16; A. III, 8; P. 19; Sc. 85–89; dorsal spines relatively short, third through eleventh being about the same size and not much longer than soft rays; mouth large, extending behind eye; eye small, being one-sixth to one-twelfth of head length; body brownish green with small, irregular brown spots on head and five oblique, irregular dark bars (becoming obscure in large adults) on sides. This long-lived fish reaches a size of about seven hundred pounds (320 kg); however, most in the northwestern Gulf are much smaller. It was formerly placed in the genus *Promicrops*. Because it is rare and easily taken, it is offered stringent protection in Texas, Louisiana, and Florida, where possession of the

species by anglers is illegal. Florida and northern Gulf through the Caribbean to south-eastern Brazil, and West Africa; in the Pacific from Mexico to Peru. Bullock et al., 1992. (6 feet; 1 2/3 m)

208. Speckled hind; calico grouper *Epinephelus drummondhayi* Goode and Bean

D. XI, 15–16 (16); A. III, 9; P. 18; Sc. 110–114; head, body, and fins profusely covered with light speckles on reddish brown background; caudal fin truncate to emarginate. According to some, this is the most beautiful of our groupers, but unfortunately it is rare in the northwestern Gulf of Mexico. North Carolina and Bermuda to Florida and the northern Gulf to Texas. (18 inches; 46 cm—rarely up to 40 inches; 1 m)

209. Red grouper *Epinephelus morio* (Valenciennes)

D. XI, 16–17 (16); A. III, 9 (rarely 10); P. 16–18 (17); Sc. 110–129; second dorsal spine longest, with interspinous membranes of dorsal not deeply incised; reddish brown with scattered pale blotches; no saddle-shaped blotch on caudal peduncle; median fins blackish with white margins; caudal truncate to emarginate. This species occurs offshore on the snapper banks but is more common in the northeastern Gulf. It reaches a size of about fifty pounds (23 kg). Bermuda and North Carolina, strays farther north, through the Caribbean to southern Brazil. (3.5 ft; 1.1 m)

210. Rock hind; calico grouper *Epinephelus adscensionis* (Osbeck)

D. XI, 16–17; A. III, 8; P. 18–19 (19); Sc. 80–99; head, body, and fins spotted orange-brown; brown spots on upper part of caudal peduncle; series of five dark blotches along base of dorsal fin; margin of caudal fin convex; posterior nostril larger or about same size as anterior nostril. This species is common about jetties and offshore oil rigs and on the snapper banks. It reaches a size of five to eight pounds (2.3–3.6 kg). Bermuda and Massachusetts through the Caribbean to southeastern Brazil, Ascension and St. Helena islands, and western South Africa. (2 feet; 61 cm)

211. Red hind; strawberry grouper *Epinephelus guttatus* (Linnaeus)

D. XI, 15–16 (16); A. III, 8; P. 17; Sc. 90–104; body with greenish yellow or light red ground color covered with large red spots; no saddle-shaped blotch on caudal peduncle; outer third of soft dorsal, anal, and caudal fins darkened. The coloration of this species is similar to that seen in *E. adscensionis*, but *E. guttatus* lacks the large dark blotches or bars along the sides and on the caudal peduncle and has small dark flecks inside the red spots. This is a common species in the Caribbean as well as off Yucatán, but in the northwestern Gulf it appears to be restricted to the offshore reefs. Bermuda and North Carolina through the Caribbean to Venezuela. (2 1/2 feet; 76 cm)

212. Nassau grouper *Epinephelus striatus* (Bloch)

D. XI, 16–18; A. III, 8; P. 17–19 (18); Sc. 95–109; third dorsal spine longest, with interspinous membranes of dorsal deeply notched; posterior nostril about twice the size of anterior nostril; background light olive brown with dark stripe running from base of dorsal fin to mouth and through eye; sides of body with irregular dark bars and saddlelike blotch on caudal peduncle. This is a rare species in the northwestern Gulf, where it is known to reach fifty-five pounds (25 kg). It exhibits a remarkable ability to change colors, and consequently the numerous color descriptions may be confusing; however, the dark, oblique stripe through the eye is usually evident. Bermuda and North Carolina, rare and uncertain in the Gulf, through the Caribbean to southern Brazil. Gunter and Knapp, 1951. (4 feet; 1 1/4 m)

213. Comb grouper *Mycteroperca acutirostris* (Valenciennes)

D. XI, 15–17; A. III, 10–12; Sc. 75–94; Gr. 18–21 + 29–36 (with no obvious rudiments); caudal fin truncate in young, becoming emarginate in adults; sides of body brown with indistinct but characteristic horizontal stripes; head with 3–5 dark bars radiating from mouth and eyes, also characteristic. This is a rather attractive fish, which may be more common than reports have indicated. Small specimens have been taken from the jetties at Ports Aransas and Isabel, and it is common on 7 1/2 Fathom Reef. It also occurs on offshore reefs in Texas and Louisiana waters, but it is a little-known grouper. Western Atlantic populations have been considered conspecific with the eastern Atlantic *M. rubra* (Bloch) and in the genus *Parepinephelus*. Recorded from scattered localities. Bermuda and western Gulf (not eastern or southern) to Brazil, rare in the Caribbean; Mediterranean and West Africa. Smith, 1971. (3 feet; 90 cm)

214. Gag *Mycteroperca microlepis* (Goode and Bean)

D. XI, 16–19; A. III, 11; Sc. 110–114; Gr. 21–29; nostrils subequal; color variable, with fish from shallow water showing greater variation than those from deeper water; generally brownish gray with or without faint spots or "kiss-shaped" markings on sides and usually with black bar or "mustache" above mouth; fins generally dark, with edges of caudal, dorsal, and anal fins and first ray of ventral fins whitish. This is a small species (usually under five pounds), which seems to be fairly common on the offshore banks. It is often confused with the black grouper, *M. bonaci,* which may not occur in the northwestern Gulf. Bermuda and Massachusetts to south Florida, throughout the Gulf; also southern Brazil, but absent in between. Gilmore and Jones, 1992; Hood and Schlieder, 1992; Smith et al., 1975. (5 feet; 120 cm)

215. Yellowmouth grouper *Mycteroperca interstitialis* (Poey)

D. XI, 16–18; A. III, 11 (12); P. 17; Sc. 110–129; Gr. 23–27 total on first arch. Posterior nostril larger than anterior. Body reddish brown, occasionally broken into reddish brown spots separated by paler yellow reticulations. Juveniles bicolored, dark above, light below. Exserted midcaudal rays of uniform length, equal to outer rays. Smith (1971) noted that this species was primarily insular, in contrast with the continental distribution of *M. phenax*. However, both species occur together in the northern Gulf. Bermuda and North Carolina to Florida through the Caribbean to southern Brazil. Bullock and Smith, 1991; Dennis and Bright, 1988a; Smith, 1971; Smith et al., 1975. (3 feet; 90 cm)

216. Scamp *Mycteroperca phenax* Jordan and Swain
D. XI, 15–18; A. III, 10–12 (11); Sc. 105–119; Gr. 3–7 + 14–18 (excluding rudiments); background light tan, with numerous small brown spots on body and fins occurring on ventral as well as dorsal sides. The scamp is a common species, occurring year-round on the snapper banks. Sometimes referred to as *M. falcata phenax* in the older literature, it is closely related to the yellowmouth grouper, which is uncommonly reported here but is definitely more common in the Caribbean. Massachusetts to Venezuela. Bright and Cashman, 1974; Gilmore and Jones, 1992; Smith, 1971; Smith et al., 1975. (3 feet; 90 cm)

217. Tiger grouper *Mycteroperca tigris* (Valenciennes)
D. XI, 16–17; A. III, 11; P. 17; Sc. 115–134; Gr. 6–7 + 4–8; first three dorsal spines low; canine teeth especially long. Color generally dark greenish brown to black with about 11 narrow pale lines, which slope downward and forward; inside of mouth yellow-orange in life. A common grouper in the Bahamas and the West Indies, this species was not discovered in the northwestern Gulf of Mexico until 1970 (Taylor and Bright, 1973), although subsequently it has been reported as the most common large grouper on the Flower Gardens reefs (Dennis and Bright, 1988a). Bermuda, the Bahamas, Florida, and the northwestern Gulf through the Caribbean to Venezuela. (2.5 feet; 75 cm)

218. Yellowfin grouper *Mycteroperca venenosa* (Linnaeus)
D. XI, 15–16; A. III, 11; Sc. 105–124; Gr. 4–5 + 10–13 (excluding rudiments); caudal fin slightly emarginate; background gray or olivaceous with dark brown blotches arranged in lengthwise rows and with numerous small, dark reddish orange spots; outer edges of pectorals sharply defined with broad orange zone. This is a medium-sized offshore grouper. Bermuda, Bahamas, southern Florida, and northern Gulf through the Caribbean to south Brazil; rare in the Gulf. (3 feet; 90 cm)

219. Black grouper *Mycteroperca bonaci* (Poey)
D. XI, 16–17; A. III, 11–13; Sc. 115–124; Gr. 2–5 + 8–11 (excluding rudiments); caudal fin usually truncate. This species closely resembles *M. venenosa* but has additional fin rays in the dorsal and anal fins. The soft dorsal, anal, and caudal fins have a broad, dark outer zone set off by a white margin. The general body coloration is dark. The pectorals are brownish orange at the tips but not as abruptly so as in *M. venenosa*. Black groupers commonly possess "kiss" marks similar to those of *M. microlepis*, with which they have

also been confused; however, the black grouper lacks the white first ventral fin rays found in the gag. The species has been reported as common near the Texas jetties and offshore reefs and from Louisiana; however, the specimens we have examined from these localities are *M. microlepis*, and we have not been able to verify the presence of *M. bonaci* in the northwestern Gulf. Bermuda and Massachusetts through the Caribbean to Brazil, apparently absent from the northwestern Gulf. Pew, 1954; C. L. Smith, 1971; G. B. Smith, 1976. (5 feet; 1 1/3 m)

220. Whitespotted soapfish *Rypticus maculatus* Holbrook

D. II, 24–26; A. 25–26; preopercle with 1–3 (usually 2) spines; body pale tan, sometimes gray or black with a few scattered, distinct, pearly spots on sides; sides often mottled in addition. Most earlier reports of *R. saponaceus* from the western Gulf appear to refer to this species. This species is not uncommon at times in the inshore Gulf, occurring over hard bottoms and reefs and near oil platforms and jetties. North Carolina to Florida and the northern Gulf. Moore, 1975b. (12 inches; 30 cm)

221. Spotted soapfish *Rypticus subbifrenatus* (Gill)

D. III, 21–23; A. 15; P. 15; preopercle with 3 spines; body pale with widely spread round, dark spots, ocellated in young and in preserved specimens. Known from the West Flower Gardens Reef. Florida, the Bahamas, and northern Gulf through the Caribbean to the northern coast of South America. Bright and Cashman, 1974; Courtenay, 1967; Retzer, 1990. (5 inches; 13 cm)

222. Greater soapfish *Rypticus saponaceus* (Schneider)

D. III, 23–24; A. 15–17 (16); P. 16. Despite several reports of this species in the literature, its occurrence in the northwestern Gulf of Mexico is problematic. Courtenay (1967) and Moore (1975b) referred all previous western Gulf records to *R. maculatus* and Bullock and Smith (1991) have done likewise for earlier Florida records. However, Dennis and Bright (1988b) have recently reported the greater soapfish from offshore banks and reefs. Bermuda and Florida through the Caribbean to Brazil. Retzer, 1990. (13 inches; 33 cm)

Priacanthidae

The bigeyes are best noted for their distinctively large eyes. As a group, the family is found over hard bottoms in relatively deep water. Three species occur in the northwestern Gulf on the middle to outer shelf. In addition to the two species discussed below, the glasseye snapper, *Priacanthus* (or *Heteropriacanthus*) *cruentatus* (Lacepède) (plate 224a), has been taken from the Flower Gardens reefs and should be looked for more frequently. (D. K. Caldwell, 1962a; Starnes, 1988)

1   Preopercular spine strong; body with blotchy or banded, red, silver, or bronze sides . . . glasseye snapper, *Priacanthus cruentatus.*
     Preopercular spine weak or absent; body uniformly reddish, rarely blotched 2
2   Scales small, more than 60 in lateral line; body oblong, with depth not one-half standard length; dorsal and anal with 12–15 rays . . . bigeye, *Priacanthus arenatus.*
     Scales large and rough, fewer than 40 in lateral line; depth of body more than one-half standard length; dorsal and anal each with 9–11 rays . . . short bigeye, *Pristigenys alta.*

223. Bigeye *Priacanthus arenatus* Cuvier

D. X, 13–15; A. III, 14–16; Sc. 61–73; Gr. 6–8 + 21–26; depth of body 33–40 percent of standard length; bright red or red stripes or mottling on lighter red background; median fins with dark edges. This fish is not uncommon on the deeper parts of snapper banks and over the twenty- to twenty-six-fathom shrimp grounds. Atlantic Ocean, in the west from Bermuda and Massachusetts through the Caribbean to Argentina. Gunter and Knapp, 1951. (12 inches; 30 cm)

224. Short bigeye *Pristigenys alta* (Gill)

D. X, 10–12; A. III, 9–11; Sc. usually 37; Gr. 6–9 + 17–21; depth of body one-half or more ot standard length; red, median fins edged with black. The short bigeye was formerly placed in the genus *Pseudopriacanthus*, where it is known as *P. altus*. It is generally found in deeper water out to about sixty fathoms. Gulf of Maine and Bermuda to Florida, with scattered localities throughout the Gulf of Mexico and the West Indies. D. K. Caldwell, 1962b; Fritzsche and Johnson, 1981. (10 inches; 25 cm).

Opistognathidae

Jawfishes are moderately small, gobylike fishes with oversized jaws. They live in burrows in relatively smooth bottoms adjacent to reefs. At least four species occur near offshore reefs.

1   Maxillary much shorter than head; caudal elongate and pointed . . . swordtail jawfish *Lonchopisthus micrognathus.*
     Maxillary almost as long as head; caudal rounded . . . *Opistognathus* spp.

225. Swordtail jawfish *Lonchopisthus micrognathus* (Poey)

D. XI, 19; A. III, 16; Sc. 60; caudal fin lanceolate, more than half as long as body. This fish has rarely been taken from shelly areas near offshore reefs off Texas and Louisiana and across the northern Gulf to off southern Florida. It was formerly known as *L. lindneri* Ginsburg. Ginsburg, 1954; Colin and Arenson, 1978. (7 inches; 18 cm)

226. Spotfin jawfish *Opistognathus* sp.

At least three species of this genus are known from offshore reefs: the yellowhead jawfish, *O. aurifrons* (Jordan and Thompson), which is distinguished by its yellow head and anterior dorsal fin; the moustache jawfish, *O. lonchurus* (Jordan and Gilbert), with a dusky snout and "mustache" above the upper jaw; and an undescribed species, the spotfin jawfish (plate 226), with a dark ocellated spot on the spinous dorsal. These burrow in patches of shelly sediment, which are more common east of the Mississippi Delta. These species are found elsewhere throughout the tropical western Atlantic. Range of the spotfin: South Carolina, Bahamas, and Florida to Texas. Dennis and Bright, 1988. (6 inches; 15 cm)

Apogonidae

Cardinalfishes are small reef fishes. They are usually red with large black spots or bars on the body, but the genus *Phaeoptyx* is silvery or bronze with many small dark spots. Many cardinalfishes live in close association with reef invertebrates and most are nocturnal. More species will probably be found on offshore reefs as divers continue their explorations. (Böhlke and Randall, 1968; Colin and Heiser, 1973: Fraser and Robins, 1970; Livingston, 1971)

1	Angle of free preopercular margin with fleshy tab extending posteriorly 2
	Angle of free preopercular margin smoothly rounded; without fleshy tab 3
2	Gill rakers on lower limb of first arch 14–16, teeth in jaws small, comblike . . . freckled cardinalfish, *Phaeoptyx conklini*.
	Gill rakers on lower limb of first arch 11–12, rarely 13; anterior teeth in upper jaw small and lateral teeth in lower jaw enlarged . . . dusky cardinalfish, *Phaeoptyx pigmentaria*.
3	Sides of body without definite dark pigmentation; gill rakers on lower limb of first arch 10–11 . . . bridle cardinalfish, *Apogon aurolineatus*.
	Sides of body with definite dark spots or vertical bars beneath second dorsal fin; gill rakers on lower limb of first arch 12–18 4
4	Sides of body with dark spot beneath second dorsal fin 5
	Sides of body with dark bar beneath second dorsal fin . . . belted cardinalfish, *Apogon townsendi*.
5	Caudal peduncle with broad, blackish saddle extending below lateral line on each side . . . flamefish, *Apogon maculatus*.
	Caudal peduncle with small, sharply defined black spot on each side, not extending below lateral line . . . twospot cardinalfish, *Apogon pseudomaculatus*.

227. Freckled cardinalfish *Phaeoptyx conklini* (Silvester)

D. VI + I, 9; A. II, 8; P. II–13; Gr. on lower limb 14–16; body silvery with dark stripes on soft dorsal and anal fins and numerous dark spots on scales, producing freckled appearance.

Bermuda, Bahamas, and Florida to Curaçao and northern South America. Bright and Cashman, 1974; Causey, 1969. (2 inches; 5 cm)

228. Dusky cardinalfish *Phaeoptyx pigmentaria* (Poey)
D.VI + I, 9; A. II, 8; P. I I–I 3; Gr. on lower limb I I–I 3; body pale with dark spots on head and on each scale, large dark blotch at base of caudal fin. In the northwestern Gulf, this species is known only from the West Flower Gardens Reef. Bahamas to Curaçao and northern South America. Bright and Cashman, 1974. (I 1/2 inches; 4 cm)

229. Bridle cardinalfish *Apogon aurolineatus* (Mowbry)
D.VI + I, 9; A. II, 8; Gr. on lower limb 10–11, body not conspicuously marked; two dusky streaks on head radiating from eye. A few specimens of this fish are known from deep water off Texas. Bahamas and Florida through the Caribbean to Curaçao and Venezuela. Hoese, 1958a. (2 inches; 5 cm)

230. Belted cardinalfish *Apogon townsendi* (Breder)
D.VI + I, 9; A. II, 8; Gr. on lower limb 16–18; body red with wide black band across caudal peduncle and second, narrower black bar beneath posteriormost rays of soft dorsal. In the northwestern Gulf, this species is known only from the West Flower Gardens Reef. Bahamas and Florida through the Caribbean to Curaçao. Bright and Cashman, 1974. (2 inches; 5 cm)

231. Flamefish *Apogon maculatus* (Poey)
D.VI + I, 9; A. II, 8; Gr. on lower limb 13–14; body red with dark spot beneath base of soft dorsal and dusky saddle across caudal. This is the commonest cardinalfish off both Texas and Louisiana, occurring on reefs and around oil platforms. New England and Bermuda through the Caribbean to Brazil. Briggs et al., 1964; Bright and Cashman, 1974; Sonnier et al., 1976. (3 inches; 8 cm)

232. Twospot cardinalfish *Apogon pseudomaculatus* Longley
D.VI + I, 9; A. II, 8; Gr. on lower limb 12–14; body red with dark spot beneath base of soft dorsal fin and sharply defined spot on caudal peduncle, not extending below lateral line. New England and Bermuda through the Caribbean to southern Brazil. Sonnier et al., 1976. (3 inches; 8 cm)

Malacanthidae

Members of the tilefish family are rather elongate fishes with long dorsal and anal fins. Most species are usually found over hard, sandy bottoms, where they construct and live in burrows; the tilefish itself, *Lopholatilus chamaeleonticeps,* usually occurs in very deep water at the edge of the shelf and on the continental slope. Aside from the sand tilefish, other tilefishes were formerly placed in a separate family, the Branchiostegidae. (Dooley, 1974, 1978, 1981, personal communication; Able et al., 1987)

1   Preopercle entire ... sand tilefish, *Malacanthus plumieri*.
     Preopercle serrate 2
2   Nape with fleshy process ... tilefish, *Lopholatilus chamaeleonticeps*.
     Nape without fleshy process 3
3   Interoperculum with scales 4
     Interoperculum without scales 5
4   Dorsal fin VIII, 23–25; a broad yellow patch extending from below eye to nostril in fresh fish
     ... goldface tilefish, *Caulolatilus chrysops*.
     Dorsal fin VII, 23–24; no broad yellow-gold patch under eye to nostril ... blackline tilefish,
     Caulolatilus cyanops.
5   Eye small, about 20 percent of head length; gill rakers 21–26 ... blueline tilefish, *Caulolatilus microps*.
     Eye larger, about 25–28 percent of head length; gill rakers 18–22 ... anchor tilefish, *Caulolatilus intermedius*.

233. Sand tilefish *Malacanthus plumieri* (Bloch)

D. IV–V, 53–57; A. I, 48–55; P. 16–17; Sc. 135–152 (143); Gr. 8–13 on first arch. Body light metallic blue, lighter ventrally; yellow and blue stripes on head; yellow spots on dorsal and anal fins. This tropical species is usually found on sandy bottoms surrounding coral reefs and is absent off deltas. Bermuda, Bahamas, and North Carolina through the Caribbean to south Brazil and Ascension Island. Baughman, 1947, 1950b; Bright and Cashman, 1974. (2 feet; 61 cm)

234. Tilefish (great northern tilefish) *Lopholatilus chamaeleonticeps* Goode and Bean

D. VII, 14–15; A. II, 13–15; Sc. about 93; fleshy appendage on nape before dorsal fin. This deepwater species is known from the edge of the continental shelf off both Texas and Louisiana, where a small commercial and sport fishery exists. Labrador to Suriname. Able et al., 1987; Katz et al., 1983; Nelson and Carpenter, 1968. (3 1/2 feet; 1m)

235. Goldface tilefish (Atlantic golden-eyed tilefish) *Caulolatilus chrysops* (Valenciennes)

D. VIII, 23–25; A. II, 22–24; P. 18–19; Sc. 79–89 (85); Gr. 17–21 (19) on first arch. Body generally bluish purple above, white below, with a small spot above pectoral axil; a bright golden-yellow bar extending from beneath eye to upper nostril; iris golden yellow. This species had not been reported from the northwestern Gulf of Mexico prior to 1978 and since then only four specimens have been taken, in 73–106 fathoms (132–192 m) from off Louisiana (Burgess and Branstetter, 1985). Elsewhere the species occurs generally in 50–72 fathoms (90–131 m). North Carolina through the Caribbean to southern Brazil. Burgess and Branstetter, 1985; Dooley, 1978. (21 inches; 54 cm)

236. Blackline tilefish *Caulolatilus cyanops* Poey
D. VII, 23–24 (24); A. I–II (first spine often small and inconspicuous), 20–23 (22); P. 16–18; Sc. 75–82 (79); Gr. 17–21 (19). Body bluish purple dorsally with an electric-blue chainlike pattern on upper sides and a dark stripe running along either side of dorsal fin base; becoming lighter on venter; large dark spot in axil of pectoral fin; head marked with a greenish blue bar from below eye to upper lip; iris silver and gold. This species was first reported from the northwestern Gulf by Dennis and Bright (1988a) based on specimens taken at the Flower Gardens reefs in 50–64 fathoms (91–117 m). Elsewhere the species occurs in 25–272 fathoms (45–495 m). North Carolina and Bermuda through the Caribbean to Venezuela. Chittenden and Moore, 1977; Dooley, 1978. (14 inches; 34 cm)

237. Blueline tilefish (gray tilefish) *Caulolatilus microps* Goode and Bean
D. VII, 25; A. II, 22–24 (23); Sc. 80–91; Gr. 21–26; plain-sided, without definite blotch in axil of pectoral fin; some yellow pigment on caudal and dorsal fins and under eye; iris gold with green spot below pupil; eye quite small, about one-fifth of head length; tail truncate, with extended uppermost and lowermost rays. This species has commonly been confused in the past with *C. cyanops,* and early reports of the latter have generally turned out to be erroneous; however, the blackline tilefish has recently been confirmed also to occur in our area (see preceding account). Virginia to Yucatán. (1 foot; 30 cm)

238. Anchor tilefish (Gulf bar-eyed tilefish) *Caulolatilus intermedius* Howell-Rivero
D. VII, 24–25; A. I–II, 22–23; Sc. 73–81; Gr. 18–22; upper body uniformly brownish gray without yellow on fins or head; small dark blotch in axil of pectoral fin and dark bar beneath eye; eye about 25–28 percent of head length. The tail in small specimens, including the type specimen, which may be damaged, is rounded; however, larger specimens may have caudal fins with produced upper, middle, and lower rays, resulting in a trilobed tail. Although this species has not been generally recognized in the northwestern Gulf, it is the most common tilefish and appears to be restricted entirely to the Gulf of Mexico, including western Cuba. Guillory et al., 1985. (1 foot; 30 cm)

Pomatomidae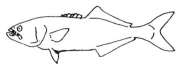

The bluefish is the only member of this family. Bluefish are more common in the Atlantic and eastern Gulf than in the northwestern Gulf. Inshore off Texas, adults occur only sporadically and young are more likely to be encountered. (Barger, 1990)

239. Bluefish *Pomatomus saltatrix* (Linnaeus)

D. VII–VIII + I, 23–26; A. II + I, 25–27; Sc. about 95; no keels on lateral line; color bluish or greenish on back, lighter below. Bluefish, which are not especially common on the Texas coast but are more so off Louisiana, resemble jacks, basses, or croakers, and many anglers mistakenly associate the bluefish with these other families. Bluefish are common along the Atlantic Coast of the United States, where they reach considerable size. Known for their voraciousness, bluefish are exciting game fish, and in addition they are well worth eating. They have been known to bite chunks out of other fish and people. In the northwestern Gulf the bluefish reflects its generally northern distribution by appearing inshore only in the cooler months. Worldwide, in the western Atlantic from Nova Scotia to Argentina, but rare or absent in the tropics. (3 1/2 feet; I m)

Rachycentridae

The cobia, also known as the ling, cabio, lemonfish, crabeater, or sergeantfish, is the only member of this family. Cobia and sharksuckers (family Echeneidae) resemble one another, especially as juveniles, and this resemblance indicates a close relationship between these two types of fish. Aside from this similarity, the cobia shows little relationship to any other living fish.

240. Cobia; ling *Rachycentron canadum* (Linnaeus)

D. VIII–IX + I, 27–33; A. II, 23–21; adults brownish, stocky-bodied, almost square in cross section; lighter on the belly, sometimes with trace of broad lateral stripe found in juveniles; juveniles darker, often almost black, with dark lateral stripe set off by light bands above and below; caudal fin of juveniles rounded to lanceolate and margined with white almost exactly like that of the sharksucker, *Echeneis naucrates;* dorsal spines low, separate, and in adults almost embedded. Small ling are found in the saltier bays during the summer. Larger fish, which may weigh fifty to one hundred pounds (23–45 kg) congregate about drifting or stationary objects in the Gulf of Mexico, where they are a favorite game and food fish for most saltwater anglers. Worldwide; in the western Atlantic from Massachusetts through the Caribbean to Argentina. Dawson, 1971c; Ditty and Shaw, 1992; Shaffer and Nakamura, 1989. (6 feet; 2 m)

Echeneidae

The sharksuckers are distinguished by the presence of a laminated adhesive disc on top of the head. The disc is actually a highly modified spinous dorsal fin. These fish attach themselves, by means of this disc, to various species of sharks, rays, bony fishes, turtles, cetaceans, and even ships and other floating inanimate objects.

There are only eight described species of echeneids in the world, five or six of which occur in our waters. Most are rather specific about the animal to which they will attach themselves; however, the less particular species are the most commonly encountered. *Echeneis naucrates* and *Remora remora* have a variety of hosts including sharks, snappers, and dolphins. *Remora brachyptera* and *R. osteochir* are found almost always on billfish (sailfish, marlin, spearfish, or swordfish); *Remora australis* only occurs on whales. The white suckerfish, *Remorina albescens,* and the slender suckerfish, *Phtheirichthys lineatus* (Menzies), although not reported from the northwestern Gulf, should be expected here. The family is believed to be related to the Rachycentridae (cobia or ling). (Schultz et al., 1966)

1 Disc lamellae 9–11 . . . slender suckerfish, *Phtheirichthys lineatus.*
   Disc lamellae 13 or more 2
2 Caudal fin of young lanceolate, with middle rays produced; lower jaw with a fleshy flap; body
   elongate, usually with dark stripe down side; pelvic fins narrowly attached to ventral surface
   . . . sharksucker, *Echeneis naucrates.*
   Caudal fin forked in young, becoming more or less emarginate in adults; lower jaw without
   flap; no lateral stripe; pelvic fins usually broadly attached to ventral surface (except in *Remorina*
   albescens) 3
3 Gill rakers numerous, more than 27 . . . remora, *Remora remora.*
   Gill rakers fewer than 21 4
4 Disc lamellae numerous, more than 24 . . . whalesucker, *Remora australis.*
   Disc lamellae fewer than 20 5
5 Pelvic fins narrowly attached to ventral surface; disc lamellae 13–14 . . . white suckerfish,
   Remorina albescens.
   Pelvic fins broadly attached to ventral surface; disc lamellae 15–19 6
6 Dorsal fin rays 27–34; disc 28–40 percent of standard length; pectoral fins flexible . . .
   spearfish remora, *Remora brachyptera.*
   Dorsal rays 20–26; disc 27–49 percent of standard length, extending well beyond ends of
   depressed pectoral fins; pectoral fins stiff to their tips . . . marlinsucker, *Remora osteochir.*

241. Slender suckerfish *Phtheirichthys lineatus* (Menzies)
D. 33; A. 33; disc lamellae 9–11 (usually 10); disc less than 22 percent of body length. This fish is an elongate species resembling the sharksucker and is found on sharks, billfishes, and barracuda. It is not reported from the northwestern Gulf, but it occurs in all tropical seas. (28 inches; 71 cm)

242. Sharksucker *Echeneis naucrates* Linnaeus
D. 33–34; A. 31–41; disc lamellae 21–27 (usually 23–24); length of disc 26–29 percent of body length; brown or dark gray above, lighter below with distinct light stripe down middle of side running from snout to eye, generally diminishing in intensity; young with

lanceolate tail with white or yellow tips on dorsal, anal, and caudal fins. The sharksucker—which generally attaches to larger fish, sometimes hitching rides on boats (while scuba divers watch)—seems to be the least particular about its hosts. The very similar whitefin sucker, *E. neucratoides* Zuieuw, may occur in our area. It looks like *E. naucrates* but is generally stouter, has fewer disc lamellae (modally 21), and has dorsal and anal fin rays modally 36 (32–41) and 33 (30–38) respectively. Sharksuckers are known from all temperate and tropical waters. (32 inches; 81 cm)

243. Remora *Remora remora* (Linnaeus)
D. 21–27; A. 20–24; disc lamellae 16–20; ventral fins connected to body for more than one-half their length; uniformly black or gray. The remora attaches to large sharks, turtles, or boats and is found worldwide in temperate and tropical waters. (3 feet; 91 cm)

244. Whalesucker *Remora australis* (Bennett)
D. 22; A. 21–23; disc lamellae 24–27; brown. The whalesucker is found on dolphins and whales. It is sometimes placed in the genus *Remilegia,* and it is believed to inhabit all tropical seas. (30 inches; 76 cm)

245. White suckerfish *Remorina albescens* (Temminck and Schlegel)
D. 22; A. 22; disc lamellae 13–14. This small remora is found in the gill cavities of manta rays and sharks. It is not reported from the northwestern Gulf but is to be expected here. Circumtropical. Lachner, 1966. (1 foot; 30 cm)

246. Spearfish remora *Remora brachyptera* (Lowe)
D. 27–34; A. 25–30; disc lamellae 15–19. The spearfish has been reported only once from our area, so it is not surprising that this sucker favoring it as a host is equally rare. Worldwide; tropical. (1 foot; 30 cm)

247. Marlinsucker *Remora osteochir* (Cuvier)
D. 21–23; A. 20–21; disc lamellae 28; body light brown; underside of head, parts of ventral fins, and ventral line light; pale spots on pectoral fins. This sucker usually attaches to species of billfish. It is often placed in the genus *Rhombochirus.* Atlantic Ocean, in the west from Massachusetts to Cuba. (1 foot; 30 cm)

Carangidae

Jacks are large, fast-swimming fishes often found schooling. All are predaceous, and several are prized game and food fishes. Identification of some species requires more precision than is needed in other groups, but most of the common species can readily be learned. The name "crevalle" is sometimes applied to the entire family, sometimes to any member of the genus *Caranx,* and sometimes only to the common jack.

Pompano *(Trachinotus carolinus)* are the most sought after member of the family, with several thousand pounds harvested annually, mostly from Louisiana. Many juvenile carangids associate with floating objects, flotsam, jellyfish, and the like in the open waters and make interesting aquarium fishes.

The most distinctive features of the family are the rather narrow caudal peduncle and the two free spines found before the anal fin. In young fish these two spines may be connected by a membrane. However, in very large fish these spines, and frequently the anteriormost spines of the dorsal, become overgrown with skin, making their detection difficult. In the African pompano all spines in the first dorsal and anal fins may be so obscured.

The pilot fish, *Naucrates ductor* (Linnaeus), has not been reported from the northern Gulf. It is a pelagic fish known from all warm seas and so should be expected here. The common name is derived from its habit of accompanying sharks and other large carnivorous fish. It is similar to *Seriola* except that it has fewer dorsal spines (IV), which are not connected by membranes except in very young fish. (Berry, 1959; Fields, 1962; Ginsburg, 1952a; Shaw and Drullinger, 1990)

1   Maxillary not protractile; soft dorsal and anal fins followed by more than one finlet . . . leatherjack, *Oligoplites saurus.*
    Maxillary protractile; dorsal and anal fins with no more than one finlet apiece 2
2   Lateral line without well-developed scutes (large modified scales) 3
    Lateral line with well-developed scutes 13
3   Dorsal contour elevated, with forehead oblique or almost vertical; lower-limb gill rakers fewer than 30 4
    Dorsal contour rounded, tapering forward to snout; lower-limb gill rakers 31 or more . . . Atlantic bumper, *Chloroscombrus chrysurus.*
4   One finlet behind dorsal and anal fins . . . rainbow runner, *Elagatis bipinnulata.*
    No finlets behind dorsal anal fins 5
5   Anterior profile straight, oblique, or nearly vertical; lower-limb gill rakers more than 22 6
    Anterior profile rounded, not straight; lower-limb gill rakers fewer than 21 7
6   Anterior profile nearly vertical; lobes of dorsal and anal fins not greatly elongate . . . Atlantic moonfish, *Selene setapinnis.*
    Anterior profile oblique; lobes of dorsal and anal fins elongated . . . lookdown, *Selene vomer.*
7   Snout blunt; second dorsal with one to four more rays than anal 8
    Snout tapering; second dorsal with seven or more rays than anal 10
8   Dorsal rays 18–21; anal rays 16–18 9
    Dorsal rays 23–27; anal rays 20–23 . . . Florida pompano, *Trachinotus carolinus.*
9   Body deep, 53–72 percent of standard length; dorsal and anal lobes reaching base of caudal fin; sides of body without vertical lines . . . permit, *Trachinotus falcatus.*

Body more slender, 37–54 percent of standard length; dorsal and anal lobes reaching beyond base of caudal fin in adults; sides of body usually with vertical stripes . . . palometa, *Trachinotus goodei*.

10　Gill rakers 25–28; lateral line scales 121–137; dorsal rays 28–32 11

　　Gill rakers 21–25 (number reduced with growth to 13–20); lateral line scales 141–187; dorsal rays 30–40 12

11　Dorsal spines seven; dark band from eye reaches base of first dorsal; body with five or six . . . almaco jack, *Seriola rivoliana*.

　　Dorsal spines eight; band from eye not reaching dorsal fin; body with seven bands . . . lesser amberjack, *Seriola fasciata*.

12　Lateral line scales 141–163; dorsal rays 30–35; body depth 32–35 percent of standard length . . . greater amberjack, *Seriola dumerili*.

　　Lateral line scales 160–187; dorsal rays 33–40; body depth 25–30 percent of standard length . . . banded rudderfish, *Seriola zonata*.

13　First dorsal reduced, with at least last four spines very small; body thin laterally, almost a knife edge . . . African pompano, *Alectis crinitus*.

　　First dorsal not reduced; body relatively thick 14

14　Pectoral never reaching beyond vertical through origin of soft anal; interorbital and interopercle scaled 15

　　Pectoral reaches beyond origin of soft anal; interorbital and interopercle scaleless 17

15　Anterior lateral line scales scutelike; shoulder girdle (under operculum) without papillae . . . rough scad, *Trachurus lathami*.

　　Anterior lateral line scales not scutelike; shoulder girdle with two papillae (fig. 6) 16

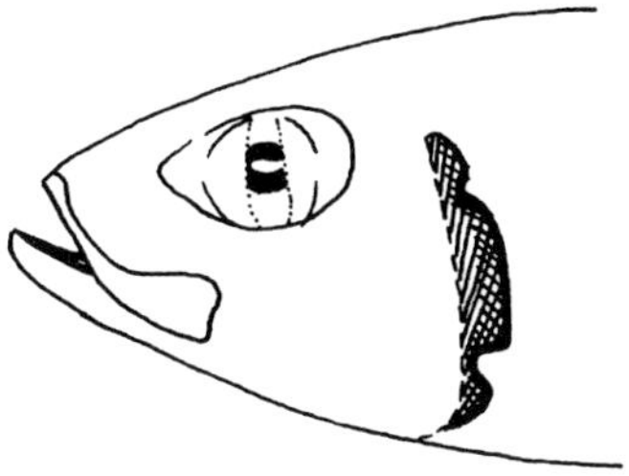

Fig. 6. Shoulder girdle of *Decapterus* and *Selar*, showing projecting lobes

16　Finlet behind dorsal and anal fins; body depth 19–23 percent of standard length . . . round scad, *Decapterus punctatus*.

　　No finlets behind dorsal or anal fins; body deeper, 25–30 percent of standard length . . . bigeye scad, *Selar crumenophthalmus*.

17　Vomer without teeth; teeth in jaw not enlarged; no keels on caudal peduncle 18

　　Vomer with teeth; teeth in outer jaw enlarged; two keels on caudal peduncle 19

18　Spines of scutes directed rearward; chest scaled . . . bluntnose jack, *Hemicaranx amblyrhynchus*.

　　Spines of scutes directed forward; chest scaleless . . . cottonmouth jack, *Uraspis secunda*.

19　Anal rays 22 or more 20

　　Anal rays 21 or fewer 21

20   Lateral line scutes 27–35; black band from below soft dorsal to lower lobe of caudal . . . bar jack, *Caranx ruber.*

Lateral line scutes 20–31; no blackish band on body . . . yellow jack, *Caranx bartholomaei.*

21   Scutes 45– 54; anal rays 19–21 . . . blue runner, *Caranx crysos.*

Scutes 42 or fewer; anal rays 15–19 22

22   Body silvery, usually with black spot on opercle; anal rays 15–17 23

Body brown to black; anal rays 17–19 . . . black jack, *Caranx lugubris.*

23   Chest mostly scaleless . . . crevalle (common jack), *Caranx hippos.*

Chest completely scaled . . . horse-eye jack, *Caranx latus.*

248. Leatherjack; leatherjacket *Oligoplites saurus* (Schneider)

D. V + I, 19–21; A. II + I, 18–21; P. 15–17; Gr. 6–9 + 13–15; sides silvery, yellow-greenish in young; vertical fins of young yellow; most rays of dorsal and anal fins fan-shaped, forming finlets joined together at bases. The spines of this fish contain a small amount of poison, so it should be handled with care. Dropping the -*et* off the name was to avoid confusion with triggerfishes, called leatherjackets in other areas of the world. Gulf of Maine through the Caribbean to Uruguay. (10 inches; 25 cm)

249. Rainbow runner *Elagatis bipinnulata* (Quoy and Gaimard)

D. VI + I, 25–26; A. II + I, 16–17; P. 20–23; Gr. 10–11 + 25–26; sides with blue, green, and reddish tones (hence the common name); light underneath; fins yellowish. This is a beautiful but uncommon species known in our area only from a few specimens. It is a good game fish and an excellent food fish as well. New England through the Caribbean to northeastern Brazil. Gunter and Knapp, 1951. (12 inches; 30 cm)

250. Florida pompano *Trachinotus carolinus* (Linnaeus)

D. V–VI + I, 23–27; A. II + I, 20–23; P. 17–19; Gr. 5–9 + 7–11; sides silvery. Small pompano abound in the surf in the summertime. The pompano is the most popular jack, sought by both sport and commercial fishermen. Massachusetts to southern Brazil. Bellinger and Avault, 1970, 1971; Fields, 1962. (17 inches; 43 cm)

251. Permit *Trachinotus falcatus* (Linnaeus)

D. VI + I, 18–20; A. II + I, 17–18; P. 16–19; Gr. 5–9 + 9–13. Although the permit's sides are usually silvery, this species exhibits considerable color changes, sometimes becoming almost black. Its body depth is greater than that of the pompano. The young—which occur in the surf, as in all pompano species—frequently have reddish fins. Permit are uncommon, and relatively little is known about their life history. New England through the Caribbean to southern Brazil. (31 inches; 79 cm)

252. Palometa; longfinned pompano *Trachinotus goodei* Jordan and Evermann

D. VI + I, 19–20; A. II + I, 16–18; P. 16–19; Gr. 5–9 + 8–12; sides silvery; adults with about five thin vertical bars on sides and very long dorsal and anal fins. An uncommon species, usually regarded as a stray from more tropical waters, this fish in older literature goes by the names *T. glaucus* or *T. palometa*. Massachusetts through the Caribbean to Argentina. Gunter and Knapp, 1951; Moore, 1975b. (12 inches; 30 cm)

253. Almaco jack *Seriola rivoliana* Valenciennes
D. VII + 1, 28–32; A. II + 1, 19–22; P. 19–22; Sc. 122–137; Gr. 7–8 + 16–18; depth of body (at point just behind end of head) 34.5–40 percent of standard length. This species is a wide-ranging but little-reported amberjack. Because of their high dorsal and anal lobes, western Atlantic populations are sometimes reported as *S. falcata*. Circumtropical, in the western Atlantic from Massachusetts through the Caribbean to Argentina. (3 feet; 91 cm)

254. Lesser amberjack *Seriola fasciata* (Bloch)
D. VIII + 1, 30–32; A. II + 1, 19–20; P. 19–20; Sc. 129–134; Gr. 7–8 + 18–20; depth of body 37–42 percent of standard length. This is another widespread but little-known jack. Small specimens occur on the shelf. It does not grow as large as other *Seriola* species. Massachusetts through the Caribbean to southern Brazil. (12 inches; 30 cm)

255. Greater amberjack *Seriola dumerili* (Risso)
D. VIII + 1, 30–35; A. II + 1, 19–22; P. 19–22; Sc. 141–163; Gr. 2–3 + 11–17; depth of body 29–31 of standard length. The largest and most common amberjack in our area, this fish is rather easily confused with the eastern Atlantic species, *S. lalandi*, reports of which in this area probably refer to *S. dumerili*. In very large fish, both the dorsal spines and the gill rakers are reduced in number. This phenomenon also occurs in the almaco jack *(S. rivoliana)*; however, the greater amberjack always has lower counts as well as a thinner body. It occurs widely throughout the tropical and temperate Atlantic Ocean; Bermuda and Nova Scotia through the Caribbean to southern Brazil. (3 feet; 91 cm)

256. Banded rudderfish *Seriola zonata* (Mitchill)
D. VII–VIII + 1, 33–40; A. II + 1, 19–21; P. 18–21; Sc. 160–180; Gr. 2–3 + 11–13; body depth 25–30 of standard length. This small jack usually retains its bands, characteristic of the younger fish, longer than do the other species of *Seriola*. Young fish are sometimes found inshore, around pilings and wharves, but more commonly this fish is seen offshore, where it associates with floating objects. Nova Scotia through the Caribbean to southern Brazil. (2 feet; 61 cm)

257. African pompano *Alectis crinitus* (Mitchill)
D. VII + 1, 18–19; A. II + 1, 15–16; P. 18–20; Gr. 5–6 + 14–16. The young of this species are characterized by extremely long, filamentous dorsal and anal fins and by well-developed scutes along the posterior lateral line. In adults the spinous portions of both the dorsal

and anal fins become overgrown and obscured, and the filamentous fins are usually lost through abrasion, although it is generally apparent that these fin rays are (were) considerably longer than normal. As with all jacks, African pompano young are banded, and traces of bands remain on the sides of the silvery adults. This is a tropical species with only scattered reports of young or adults inshore off southern Texas, but adults are fairly common offshore of Louisiana. Both coasts of the Atlantic and in the eastern Pacific as well. Circumtropical, in the western Atlantic from Massachusetts through the Caribbean to southern Brazil. (45 inches; 1.1 m)

258. Atlantic moonfish *Selene setapinnis* (Mitchill)
D. VIII + 1, 20–23; A. II + 1, 17–19; P. 17–19; Gr. 5–8 + 25–29. The young of this species are similar to *Alectis* except that they lack the filamentous fins and have a black spot on the sides. The silvery adults are more elongate and also lack the produced fin rays. This is a common small fish inshore, occurring in large schools in the bays during the summer. Formerly placed in the genus *Vomer*. Eastern Pacific and both sides of the Atlantic, in the west from Nova Scotia to Argentina. (15 inches; 38 cm)

259. Lookdown *Selene vomer* (Linnaeus)
D. VIII + 1, 21–23; A. II + 1, 18–20; P. 20–21; Gr. 6–8 + 23–27. Lookdown young look rather like those of *Alectis* but lack developed scutes. They differ from *S. setapinnis* in having filamentous dorsal, anal, and ventral fins. The young are silvery but with dark bands sometimes apparent; adults are silvery with moderately produced dorsal and anal lobes. Worldwide, in the western Atlantic from Nova Scotia through the Caribbean to Uruguay. (12 inches; 30 cm)

260. Rough scad *Trachurus lathami* Nichols
D. VIII + 1, 28–32; A. II + 1, 25–27; P. 21–22; Gr. 12–14 + 34–37; body elongate, spindle-shaped, with scutes posteriorly and scutelike scales anteriorly on lateral line. This little-known schooling fish occurs commonly on the inshore continental shelf. Gulf of Maine to Argentina. (8 inches; 20 cm)

261. Round scad; cigarfish *Decapterus punctatus* (Agassiz)
D. VIII + 1, 28–32; A. II + 1, 25–27; P. 19–21; Sc. 36–44; Gr. 12–15 + 34–40; two papillae on shoulder girdle under opercular flap (fig. 6). This poorly known but widespread jack is not uncommon on the outer shelf and occurs inshore east of the Mississippi. Two other species, *D. tabl* and *D. macarellus,* have recently been reported from the northwestern Gulf of Mexico by Retzer (1990). Both of these species occur more commonly in the eastern Gulf and Atlantic. *D. tabl* may be distinguished by its bright red caudal fin, enlarged posterior scutes, and lack of spots along the lateral line. *D. macarellus* has only a single spot near the edge of the opercle and none along the lateral line, and its caudal peduncle scutes are only slightly enlarged in comparison with those along the sides.

Atlantic Ocean, in the west from Bermuda and Nova Scotia through the Caribbean to southern Brazil. Berry, 1968. (7 inches; 18 cm)

262. Bigeye scad *Selar crumenophthalmus* (Bloch)

D. VIII + 1, 24–26; A. II + 1, 21–23; P. 20–22, Sc. 30–40; Gr. 9–11 + 27–30; two papillae on shoulder girdle under opercular flap (fig. 6). This little-known fish, not commonly taken on the inshore shelf at least west of the Mississippi, is normally found closer inshore in the northeastern Gulf. Circumtropical, in the western Atlantic from Nova Scotia to southern Brazil. (12 inches; 30 cm)

263. Atlantic bumper *Chloroscombrus chrysurus* (Linnaeus)

D. VIII + 1, 26–28; A. II + 1, 25–27; P. 19–20; Gr. 9–11 + 31–35. This small species is common in the Gulf and high-salinity bays. Aside from its slender caudal peduncle and free anal spines, the Atlantic bumper is identified by its yellow tail and dark spot atop the caudal peduncle. Atlantic Ocean, in the west from Massachusetts to Uruguay. Lefler and Shaw, 1992. (12 inches; 30 cm)

264. Bluntnose jack *Hemicaranx amblyrhynchus* (Cuvier)

D. VII + 1, 27–29; A. II + 1, 23–25; P. 19–22; Sc. 45–54; Gr. 8–10 + 19–23. This is a small jack seldom exceeding about ten inches (25 cm). Its young hide in the bell and among the tentacles of several common jellyfishes. This species is distinguished from *Caranx* by the lack of keels on the caudal peduncle, generally darker coloration, a more strongly arched lateral line, and the absence of vomerine and enlarged jaw teeth. The bases of the soft dorsal and anal fins are sheathed. Young fish between one and six inches (22–150 mm) have vertical bars, the last one farther forward than in *Caranx* young. North Carolina to southern Brazil. (11 inches; 28 cm)

265. Cottonmouth jack *Uraspis secunda* (Poey)

D. VIII + 1, 29; A. I, 21; P. 23; Sc. about 38; Gr. 6 + 14; tongue milky white; soft dorsal and anal fins with almost vertical margin over middle of caudal peduncle. This is the only carangid in which scute spines point forward. Although a distinctive species, it may have been confused with *Hemicaranx,* from which it differs by the above traits. New Jersey to southern Brazil. (8 inches; 20 cm)

266. Bar jack *Caranx ruber* (Bloch)

D. VIII + 1, 27–28; A. II+1, 24; P. 19–21; Sc. 20–27; Gr. 12–15 + 29–34; general body form that of an elongate *Caranx,* but distinguished by dark bar running along base of dorsal fin onto lower lobe of caudal. A rare species in the northwestern Gulf, this fish is generally confined to areas farther offshore and is more common in more tropical waters. New Jersey through the Caribbean to Brazil. Baughman, 1947; Berry, 1959. (22 inches; 56 cm)

267. Yellow jack *Caranx bartholomaei* Cuvier

D. VIII + I, 25–27; A. II + I, 22–24; P. 20–21; Sc. 20–31; Gr. 7–9 + 19–21. This fish is similar to *C. ruber* but without the dark band. All its fins, especially the caudal, are yellow, but this is not uncommon in most species of *Caranx*. The young, however, are known to have yellow blotches on their sides. The yellow jack is another uncommon, tropical species. Adults are known only from offshore, although young occur inshore. Massachusetts through the Caribbean to eastern Brazil. (36 inches; 91 cm)

268. Blue runner (hardtail) *Caranx crysos* Mitchill

D. VIII + I, 23–24; A. II + I, 19–20; P. 21–23; Sc. 45–54; Gr. 12–14 + 23–28. Another elongate *Caranx, crysos* is distinguished from *ruber* and *bartholomaei* by its more numerous scutes, lack of coloration as described for these other species, and generally black lobes on the caudal fin as well as a black opercular spot. The blue runner is a jack occasionally caught inshore. Some authorities combine eastern and western Atlantic populations as *C. fusus*. Nova Scotia through the Caribbean to Brazil. Goodwin and Johnson, 1986. (26 inches; 66 cm)

269. Black jack *Caranx lugubris* Poey

D. VIII+I, 21–22; A. II + I, 17–19; P. 20–22; Sc. 26–33; Gr. 6–8 + 18–20. A distinctively shaped and colored jack, this fish is rarely encountered, and only far offshore. Circumtropical, in the western Atlantic from Bermuda, the Bahamas, and northern Gulf through the Caribbean to southern Brazil. Sonnier et al., 1976. (36 inches; 91 cm)

270. Crevalle; common jack *Caranx hippos* (Linnaeus)

D. VIII + I, 15–21; A. II + I, 15–17; P. 20–21; Sc. 24–39; Gr. 6–8 + 14–16. This is the common jackfish of inshore waters, both juveniles and adults often being found inshore. The young have dark bars similar to those of *Hemicaranx,* with which it can be confused, but young *Caranx* are more silvery, have a low arch in the anterior lateral line, and usually have the anterior soft dorsal and anal fins lobed. This is a very large species, reaching over forty pounds (18 kg). Although it is not generally considered a food fish (jacks are edible), it is most prized as a hard-fighting game fish. Crevalle are voracious scavengers that may follow boats dumping trash. Worldwide in tropical and temperate waters, in the western Atlantic from Nova Scotia to Uruguay. (40 inches; 1 m)

271. Horse-eye jack *Caranx latus* Agassiz

D. VIII + I, 20–22; A. II + I, 16–17; P. 19–21; Sc. 30–42; Gr. 6–8 + 14–18. The horse-eye jack is less common than *C. hippos,* but young of the two species often occur together and are easily confused. *C. latus* possesses a fully scaled chest, a smaller dark spot on the opercle, and usually a black spot on the lobe of the dorsal fin. It occasionally enters the bays. New Jersey and Bermuda through the Caribbean to Brazil. (22 inches; 56 cm)

Coryphaenidae

The dolphins or dorados are a small family of epipelagic fishes. Both known species occur in our range as well as in all warm seas around the world. Dolphins are elongate, compressed fish with small scales and are capable of rapid changes in color. Although little is known of dolphin behavior, it is likely that color changes play an important role in communication among these fish. Many fishermen are familiar with the dramatic and rapid changes in color of freshly caught dolphin. The young as well as adults of both species commonly associate with *Sargassum* and other drifting materials (Dooley, 1972).

Generally speaking, the pompano dolphin does not grow as large as the common dolphin. In the western Gulf, most moderately small dolphin—up to eighteen inches (46 cm)—are *Coryphaena equisetis,* while any dolphin over thirty inches (76 cm) and most over two feet (61 cm) are *C. hippurus.* Large males of *C. hippurus* develop high, almost vertical foreheads, leading to their being called bull dolphin. (Ditty, Shaw, Grimes, and Cope, 1994; Gibbs and Collette, 1959; Palko et al., 1982)

1   Small fish, less than 8 inches (200 mm) 2
     Large fish, more than 8 inches (200 mm) 3
2   Sides with alternating light (orange in life) and black bars, continuing onto dorsal, anal, and caudal fins, dark except for tips of lobes . . . dolphin, *Coryphaena hippurus.*
     Sides uniformly colored; dorsal and anal fins weakly barred; posterior margin of caudal and sometimes entire fin unpigmented . . . pompano dolphin, *Coryphaena equisetis.*
3   Depth of body less than one-fourth of standard length; margin of anal fin concave; pectoral fin length half head length; small, oval tooth patch on tongue; lateral line scales 240–280; total dorsal rays (including buried anteriormost rays) more than 55 . . . dolphin, *Coryphaena hippurus.*
     Depth of body more than one-fourth of standard length; margin of anal fin convex; pectoral fin length about half head length; broad, square tooth patch on tongue; lateral line scales fewer than 200; total dorsal rays 55 or fewer . . . pompano dolphin, *Coryphaena equisetis.*

272. Dolphin; mahi-mahi *Coryphaena hippurus* Linnaeus

D. 58–66 (usually 59–65); A. 25–31 (27); P. 17–21 (20); Sc. 240–280; large males over 38 inches (95 cm) with high crested forehead; body in life colorful, in various shades of blue, violet, yellow, orange, and white, with many small blue spots. Dark vertical bands present in small fish are sometimes seen also in adults. This species occurs more inshore than does *C. equisetis* and also ranges into cooler waters. Young fish have been reported from saltier bays. Dolphin, like sailfish, apparently are rapidly growing fish with short lives of only two or three years. Highly prized as sport fish reaching forty pounds (18 kg), dolphin are generally regarded as one of the best-tasting fishes in the Gulf. Recently they have been extensively marketed in restaurants and fish houses under the Hawaiian name mahi-mahi, to avoid the misconception that the meat is that of the marine mammal (and arguably because this exotic sounding name commands a higher price). Circumtropical, in the western Atlantic from Nova Scotia and Bermuda through the Caribbean to southeastern Brazil. Baughman, 1941c; Pew, 1957. (5 feet; 1.5 m)

273. Pompano dolphin; blue dolphin *Coryphaena equisetis* Linnaeus

D. 52–58 (usually 53); A. 23–29 (26); P. 18–21 (20); Sc. 170–200; coloration much like *C. hippurus,* except that dark banding is never apparent and dark spots are more obvious. In the Gulf most fish are under 18–24 inches (45–60 cm) long. Fish over nine inches (230 mm) long are in breeding condition from April through August. Circumtropical, in the western Atlantic from New Jersey and Bermuda through the Caribbean to Brazil. (30 inches; 76 cm)

Bramidae

The pomfrets are a remarkable family famous for undergoing great changes in body shape with growth. They are probably closely related to the dolphins (Coryphaenidae), but their general body form is more like that of the butterfishes. Pomfrets have long, lunate dorsals and anals and very small ventral fins. Juveniles of several species occur rarely on the shelf, but they are mainly deeper-water animals. Of five species in the Gulf, *Taractes rubescens* and *Brama dussumieri* are the most common on the shelf. (Mead, 1957; Mead and Maul, 1958; Russo, 1981; Thompson and Russell, in press)

Lutjanidae

The snappers are large, carnivorous fishes native to the offshore reefs or snapper banks at from forty to one hundred fathoms in the northwestern Gulf of Mexico. Snappers are generally bottom-dwelling fishes, but they often feed well away from the bottom or over more open bottoms and occasionally are found far from reefs. The young of most species occur in shallower water than do the adults, and one species, the gray snapper, occurs commonly inshore as an adult and in low salinities as young. *Lutjanus* and *Rhomboplites* occur in the shallowest water, and other snappers not included here are found in water one hundred to three hundred fathoms deep.

The Gulf red snapper supports a considerable commercial fishery and is highly regarded as a sport fish as well, especially where it is caught around oil platforms and wrecks. A sizable harvest is landed in Florida and Texas, but the largest catches are probably made off Louisiana and the Campeche Bank off Mexico. Other snappers are frequently caught together with the red snapper; however, none except the vermilion snapper is as common. (Allen, 1985; Anderson, 1967; Baughman, 1943c; Domeier and

Clarke, 1992; Loftus, 1992; Polovina and Ralston, 1987; Randall and Caldwell, 1966; Rivas, 1966, 1970)

1   Dorsal spines X, lateral line scales fewer than 62 2

       Dorsal spines XII; lateral line scales more than 60 ... vermilion snapper, *Rhomboplites aurorubens*.

2   No scales on soft dorsal and anal fins 3

       Scales on soft dorsal and anal fins, with last rays of these fins not produced; dorsal rays 12–14; gill rakers on lower limb of first arch few (7–10) or numerous (19–20) 5

3   Dorsal fin deeply notched between spinous and soft portions . . . queen snapper, *Etelis oculatus*.

       Dorsal fin not deeply notched 4

4   Last rays of soft dorsal and anal fins produced as filaments (which may be broken); dorsal rays 10–11; gill rakers on lower limb of first arch 16–17 ... wenchman, *Pristipomoides aquilonaris*.

       Last rays of soft dorsal and anal fins not produced . . . black snapper, *Apsilus dentatus*.

5   Gill rakers on lower limb of first arch few (7–10); caudal lobes not produced in adults; no pterygoid teeth 6

       Gill rakers on lower limb of first arch numerous, 19–21; caudal lobes produced in adults; pterygoid teeth present . . . yellowtail snapper, *Ocyurus chrysurus*.

6   Dorsal rays usually 14, rarely 13 7

       Dorsal rays normally 12 . . . lane snapper, *Lutjanus synagris*.

7   Large black spot at base of pectoral fin . . . blackfin snapper, *Lutjanus buccanella*.

       No large black spot at base of pectoral fins 8

8   Vomerine tooth patch with posterior extension 9

       Vomerine tooth patch without posterior extension 11

9   Gill rakers on lower limb of first arch 7–8; anal rays usually 8 10

       Gill rakers on lower limb of first arch 9–10; anal rays usually 9 (8 in 11 percent of Gulf specimens) . . . red snapper, *Lutjanus campechanus*.

10   Lateral line scales 45–47; body depth 29–32 percent of standard length; caudal without pointed lobes . . . cubera snapper, *Lutjanus cyanopterus*.

       Lateral line scales 47–51; body depth 31–40 percent of standard length; caudal with pointed lobes . . . mutton snapper, *Lutjanus analis*.

11   Body comparatively stout, with greatest depth 36–43 percent (usually 37–42 percent) of standard length; pectoral fin in adults longer than distance from tip of snout to posteriormost edge of preopercle (in juveniles pectoral fin as in *Lutjanus griseus*) 12

       Body comparatively slender, with greatest depth 31–38 percent (usually 32–37 percent) of standard length; pectoral fin in adults as long as distance from tip of snout to posteriormost edge of preopercle . . . gray snapper, *Lutjanus griseus*.

12   Anal fin rounded at all sizes, middle rays less than one-half head length; no black spot on sides 13

       Anal fin pointed in mature fish (greater than 6 cm standard length); middle rays greater than one-half head length; black spot beneath the dorsal fin in young fish, often disappearing in older fish 14

13 Scales large, with 39–44 (usually 40–43) transverse rows between scale bone (an enlarged scale above and behind the gill slit) and base of caudal fin; 40–45 pored scales in lateral line; 5–7 rows between base of dorsal and lateral line ... schoolmaster, *Lutjanus apodus*.

Scales small, with 45–49 transverse rows between scale bone and base of caudal; 46–48 pored scales in lateral line ... dog snapper, *Lutjanus jocu*.

14 Scales below lateral line 16–19; scales above lateral line 9–11 and smaller than those below on anterior portion of body; black spot as large as or larger than eye; iris red in live or fresh specimens ... southern red snapper, *Lutjanus purpureus*.

Scales below lateral line 20–24; scales above lateral line 10–12 and equal in size to those below; black spot, if present, smaller than eye; iris yellow in live or fresh specimens ... silk snapper, *Lutjanus vivanus*.

274. Vermilion snapper; bastard snapper; B-liner *Rhomboplites aurorubens* (Cuvier)

D XII, 11; A. III, 8; Sc. about 72; Gr. 6 + 21; vomer with diamond-shaped (rhomboid) patch of teeth; vermilion red to pink, paler below, with series of yellow lines along sides; yellow-orange edges on dorsal and anal fins. As common as or more common than the red snapper, the vermilion snapper is found year-round on the snapper banks. Apparently this species occurs most commonly on the level areas on the reefs or about their bases instead of on the steep slopes. North Carolina through the Caribbean to southern Brazil. Fable, 1980; Laroche, 1977. (23 inches; 60 cm)

275. Queen snapper; ball bat *Etelis oculatus* (Valenciennes)

D. X, 11; A. III, 8; P. 16–17; Sc. 48–50; Gr. 7–10 + 16–18. Back and upper sides reddish pink, lower sides and belly pale pink; fins pink except spinous dorsal; caudal fin brilliant red. Body elongate and slender; eye large, snout shorter than eye diameter; both jaws with bands of caninelike teeth; vomerine tooth patch a narrow V. This is an increasingly commonly caught fish over rocky bottoms between 74 and 248 fathoms (135 and 450 m). Bermuda and North Carolina through the Caribbean to eastern Brazil. Anderson, 1981; Burgess and Branstetter, 1985. (28 inches; 71 cm)

276. Wenchman *Pristipomoides aquilonaris* (Goode and Bean)

D. X, 10–11; A. III, 8; Sc. 47–52; Gr. 7–9 + 17–19. The wenchman is one of the most common fish over the hard-bottomed regions on the middle to outer shelf. References to *P. macrophthalamus* and *P. andersoni* from this area usually refer to this *P. aquilonaris*, but *macrophthalamus* has been reported in deeper water. It differs from the wenchman by having smaller scales (54–57) and fewer gill rakers (20–23). North Carolina through the Caribbean to French Guiana. Allen, 1985; Anderson, 1966; Randall and Vergara, 1978. (9 inches; 23 cm)

277. Black snapper *Apsilus dentatus* Guichenot

D. X., 9–10; A. III, 8; P. 15–16; Sc. 58–63; Gr. 7–8 + 15–16. Back and upper sides violet or dark brown, head darker, lower sides and belly lighter; juveniles are mainly blue. Body oblong, relatively deep, head relatively small; interorbital convex, snout short and pointed; anterior teeth in upper jaw enlarged, caninelike; vomerine tooth plate V-shaped without median extension. Black snapper inhabit rocky bottoms between 66 and 100 fathoms (120 and 180 m). North Carolina and northern Gulf through the Bahamas and Antilles. Trimm and Searcy, 1989. (26 inches; 65 cm)

278. Yellowtail snapper *Ocyurus chrysurus* (Bloch)

D. X, 12–14; A. III, 8–9; Sc. 48–49; Gr. 21–22; vomerine teeth in arrow-shaped patch; caudal fin deeply forked; prominent midlateral yellow stripe beginning on snout, broadening as it passes along body, and continuing onto tail; yellow spots on blue background above this line, with narrow yellow stripes on lighter background below. More pelagic than the other snappers, it is seldom seen here in abundance. Massachusetts through the Caribbean to Brazil. (27 inches; 70 cm)

279. Lane snapper; candy snapper *Lutjanus synagris* (Linnaeus)

D. X, 12–13; A. III, 8; Sc. 47–52; Gr. 8–11 on lower limb, excluding rudiments, which may be fused in adults; vomerine teeth in arrow-shaped patch; diffuse black spot, as large as eye, below soft dorsal, with lateral line passing through bottom of this spot or running just beneath it. Body pink to red with seven or eight yellow longitudinal stripes; caudal fin light red; soft dorsal, anal, and ventrals yellow. This fish is frequently encountered on the snapper banks, the young occurring regularly inshore, where they are caught in shrimp trawls. North Carolina through the western Caribbean to Brazil. Domeier and Clarke, 1992. (20 inches; 50 cm)

280. Blackfin snapper *Lutjanus buccanella* (Cuvier)

D. X, 14; A. III, 8; P. 14–18 (16–17); Sc. 47–50; Gr. 7–9 + 17–19, including rudiments. Dorsum scarlet, sometimes with yellow posteriorly, silvery below; fins yellowish orange with a prominent black spot at base and in axil of pectoral fin. Juveniles light colored with bright yellow extending from beneath the soft dorsal onto the caudal fin. Anal fin rounded; body moderately deep; vomerine tooth patch V-shaped with median posterior extension. Blackfin snapper are sometimes taken with queen and silk snapper and are generally caught in water deeper than 44 fathoms (80 m). North Carolina through the Caribbean to northeast Brazil (2 feet; 62 cm)

281. Red snapper *Lutjanus campechanus* (Poey)

D. X, 14; A. III, 9; Sc. 46–50; Gr. 8–11; vomerine teeth broadly arrow-shaped; various intensities of red, often composed of alternating dark and lighter vertical red bands;

diffuse black spot above lateral line and below soft dorsal, disappearing in larger specimens. This is the commercial red snapper of the Gulf of Mexico. It is replaced to the south by the similar *L. purpureus* (see species key). Literature before 1966 referred to this species as either *L. blackfordi* (Goode and Bean) 1878 or *L. aya* (Bloch) 1790. Massachusetts (rare north of Cape Hatteras) through the Gulf to Yucatán. Arnold et al., 1978; Bradley and Bryan, 1975; Camber, 1955; Carpenter, 1965; Collins et al., 1979; Fable, 1980; Holt and Arnold, 1982; Moseley, 1966b; Nelson and Manooch, 1982; Wakeman et al., 1979. (39 inches; 1 m)

282. Cubera snapper *Lutjanus cyanopterus* (Cuvier)

D. X, 14; A. III, 7–8; P. 16–18; Sc. 45–57; Gr. 6–8 on lower limb, excluding rudiments; vomerine teeth without median extension; upper and lower canines equally developed, very strong; body depth less than 32 percent of standard length for a 10-inch or larger fish. The largest species of *Lutjanus,* known to exceed one hundred pounds (45 kg), the cubera snapper is rarely reported from scattered Gulf locations and juveniles are very rare. Its status is uncertain because of confusion with large dog and gray snapper. Bahamas, Florida, and northern Gulf through the Caribbean to northern Brazil. Moe, 1968. (5 feet; 1.6 m)

283. Mutton snapper *Lutjanus analis* (Cuvier)

D. X (rarely IX or XI), 13–14; A. III, 8 (rarely 7); Sc. 47–51; Gr. 7–9 on lower limb, excluding rudiments; vomerine teeth in crescent-shaped patch; black spot, smaller than eye, present above lateral line and below soft dorsal; often with wavy blue line beneath eye and another from snout to middle of anterior edge of orbit and continuing behind eye for a short distance; fins reddish, especially ventrals, anal, and lower portion of caudal; posterior edge of caudal dusky. The status of this moderate-sized snapper—up to thirty pounds (14 kg)—here is uncertain. Massachusetts (rare north of the Carolinas) through the Caribbean to southeast Brazil. (2 1/2 feet; 76 cm)

284. Gray snapper; black snapper; mangrove snapper *Lutjanus griseus* (Linnaeus)

D. X, 14; A. III, 7–8; Sc. 43–47; Gr. 7–9 on lower limb, excluding rudiments; vomerine teeth in arrow-shaped patch; dark gray-green to brown on body and fins; no black spot on side of body; median fins dark brown to black, often edged with white or yellow; young with black bar from tip of snout through eye and often with blue streak beneath eye and generally lighter color; large adults on offshore banks more reddish in color. This is a common snapper inshore; young and adults regularly occur in saltier bays. In the southern Gulf this species frequents mangrove swamps. Bermuda and North Carolina, rare to Massachusetts, through the Caribbean to southeast Brazil. (3 feet; 91 cm)

285. Schoolmaster *Lutjanus apodus* (Walbaum)

D. X, 14; A. III, 8; Sc. 40–45; Gr. 7–9 on lower limb, excluding rudiments; vomerine tooth patch arrow-shaped; body brown with series of pale vertical bars but sometimes partly blotches; median and ventral fins yellow; young with blue stripe below eye, often broken into series of blue spots. This is the most common snapper of Caribbean reefs, but it is fairly rare in the northwestern Gulf. Massachusetts through the Caribbean to Brazil. (2 feet; 61 cm)

286. Dog snapper *Lutjanus jocu* (Bloch and Schneider)

D. X, 13–14; A. III, 8; P. 16–17; Sc. 45–49; Gr. 8–11 on lower limb, excluding rudiments; body deep, 36–43 percent of standard length; arrow-shaped vomerine tooth patch; canines in upper jaw enlarged. The most characteristic coloration of this species is a pale bar running from beneath the eye to the posterior corner of the maxillary, broadening ventrally, but unfortunately this trait is sometimes not apparent. A row of blue spots or a blue bar appears beneath the eye in some small fish. This is a rare but regularly occurring snapper. Bermuda (introduced) and Massachusetts through the Caribbean to eastern Brazil. (29 inches; 74 cm)

287. Silk snapper; yellow eye snapper *Lutjanus vivanus* (Cuvier)

D. X, 13–14; A. III, 8; P. 16–18 (17); Sc. 50–53 (51); Gr. 7–9 + 9–12, including rudiments. Dorsum reddish, silvery below, caudal margined in black; adults without lateral spot, lateral line running through middle of spot in juveniles; iris yellow in live or fresh specimens. This is a deepwater snapper usually found in 40–120 fathoms (73–218 m). Bermuda and North Carolina through the Caribbean to eastern Brazil. (31 inches; 80cm)

Lobotidae

The tripletail is the single representative of this family.

288. Tripletail *Lobotes surinamensis* (Bloch)

D. XII, 15; A. III, 11; Sc. 47; body deep brown to olivaceous above grayish yellow below, often blotched; color changeable from yellow to brown and often variously mottled. A fish of sluggish habits, the tripletail often floats horizontally on the surface like the ocean sunfish, *Mola mola*. Small fish associate with flotsam in open waters and occur around pilings and bulkheads in enclosed areas. This species is uncommon in the bays and shallow Gulf during the warmer months but is often caught in Matagorda Bay. Although bony, it is an excellent eating fish, reaching twenty pounds. Circumtropical; in the western Atlantic from Cape Cod through the Caribbean to Argentina. Baughman, 1941a, 1943d; Ditty and Shaw, 1994. (3 feet; 91 cm)

Gerreidae

The mojarras, family Gerreidae (often misspelled Gerridae), are silvery, high-bodied fishes with deeply forked tails and greatly protrusible jaws. Although our understanding of the taxonomy of local species has improved in recent years, the family is still poorly known ecologically, and the relationship of closely related forms remains uncertain. The family has sometimes been combined with the Indo-Pacific Leiognathidae. (Curran, 1942; Deckert and Greenfield, 1987; Matheson and McEachran, 1984)

1   Body with narrow, dark bars, more obvious in life than in preserved specimens . . . yellowfin
     mojarra, *Gerres cinereus.*
     Body without narrow, dark vertical bars; young of some species mottled, blotched, or with
     diagonal bars, but none with vertical bars 2
2   Anal spines three 3
     Anal spines two . . . mottled mojarra, *Eucinostomus lefroyi.*
3   Preopercle entire; second interhaemal bone enlarged, hollowed, and surrounding posterior
     extension of swimbladder 4
     Preopercle serrate; second interhaemal bone normally developed, not hollow and not sur-
     rounding part of swimbladder . . . Irish pompano, *Diapterus auratus.*
4   Lower arch gill rakers eight, dorsal not tricolored, but may have black tip 5
     Lower arch gill rakers nine, dorsal tricolored with black tip . . . flagfin mojarra, *Eucinostomus
     melanopterus.*
5   Premaxillary groove continuous, naked, uninterrupted by a transverse row of scales; spinous
     dorsal sometimes with black spot; depth about one-third of standard length . . . spotfin
     mojarra, *Eucinostomus argenteus.*
     Premaxillary groove interrupted by transverse row of scales across anterior end; spinous
     dorsal usually without black spot; depth 40 percent or less of standard length . . . silver jenny,
     Eucinostomus gula.

289. Yellowfin mojarra *Gerres cinereus* (Walbaum)
D. IX, 10; A. III, 7; Sc. 39–44; body depth 37–43 percent of standard length; sides silvery with seven darker, vertical bars; ventral and anal fins yellow. This species is found mostly in the fall in the bays and shallow Gulf. Eastern Pacific and western Atlantic from Florida and Bermuda through the Caribbean to southern Brazil. (15 inches; 38 cm)

290. Mottled mojarra *Eucinostomus lefroyi* (Goode)
D. IX, 10; A. II, 8; Sc. 44–47; body depth 28–32 percent of standard length; sides silvery; dark, irregular markings about base of dorsal fin rays. This mojarra is a rarely reported form not known from Louisiana. Bermuda and North Carolina through the Caribbean to Brazil. (9 inches; 23 cm)

291. Irish pompano *Diapterus auratus* Ranzani

D. IX, 10; A. III, 8; Sc. 37–40; Gr. 12–15 on lower limb; body rhomboid, with depth one-half standard length; anterior profile steep, with prominent notch above eye; dorsal fin margin concave; second dorsal spine well developed, about as long as head; second anal spine strong, about three-fourths head length; third anal spine thinner but slightly longer than second. The similar species *D. rhombeus,* which possesses only two anal spines, was incorrectly reported from Texas; however, that species as well as the striped mojarra previously put in *Diapterus, Eugerres plumieri,* with more gill rakers, are known from the Laguna Madre de Tamaulipas. New Jersey and South Texas (rarely Louisiana) through the Caribbean to Brazil. Deckert, 1973. (12 inches; 30 cm)

292. Spotfin mojarra *Eucinostomus argenteus* Baird and Girard

D. IX, 10; A. III, 7; Sc. 44–48; depth 30–36 percent of standard length; premaxillary groove not interrupted by transverse scale row; body silvery with irregular blotches or diagonal bars on upper half. Boschung (1992) reports that freshwater records of this species are *E. harengulus* Goode and Bean, which differs in snout pigmentation but may only be a variant. Both coasts of Central America; in the western Atlantic from New Jersey and Bermuda through the Caribbean to Brazil. (8 inches; 20 cm)

293. Silver jenny *Eucinostomus gula* (Quoy and Gaimard)

D. IX, 10; A. III, 8; Sc. 42; depth 42 percent of standard length; premaxillary groove crossed by scale row. *E. gula* tends to be found more commonly in the Gulf and *E. argenteus* more commonly in bays and inland waters. New England through the Caribbean to Argentina. (7 inches; 18 cm)

294. Flagfin mojarra *Eucinostomus melanopterus* Bleeker

D. IX, 10; A. III, 7; Sc. 44–47; depth 35–39 percent of standard length; distinctive black-tipped dorsal separated from a lighter black area at its base by a clear area. Omitted from the first edition, this seems to be a common species, although frequently overlooked by many workers. S.C. through the Caribbean to southeastern Brazil. Matheson, 1981. (7 inches; 18 cm)

Haemulidae

The grunts are a family of fishes (sometimes referred to as the Pomadasyidae) allied to the snappers but lacking the canines and vomerine teeth found in all lutjanids. The common name of the group is derived from the noise they make when they rub their pharyngeal teeth together. Only the pigfish is common inshore, but others are important predators on offshore reefs. The adults and young of each species are quite distinct.

Other species may be expected rarely; for example, Gunter (1935) reported the small-mouth grunt, *Haemulon chrysargyreum*, which has not been verified since. For identification of the young of *Haemulon* see Böhlke and Chaplin, 1968, 1993; Courtenay, 1961; Lindeman, 1986.

1   Soft dorsal and anal fins densely scaled to their margins 2

    Soft dorsal and anal fins not scaled except at bases 7

2   Dorsal spines XIII (XII + I) 3

    Dorsal spines XII (XI + I), rarely XI 4

3   Scales around caudal peduncle 22; gill rakers 24–28, dorsal rays 14–15; anal rays usually 9 ... tomtate, *Haemulon aurolineatum*.

    Scales around caudal peduncle 24 or more, usually 26; gill rakers 27–36; dorsal rays 13–14; anal rays 7–8 ... striped grunt, *Haemulon striatum*.

4   Scales around caudal peduncle 23 or more; scales below lateral line 13–14; dark stripe along base of soft dorsal fin extending onto upper lobe of caudal ... cottonwick, *Haemulon melanurum*.

    Scales around caudal peduncle 22 or fewer; scales below lateral line 12 or 13; color not as above 5

5   Pectoral fins scaled for more than one third of their length; dorsal fin rays 16–18, usually 17–18 ... sailor's choice, *Haemulon parra*.

    Pectoral fins not scaled 6

6   Scales above lateral line larger than those below; pectoral rays 17, rarely 16 ... white grunt, *Haemulon plumieri*.

    Scales above lateral line not larger than those below; pectoral rays 17–18, usually 18 ... Spanish grunt, *Haemulon macrostomum*.

7   Preopercle strongly serrate, with serration on lower margin directed anteriorly; two enlarged spines at angle ... barred grunt, *Conodon nobilis*.

    Preopercle moderately, or not at all, serrate, with none of serrations directed anteriorly 8

8   Body elongate, depth 33–36 percent of standard length 9

    Body deep, depth 43–48 percent of standard length 10

9   Anal rays 12–13; gill rakers on lower limb of first arch... pigfish, *Orthopristis chrysoptera*.

    Anal rays 6–7; gill rakers on lower limb of first arch 7–9 ... burro grunt, *Pomadasys crocro*.

10 Body marked with alternating blue and yellow stripes; scales small, 10–11 in vertical row between base of spinous dorsal and lateral line ... porkfish, *Anisotremus virginicus*.

    Body without alternating blue and yellow stripes; scales larger, 6–7 in oblique row between base of spinous dorsal and lateral line ... black margate, *Anisotremus surinamensis*.

295. Tomtate *Haemulon aurolineatum* Cuvier

D. XII–XIV, 14–15 (usually XIII, 15); A. III, 9; P. 17–18; Sc. 49–52; Gr. 24–28; depth of body 27–37 percent of standard length; body silvery with golden stripe running from eye to round black spot located at base of caudal; second narrow stripe on sides above lateral line; inside of mouth red. Only this species and *H. striatum* have thirteen dorsal spines. Because of this characteristic, these two species were placed in the genus *Bathystoma*. Northwestern Gulf members of this species are sometimes separated into the subspecies (or species) rimator. This is a common fish around offshore reefs, and it is occasionally found near platforms. Massachusetts and Bermuda through the Caribbean to Brazil. Darcy, 1983a; Manooch and Barans, 1982. (9 inches; 23 cm)

296. Striped grunt *Haemulon striatum* (Linnaeus)

D. XIII, 13–14; A. III, 7–8 (usually 8); P. 17–19; Sc. 51–53; Gr. 28–34; body more elongate than in other grunts, depth 26–32 percent of standard length; body silvery gray with five dusky yellow stripes. The striped grunt is known here only from a specimen collected offshore of Texas. South Texas and the Bahamas through the Caribbean to Brazil. Courtenay, 1961. (9 inches; 23 cm)

297. Cottonwick *Haemulon melanurum* (Linnaeus)

D. XII, 15–17; A. III, 8–9 (usually 8); P. 16–18, Sc. 49–52, Gr. 20–23; body silvery white with five or six yellow stripes on sides and strong black stripe running from dorsal fin origin to caudal peduncle, then separating into two stripes running to each lobe of caudal fin; sometimes with additional longitudinal black stripes on body. In the northern Gulf, this grunt is not uncommon around offshore reefs, and it is commonly exhibited in aquaria. Bermuda, Bahamas, and the northern Gulf through the Caribbean to Brazil. Nelson, 1985. (12 inches; 30 cm)

298. Sailor's choice *Haemulon parra* (Desmarest)

D. XII, 16–18, A. III, 8; P. 17; Sc. 51–52; Gr. 21–26; body silvery, with each scale edged with brown; scales on upper half of body with brownish spots, which form oblique rows; black blotch usually present under opercular edge; inside of mouth red. There is one report of this fish from Texas, but its status in the northern and western Gulf is not clear. Bahamas, Yucatán, and Florida through the Caribbean to Brazil. Reed, 1941. (16 inches; 41 cm)

299. White grunt *Haemulon plumieri* (Lacepède)

D. XII, 15–17; A. III, 8–9 (usually 9); P. 16–17; Sc. 48–52; Gr. 21–27; scales above lateral line larger than those below; usually yellowish; head with narrow blue stripes; scales on upper part of body with blue or white spots—inside of mouth red; black blotch possibly present beneath free edge of opercle. This grunt is known in the Gulf only from a few specimens taken far offshore. Bermuda (introduced) and Virginia through the Caribbean to Brazil. Darcy, 1983a. (18 inches; 46 cm)

300. Spanish grunt *Haemulon macrostomum* (Günther)

D. XII, 15–17; A. III, 9; P. 17–18 (usually 18); Sc. 50–52; Gr. 26–28; body silvery gray with faint dark stripes on upper portion; caudal peduncle yellow. There is one report of this species from Texas. Bermuda, Florida, and Texas through the Caribbean to Brazil. (14 inches; 36 cm)

301. Barred grunt *Conodon nobilis* (Linnaeus)

D. XI + I, 13; A. III, 7; Sc. 55; dorsal fin divided; preopercle strongly serrated; silver with eight broad vertical bars; sides with yellowish stripes underlying bars; ventral, anal, and caudal fins yellow; belly and lower sides with yellow during breeding season. The barred grunt is common during the late spring and summer on the South Texas coast but less common on the northern Gulf coast. Northern Gulf through the Caribbean to Brazil; not in northeastern Gulf or Florida. Dawson, 1962a. (1 foot; 30 cm)

302. Pigfish *Orthopristis chrysoptera* (Linnaeus)

D. XII–XIII, 16; A. III, 12–13; Sc. 60; body blue above, silvery below, each scale with blue center and bronze edge, forming series of yellow-brown stripes on sides; snout and head sometimes with orange bands. This is a very common fish in the saltier bays and shallow Gulf; its young live in grass beds. Bermuda and Massachusetts to Florida and throughout the Gulf. Darcy 1983b. (1 foot; 30 cm)

303. Burro grunt *Pomadasys crocro* (Cuvier)

D. XIII, 11–12; A. III, 6–7; Sc. 54; brown with 3–4 ill-defined dark stripes on sides, one from point of snout to base of caudal fin. There have been several reports of this species from Texas, including young from the Port Aransas jetties. South Florida and South Texas through the Caribbean to Brazil. Hoese, 1965; Pezold and Edwards, 1983. (1 foot; 30 cm)

304. Porkfish *Anisotremus virginicus* (Linnaeus)

D. XII, 16–17; A. III, 9–11; P. 17–18; Sc. 51–53; Gr. 27–29; diagonal black band from mouth through eye, another running from opercular opening to origin of dorsal fin; behind this bar, body with alternating blue and yellow stripes. Bermuda, Bahamas, southern Florida, and South Texas through the Caribbean to Brazil. Briggs et al., 1964. (1 foot; 30 cm)

305. Black margate *Anisotremus surinamensis* (Bloch)

D. XII, 16–18; A. III, 8–10 (usually 9); P. 18–19; Sc. 50–53; Gr. 30–36; body silvery, each scale with dark center, tending to form dark diagonal lines on sides; large irregular dark area on lower body behind opercular opening; soft dorsal and anal fins dusky. The range of this species is the same as that of the porkfish. (2 feet; 61 cm)

Sparidae

The porgies are a family of moderately sized fish, some of which resemble the grunts. They are best characterized by their anteriormost teeth, which are either flattened incisors or peglike canines. Most species are omnivorous, feeding on attached vegetation or invertebrates. The genus *Calamus* was revised by Randall and Caldwell (1966), who noted that the sheepshead porgy, *C. penna* (plate 311b), reported by Baughman (1950b) from off Galveston, does not occur in the northwestern Gulf. This species is however known from the northeastern Gulf, at least as far west as Alabama (Boshung, 1992). The sea bream, *Archosargus rhomboidalis* (Linnaeus), is found on grass flats and in mangrove swamps in the tropics, but we have not verified it from the northwestern Gulf. It occurs in the northeastern Gulf and possibly west to Louisiana (Randall and Vergara, 1978). The sea bream superficially resembles the pinfish, from which it can be distinguished by its teeth and a typically deeper body (sea bream body depth goes into standard length about twice vs. greater than 2.3 times in the pinfish).

1   Teeth in front of jaws flattened, incisorlike, not molar 2
    Teeth in front of jaws conical or caninelike 6
2   First and second dorsal spines short, about one-third of eye diameter in length; third dorsal spine greatly elongate, often longer than head . . . longspine porgy, *Stenotomus caprinus.*
    First and second dorsal spines as long as or longer than diameter of eye 3
3   Broad dark bar across top of caudal peduncle . . . spottail pinfish, *Diplodus holbrooki.*
    Color variable, but not as above 4
4   Incisors deeply notched; lateral line scales 65–70 . . . pinfish, *Lagodon rhomboides.*
    Incisors not notched; lateral line scales 45–50 5
5   Dorsal rays 12; five or six (rarely four) broad, black, vertical bands on sides . . . sheepshead, *Archosargus probatocephalus.*
    Dorsal rays 13; dark bars on sides not conspicuous; sides usually with longitudinal lines . . . sea bream, *Archosargus rhomboidalis.*
6   Anal rays 8 . . . red porgy, *Pagrus pagrus.*
    Anal rays 10 or 11 7
7   Pectoral rays usually 14 or 15 8
    Pectoral rays usually 16 (rarely 15) 12
8   Pectoral rays typically 14 9
    Pectoral rays typically 15 11
9   Anal rays 10 . . . littlehead porgy, *Calamus proridens.*
    Anal rays 11 10
10 Third and sometimes fourth canine in upper jaw enlarged and outcurved . . . saucereye porgy, *Calamus calamus.*
    Third canine in upper jaw not enlarged, no enlarged canines in jaw . . . knobbed porgy, *Calamus nodosus.*
11 Lateral line scales typically 49 or fewer . . . Campeche porgy, *Calamus campechanus.*
    Lateral line scales typically 51 or more . . . jolthead porgy, *Calamus bajonado.*
12 Humeral spot absent or diffuse; pectoral fin goes 2.4–3.4 times into standard length; depth goes 1.8–2.3 times into standard length; snout purplish . . . whitebone porgy, *Calamus leucosteus.*

Humeral spot conspicuous, usually larger than pupil; pectoral fin goes 3.0–3.6 times into standard length; depth goes 2.0–2.5 times into standard length; snout olive, mottled with blue; yellow bars in front of eye ... grass porgy, *Calamus arctifrons*.

306. Longspine porgy *Stenotomus caprinus* Bean

D. XII, 12; A. III, 12; Sc. 50; 5 scales above and 15 below lateral line; deep-bodied; silvery-sided, with third, fourth, and fifth dorsal spines greatly elongated. A close relative, *S. chrysops*, which occurs off the Atlantic Coast, has also been reported from Texas waters, but it probably does not occur here. In addition, Atlantic populations may be divisible into two species, the northern porgy, *S. chrysops*, and the southern porgy, *S. aculeatus*, The latter form is more similar to *S. caprinus* than is *S. chrysops*; that fact may be responsible for a lot of the apparent confusion in the common and scientific names of these fishes. Throughout the Gulf except the Florida west coast, but commonest on the middle shelf off Louisiana and East Texas. Caldwell, 1955a; Geoghegan and Chittenden, 1982; Henwood et al., 1978. (6 inches; 15 cm)

307. Spottail pinfish *Diplodus holbrooki* (Bean)

D. XII, 14–15; A. III, 13; Sc. 55–57; 7 scales above and 14 below lateral line; silvery-sided, with dark saddle or spot on dorsal surface of caudal peduncle. Juveniles are sometimes found schooling with the common pinfish. A similar fish occurs in the Caribbean. North Carolina to Florida and the northern Gulf to southern Texas. Caldwell, 1955b; Darcy, 1985a. (7 inches; 18 cm)

308. Pinfish; pin perch *Lagodon rhomboides* (Linnaeus)

D. XII, 11; A. III, 11; Sc. 65–70; 10 scales above and 17 below lateral line; body olivaceous above, lighter below, with numerous blue and yellow stripes and spots; adults with traces of six vertical bars on sides (becoming more prominent after death) and prominent humeral spot. One of the most common inshore fishes except in the highly turbid brackish waters of western Louisiana, the pinfish is usually found around wharves and pilings and over grass flats. A voracious feeder, noted for its bait-stealing activities, it is edible, but it rarely reaches sufficient size to warrant keeping unless it is cooked whole. Massachusetts and Bermuda to Florida and throughout the Gulf, rarely crossing the Gulf Stream. Caldwell, 1957; Darcy, 1985b. (15 inches; 40 cm)

309. Sheepshead *Archosargus probatocephalus* (Walbaum)

D. XII, 10–12; A. III, 10–11; Sc. 48; 8 scales above and 15 below lateral line; six to seven vertical black bands on sides and no distinct humeral spot. Western Gulf populations of the sheepshead were considered to be a separate species, *A. oviceps*, distinguished by 5 instead of 6 stripes; however, the differences between eastern and western Gulf populations are probably not at the species level. A common inshore sport fish, the sheepshead is often caught using fiddler crabs or barnacles for bait. Massachusetts through the Caribbean to Brazil. Beckman et al., 1991; Caldwell, 1965; Ginsburg, 1954; Hildebrand, 1955; Mook, 1977. (2 feet; 61 cm)

310. Red porgy; silver snapper; white snapper *Pagrus pagrus* Linnaeus

D. XII, 9–11; A. III, 8; Sc. 56–59. A common fish on the Atlantic Coast of the United States, the red porgy has been reported only once from the western Gulf but is common off the Florida panhandle. The western Atlantic form was previously considered a distinct species from the eastern Atlantic form and was known as *Pagrus sedicim* Ginsburg. Huntsman, 1992. (18 inches; 46 cm)

311. Littlehead porgy *Calamus proridens* Jordan and Gilbert

D. XII, 12; A. III, 10; P. 14; Sc. 52–57. Snout and cheek blue-gray with many wavy blue lines; diffuse blue blotch at upper end of gill opening; alternating narrow blue and wide yellow horizontal lines on cheek. This is a shallow reef species usually found out to the middle shelf. Louisiana and southern Florida to Campeche and the Greater Antilles. Darcy, 1986. (18 inches; 46 cm)

312. Saucereye porgy *Calamus calamus* (Valenciennes)

D. XII, 12; A. III, 11; P. 14–15; Sc. 51–55. Cheeks blue with closely spaced yellow spots arranged in lines; head frequently with yellow wash, at least corner of mouth yellow; third (sometimes fourth) upper canine enlarged and outcurved. North Carolina, Bermuda, Bahamas, and northeastern Gulf to Brazil. (15 inches; 36 cm)

313. Campeche porgy *Calamus campechanus* Randall and Caldwell

D. XII, 12; A. III, 10; P. 14–15; Sc. 44–49; 6 scales above and 13–14 below lateral line; Gr. 12; body with five or six indistinct blotches on sides and pattern of wavy horizontal lines on cheek and snout. Presently known only from the Campeche Bank, this porgy may range north along the Mexican coast to southern Texas. Randall and Vergara, 1978. (8 inches; 20 cm)

314. Whitebone porgy *Calamus leucosteus* Jordan and Gilbert

D. XII, 12; A. III, 10; P. 16; Sc. 51; 7–8 scales above and 14 below lateral line; body silvery with faint crossbars; dorsal and anal fins with dark blotches; ventrals dusky; axil of pectoral not distinctly colored. The porgy occurs mainly in deeper water. Southeastern Atlantic states and throughout the Gulf. Dennis and Bright, 1988a. (14 inches; 36 cm)

315. Jolthead porgy *Calamus bajonado* (Bloch and Schneider)

D. XII, 12; A. III, 10; Sc. 50–57; 7 scales above and 17 below lateral line; eye diameter about 40 percent of head length of adults; body silvery with faint blue or violet iridescence;

blue line under eye; axil of pectoral with blue spot; two horizontal white bands on cheek, most obvious in live specimens seen underwater. Records of *C. macrops* refer to this species, according to Randall and Caldwell (1966), who have synonymized the two forms. Dennis and Bright (1988b) referred all of Baughman's records (1950b) of *C. bajonado* to *C. leucosteus;* however, the jolthead porgy is occasionally reported and Randall and Vergara (1978) include the Louisiana and Texas coasts in their reported range. Bermuda through the Caribbean and Rhode Island to Belize. (20 inches; 51 cm)

316. Knobbed porgy *Calamus nodosus* Randall and Caldwell
D. XII, 12; A. III, 11; P. 13–15 (14); Sc. 52–57; 7–8 scales above and 17–20 below lateral line; body silver, no obvious bars on sides; snout, unscaled part of cheek, and preopercle dark purple with irregular yellowish spots and darker stripes; often with large, diffuse dark spot in axil of pectoral. The knoblike tubercle found above the posterior nostril helps identify this species. This the commonest *Calamus* in the area, usually in six to forty-three fathoms. Reports of *C. calamus* from Texas probably refer to this species; however, *C. calamus* occurs in the eastern Gulf and west to Louisiana. North Carolina to Yucatán. (2 feet; 61 cm)

317. Grass porgy *Calamus arctifrons* Goode and Bean
D. XII, 12; A. III, 10; P. 16; Sc. 43–49; 6 scales above and 13 below lateral line; Gr. 10; body olivaceous with dark bars on sides, sometimes confined to 6–8 spots along lateral line; a conspicuous blotch, larger than pupil, behind gill opening. This species is smaller than most other porgies. It is found over shallow grass flats and reefs, to 17 fathoms (30 m), on the Florida Gulf Coast and rarely strays west. Louisiana to southern Florida. Bullis and Thompson, 1965; Darcy, 1986; Randall and Caldwell, 1966; Randall and Vergara, 1978. (8 inches; 20 cm)

Polynemidae

The threadfins are a group of warm-water fishes characterized by detached rays of the pectoral fins (hence their common name). These rays serve as feelers or scoops as the fish feed over hard, sandy bottoms. There is one species in the northern Gulf, with others in the tropics.

318. Atlantic threadfin; eight-fingered threadfin (whiskerfish)
Polydactylus octonemus (Girard)
D. VIII + I, 12–13; A. III, 13–15; Sc. 70; pectoral filaments 8; sides silvery; snout nearly transparent. This species is abundant in the surf zone during the summer and never occurs farther out than the inner shelf. New York to southern Florida, across to at

least South Texas, possibly in South Atlantic. Dentzau and Chittenden, 1990. (8 inches; 20 cm)

Sciaenidae

The croakers are perhaps the most characteristic group of large northern Gulf inshore fishes. In numbers of species they exceed all other families, and in numbers of individuals, or biomass, they are among the top three (the others being the mullets and the much smaller anchovies). Many croaker species grow to a large size and are important commercial and sport fish. Most spawn in the shallow Gulf, with the larvae entering the bays, where they spend their first summer in brackish water. Most are fast-growing and short-lived, but recent work has shown that the larger species are long-lived (at least two decades). Although most species are adapted to living on muddy bottoms, a few are found in sandier habitats or are adapted to rocky habitats. In some species, individuals move from soft, muddy substrates to harder ones as the fish grow older. (Cowan and Shaw, 1988; Ditty, 1989; Hildebrand and Cable, 1934; King et al., 1987; McMichael and Ross, 1987; Pearson, 1929; Vetter, 1982; Welsh and Breder, 1923;)

1	Second dorsal rays fewer than 32	2
	Second dorsal rays more than 36	17
2	Lower jaw with one or more barbels	3
	Lower jaw without barbels	8
3	One thick barbel on front underside of lower jaw	4
	Many barbels, minute to large, sometimes wearing off	7
4	Two anal spines; thin vertical bars on sides of body sand drum, *Umbrina coroides*.	
	One anal spine; sides may be blotched, but without definite thin vertical bars	5
5	Second dorsal spine elongate, extending to twice height of rest of fin; body with V-shaped blotch on each side . . . northern kingfish, *Menticirrhus saxatilis*.	
	Second dorsal spine only slightly elongate, barely extending beyond others; body silvery, blotched or with oblique bars	6
6	Inside of operculum dusky; body with irregular dark stripes or blotches; pectoral rays 21–22 . . . southern kingfish, *Menticirrhus americanus*.	
	Inside of operculum silvery; body plain, silvery; pectoral rays 18–19 . . . Gulf kingfish, *Menticirrhus littoralis*.	
7	Many large barbels on lower jaw; body with about five dark vertical bars . . . black drum, *Pogonias cromis*.	
	Row of minute barbels on each side of lower jaw (often worn off in larger fish, with series of small pits along edge of jaw to show their former location); no vertical bars . . . Atlantic croaker, *Micropogonias undulatus*.	

8   Black spot at base of pectoral fin . . . reef croaker, *Odontoscion dentex.*

No spot at base of pectoral fin (*Cynoscion* with some black pigment on pectoral, but with large canines) 9

9   Lower jaw projecting; one pair of enlarged canine teeth in upper jaw 10

Lower jaw not projecting; mouth terminal or inferior; no enlarged canines in upper jaw 13

10   Upper portions of sides of body with well-defined spots 11

Upper portions of sides of body without definite spots 12

11   Spots on upper portions relatively large; gill rakers 11–13 . . . spotted seatrout, *Cynoscion nebulosus.*

Spots on upper portions relatively small and in oblique streaks; gill rakers 14–17 . . . weakfish, *Cynoscion regalis.*

12   Anal rays 10–11; scales firm; second dorsal . . . sand seatrout, *Cynoscion arenarius.*

Anal rays 8–9; scales deciduous; second dorsal . . . silver seatrout, *Cynoscion nothus.*

13   Mouth inferior, below horizontal line drawn from lower edge of eye 14

Mouth terminal, with at least tip of upper jaw above line drawn through lower edge of eye 15

14   Dark spot present above lateral line in front of caudal fin (possibly several such spots); no shoulder spot . . . red drum, *Sciaenops ocellatus.*

No dark spot at base of caudal fin, but spot on shoulder . . . spot, *Leiostomus xanthurus.*

15   Space between eyes (interorbital) hollow; caudal lanceolate . . . star drum, *Stellifer lanceolatus.*

Space between eyes slightly convex, caudal truncate 16

16   Edge of preopercle serrate; mouth oblique; body with vertical bars . . . banded drum, *Larimus fasciatus.*

Edge of preopercle smooth; body without bars; mouth only slightly oblique . . . silver perch, *Bairdiella chrysoura.*

17   First dorsal height about half of head length; broad black from base of spinous dorsal to abdomen; horizontal stripes thicker than eye . . . blackbar drum, *Equetus iwamotoi*

First dorsal more than twice head length or a series of horizontal bars thinner than eye 18

18   Dorsal soft rays fewer than 40; midlateral dark stripe extending from caudal fin to eye; dorsal and caudal fins not greatly elongate in adults, and in young still less than one-half body length . . . cubbyu, *Equetus umbrosus.*

Dorsal soft rays more than 45; midlateral dark stripe curving upward to join dark bar on spinous dorsal fin; dorsal and caudal fins greatly elongate, especially in young 19

19   Pectoral and anal fins pale; median fins not spotted; more than 48 dorsal rays . . . jackknife fish, *Equetus lanceolatus.*

Pectoral and anal fins dark; median fins (except anal) spotted; fewer than 48 dorsal rays . . . spotted drum, *Equetus punctatus.*

319. Sand drum (roncador) *Umbrina coroides* Cuvier
D. X + I, 27–28, A. II, 6–7; Sc. 48; Gr. 5 + 9; body silvery with nine dark crossbands; undulating streaks along rows of scales; spinous dorsal darkish. The sand drum is a tropical sand-beach species, usually from Port Aransas south. Chesapeake Bay through the Caribbean to northeast Brazil but not in the northern and eastern Gulf. Gilbert, 1966. (1 foot; 30 cm)

320. Northern kingfish; king whiting *Menticirrhus saxatilis* (Bloch and Schneider)
Gulf of Mexico specimens with D. X + I, 24–25; A. I, 8; Sc. 75–86; Gr. 5 + 7–10; dusky gray above, sometimes blackish; sides and back with distinct dark oblique blotches forming V-shaped pattern; second ray of spinous dorsal elongate. This is a rare but characteristic species known only from the inshore shelf. Fish from the Gulf of Mexico were once described as a separate species, *M. focaliger* Ginsburg, but the two forms intergrade along the Florida coast. Cape Cod to Florida, throughout the Gulf. Ginsburg, 1952a; Harding and Chittenden, 1987; Irwin, 1970. (1 foot; 30 cm)

321. Southern kingfish; sea mullet *Menticirrhus americanus* (Linnaeus)
D. X + I, 24–25; A. I, 7; P. 21–22; Sc. 80–90; body silver gray to coppery with irregular dark patches; gill cavity dusky. This common inshore and bay species is found mostly in deeper water than the Gulf kingfish. New York to Argentina. Crowe, 1984; Harding and Chittenden, 1987. (16 inches; 47 cm)

322. Gulf kingfish; Gulf whiting *Menticirrhus littoralis* (Holbrook)
D. X + I, 23–25; A. I, 7; P. 18–19; Sc. 70–74; body silvery out of the water, but mottled gray in, not blotched; gill cavity pale. The Gulf whiting is almost entirely a surf species, but the young are sometimes found in the bays, especially in shallow water. Virginia to Florida and throughout the Gulf. (1 foot; 30 cm)

323. Black drum *Pogonias cromis* (Linnaeus)
D X + I, 21; A. II, 5–6; Sc. 41–47; Gr. 4 + 12; four to five broad, dark bands on sides of body, becoming obscured in large fish, which are more uniformly dark; underside of lower jaw with numerous large barbels. The largest of the family (up to 150 pounds—68 kg), it is predominantly a bay species. Massachusetts to Argentina. Beckman et al., 1990; Fitzhugh et al., 1993; Nieland and Wilson, 1993; Saucier and Baltz, 1993; Simmons and Breuer, 1962; Wakeman et al., 1990. (3 feet; 91 cm)

324. Atlantic croaker *Micropogonias undulatus* (Linnaeus)
D. X + I, 28–29; A. II, 7; Sc. 64–72; Gr. 7 + 16; young silvery, older fish brassy yellow; middle of body with short, irregular brown streaks formed by spots on scales. This is perhaps the commonest bottom-dwelling estuarine species, with the young occurring in the

deeper parts of the bays in summer but departing in the fall. Only a few large fish live past their first year; very large croakers were formerly found off the mouth of the Mississippi but are less common today. From Mexico to Argentina it seems to be replaced by *M. furnierei* (Desmarest), which has often been confused with *M. undulatus*. It differs because of its larger scales (seven between the dorsal origin and the lateral line vs. nine in *M. undulatus*) and because its spots on the scales above the lateral line form more continuous vertical lines. Older literature places this species in the genus *Micropogon*. Massachusetts to Yucatán. Avault et al., 1969; Fruge and Truesdale, 1978; Knudsen and Herke, 1978; Suttkus, 1954. (2 feet; 61 cm)

325. Reef croaker *Odontoscion dentex* (Cuvier)
D. XI or XIII + I, 23; A. II, 8; Sc. 49–52; Gr 5 + 14; body silvery with distinct black blotch at base and in axil of pectoral fin. This rare species, known off Texas only from 7 1/2 Fathom Reef and the Flower Gardens reefs. Florida and northern Gulf to Brazil, rare in the Caribbean. (7 inches; 18 cm)

326. Spotted seatrout; speckled trout (spotted weakfish; spotted squeteague) *Cynoscion nebulosus* (Cuvier)
D. X I I, 24–26, A. II, 10–11, Sc. 66 or more; Gr. 4 + 7–9, short and thick (the longest about as long as width of pupil); mouth orange inside; body silvery, greenish above, with numerous dark spots on upper sides and on dorsal and caudal fins; young fish similarly spotted and with lanceolate caudal fin, which becomes truncate or slightly concave with growth. The spotted seatrout is an important inshore sport and commercial fish. It spawns in the bays, and the young often spend their first year in or near grass flats, where those are present. The adults are commonest in deeper areas and are sometimes found over oyster reefs. Very large "specks" are believed to feed almost exclusively on fish, mostly mullet. Because of the size of their prey, they probably feed only once or twice a week, which results in disproportionately low sport catches of these large (but most under three feet) fish. They may be more common in the Laguna Madre, where they have recently been very common and large. North Atlantic, in the west from New York to Tampico. Guest and Gunter, 1958; Hein and Shepard, 1979; Saucier and Baltz, 1993; Sundararaj and Suttkus, 1962; Wakeman and Wohlschlag, 1977. (4 feet; 1 1/4 m)

327. Sand seatrout; sand trout; white trout *Cynoscion arenarius* (Ginsburg)
D. X + I, 25–27; A. II, 11; Sc. about 60; Gr. 3–4 + 10; body silvery, greenish above, often with large, irregular dark blotches on back when viewed from above; mouth large, orange on inside. This species is a sport fish of some importance. Although it does not grow as large as *C. nebulosus*, the sand trout is a popular fish with most anglers. These fish spawn in the deeper channels of the bays or in the shallow Gulf, the young staying over muddy bottoms. They become almost entirely piscivorous (fish-eating) at a smaller size than does *C. nebulosus*. For many years this species, the common seatrout of the bays

and shallow Gulf, was confused with *C. nothus,* the silver seatrout, which is usually found farther offshore. The sand seatrout is confined to the Gulf of Mexico. Recent biochemical work suggests that it its an unspotted version of the Atlantic weakfish, *Cynoscion regalis,* which ranges to Nova Scotia. A greater mystery surrounds the discovery of two larval forms in Louisiana, differing in their pigmentation, distribution, and growth. Throughout the Gulf. Cowan et al., 1989; Ditty et al., 1991; Shlossman and Chittenden, 1982. (16 inches; 41 cm)

328. Silver seatrout *Cynoscion nothus* (Holbrook)
D. X + I, 27–29; A. II, 9; Sc. 55–58; Gr. 3 + 10, long and slender (the longest greater than diameter of eye); scales very deciduous; flesh weaker than that of other trouts; mouth orange inside. This species is usually found more offshore. During the summer it first appears at about eight fathoms; between eight and twelve fathoms it gradually replaces *C. arenarius,* and it is the only *Cynoscion* normally found in waters deeper than twelve fathoms. During the colder months silver seatrout come inshore and may even be found in the bays. New York to Florida and throughout the Gulf of Mexico. Brown-Peterson et al., 1988; DeVries and Chittenden, 1982; Ginsburg, 1931. (1 foot; 30 cm)

329. Red drum; redfish (channel bass) *Sciaenops ocellatus* (Linnaeus)
D. X + I, 24; A. II, 8; Sc. 45–50; Gr. 5 + 7; body in young silvery, becoming coppery brown or reddish in older fish; all sizes with one large black spot above lateral line at base of caudal, sometimes with additional spots located anteriorly. The redfish is one of the largest of the sciaenids and historically was the most important commercially; from a sportfishing standpoint it is probably the most highly prized croaker. The young are numerous around the mouths of passes in the spring and early summer; subadults are largely solitary fish living in quite shallow water in the bays, where they may be seen swimming about with their dorsal fins protruding from the water. Large numbers of redfish migrate to the Gulf in the fall and return in the spring. These "runs" attract large numbers of anglers, and it is during those times that larger fish are caught. The largest, the mature fish, stay offshore, where they occur in large schools during late summer–early fall spawning. Large fish are known as bull reds. Males usually mature in three years, females in five, with many fish living over two decades. Massachusetts to northern Mexico. Beckman, 1989; Beckman et al., 1989; Boothby and Avault, 1971; Holt et al., 1983; Simmons and Breuer, 1962. (5 feet; 1 1/2 m)

330. Spot; flat croaker (Lafayette) *Leiostomus xanthurus* Lacepède
D. X + I, 31; A. II, 12; Sc. 60–70; Gr. 8 + 22; body silvery, with shades of yellow during spawning season (fall); irregularly wavy lines on sides; black humeral spot; fins olivaceous except for clear caudal. The spot is a very common bay and shallow Gulf species, the young maturing in shallow bay waters and moving to deeper water as they grow. Like the croaker, most spot probably live only one year. During the spawning season this fish

is known as the golden croaker (the Atlantic croaker is also called golden croaker during this same time). Cape Cod to northern Mexico. Fruge and Truesdale, 1978; Stickney and Cuenco, 1982. (10 inches; 25 cm)

331. Star drum *Stellifer lanceolatus* (Holbrook)
D. XI + 1, 20–23; A. II, 7–8; Sc. 47–50; Gr. 13 + 22; body silvery, plain, and more rounded than in other croakers; caudal fin lanceolate at all sizes; interorbital space broad, concave. This small croaker is common in the shallow Gulf and deeper parts of the bays. It is predominantly a mud-bottom species. The center of its abundance in the northwestern Gulf is off Louisiana, and it becomes less common along the Texas coast. Virginia to Texas. (6 inches; 15 cm)

332. Banded drum; banded croaker *Larimus fasciatus* Holbrook
D. X + 1, 24–26; A. II, 5–6; Sc. 49; Gr. 12 + 24; body long, fairly deep, with 7–9 conspicuous vertical black bands on sides; mouth very oblique (greater than 45 degrees). Found in the shallow Gulf, this small croaker rarely enters the bays. It has no commercial value, but larger individuals are big enough to be a nuisance to fishermen. It is somewhat more common off Louisiana. Massachusetts to northern Mexico. (8 inches; 20 cm)

333. Silver perch *Bairdiella chrysoura* (Lacepède)
D. XI + 1, 22; A. II, 10; Sc. 52; Gr. 8 + 16; sides silvery; fins yellow. This species occurs in the saltier bays, the young often in grass beds. It rarely reaches a size large enough to warrant its exploitation as either a commercial or sport fish, but it is locally very common. New York to Mexico. (9 inches; 23 cm)

334. Cubbyu *Equetus umbrosus* Jordan and Eigenmann
D. X + 1, 38–40; A. II, 7; Sc. 45–50; Gr. 6 + 9; nearly black, with long white stripes on body (or color white with long black stripes on body and fins); dorsal fin somewhat elevated. The cubbyu is a rock-dwelling species found on the offshore reefs and rarely near the jetties. It is closely related to the reef-living high hat, *E. acuminatus,* of the Caribbean and Florida, which lacks a continuous median stripe from the first dorsal to beyond the nostrils and has a higher dorsal. This species and *E. iwamotoi* are sometimes placed in *Eques* or *Pareques*. Range uncertain. (8 inches; 20 cm)

335. Blackbar drum *Equetus iwamotoi* (Miller and Woods)
D. IX–XI, 33–40; A. II, 7–8; Sc. 47–52; Gr. 4–7 + 9–12. A dark-colored form of *Equetus,* especially in older individuals, the blackbar drum lacks the thin horizontal bars of typical *E. umbrosus* but instead has a thick bar extending in a curve from the first dorsal to the caudal, or separating into a thick bar to the venter and a thinner one to the tail, much like in other species of *Equetus*. A fish of the outer shelf, its first dorsal is about the same in

height as the cubbyu. North Carolina through the Caribbean to Brazil. Miller and Woods, 1988. (8 inches; 20 cm)

336. Jackknife fish *Equetus lanceolatus* (Linnaeus)
D. XIV–XVI + 1, 53; A. II, 5; Sc. 49–55; Gr. 9 + 12; body white with three dark stripes, each bordered with silver; first stripe nearly vertical through eye; second stripe running posteriorly from top of head above eye to base of ventral fin and onto fin; third stripe V-shaped, covering forward edge of spinous dorsal and then running from base of spinous dorsal posteriorly along midline of body and onto caudal fin. This tropical species is known from a few reefs offshore. Young of this and other *Equetus* species are similar, but apparently only the spotted drum has a spot on its snout, and only the cubbyu has several horizontal stripes. Juvenile jackknife fish are distinguished by elimination. Bermuda and South Carolina through the Caribbean to Brazil. (9 inches; 23 cm)

337. Spotted drum *Equetus punctatus* (Bloch and Schneider)
D. XI–XII + 1, 46; A. II, 6–7; Sc. 52–56; Gr. 6 + 11; body with alternating light and dark stripes running more or less vertically on anterior body and becoming horizontal on posterior; largest stripe black, running along forward edge of spinous dorsal fin and then back along midline of side to base of caudal fin; soft dorsal, anal, and caudal fins with pale spots, with young lacking the spots; spinous dorsal greatly elongate. This is another tropical reef species known rarely from offshore reefs. It is very secretive, so it may be more abundant than has been recorded. South Florida, northern Gulf, and Bahamas through the Caribbean to Hispaniola. (10 inches; 25 cm)

Mullidae

The goatfishes are unfamiliar to most people since they occur only on reefs or in the open Gulf, but one species is frequently caught by shrimpers. They are easily recognized by the two distinct dorsal fins and the two barbels on the lower jaw. (M. C. Caldwell, 1962)

1   Teeth present on upper jaw and roof of mouth; opercular spine absent 2
    Teeth absent from roof of mouth or upper jaw; opercular spine usually present 3
2   Caudal, dorsal, and anal with black bands ... dwarf goatfish, *Upeneus parvus.*
    Median fins without dark bands ... red goatfish, *Mullus auratus.*
3   Lateral yellow stripe present, sometimes faint, running from eye to tail; lateral line scales 34–39 ... yellow goatfish, *Mulloidichthys martinicus.*
    Dark blotches on sides; lateral line scales 27–31 ... spotted goatfish, *Pseudupeneus maculatus.*

338. Dwarf goatfish *Upeneus parvus* Poey
D.VII + 1, 8; A. II, 6; P. 14–16; Sc. 36–38; Gr. 24–27; body reddish orange with dark bars on dorsal, anal, and lobes of caudal; small teeth on roof of mouth often hard to locate in fresh specimens, but more easily found in preserved fish. This fish is commonly encountered in shrimpers' trawls over the inner continental shelf. North Carolina, northern Gulf of Mexico to Brazil (6 inches; 15 cm)

339. Red goatfish *Mullus auratus* Jordan and Gilbert
D.VIII (first minute) + 1, 8; A. II, 6; P. 15–17; Sc. 29–35; Gr. 18–21; body blotched with red, without other distinguishing markings, but often with light red bars on median fins. This is an uncommon form probably occurring mostly over the outer shelf. Bermuda and Nova Scotia through the Caribbean to Guyana. (9 inches; 23 cm)

340. Yellow goatfish *Mulloidichthys martinicus* (Cuvier)
D.VIII (first minute) + 1, 8; A. II, 6; P. 15–17; Sc. 34–39; Gr. 26–33; body and fins pale yellow with yellow stripes on sides. It is known only from areas around offshore reefs. Northern Gulf, Bermuda, and Florida, through the Caribbean to Brazil. (12 inches; 30 cm)

341. Spotted goatfish *Pseudupeneus maculatus* (Bloch)
D.VIII (first minute) + 1, 8; A. II, 6; P. 13–16; Sc. 27–31, Gr. 26–32; body pale with usually three blotches on sides. This is another rare offshore reef fish. New Jersey, Bermuda, and the Gulf of Mexico, through the Caribbean to Brazil. (10 inches; 25 cm)

Kyphosidae

The chubs or rudderfishes are schooling reef fishes that are seldom seen. Juveniles are sometimes associated with sargassum. The two closely related species are both capable of extensive variation in coloration and are therefore difficult to distinguish. For example, both species may display a checkered pattern. (Moore, 1962)

1 Anal rays usually 11; dorsal rays usually 12; base of pectoral dark ... Bermuda chub, *Kyphosus sectatrix.*
  Anal rays always 12 or 13; dorsal rays almost always 13 or 14; base of pectoral pale ... yellow chub, *Kyphosus incisor.*

342. Bermuda chub *Kyphosus sectatrix* (Linnaeus)
D. XI, 12 (rarely 11 or 13); A. III, 11 (rarely 10 or 12); Sc. 51–58; Gr. 6–8 + 16–18. Rarely seen despite being more of an inshore species than is *K. incisor,* this fish is found around jetties and some reefs and oil platforms. Massachusetts and Bermuda through the Caribbean to Brazil. (18 inches; 46 cm)

343. Yellow chub *Kyphosus incisor* (Cuvier)

D. XI, 13–15; A. III, 12–13; Sc. 54–62; Gr. 6–8 + 11–22. More of an offshore species, this chub tends to be more yellow in life than the Bermuda chub. It has only rarely been recorded from offshore, with one record inshore in South Texas. Its range is about the same as that of the Bermuda chub. Pezold and Edwards, 1983. (3 feet; 91 cm)

Cirrhitidae

Hawkfishes are a small family of perchlike fishes distinguished by their lower pectorals having thickened, separate rays somewhat like those of the scorpionfishes. Hawkfishes are colorful reef fishes, with only one species known in the western Atlantic. (Randall, 1963)

344. Redspotted hawkfish *Amblycirrhitus pinos* (Mowbray)

D. X, 11; A. III, 6; P. 14; Sc. 41–44; greenish, perchlike, with brownish vertical bands; large black bar on caudal peduncle; large spot under posterior soft dorsal fin; anterior body and dorsals covered with red spots. A poorly known fish from offshore reefs and wrecks, it is probably not rare but is hard to collect. Bahamas, southern Florida, northern Gulf, through the Caribbean to the Lesser Antilles and Saint Helena. Bright and Cashman, 1974; Dennis and Bright, 1988b; Sonnier et al., 1976. (3 1/2 inches; 9 cm)

Chaetodontidae

The butterflyfishes are some of the most beautiful of tropical reef fishes. All of the following species may be found offshore, but the juveniles of many species occur inshore as well. Very small juveniles differ appreciably from the adults in color and form; these differences are incorporated in the keys to the species. Formerly the angelfishes, family Pomacanthidae, were also included in this family. (Allen, 1979; Burgess, 1974; Feddern, 1972; Motta, 1989)

1   Lateral line scales fewer than 28, usually 25; snout greatly elongated; diffuse bar on head through eye and another diffuse bar along base of soft dorsal, but sides and head otherwise without distinct color pattern . . . longsnout butterflyfish, *Chaetodon aculeatus*.
     Lateral line scales more than 26, usually more than 29; snout elongated only slightly, if at all; sides of body and head usually with definite bands or spots 2
2   Dorsal spines XIII or XIV (rarely XV) 3
     Dorsal spines XII 5
3   Lateral line scales 36 or more; anal rays 18 or more; soft dorsal rays 21 or more . . . reef butterflyfish, *Chaetodon sedentarius*.

Lateral line scales 26–35, usually 29–33; anal rays 14–17; soft dorsal rays 18–20 4

4   Lateral line scales 31–35; anal rays 16–17; dorsal rays 19–20; ocellated spot on side of adults; juveniles with two ocellated spots, one on side and one on soft dorsal above first spot ... foureye butterflyfish, *Chaetodon capistratus.*

Lateral line scales 26–32, usually 29; anal rays 15, rarely 14; dorsal rays 18–19; no ocellated spot on sides of adults or juveniles; snout moderately elongated ... bank butterflyfish, *Chaetodon aya.*

5   Sides of body with four distinct stripes, juveniles also have ocellated spot at base of soft dorsal; dorsal rays usually 21 or 22 ... banded butterflyfish, *Chaetodon striatus.*

Sides of body with one or two stripes, adults with unocellated spot at base of soft dorsal; juveniles with additional spot at edge of soft dorsal; dorsal rays usually 19 to 21 ... spotfin butterflyfish, *Chaetodon ocellatus.*

345. Longsnout butterflyfish *Chaetodon aculeatus* (Poey)

D. XIII, 18–19; A. III, 14–16; Sc. 22–28; snout prolonged (43–45 percent of standard length); upper half of body yellow-orange, becoming nearly black at base of dorsal fin; lower half of body white; soft dorsal, anal, and caudal fins with black margins. This is a deep-dwelling species, more common in one hundred feet and deeper, and in our area uncommon even there. Formerly placed in the genus *Prognathodes.* North Carolina and the Bahamas through the West Indies to the Caribbean coast of South America. (3 inches; 8 cm)

346. Spotfin butterflyfish *Chaetodon ocellatus* Bloch

D. XII, 19–21; A. III, 16–18; Sc. 33–34; body silvery; median fins and caudal peduncle yellow; black spot at base of soft dorsal fin; black bar extending from origin of dorsal through eye; axil of pectoral yellow, continuing upward along opercular flap. The spotfin is the most common butterflyfish in our area. Adults occur offshore for the most part, but juveniles and occasional adults appear inshore near the jetties and occasionally in the saltier bays. New England through the Caribbean to Brazil. (6 inches; 15 cm)

347. Foureye butterflyfish *Chaetodon capistratus* Linnaeus

D. XIII, 19–20; A. III, 16–17; Sc. 31–35; single large ocellus in adults, sometimes accompanied by two broad, dusky bars on sides, but more usually sides are white with series of chevron-shaped lines; dark bar through eye. This is one of the more wide-ranging "tropical" fishes, but it is more common in the northeastern Gulf. Massachusetts through the Caribbean to northern South America. (6 inches; 15 cm)

348. Banded butterflyfish *Chaetodon striatus* Linnaeus

D. XII, 21–22; A. III, 16–18; Sc. 33–36; background silvery with five broad, black bars on body and fins; bar crossing caudal peduncle less distinct than others and sometimes interrupted. In our area this species is known so far only from offshore reefs. Tropical

Atlantic, in the west from New Jersey and Bermuda through the Caribbean to southern Brazil. (6 inches; 15 cm)

349. Bank butterflyfish *Chaetodon aya* Jordan

D. XII, 18; A. III, 14–16; Sc. 34–36; two diverging black bands mark this species distinctively. A deep-dwelling species originally named for the red snapper (then called *Lutjanus aya*) because the first specimen was collected from a snapper stomach, the bank butterflyfish is now known from the Flower Gardens reefs as well as from the shelf edge in the northeastern Gulf, and probably occurs on other, deeper reefs as well. North Carolina to Yucatán. Bright et al., 1974; Hubbs, 1963. (5 inches; 13 cm)

350. Reef butterflyfish *Chaetodon sedentarius* Poey

D. XIII (rarely XIV), 21–23; A. III, 18–19; Sc. 36–39; body silvery, with dark band through eye similar to that of other *Chaetodon* species and with diffuse black band posteriorly from dorsal to anal fin, covering caudal peduncle. It is an uncommon species in our area, with adults occurring offshore and young inshore. Florida, northern Gulf through the Caribbean to southern Brazil. (6 inches; 15 cm)

Pomacanthidae

Angelfishes are among the most attractive and conspicuous of tropical reef fishes that occur in our area. They were formerly included in the family Chaetodontidae but are distinguished from the butterflyfishes by possessing a large spine on their preopercle as well as by less obvious internal anatomical features (Allen, 1979).

1   Dorsal spines XII–XIV 2
    Dorsal spines IX–X.. 5
2   Two well-developed spines beneath eye (on preorbital bone) . . . cherubfish, *Centropyge argi.*
    Two knobby spines, or no spines at all, on preorbital bone beneath eye 3
3   Head, caudal fin, and front of body yellow, with rest of body black; upper rays of caudal fin prolonged (juveniles yellow with black spot on side which enlarges with growth to cover entire posterior half of body) . . . rock beauty, *Holacanthus tricolor.*
    Body not tricolored, caudal completely rounded 4
4   Dark spot on nape of neck surrounded by light blue ring, often with small light spots in its interior; caudal fin bright yellow; soft dorsal and anal fins tinged with blue (juveniles yellow and black with dark bar from nape through eye, narrow blue stripes on sides, and caudal fin clear yellow) . . . queen angelfish, *Holacanthus ciliaris.*
    Dark spot on nape not surrounded by light blue and without small light spots in its interior; caudal fin yellow at tips; soft dorsal and anal also yellow-tipped (juveniles colored like

H. ciliaris but with yellow on trailing edges of soft dorsal and anal fins) . . . blue angelfish, *Holacanthus bermudensis.*

5   Caudal fin rounded, without light margin in adults; dorsal spines X; juveniles with yellow margin surrounding dark central spot on caudal fin . . . French angelfish, *Pomacanthus paru.* Caudal fin truncate, with light margin in adults; dorsal spines IX; color gray; juveniles similar to *P. paru* except for yellow mid-dorsal stripe extending below lower lip onto chin and caudal fin crossed entirely by central black area . . . gray angelfish, *Pomacanthus arcuatus.*

351. Cherubfish *Centropyge argi* Woods and Kanazawa
D. XIV–XV, 15–16 (usually XIV, 16); A. III, 17; Sc. 32–34; lateral line ending beneath soft dorsal fin; lower part of head yellow, with light blue about eye and on opercle and yellow extending to base of pectoral fin; rest of body dark blue with light margins on soft dorsal and anal fins. In addition to coloration, the character of the lateral line, the spine on the preopercle, and the two free spines on the preorbital make this small chaetodontid distinct. It is an uncommon, generally deep-dwelling fish in our area. Bermuda, Florida, and the northern Gulf to Colombia and Curaçao. (2.5 inches; 6 cm)

352. Rock beauty *Holacanthus tricolor* (Bloch)
D. XIV, 17–19; A. III, 18–20; Sc. 43–46; head, lower part of body, and caudal fin yellow, rest of body black. Juveniles one inch (25 mm) long and smaller are more or less entirely yellow except for a blue-edged black spot on the side, which enlarges with growth to become a black area covering most of the posterior body, including soft dorsal and anal fins. This species is found often on the offshore reefs in the northwestern Gulf. Georgia through the Caribbean to southern Brazil. (12 inches; 30 cm)

353. Queen angelfish *Holacanthus ciliaris* (Linnaeus)
D. XIV, 19–21; A. III, 20–21; Sc. 45–49; body green with yellow on caudal peduncle and on anterior portion of caudal fin and on ventral fins; dorsal and anal fins edged with blue; opercle, base of pectoral, and underside of head blue; black spot edged with blue on nape; juveniles greenish yellow with five or six narrow, vertical blue stripes. This species is rarely encountered about rigs, reefs, and other offshore structures. It is known to hybridize with *H. bermudensis;* the hybrid has been named *H. bermudensis* or *H. townsendi.* Bahamas through the Caribbean to eastern Brazil. Feddern, 1968. (12 inches; 30 cm)

354. Blue angelfish *Holacanthus bermudensis* Goode
Meristics essentially same as those of *H. ciliaris;* body blue-gray to purple; ventral fins and trailing edges of soft dorsal, anal, and caudal fins yellow; upper edge of soft dorsal blue; pectoral fin with blue axil, yellow and blue bands distally. The most distinctive feature of adults is the large spot on the nape, which in this species is not surrounded by a lighter blue ocellus and which lacks light spots in its interior. The queen angelfish possesses both the ocellus and small light spots within the larger dark spot. This is among the most

common of our angelfishes, especially on the deeper reefs. An older name is *H. isabelita*. Bahamas through the Caribbean to Brazil (18 inches; 46 cm)

355. French angelfish *Pomacanthus paru* (Bloch)
D. X, 29–31; A. III, 22–24; adults dark purple to black with yellow on edge of each scale; mouth and tip of snout blue; juveniles black-and-yellow striped, with median yellow band on forehead that stops at upper lip. This is a fairly common species offshore, and young occur uncommonly inshore. Some old records of *P. arcuatus* probably refer to this species. Tropical Atlantic, in the west from Florida, Bahamas, and northern Gulf through the Caribbean to Brazil. (14 inches; 36 cm)

356. Gray angelfish *Pomacanthus arcuatus* (Linnaeus)
D. IX, 31–33; A. III, 23–25; body grayish brown with black spots on each scale; mouth and tip of snout white in adults; juveniles colored similarly to *P. paru* except median yellow stripe on forehead extends below lower lip onto chin. The juvenile pattern of bars persists longer in this species than in the French angelfish, with pale bars still being present even after the spotted adult coloration has been assumed. In our area the species is rare on offshore reefs. Old records of *P. aureus* refer to this species. New England through the Caribbean to southeastern Brazil. (14 inches; 36 cm)

Pomacentridae

The damselfishes are small, colorful reef fishes, with several species also appearing at saltier inshore localities. All make good aquarium fishes, although they may be somewhat pugnacious. Young of most pomacentrids may vary extensively from the color patterns found in adults. The adults themselves vary in color depending on the time of day and their mood. Additional deepwater species occur at the edge of the shelf, but those species are not well known. The beaugregory, *Pomacentrus leucostictus* Müller and Troschel, once believed likely to inhabit Gulf waters, does not seem to occur west of Florida. (Böhlke and Chaplin, 1968; Dennis and Bright, 1988b; Emery, 1973a; Emery and Burgess, 1974; Randall, 1968; Rivas, 1960; Smith-Vaniz and Emery, 1980; Thresher, 1975)

1	Teeth fixed, not movable 2
	Teeth movable; distinct notch in preorbital bone bordering upper jaw … yellowtail damselfish, *Microspathodon chrysurus*.
2	Teeth incisorlike, in single row 3
	Teeth conical, in two or three rows 9
3	Preopercle serrate; body without wide vertical bars 4
	Preopercle smooth; body with wide vertical bars 8
4	Three rows of scales on cheek between suborbital and margin of preopercle; body distinctly

bicolored, dark anteriorly, including belly, and light posteriorly ... bicolor damselfish, *Pomacentrus partitus*.

Four rows of scales on cheek (lowermost row may be reduced); body not colored as above 5

5   Profile of forehead straight or sharply angled at eye; juveniles and some adults bright yellow with black spot in dorsal fin and two other black spots in axil of pectoral and on caudal peduncle; other adults dusky, without spot on dorsal and with vertical bars ... threespot damselfish, *Pomacentrus planifrons*.

Profile of forehead convexly rounded; color variable, but not as above 6

6   Three rows of scales on opercle between margin of preopercle and opercular spine; spot on dorsal surface of caudal peduncle usually present; dusky bars on sides of body in adult ... cocoa damselfish, *Pomacentrus variabilis*

Two rows of scales on opercle between preopercle margin and spine; spot on dorsal surface of caudal peduncle may or may not be present; sides without dusky bars 7

7   Lowest row of cheek scales reduced in size, not extending to margin of preopercle; usually without a spot on caudal peduncle; most of body yellow, but upper and anterior body blue, with pearly blue spots on sides and head ... beaugregory, *Pomacentrus leucostictus*.

Lowest row of cheek scales of normal size, extending to margin of preopercle; dark spot on caudal peduncle of juveniles; most of body blue with yellow or orange on upper and anterior parts of body and head; adults more uniformly dark ... dusky damselfish, *Pomacentrus fuscus*.

8   Anal rays 12–13 ... sergeant major, *Abudefduf saxatilis*.

Anal rays 9–10 ... night sergeant, *Abudefduf taurus*.

9   Caudal fin deeply cleft, the tips pointed 10

Caudal fin not deeply cleft, the tips rounded or only slightly pointed 11

10   Body blue; no light spot on top of caudal peduncle; dorsal, anal, and caudal fins with dark margins ... blue chromis, *Chromis cyanea*.

Body pale (yellowish green) or dusky; light spot on top of caudal peduncle; dorsal margin and anal fin light; caudal margins usually dark ... brown chromis, *Chromis multilineata*.

11   Body and fins almost entirely blue or purple (uniformly brown in preservative) ... purple reeffish, *Chromis scotti*.

Body countershaded, not uniformly colored 12

12   Upper body blue (dark brown in preservative); caudal fin, posterior dorsal fin, and lower body yellow; light blue lines running from upper lip over top of eyes and along sides above lateral line (juveniles more uniformly colored blue, but with yellow fins and light blue lines) ... yellowtail reeffish, *Chromis enchrysurus*.

Upper body dark green or lime green; greenish gray or brown below; posteriormost half of caudal fin light; no blue lines on head and sides ... sunshinefish, *Chromis insolata*.

357. Yellowtail damselfish *Microspathodon chrysurus* (Cuvier)
D. XII, 14–15; A. II, 12–13; P. 20–22; Sc. 20–22; Gr. 15–20 on lower limb; adults dark green with yellow tail; young similarly colored but with more prominent metallic blue spots on sides of body. It is known from several offshore reefs. Bermuda, Florida, and the northern Gulf to Panama; also in the eastern Atlantic. Causey, 1969. (6 inches; 15 cm)

358. Bicolor damselfish *Pomacentrus partitus* Poey
D. XII, 14–17; A. II, 13–15; P. 18–20; Sc. 18–21; sharp, vertical demarcation between dark anterior parts of body and light posterior parts, with dark margins on median fins. Apparently a deeper-water species than most damselfishes, the bicolor damselfish is not rare on offshore reefs. Florida, northern Gulf, and Caribbean. Emery, 1973b. (6 inches; 15 cm)

359. Threespot damselfish; yellow damselfish *Pomacentrus planifrons* Cuvier
D. XII, 15–17; A. II, 13–14; P. 18–20; Sc. 18–20; profile steep (45 degrees) and nearly straight; young bright yellow with dark spots on soft dorsal fin, caudal peduncle, and pectoral axil; adults plainer, brownish yellow with narrow dark bars on sides. Florida and the northern Gulf through the Caribbean. Bright and Cashman, 1974. (5 inches; 13 cm)

360. Cocoa damselfish *Pomacentrus variabilis* Castelnau
D. XII, 14–17; A. II, 12–15; P. 18–21; Sc. 18–20; body yellowish with blue on upper half of head and anterior part of body and dorsal fin, reaching back to cover black spot on dorsal fin at junction of spinous and soft parts. A common fish on offshore reefs, oil platforms, and wrecks, with occasional juveniles appearing inshore, this fish has often been misidentified as the beaugregory, which we have not been able to verify from the northern Gulf. Florida, Gulf of Mexico, and Caribbean. (4 inches; 10 cm)

361. Dusky damselfish *Pomacentrus fuscus* Cuvier
D. XII, 14–17; A. II, 13–15; P. 20–22; Sc. 18–21; anal fin short, longest rays not reaching base of caudal fin or just barely reaching it (*variabilis, leucostictus,* and other species have longer anals); adults dark gray to blackish with vertical dark lines on sides of body; young (one inch long) lighter with orange-red coloration on spinous dorsal, adjacent region of back, and nape; large blue-edged black spot at base of dorsal fin near posterior spines; smaller blue-edged black spot on upper edge of caudal peduncle. This fish is the second most common *Pomacentrus* on the southern Texas jetties. It has often reported as *P. dorsopunicans* (Cuvier), and Rivas (1960) synonymized the two names, but Emery and Burgess (1974) considered them distinct. Florida and Bermuda through the Caribbean to Brazil; also in the eastern Atlantic. (2 inches; 5 cm)

362. Sergeant major *Abudefduf saxatilis* (Linnaeus)

D. XIII, 12–13; A. II, 10–12; P. 18–19, Sc. 21; relatively high-bodied and short-snouted; five distinct vertical bars on sides; background color between bars whitish or yellow. Young members of this species are often abundant near the southern Texas jetties. A year-round resident of 7 1/2 Fathom Reef, this fish may be common on other shallow reefs as well. Both sides of Atlantic and possibly conspecific with Pacific Ocean forms; Bermuda and Rhode Island through the Caribbean to Uruguay. (7 inches; 18 cm)

363. Night sergeant *Abudefduf taurus* (Müller and Troschel)

D. XIII, 11–12; A. II, 10; P. 18–19; Sc. 19–20; light brown or yellowish brown with five broad, dark brown bars on sides, with anterior bars often broader than those near tail; sixth bar on prominent black saddle on top of caudal peduncle; black spot at upper base of pectoral fin. This is a rare form so far known in our area only from the Port Aransas jetties. Elsewhere from Florida and throughout the Caribbean. (7 inches; 18 cm)

364. Blue chromis *Chromis cyanea* (Poey)

D. XII, 12; A. II, 12; P. 16–18; body shape similar to that of the brown chromis, but blue all over; upper margin of spinous dorsal and outer rays of caudal fin dark. The blue chromis is a very common fish on some offshore reefs. Florida, Bahamas, and Caribbean. Bright and Cashman, 1974. (5 inches; 13 cm)

365. Brown chromis *Chromis multilineata* (Guichenot)

D. XII, 12; A. II, 12; P. 18–20; moderately elongate, with deeply forked tail, brownish overall with light (yellow) edges of dorsal and tips of caudal fin and distinctive light spot on top of caudal peduncle. This is another species so far known only from offshore reefs. Florida, Bermuda, and through the Caribbean. Briggs et al., 1964; Bright and Cashman, 1974. (5 inches; 13 cm)

366. Purple reeffish *Chromis scotti* Emery

D. XIII, 12; A. II, 12; P. 17–19 (usually 18), body and fins (except clear pectoral) uniformly blue, sometimes lighter on belly, with bright pearly blue spots on head. Florida and Gulf of Mexico to Curaçao and Colombia. Bright and Cashman, 1974; Hensley and Smith, 1977. (3 inches; 8 cm)

367. Yellowtail reeffish *Chromis enchrysurus* Jordan and Gilbert

D. XIII, 11–13 (usually 12); A. II, 12; upper body dark gray, lower body light gray, with raised light blue line from lip over upper eye and along side above lateral line; distal half of anal, soft dorsal, and caudal fins yellow. This is a deeper-dwelling species than most damselfish. In our previous edition the plate identified as a yellowtail was actually a sunshinefish. North Carolina through the Caribbean to Brazil. Emery and Smith-Vaniz, 1982. (4 inches; 10 cm)

368. Sunshinefish *Chromis insolata* (Cuvier)

D. XII, 12; A. II, 12; P 17; short-bodied, lacking deeply cleft tail and dark outer margins of caudal fin found in some other species of *Chromis* treated here; upper parts bright green; lower parts olive green; large fish olive colored overall. This is a little-known species, known in this area only from Stetson Reef and a few deeper reefs. It is apparently a deeper-water species in most of its range. Older records of *C. insolata* may refer to the recently described *C. scotti.* Florida and northern Gulf through the Caribbean to Brazil. Briggs et al., 1964. (5 inches; 13 cm)

Labridae

The wrasses are an abundant family of tropical and temperate fishes related to the parrotfishes, from which they differ by having individual teeth not fused into a beak. Two temperate species occurring on the Atlantic Coast, usually north of Cape Hatteras, are the tautog or blackfish, *Tautoga onitis,* and the cunner, *Tautogolabrus adspersus.* Gulf of Mexico and southeastern Atlantic Coast species are primarily tropical. It is still uncertain how many species occur in the northwestern Gulf of Mexico, but the following have been recorded. (Böhlke and Chaplin, 1968, 1993; Briggs et al., 1964; Bright and Cashman, 1974; Causey, 1969; Dennis and Bright, 1988b; Hildebrand and Schroeder, 1928; Randall, 1968; Randall and Böhlke, 1965; Sonnier et al., 1976)

1   Dorsal spines XI–XIV 2
    Dorsal spines VIII or IX 6
2   Dorsal spines XIV, the first three extending distally as filaments . . . hogfish, *Lachnolaimus maximus.*
    Dorsal spines XI or XII, rarely XIII; no filaments 3
3   Posterior canines present; anterior canines large 4
    Posterior canines absent; anterior canines small; upper body purple; lower body pale, with small amount of yellow . . . Creole wrasse, *Clepticus parrae.*
4   Soft dorsal and anal with scaly bases... 5
    Soft dorsal and anal without scaly bases; body pink with red spots or blotches . . . red hogfish, *Decodon puellaris.*
5   Back bluish or purple; remainder of body yellow; no produced rays on fins; gill rakers 15–16 on first arch . . . spotfin hogfish, *Bodianus pulchellus.*
    Back reddish anteriorly; rest of body yellow; soft dorsal, anal, and outer caudal rays produced; gill rakers 17–19 on first arch . . . Spanish hogfish, *Bodianus rufus.*
6   Lateral line complete; body oval or rounded in cross section 7
    Lateral line interrupted posteriorly; body flattened laterally . . . pearly razorfish, *Hemipteronotus novacula.*

7   Dorsal spines VIII; no posterior canines present ... bluehead, *Thalassoma bifasciatum*.
     Dorsal spines IX; posterior canines present 8
8   Gill rakers 21–23; depth of body 28–37 percent of standard length; head with narrow dark
     (blue) bands radiating from eye; small black spot at upper pectoral fin base and four or five
     broad dark bands on sides (small specimens with a black spot above midline at caudal
     peduncle) ... puddingwife, *Halichoeres radiatus*.
     Gill rakers 15–20; depth of body 22–30 percent of standard length; color variable, but not as
     above 9
9   Anterior lateral line scales with more than one pore (usually three or more) per scale;
     caudal fin rounded 10
     Anterior lateral line scales with single pore; caudal fin double emarginate in large adults ...
     painted wrasse, *Halichoeres caudalis*.
10   Two lengthwise dark stripes on side of body; pale-edged dark spot near edge of opercle
     (within upper stripe); small black spot at rear base of dorsal fin ... slippery dick, *Halichoeres
     bivittatus*.
     Single broad black band down sides, disappearing in larger fish; two dark wavy lines radiating
     from eye ... yellowhead wrasse, *Halichoeres garnoti*.

369. Hogfish *Lachnolaimus maximus* (Walbaum)

D. XIV, 11; A. III, 10; first three spines of dorsal filamentous; body red with dark spot at
base of soft dorsal; outer margins of soft dorsal, anal, and caudal fins with dark bars;
mature males with long snout. This rare fish is known so far only from offshore reefs in
deep water. Bermuda and North Carolina through the Caribbean to Columbia. Gunter,
1944. (3 feet; 91 cm)

370. Creole wrasse *Clepticus parrae* (Bloch and Schneider)

D. XII, 10; A. III, 12–13; body and fins mostly purple. This wrasse is apparently common on
offshore reefs. Bermuda and Florida through the West Indies. (1 foot; 30 cm)

371. Red hogfish *Decodon puellaris* (Poey)

D. XI, 10; A. III, 10; Sc. 30; body pink to light red, with deeper red blotches. This colorful fish
is deepest-dwelling wrasse known from our area. It is apparently common in waters
deeper than about fifty fathoms. Bermuda and North Carolina through the Caribbean
to Brazil. (15 inches; 38 cm)

372. Spotfin hogfish *Bodianus pulchellus* (Poey)

D. XI–XII, 9–10; A. III, 11–13; Gr. 15–16; soft dorsal, anal, and outer caudal rays only
slightly if at all produced; back bluish, usually purple; remainder of body yellow. This
species occurs on offshore reefs, but only rarely. Atlantic Ocean, in the west from Bermuda, Florida, and the northern Gulf throughout the Caribbean to Brazil. (2 feet; 61 cm)

373. Spanish hogfish *Bodianus rufus* (Linnaeus)
D. XI–XII, 9–11 (usually XII, 10); A. III, 11–13 (12); Gr. 17–19; soft dorsal and anal fins as well as outer rays of caudal produced; body red anteriorly and dorsally, becoming yellow ventrally and posteriorly; spinous dorsal, ventral, and anal fins purple. This species is common on offshore reefs in fairly deep water. Bermuda, South Carolina, and the northern Gulf through the Caribbean to Ascension Island. (1 foot; 30 cm)

374. Pearly razorfish *Hemipteronotus novacula* (Linnaeus)
D. IX, 12; A. III, 12; lateral line interrupted posteriorly; body light pink to yellow, with red and green on median fins; anterior profile nearly vertical. This laterally flattened wrasse has the remarkable ability to dive sideways into the sand. It is probably common where coarse sand occurs and is more common in the northeastern Gulf. Atlantic Ocean, in the west from South Carolina through the Caribbean to Brazil. Chittenden and Moore, 1977. (9 inches; 23 cm)

375. Bluehead *Thalassoma bifasciatum* (Bloch)
D. VIII, 12–13; A. III, 10–11; males with blue head and green body separated by two black stripes; females, some males, and young yellow with broad longitudinal black stripe. This is a common wrasse on offshore reefs. Tropical Atlantic; Bermuda, Bahamas, Florida, and the northern Gulf of Mexico through the Caribbean to Colombia. (6 inches; 15 cm)

376. Puddingwife *Halichoeres radiatus* (Linnaeus)
D. IX, 11; A. III, 12; Gr. 7–8 + 13–16; depth of body 28–37 percent of standard length; caudal fin truncate; anterior lateral line scales with three or more pores per scale; background brownish with dark streaks radiating from eye and four or five dark bands on side of body, most distinct near base of dorsal fin; small dark spot at upper base of pectoral fin; young with prominent spot at base of caudal fin. This is the largest species of *Halichoeres* (the others rarely exceed eight inches, or about 200 mm). North Carolina and Bermuda through the Caribbean to Brazil. Hildebrand et al., 1964. (20 inches; 51 cm)

377. Painted wrasse (eared wrasse) *Halichoeres caudalis* (Poey)
D. IX, 11; A. III, 12; Gr. 6–7 + 11–13; anterior lateral line scales with only single pore per scale; caudal fin emarginate; body without distinct dark markings except for dark spots behind each eye and rather diffuse dark area at base of caudal fin. This species is very similar to *H. poeyi*, which is found on Caribbean reefs, but it appears to be restricted to continental tropical America. North Carolina to Brazil. (7 inches; 18 cm)

378. Slippery dick *Halichoeres bivittatus* (Bloch)
D. IX, 11; A. III, 12; Gr. 5–7 + 9–14; anterior lateral line scales with more than one pore (usually four or five) per scale; caudal fin rounded; body with two longitudinal stripes

sometimes broken into spots; greenish above and below these stripes, white between. This is probably the most common inshore member of the genus in the northern Gulf. Bermuda and North Carolina through the Caribbean to Brazil. Causey, 1969; Springer and Hoese, 1958. (9 inches; 23 cm)

379. Yellowhead wrasse (variegated wrasse) *Halichoeres garnoti* (Valenciennes)

D. IX, 11; A. III, 12; Gr. 4–7 + 8–14; depth of body usually less than 30 percent of standard length; caudal fin rounded, anterior lateral line scales with more than one pore per scale; juveniles yellow with single dark blue stripe down middle of side (appearing as two closely spaced narrow stripes in preserved specimens); older fish with characteristic diagonal wavy lines running back from eye and yellowish brown dorsally and lighter ventrally; large adult males yellowish with large black blotch or bar about halfway along side and wavy lines behind eye. Bermuda, Florida, and northern Gulf through the Caribbean to Brazil. (6 inches; 15 cm)

Scaridae

Parrotfishes are members of the tropical reef fish community. One species is known from inshore waters in Texas and two from such habitats in the Florida panhandle; the others are known only from the offshore reefs such as the Flower Gardens. Parrotfishes are almost strictly coral reef fishes, with a few in grass beds; their parrotlike beaks (teeth joined only at the base in *Cryptotomus* and *Nicholsina*) are used to break coral apart to reach attached animals. They are highly colorful, and the sexes often look quite different. For identification of small parrotfishes (less than four inches or 100 mm long) and species not included, see Böhlke and Chaplin, 1968, 1993, and Humann, 1994. Two species are rarely known from deeper water of the Flower Garden: the redband parrotfish, *Sparisoma aurofrenatum* (Valenciennes), and the greenblotch parrotfish, *S. atomarium* (Poey). (Böhlke and Chaplin, 1968, 1993; Dennis and Bright, 1988a, b; Randall, 1968)

1 Teeth fused; lower plate overlaps upper 2
   Teeth separated except at base; neither jaw overlaps . . . emerald parrotfish, *Nicholsina usta*.
2 Three or four rows of scales present below eye; front edge of dental plate of lower jaw inside that of upper jaw when mouth is closed 3
   Single row of scales below eye; front edge of dental plate of lower jaw outside that of upper jaw when mouth is closed 4
3 Four rows of scales below eye . . . queen parrotfish, *Scarus vetula*.
   Three rows of scales below eye . . . princess parrotfish, *Scarus taeniopterus*.
4 Fleshy flap on anterior nostril ribbonlike . . . bucktooth parrotfish, *Sparisoma radians*.

Fleshy flap on anterior nostril incised, with several lobes 5

5　Saddle-shaped white area behind dorsal fin; horizontally elongate white bar on operculum
   ... redband parrotfish, *Sparisoma aurofrenatum.*

   No saddle-shaped area behind dorsal; no white bar on opercle . . . stoplight parrotfish,
   Sparisoma viride.

380. Queen parrotfish *Scarus vetula* Schneider
D. IX, 10; A. III, 9; P. 14; males predominantly green, with yellow and blue streaks on fins
and head; females overall drab purplish green, with white streak on side. This large parrotfish
is quite common over most of the tropical coral reef areas of the western Atlantic.
Bahamas, Bermuda, and the northern Gulf through the Caribbean to Colombia. Bright
and Cashman, 1974. (2 feet; 61 cm)

381. Princess parrotfish *Scarus taeniopterus* Desmarest
D. IX, 10; A. III, 9; P. 12; much more highly colored than *S. vetula;* females tan, with three
dark, longitudinal stripes; males in two color phases, with blues and oranges predominating. This fish is easily confused with the striped parrotfish, *S. croicensis* Bloch, which in our
area may occur along with the princess. Bermuda, Bahamas, and northern Gulf, southern
range in Caribbean uncertain. (1 foot; 30 cm)

382. Bucktooth parrotfish *Sparisoma radians* (Valenciennes)
D. IX, 10; A. III, 9; Gr. 10–13; light-colored, with numerous speckles on sides but no
distinct color pattern; males with black edges on caudal and anal fins and black pectoral
axil; drab olivaceous color phase is also known. This is the smallest parrotfish in our area,
both sexes maturing at about three inches (75 mm). It is known from inshore and bay
waters of Texas and is more common in Florida turtlegrass beds. Tropical Atlantic, in the
west from Bermuda, Bahamas, and northern Gulf through the Caribbean to Brazil. Leary,
1956; Springer and Hoese, 1958. (8 inches; 20 cm)

383. Redband parrotfish *Sparisoma aurofrenatum* (Valenciennes)
D. IX, 10; A. III, 9; Gr. 11–16; white spot behind dorsal fin; general coloration mottled
brown, orange, white, and greenish. Tropical Atlantic, in the west from Bermuda, Bahamas, and the northern Gulf through the Caribbean to Brazil. Bright and Cashman, 1974;
Sonnier et al., 1976. (11 inches; 28 cm)

384. Stoplight parrotfish *Sparisoma viride* (Bonnaterre)
D. IX, 10; A. III, 9; Gr. 17–21; females reddish drab; males with blue and yellow streaks on
head and fins. This is a rare species known from offshore reefs. Bermuda, Bahamas,
southern Florida, and northern Gulf through the Caribbean to Brazil. (21 inches; 53 cm)

385. Emerald parrotfish *Nicholsina usta* (Valenciennes)
Teeth separated except at base. This species is distinguished from the closely related slender parrotfish, *Cryptotomus roseus* Cope, by the presence in emerald parrotfish of a cirrus on the nostril. New Jersey to Brazil, West Indies but not Bahamas; northern Gulf at least in the Florida panhandle. (10 inches; 40 cm)

Uranoscopidae

Stargazers are burrowing fishes with electric organs capable of delivering a mild shock. Their eyes are set directly on top of the head. Two species of stargazers are found inside one hundred fathoms. A third species, the freckled stargazer, *Gnathagnus egregius* (plate 387a), with winglike projections from the lower edge of the opercular membrane, occurs near the edge of the continental shelf. Juvenile stargazers have considerably larger heads relative to body size than do adults and have several projecting skull bones, unlike adults. (Berry and Anderson, 1961)

> Spinous dorsal fin present ... southern stargazer, *Astroscopus y-graecum*.
> Spinous dorsal fin absent ... lancer stargazer, *Kathetostoma albigutta*.

386. Southern stargazer *Astroscopus y-graecum* (Cuvier)
D. IV + I, 12–13; A. 13; Sc. 80; body blue-gray or brown with numerous white spots on back and upper sides; prominent dark bars on caudal, soft dorsal, and pectoral fins. Bones on top of the head form a Y (hence the name), and the naked area on top of head is the site of the electric organs. North Carolina to Brazil. (17 inches; 43 cm)

387. Lancer stargazer *Kathetostoma albigutta* (Bean)
D. 10; A. 12; upper body light brown with minute dark spots; dorsal, caudal, and anal fins with dark blotches. A deeper-living species than the southern stargazer, the lancer stargazer is caught from the middle to the outer shelf. North Carolina to Florida Keys and throughout the Gulf. (10 inches; 25 cm)

Dactyloscopidae

Sand stargazers resemble and are closely related to the stargazers proper (Uranoscopidae), also having eyes on top of the head, but sand stargazers have three instead of five ventral fin rays and more rounded instead of squarish bodies. They are tropical, replacing the uranoscopids in coral reef environments. A deepwater species, the masked stargazer, *Gillellus healae* Dawson, is known from off the northeastern Gulf and South Carolina. (Dawson, 1982a; Moe and Martin, 1965; Yerger, 1961)

388. Speckled stargazer *Dactyloscopus moorei* (Fowler)

D. IX–XIII, 26–30; A. 30–34; Sc. 43–47. This is a tropical species rarely taken in the Gulf but more common in Florida; there is one record for Port Aransas. Sand-colored, with speckles forming lines down the scale rows, it burrows into the bottom in shallow water near beaches out to 35 meters in places. North Carolina to Key West and Cape Sable to Corpus Christi. (3 inches; 8 cm)

Chaenopsidae

The chaenospid blennies are small, tropical fishes that associate with benthic organisms, shells, and stony corals. They are not well known in the area. (Butter et al., 1980; Greenfield and Johnson, 1981)

> Dorsal spines XXI; snout short and blunt ... sailfin blenny, *Emblemaria pandionis*.
> Dorsal spines XXII; snout pointed ... banner blenny, *Emblemaria atlantica*.

389. Sailfin blenny *Emblemaria pandionis* Evermann and Marsh

D. XXI, 15–16; A. II, 22–24; P. 13; snout short and blunt, anterior dorsal fin greatly elevated in males, less so in females; supraorbital cirrus with three branches. In the northwestern Gulf this blenny is known only from the West Flower Gardens Reef. Northern Gulf, Florida, Bahamas, and Caribbean. Bright and Cashman, 1974; Shipp, 1975; Stephens, 1963, 1970. (2 inches; 5 cm)

390. Banner blenny *Emblemaria atlantica* Jordan and Evermann

D. XXII, 15; A. II, 22; P. 14; snout pointed. Known in our area from the Flower Gardens, this is a rare species originally found in the stomach of a snapper. Bermuda, Georgia, and Bahamas to the northern Gulf. Dennis and Bright, 1988a. (2 inches; 5 cm)

Labrisomidae

The labrisomids are tropical fishes set apart from the Blenniidae by the possession of fixed conical teeth. They are sometimes included with the Chaenopsidae in the family Clinidae. Some species are the largest of the blennies. (Dennis and Bright, 1988b)

> First two anal spines detached from fin; orbital cirrus single ... checkered blenny, *Starksia ocellata*.
> First two anal spines attached to fin; orbital cirri numerous ... hairy blenny, *Labrisomus nuchipinnis*.

391. Checkered blenny *Starksia ocellata* (Steindachner)

D. XX–XXII, 7–9; A. II, 16–19; sides of body mottled; ocellated brownish spots as large as eye on head; free anal spines in males serving as intromittent organ. In the northwestern Gulf this blenny is known only from West Flower Gardens Reef. North Carolina through the Caribbean to Brazil. Böhlke and Springer, 1961; Bright and Cashman, 1974; Gilbert, 1971. (2 inches; 5 cm)

392. Hairy blenny *Labrisomus nuchipinnis* (Quoy and Gaimard)

D. XVIII, 12–13; A. II, 17–19; body plain or banded, with prominent black ocellated spot on opercle and dark spot on anterior dorsal fin. This species is abundant on the southern Texas jetties and is occasionally caught by anglers. Both sides of the Atlantic, in the west from Bermuda, Florida, and the northern Gulf of Mexico through the Caribbean to Brazil. Springer, 1958. (8 inches; 20 cm)

Blenniidae

The combtooth blennies are small, personable fishes that live in and around rocks, reefs, and other hard substrates. While the inshore species are fairly well known, the offshore species, although common, include many little-known tropical forms. The distribution and structure of hairlike cirri on the head and nape are important taxonomic features. (Böhlke and Chaplin, 1993; Dennis and Bright, 1988a, b)

1 Branchiostegal membranes not fused to body but forming well-developed fold beneath which probe may be inserted 2

   Branchiostegal membranes fused to body at sides or in ridge across breast; in any case, no distinct fold 4

2 Upper lip smooth 3

   Upper lip with lobes or papillae . . . redlip blenny, *Ophioblennius atlanticus.*

3 Median rows of cirri on raised fleshy ridge between dorsal fin and eye . . . molly miller, *Scartella cristata.*

   No cirri on head between dorsal in origin and posterior margin of eye . . . seaweed blenny, *Parablennius marmoreus.*

4 Pectoral rays usually 12; interorbital flat; anterior lateral line pores simple; no posterior canines in jaws 5

   Pectoral rays usually 14; interorbital concave; anterior lateral line pores paired; canines may be present posteriorly in jaws of males 6

5 Snout long and relatively pointed; teeth in lower jaw slender, pointed, and usually recurved . . . striped blenny, *Chasmodes bosquianus.*

   Snout short and rounded, teeth in lower jaw short, bluntly rounded, and at most only slightly recurved . . . Florida blenny, *Chasmodes saburrae.*

6　Canine teeth posterior in one or both jaws 7

No canine teeth posterior in either jaw 8

7　Dorsal with 26 or 27 total elements (spines plus rays); anal with 20 total elements ... crested blenny, *Hypleurochilus geminatus.*

Dorsal with 25 total elements; anal with 16 total elements ... barred blenny, *Hypleurochilus bermudensis.*

8　Segmented dorsal fin rays 11–12; pectoral with numerous orange spots . . . tessellated blenny, *Hypsoblennius invemar.*

Segmented dorsal fin rays 13; no pectoral spots 9

9　Orbital cirrus featherlike, with numerous branches between base and tip; lower lip linear in lateral view ... feather blenny, *Hypsoblennius hentz.*

Orbital cirrus with only terminal branch, and sometimes second branch at base; lower lip semicircular in lateral view ... freckled blenny, *Hypsoblennius ionthas.*

393. Molly miller *Scartella cristata* (Linnaeus)

D. XII, 14–15; A. II, 16–17; numerous cirri, often in distinct rows between orbital and base of dorsal fin; color variable, in southern Texas usually plain brownish gray to purple with reddish cirri. This fish is a common blenny on the southern Texas and western Florida jetties. It is basically herbivorous, but larger individuals may take bait. Earlier works referred to this species as *Blennius cristatus*. Tropical Atlantic, in the west from Florida, Bermuda, and the northern Gulf through the Caribbean to Brazil. (4 inches; 10 cm)

394. Seaweed blenny *Parablennius marmoreus* (Poey)

D. XII, 17–18; A. II, 19–20; cirri clustered above orbit, none on nape; dark above, light below, often with dark spot between first and second dorsal spines. Juveniles may be entirely yellow. Apparently a resident population exists on 7 1/2 Fathom Reef and this blenny is known from several oil platforms. Earlier works referred this species to the genus *Blennius*. New York through the Caribbean to Venezuela. Briggs et al., 1964; Causey, 1969; Rauch, 1995. (3 inches; 8 cm)

395. Redlip blenny *Ophioblennius atlanticus* (Valenciennes)

D. XII, 19–21; A. II, 20–21; lateral line interrupted about middle of body; single large cirrus (tentacle) above each eye, cluster of cirri above nostril (before eye), and isolated cirrus to either side of dorsal origin; body brownish; median fins dark with light borders (orange, pink, or red in life). In the western Gulf the redlip blenny is known only from offshore reefs, except for one old record from Freeport jetties. North Carolina through the Caribbean to Brazil; also in the eastern Atlantic and eastern Pacific. Baughman, 1950b; Bright and Cashman, 1974. (4 1/2 inches; 11 cm)

396. Striped blenny *Chasmodes bosquianus* (Lacepède)

D XI, 17–19; A. II, 18–19; teeth in lower jaw slender, pointed, and recurved; snout rather long and pointed; maxillary reaching center of eye; sides of body and dorsal and anal fins striped; females variously mottled; dorsal fin of males blue anteriorly. This is a common species, especially on grass flats. New York to northeast Florida and in the Gulf from Pensacola to Veracruz. Absent from most of Florida (see Florida blenny, *C. saburrae*). Springer, 1959b; Williams, 1983. (3 inches; 8 cm)

397. Florida blenny *Chasmodes saburrae* Jordan and Gilbert

D. XI, 17–19; A. II, 18–19; teeth in lower jaw stout, rounded, and never recurved; snout rather blunt and rounded; maxillary reaching front of eye; coloration duller than that of the striped blenny. The Florida blenny is found from northeastern Florida to the Chandeleur Islands, primarily on grass flats; it occurs together with *C. bosquianus* only in the north-central Gulf from Alabama to the Chandeleurs. Springer, 1959; Williams 1983. (3 inches; 8 cm)

398. Crested blenny *Hypleurochilus geminatus* (Wood)

D. XI, 15 to XIII, 14 (26 or 27 total rays); A. II, 18 (20 elements); body brown, usually with four quadrate blotches on sides, these often with white centers; anterior dorsal fin dark, supraorbital cirrus long in males, short in females, but usually with a cluster of four or five smaller cirri at base. This is the commonest blenny on the southern Texas jetties and oil platforms and in the shallow Gulf and saltier bays. North Carolina to Brazil. (3 inches; 8 cm)

399. Barred blenny *Hypleurochilus bermudensis* Beebe and Tee-Van

D XII, 13 (25 total elements); A. II, 14 (16 total elements); appearance rather like that of crested blenny, except anterior dorsal fin never dark and supraorbital cirrus usually shorter. In our area this blenny is known only from the West Flower Gardens Reef, but it may occur on other offshore reefs as well. Bermuda, Florida, and the northern Gulf. Bright and Cashman, 1974. (3 inches; 8 cm)

400. Feather blenny *Hypsoblennius hentz* (Lesueur)

D. XII, 15; A. II, 16; jaws without canines; sides of body brownish olive, with a few scattered dark spots on head; supraorbital cirrus featherlike. This species apparently prefers a softer, muddy-bottomed habitat (but may be found on oyster reefs and grass flats) with higher salinities. It is more common off southern Texas than off eastern Texas or Louisiana. Nova Scotia through Florida to Texas and Yucatán. Hubbs, 1939; Smith-Vaniz, 1980. (4 inches; 10 cm)

401. Freckled blenny *Hypsoblennius ionthas* (Jordan and Gilbert)
D. XII, 15; A. II, 16; similar in appearance to *H. hentz* except spots on head usually more distinct and series of dark lines between eye and mouth. This little-studied species appears to prefer harder bottoms and lower salinities, although it has been taken in the Gulf. North Carolina to north Florida and across the northern Gulf to Mexico. The photo identified as a freckled blenny in our previous edition was a feather blenny. Hubbs, 1939; Smith-Vaniz, 1980. (4 inches; 10 cm)

402. Tessellated blenny *Hypsoblennius invemar* Smith-Vaniz and Acero
D. XI–XII, 12–13; A. II, 13–14. Possibly a recent introduction, this blenny lives in Mediterranean barnacle shells at the surface of oil platforms from off Cameron to South Texas. It can be easily distinguished from other blennies by the numerous and brilliant orange spots on the head. Range uncertain, at least Louisiana and Lesser Antilles to Venezuela. (2 inches; 5 cm)

Gobiesocidae

Clingfishes are a group of small, bottom-dwelling fishes often called skilletfishes because of their large, flat heads and slender bodies. They have a complicated sucker composed jointly of the pectoral and ventral fins and underside of the body. Only one species is common inshore. *Gobiesox punctulatus* (Poey) has been doubtfully reported from South Texas but not verified, and other species may be expected to occur on offshore reefs. *G. punctulatus* typically has fewer pectoral rays (19–21; modally 20) than *G. strumosus*. (Johnson and Greenfield, 1983)

403. Skilletfish *Gobiesox strumosus* Cope
D. 10–13; A. 9–11; P. 22–26; C. 11–13; body usually plain, sometimes with longitudinal streaks; vertical fins dark, often black; pectoral fins lighter than vertical fins; upper lip and head with well-developed papilla. This fish occupies oyster reefs and other protected habitats, frequently laying its eggs in attached oyster shells. It is little studied but occurs in a wide range of salinities. New Jersey to Brazil. Briggs, 1955; Johnson and Greenfield, 1983. (3 inches; 8 cm)

Eleotridae

The sleepers are quiet, euryhaline fishes usually found in very low salinities near the coast. All are poorly known. The sleepers are often separated from the gobies proper since the gobies have a sucking disc made from the fused pelvic fins whereas sleepers have normal, separated fins. The two groups are sometimes combined because there are intermediates with partially fused pelvics (see blue and spotted gobies). Sleepers are secretive but make good aquarium subjects.

1 Fewer than 40 scale rows; maxillary reaches anterior orbit ... fat sleeper, *Dormitator maculatus*. More than 50 scale rows; maxillary reaches back of pupil 2

2 Vomer with teeth; no spine on preopercle ... bigmouth sleeper, *Gobiomorus dormitor*. Vomer without teeth; preopercle may have a ventrally directed spine 3

3 About 100 scale rows; all scales cycloid; dorsal VI + 12 .... emerald sleeper, *Erotelis smaragdus*. About 50–70 scale rows; posterior scales ctenoid; dorsal VI + 9 . . . spinycheek sleeper, *Eleotris pisonis*.

404. Fat sleeper *Dormitator maculatus* (Bloch)

D. VII + 9; A. 10; P. 14; Sc. 33–36; body depth about 25 percent of standard length; brown or tan, paler ventrally, each scale with cluster of brown melanophores; younger fish with eight to ten broad bars on sides. Moderately common in marshes and ponds of upper estuaries and known to bury. North Carolina and Bahamas through the Caribbean to Brazil. (10 inches; 25 cm)

405. Bigmouth sleeper *Gobiomorus dormitor* Lacepède

D. VI + 10; A. 10; Sc. 55–57; dark brown or olive sides interrupted by dark lateral band from under base of pectoral to base of caudal. Known in our area only from southern Texas, where it is common in the Rio Grande and in the Nueces, but known as far north as the Aransas River. Southern Florida and southern Texas to the Guianas. (2 feet; 61 cm)

406. Emerald sleeper *Erotelis smaragdus* (Valenciennes)

D. VI + 12; A. 10; P. 17; Sc. about 100; depth of body about 12 per cent of standard length; brown above, tan below, median fins light tan with traces of brown lines. Rare in the area, this fish is known only in scattered localities from Grand Isle to Port Isabel. Bahamas, Florida, and northern Gulf through the Caribbean to Brazil. (6 inches; 15 cm)

407. Spinycheek sleeper *Eleotris pisonis* (Gmelin)

D. VI + 9; A. 9; P. 17; Sc. 56–60; depth about 22 percent of standard length; brown, frequently with darker brown lines radiating from eyes. This sleeper is restricted to low-salinity areas and is known from fresh water. Its coloration is variable depending on background and illumination, but it has a light dorsal area and a spot at the upper pectoral base. The preopercular spine is not always developed. Bermuda and South Carolina to Brazil. (8 inches; 20 cm)

Gobiidae

Gobies are usually small, secretive fishes that are very common in certain habitats, although they either hide so well or have such protective coloration that the average coastal resident rarely sees one. Gobies often enter into symbiotic relationships with other animals and some are fairly tightly restricted to certain habitats. Although most species are cryptically colored to match their backgrounds, the fins of the males are often strikingly flashy during the breeding season. Reef gobies are usually more colorful than their estuarine relatives.

Several rarely seen species of highly colored tropical gobies—including the neon goby, *Gobiosoma oceanops,* and members of *Lythrypnus, Quisquilius,* and *Gnatholepis*—occur on offshore reefs (Rezak et al., 1985). Even more species are known in the eastern Gulf (Gilbert, 1977). The river goby, *Awaous tajasica,* is known rarely from the Rio Grande. It has distinctive flaps on the shoulder girdle extending into the gill chamber. (Baird, 1965; Bright and Cashman, 1974; Dawson, 1966d, 1969; Gilbert and Randall, 1979; Ginsburg, 1932, 1933)

1   Ventral fin joined only by a small membrane at base 2
      Ventral fin completely joined 3

2   More than 100 scale rows . . . blue goby, *loglossus calliurus.*
      Fewer than 100 scale rows . . . spotted goby, *Coryphopterus punctipectophorus.*

3   Dorsal fins continuous and connected; body very long and slender; standard length more than seven times as long as greatest depth . . . violet goby, *Gobioides broussoneti.*
      Dorsal fins separate; body stout and robust; standard length less than seven times maximum depth 4

4   Upper pectoral rays free; tongue notched . . . frillfin goby, *Bathygobius soporator.*
      Upper pectoral rays united; tongue indented but not notched 5

5   Body without scales, except possibly two small scales at base of caudal fin 6
      Body mostly covered by scales 9

6   Body with colored horizontal stripe . . . neon goby, *Gobiosoma oceanops.*
      Body stripes vertical 7

7   Two small ctenoid scales at base of caudal fin; seven or eight dark bars on sides . . . twoscale goby, *Gobiosoma longipala.*
      No scales at base of tail, more than eight vertical bars on sides, although some may be interrupted 8

8   Body bars mostly interrupted, almost splotched; dorsal VII + 12; pelvic fin reaching to anus . . . code goby, *Gobiosoma robustum.*
      Body bars not interrupted; dorsal VII + 13; pelvic fins not reaching one-half distance to anal fin origin . . . naked goby, *Gobiosoma bosc.*

9   Second dorsal rays 15–16; anal 16–17 10
      Second dorsal rays 11–14; anal 12–15 11

10   Body spotted with large blotches; 22 pectoral rays; outer teeth enlarged ... clown goby, *Microgobius gulosus*.

　　　Body dusky, without blotches; 21 pectoral rays; outer teeth same size as inner ... green goby, *Microgobius thalassinus*.

11   Dorsal spines VII; pectoral rays 22; scales deciduous ... ragged goby, *Bollmannia communis*.

　　　Dorsal spines VI; pectoral rays 16–19 12

12   Tusklike recurved canine on lower jaw projects outside of closed mouth ... blackfin goby, *Gobionellus claytoni*.

　　　No recurved canine as above 13

13   Patch of scales on upper margin of opercle 14

　　　No patch of scales on opercle 15

14   Fewer than 50 scales rows; eye more than one-half upper jaw length ... lyre goby, *Evorthodus lyricus*.

　　　More than 60 scale rows; eye less than one-half upper jaw length ... highfin goby, *Gobionellus oceanicus*.

15   Dorsal rays 12; anal rays 13; lateral line scales 35–40; horizontal bar on cheek ... freshwater goby, *Gobionellus shufeldti*.

　　　Dorsal rays 11; anal rays 12, lateral line scales 29– 33; large dark spot on body above opercle ... darter goby, *Gobionellus boleosoma*.

408. Blue goby *Ioglossus calliurus* Bean
D. VI + 22–24; A. 22–24; Sc. 100+ (120–160); body tan in preservative, bluish in life, densely spotted; fins edged with black or blue; caudal reddish. A widespread fish, the blue goby is to be expected around all reefs, where it burrows in shell rubble. North Carolina through southern Florida and the Gulf of Mexico. (4 inches; 10 cm)

409. Spotted goby *Coryphopterus punctipectophorus* Springer
D. VI + 11; A. 10; P. 17–20; body plain, with dark spot on lower half of pectoral base. This is an offshore reef species, rarely found. Florida, Gulf of Mexico, and Caribbean. Causey, 1969; Springer, 1960. (2 inches; 5 cm)

410. Violet goby *Gobioides broussoneti* Lacepède
D. VII, 15; A. 16; P. 19; depth about 9 percent of standard length; body very long and tapering; dorsal fins continuous; color purplish brown, interrupted with white; 25–30 dark, anteriorly directed chevrons along myomeres. This large, slim goby is usually taken individually over soft mud bottoms. It is found from inshore marsh channels out across the continental shelf. Georgia and northern Gulf to Brazil. (18 inches; 46 cm)

411. Frillfin goby *Bathygobius soporator* (Valenciennes)
D. VI + 10; A. 9; P. 19; Sc. 42; depth about 21 percent of standard length, body brown with darker bars and blotches, fins densely spotted with brown. This tropical form is known

from the Port Aransas jetties and can be expected in any rocky area, especially on the South Texas coast. North Carolina to Florida, Gulf of Mexico; other subspecies occur in the Caribbean. (5 inches; 13 cm)

412. Neon goby *Gobiosoma oceanops* (Jordan)
D.VII + 12 ; A. 13; colorful body with brilliant blue stripes (not joined) through eye to tail. This is a well known cleaner fish, usually found around coral. Similar brightly colored species can be expected on the Flower Gardens and other reefs, but these have the stripes joined on the head. Because these others are secretive, more tropical gobies may be expected, especially in sponges. North Carolina to Belize. (2 inches; 5 cm)

413. Twoscale goby *Gobiosoma longipala* Ginsburg
D.VII + 12; A 10; P. 17; depth about 12–18 percent of standard length, body lacking scales except for two relatively large ctenoid scales on caudal peduncle; body with 1–8 broad vertical bars, each bar with darker mid-dorsal line. This small goby is apparently not uncommon in the deeper bays and shallow Gulf. It may prove to be conspecific with the Atlantic coast *G. ginsburgi,* with which it is closely allied; both occur around shells and other protected habitats. West Florida to Texas. (1 1/2 inches; 4 cm)

414. Code goby *Gobiosoma robustum* Ginsburg
D.VII + 12; A. 10; P. 16; depth 16–23 percent of standard length; body without scales; sometimes 10–12 indistinct vertical bars on sides. This common species is usually found in grass beds, particularly turtle grass, *Thalassia.* Chesapeake Bay to Florida, through the Gulf to Yucatán. (2 inches; 5 cm)

415. Naked goby *Gobiosoma bosc* (Lacepède)
D.VII + 13, A 11; P. 18; depth 14–20 percent of standard length; 9–10 dark vertical bars on sides, usually separated by narrow light space. This is the goby most commonly found on oyster reefs, usually hiding so well that it is not seen. Large populations sometimes develop in marsh ponds. This species closely resembles *G. robustum,* but in *G. bosc* the bars are straighter and the meristic counts are distinctive. Long Island Sound to Campeche. Conn and Belcher, 1996; Hoese, 1966b. (2 1/2 inches; 6 cm)

416. Clown goby *Microgobius gulosus* (Girard)
D.VII + 16; A. 17; P. 22, Sc. 45–52; body spotted with dark brown; two or three dark vertical bars below second dorsal; often longitudinal bar beneath eye; outer edges of second dorsal, anal, and caudal dusky in males, spotted in females. This is a common goby on mud bottoms in shallow bays and adjacent ponds in all salinities. Chesapeake Bay to Corpus Christi. Birdsong, 1981. (3 inches; 8 cm)

417. Green goby *Microgobius thalassinus* (Jordan and Gilbert)
D. VII + 16; A. 16; P. 21; Sc. 43–50; body more elongate and lighter in color than that of *M. gulosus,* with mouth more vertically inclined in *M. thalassinus;* females with prominent dark spot on first dorsal. This goby is generally considered to be very rare, probably because of its habitat. These small fish associate with and live inside sponges, particularly *Microciona,* and bryozoans. Chesapeake Bay to Corpus Christi. Birdsong, 1981. (2 inches; 5 cm)

418. Ragged goby *Bollmannia communis* Ginsburg
D. VII + 14; A. 14; P. 22; body bluish, iridescent in life; middle rays of dorsal fin elongate, darkened; center rays of caudal also produced. This is the common goby over muddy bottoms in the shallow Gulf. The common name refers to its usual loss of scales with handling. Known only from the western Gulf of Mexico, Mississippi to Campeche. (8 inches; 8 cm)

419. Lyre goby *Evorthodus lyricus* (Girard)
D. VI + 11, A. 12; P. 16; Sc. 30–35; depth 20 percent of standard length; brown or gray with five or six indistinct vertical bars; two dark spots on caudal fin base. An uncommon shallow-water form, usually found in salty tidal pools where it burrows, but also in coastal freshwater. Chesapeake Bay to Surinam and in the West Indies. Foster and Fuiman, 1987. (3 inches; 8 cm)

420. Highfin goby *Gobionellus oceanicus* (Pallas)
D. VI + 14; A. 15; P. 19; Sc. variable, extreme range 60–93; silvery, with a dark shoulder spot; another dark spot at base of lanceolate caudal fin. This large goby is a wide-ranging species found in muddy bottoms from low salinities in bays almost to the middle shelf. Confusion has existed about this highly variable goby, with specimens also identified as *G. gracillimus* and *G. hastatus.* North Carolina to Campeche. (8 inches; 20 cm)

421. Freshwater goby *Gobionellus shufeldti* (Jordan and Eigenmann)
D. VI + 12; A. 13; P. 17; Sc. 33–40; tan with four or five irregular blotches (often squares) on sides; posterior stripe on snout not extending onto lip. This goby is limited to fresh water and low salinities in bays and channels. It is not known south of Galveston Bay. Antitropical—North Carolina to Texas and Venezuela to southern Brazil. Pezold and Cashner, 1983. (3 inches; 8 cm)

422. Darter goby *Gobionellus boleosoma* (Jordan and Gilbert)
D. VI + 11; A. 12; P. 16; Sc. 28–33; tan with four or five narrow, longitudinal bars; distinct V-shaped markings on upper half of body; posterior stripe on snout usually extending onto lip. The darter is the most ubiquitous of gobies, being found in nearly all bay habi-

tats and in the shallow Gulf. Chesapeake Bay through the Caribbean to Brazil. Pezold and Cashner, 1983. (2 1/2 inches; 6 cm)

423. Blackfin goby *Gobionellus claytoni* (Meek)

D. VI + 11; A. 12; P. 16. Reported as *G. atripinnis* Gilbert and Randall only from the Rio Grande near Brownsville. Other species of *Gobionellus,* including *smaragdus* and *stigmaturus,* have also been reported from the area and need confirmation. Veracruz perhaps to Louisiana. Bryan, 1971; Pezold and Edwards, 1982. (1 1/2 inches; 4 cm)

Microdesmidae

The wormfishes are a peculiar group of nocturnal, burrowing, gobylike fishes with pale colors and long, slender bodies. They seem to be rare but might be expected anywhere inshore. (Dawson, 1962b, 1969)

> Fewer than 50 anal rays; caudal fin rounded ... pink wormfish, *Microdesmus longipinnis.*
> More than 50 anal rays, caudal fin lanceolate ... lancetail wormfish, *Microdesmus lanceolatus.*

424. Pink wormfish *Microdesmus longipinnis* (Weymouth)

D. XX–XXI, 50; A. usually about 44; caudal fin rounded. This is a rare fish found in the northern Gulf and bays, mostly in quite shallow water. S.C. to Cedar Bayou; Bermuda and Cayman Islands. (10 inches; 25 cm)

425. Lancetail wormfish *Microdesmus lanceolatus* Dawson

D. XII, 56; A. usually about 55; caudal fin lanceolate. This rare species is found in a few locations in ten to twenty fathoms off Louisiana and Texas. Dennis and Bright, 1988a. (2 inches; 5 cm)

Ephippidae

The spadefishes are large, laterally flattened, schooling fishes that are valued as food. There is not much market for them in our area, but they are often caught by anglers or speared by divers. This is a successful but little studied fish. (Ditty, Shaw, and Cope, 1994)

426. Atlantic spadefish; angelfish *Chaetodipterus faber* (Broussonet)

D. VIII + 1, 20; A. III, 18; Sc. 65–75. Very small spadefish are dark and quite round and often float on the surface, mimicking pieces of wood and seeds; however, they soon take on the black-and-white banded pattern characteristic of the species. The bars tend to be lost in old fish. Fish up to one pound are found inshore around jetties and wharves and in open water off the beaches. Larger fish occur offshore around wrecks, reefs, and oil rigs, and sometimes schools are seen in open water. Cape Cod through the Caribbean to Brazil. (3 feet; 91 cm)

Acanthuridae

The surgeonfishes or tangs are laterally flattened reef fishes and have retractable sharp spines on each side of the caudal peduncle, which serve to discourage predators and which can cut humans.

All three of our species are found throughout the tropical western Atlantic, and one additional species *(A. randalli)* is thought to replace the ocean surgeon from Miami to Mississippi. They occupy offshore reefs, with the young sometimes occurring inshore (Randall, 1956)

1 Body blue in life with longitudinal stripes; anal rays usually 24–25 . . . blue tang, *Acanthurus coeruleus.*

   Body dark brown; anal rays usually 22–23 2

2 Brown vertical bars on body; caudal fin margin slightly concave . . . doctorfish, *Acanthurus chirurgus.*

   Brown vertical bars lacking; caudal fin lunate . . . ocean surgeon, *Acanthurus bahianus.*

427. Blue tang *Acanthurus coeruleus* Bloch and Schneider
D. IX, 26–28; A. III, 24–26; body blue with lighter, wavy longitudinal stripes; young yellow overall; intermediate fish mixed, often blue with yellow fins, caudal spine surrounded by yellow in all sizes. The blue tang is a very rare fish on offshore reefs. Bermuda and New York through the Caribbean to Brazil. Bright and Cashman, 1974; Sonnier et al., 1976. (14 inches; 36 cm)

428. Doctorfish *Acanthurus chirurgus* (Bloch)
D. IX, 24–25; A. III, 22–23; body brown or light blue with narrow, darker vertical bars; median fins sometimes bluish. Occasionally found on offshore reefs, this is probably the most common surgeonfish here. Bermuda and New York through the Caribbean to Brazil. Sonnier et al., 1976. (13 inches; 33 cm)

429. Ocean surgeon *Acanthurus bahianus* Castelnau
D. IX, 23–26; A. III, 21–23; brown or light blue, but without dark vertical bars; usually with light area posterior to caudal spine (sometimes present in *A. chirurgus*) and broad light margin on caudal fin; short blue lines around eye. Fish resembling ocean surgeons in the northeastern Gulf but with a squarer tail and a shorter pectoral (more than 27 percent

of head length compared to less than 26 percent in *A. bahianus*) have been described as the Gulf surgeon, *A. randalli* Briggs and Caldwell. The Gulf surgeon has been listed by McEachran (1994) as occurring in Texas waters occasionally, on offshore reefs. Briggs and Caldwell, 1957; Sonnier et al., 1976. (14 inches; 36 cm).

Sphyraenidae

The barracudas are large, predatory fishes, of which three species occur here. De Sylva (1963) gives keys for identifying all juveniles and larvae as well as larger fishes and provides life history information on the species. Barracudas are considered to be game fish, and all are edible, but in the tropics the great barracuda often causes ciguatera poisoning. No cases of this poisoning are known from our region.

1 Spinous dorsal placed well behind origin of pelvic fin; maxillary extending backward to beyond margin of eye; pectoral fin reaches origin of pelvic fin; lower jaw without fleshy tip 2
Spinous dorsal placed above or slightly in advance of origin of pelvic fin; maxillary not reaching anterior margin of eye; pectoral fin does not reach origin of pelvic fin; lower jaw with fleshy tip . . . northern sennet, *Sphyraena borealis*.

2 Last rays of soft dorsal and anal fins produced and longer than anterior rays when fin is depressed; teeth noticeably directed backward; lateral line scales raised, distinct, larger than surrounding scales, 108–114 in number. . . guaguanche, *Sphyraena guachancho*.
Last rays of soft dorsal and anal fins not produced, equal in length to anterior rays when fin is depressed; teeth nearly vertical in jaws; lateral line scales not raised, no different in size from surrounding scales, 75–87 in number . . . great barracuda, *Sphyraena barracuda*.

430. Northern sennet *Sphyraena borealis* DeKay
D.V + I, 9; A. II, 9; Sc. 107–116 in local populations; eye diameter about 19–21 percent of head length; interorbital flattened; two faint longitudinal stripes in life, sometimes appearing as rows or spots in preserved specimens. This species and the southern sennet, *S. picudilla* (Poey), are here regarded as conspecific, the name *S. borealis* having priority. Very small individuals (larvae to postjuveniles) of this species are apparently common in spring in the northwestern Gulf, although at this size confusion with *S. guachancho* is possible. Massachusetts through the Caribbean to Uruguay. (18 inches; 46 cm)

431. Guaguanche *Sphyraena guachancho* Cuvier
D.V + I, 9; A. II, 7–8; Sc. 108–114; interorbital convex; three encircling bands on posterior portion of trunk in small fish taking hourglass shape; silvery to olive, with faint golden longitudinal stripe along enlarged lateral line scales; margin of pelvic and anal fins black; tips of middle caudal rays black. This is the most common barracuda in the Gulf. It is

found in open waters and therefore often caught by shrimpers. Atlantic Ocean, in the west from Massachusetts through the Caribbean to Brazil. (2 feet; 61 cm)

432. Great barracuda *Sphyraena barracuda* (Walbaum)

D.V + 1, 9; A. II, 7–8; Sc. 75–87; head small; fish with longitudinal series of blotches, often H-shaped, but never with encircling bands; deep green to gray on back, silver-white below; upper sides with 18–22 oblique dark bands; lower sides with inky blotches; soft dorsal and caudal fins black with white tips. The great barracuda is common around oil platforms, wrecks, and reefs. Circumtropical, except the eastern Pacific and the Mediterranean; in the western Atlantic from Massachusetts through the Caribbean to Brazil. (6 feet; 1.6 m)

Trichiuridae

The Atlantic cutlassfish, *Trichiurus lepturus,* is the sole inshore representative of this family occurring in our range; however, current opinion also includes the deeper-dwelling snake mackerels (formerly placed in the family Gempylidae) in this family (Nakamura and Parin, 1993). The snake mackerel, *Gempylus serpens* Cuvier, is distributed circumtropically in the open ocean, in the Western Atlantic from New York, Bermuda, and the northern Gulf to South America. Other gempylids are to be expected on the outer shelf, but they are pelagic fishes of the continental slope. The oilfish, *Ruvettus pretiosus* Cocco, derives its name from the high oil content of its flesh, which spoils rapidly. It is known to cause food poisoning, more commonly acting as a purgative, and has been reported in the eastern but not the western Gulf. It is normally found in 55–330 fathoms (100–600 m). (Nakamura and Parin, 1993)

1 Caudal fin absent ... Atlantic cutlassfish, *Trichiurus lepturus.*
 Caudal fin present 2
2 Caudal peduncle keeled, one large keel and with two smaller keels above and below on each side; lateral line single ... escolar, *Lepidocybium flavobrunneum.*
 Caudal peduncle without keels; lateral line obscure or double 3
3 Lateral line single, but obscure; scales interspersed with spinous bony tubercles ... oilfish, *Ruvettus pretiosus.*
 Lateral line double, upper running next to base of dorsal, lower along midline of body; body with smooth cycloid scales .. snake mackerel, *Gempylus serpens.*

433. Atlantic cutlassfish; ribbonfish *Trichiurus lepturus* Linnaeus

D. 135; A. 100; no scales; body elongate, silvery; eye and mouth large; upper jaw with about four large barbed teeth anteriorly. Ribbonfish are common in the inshore Gulf and bays during the warmer months. Although very common in Texas, they are more abundant in Louisiana. Smaller individuals are used as trolling bait for kingfish, *(Scomberomorus cavalla)*, while larger fish are notorious bait stealers, often breaking leaders with their sharp teeth or devouring other hooked fish before the angler can land them. The flesh of the cutlassfish is edible and reportedly good eating, and the species supports a commercial fishery in other areas. It is fortunate that it dies rapidly, because its large teeth (fangs with barbs) are capable of inflicting a painful bite. These teeth have been taken from seismic cable, apparently deliberately bitten. Circumtropical—temperate, in the western Atlantic from Massachusetts to south Brazil; also in the Pacific from Panama to Mexico (Gulf of California). Dawson, 1967; Mericas, 1981. (5 feet; 1.2 m)

434. Escolar *Lepidocybium flavobrunneum* (Smith)
D. VII–IX + 16–18 + 4–6 finlets; A. 13–15 + 4–5 finlets; P. 15; lateral line single, wavy. Normally in 45–110 fathoms (80–200 m). This fish is now sometimes sold in restaurants in Louisiana and Texas. The somewhat similar oilfish, *Ruvettus pretiosus* Cocco, has a nearly straight lateral line. Circumtropical, in the Western Atlantic from Nova Scotia, Bermuda and the northern Gulf to southern Brazil. (6 1/2 feet; 2 m)

Scombridae

The mackerels are typified as fast-swimming, oceanic fishes. A streamlined body, stiff fins, and rigid caudal peduncle enable these fishes to swim constantly at high speeds. Indeed, in some species of scombrids, the branchiostegal respiratory pump has so degenerated that the fishes must remain in motion in order to pass sufficient water over their gills to meet their respiratory needs. Some tunas as well as other fast-swimming fish, such as marlins and some sharks, can maintain body temperatures up to 10°C above that of the surrounding water. These elevated temperatures allow for high metabolic rates, which in turn provide the large quantities of energy required for constant, high-speed swimming.

Most species travel in schools and feed on smaller fish or squid. They are highly regarded as both game and food fish, and most of the larger species support commercial fisheries. The mackerels superficially resemble the carangids (jacks) but lack bony scutes on the posterior lateral line and the pair of free anal spines characteristic of the Carangidae. Instead, they appear to be more closely related to the billfishes, with which they are usually grouped in the suborder Scombroidei. (Collette, 1978; Collette and Chao, 1975; Collette and Nauen, 1983; Collette and Russo, 1984; Gibbs and Collette, 1967; Klawe and Shimada, 1959; Lang et al., 1994; Rivas, 1951, 1964; Russo, 1981)

1   Dorsal fins far apart, with distance between fins greater than length of snout; dorsal spines IX–X 2
     Dorsal fins close together, with distance between fins less than length of snout; dorsal spines

2   Body entirely scaled; dorsal finlets V; anal finlets V; caudal peduncle without keel . . . chub mackerel, *Scomber japonicus.*

Body scaled only anteriorly, along lateral lines and along back to origin of second dorsal fin; dorsal finlets VIII or IX; anal finlets VII; caudal peduncle with median keels 3

3   Posterior extension of corselet narrow, only 1–5 scales wide beneath origin of second dorsal . . . frigate mackerel, *Auxis thazard.*

Posterior extension of corselet wide, 10–15 scales wide beneath origin of second dorsal . . . bullet mackerel, *Auxis rochei.*

4   Dorsal spines XIII–XXII; gill rakers present; snout shorter than rest of head 5

Dorsal spines XXI–XXVII; gill rakers absent; snout about equal to rest of head . . . wahoo, *Acanthocybium solanderi.*

5   Gill rakers 36–40 on lower limb of first arch; distance between origin of second dorsal and last dorsal finlet less than distance between tip of snout and origin of first dorsal; three to five dark longitudinal stripes on lower sides of body, converging toward caudal peduncle . . . skipjack tuna, *Euthynnus pelamis.*

Gill rakers 7–29 on lower limb of first arch; distance between origin of second dorsal and last dorsal finlet greater than distance between tip of snout and origin of first dorsal; no longitudinal stripes 6

6   Scales present only on anterior portion of body, along anterior lateral line, and along back to origin of second dorsal fin; irregularly scattered dark blotches, as large as pupil of eye, on sides of body below pectoral fin . . . little tuna, *Euthynnus alletteratus.*

Scales covering entire body, sometimes enlarged in pectoral region; no dark blotches below pectoral fin 7

7   Dorsal spines XIII–XV; first spine as long as or longer than second and third spines; pectoral fin long, reaching beyond vertical through tenth dorsal spine 8

Dorsal spines XV–XXII; first spine shorter than second; pectoral fin short, not reaching vertical through tenth dorsal spine 10

8   Pectoral fin not reaching beyond vertical through twelfth dorsal spine; gill rakers 25–28 on lower limb of first arch . . . bluefin tuna, *Thunnus thynnus.*

Pectoral fin reaching beyond vertical from twelfth dorsal spine; gill rakers 15–22 on lower limb of first arch 9

9   Gill rakers 15–19 on lower limb of first arch; dorsal finlets VII–IX, usually VIII; anal finlets VII–VIII; second dorsal and anal fins not greatly produced in older specimens . . . blackfin tuna, *Thunnus atlanticus.*

Gill rakers 20–22 on lower limb of first arch; dorsal finlets VIII–XI, usually IX–X; anal finlets VIII–X; second dorsal and anal fins produced . . . yellowfin tuna, *Thunnus albacares.*

10 Maxillary reaching beyond vertical from posterior margin of eye; dorsal spines XX–XXII; dark oblique stripes on back . . . Atlantic bonito, *Sarda sarda.*

Maxillary reaching no further than vertical from posterior margin of eye; dorsal spines XV–XVIII; no dark oblique stripes on back 11

11 Gill rakers 7–9 on lower limb of first arch; dorsal spines XV–XVI; lateral line curving abruptly downward below second dorsal fin . . . king mackerel, *Scomberomorus cavalla*.

Gill rakers 10–13 on lower limb of first arch; dorsal spines XVII–XVIII; lateral line not abruptly curving downward below second dorsal 12

12 Gill rakers 12–13 on lower limb of first arch; maxillary not quite reaching vertical from posterior margin of eye; pectoral fin scaled; sides of body with spots and one or two longitudinal stripes . . . cero, *Scomberomorus regalis*.

Gill rakers 10–11 on lower limb of first arch; maxillary just reaching to posterior margin of eye; pectoral fin not scaled; sides of body with spots but without longitudinal stripes . . . Spanish mackerel, *Scomberomorus maculatus*.

435. Chub mackerel *Scomber japonicus* Houttuyn

D. IX + I, 12 + V–VI; A. I, 11 + V; Sc. 200; small scales covering entire body; elongate, silvery, with widely separated first and second dorsal fins; back greenish blue with wavy dark lines. The chub mackerel is sometimes separated from the Pacific mackerel and referred to as *Scomber* (or *Pneumatophorus*) *colias* Gmelin. It is a small mackerel sporadically caught near the outer shelf in the northern Gulf. Worldwide in temperate and tropical seas, in the western Atlantic from Nova Scotia and Bermuda to Brazil. Matsui, 1967. (20 inches; 50 cm)

436. Frigate mackerel; frigate tuna *Auxis thazard* (Lacepède)

D. X–XII + 10–13 +VIII; A. VII, 8–11 +VII; Gr. 9–10 + 1 + 27–32. Scales covering anterior portion of body; unscaled portion of back with wavy, oblique dark lines; first and second dorsal fins widely separated. This and the next species are small scombrids not commonly caught. Circumtropical, in the western Atlantic from Massachusetts through the Caribbean to Columbia. Uchida, 1981. (2 feet; 61 cm)

437. Bullet mackerel *Auxis rochei* (Risso)

D. X + 13 +VIII; A. II, 6–7 +VII; Gr. 8–12 + 1 + 31–37. Scales covering anterior portion of body; unscaled portion of back with about 15 broad nearly vertical bars; dorsal fins widely separated. Circumtropical, in the western Atlantic from Massachusetts to Argentina. Uchida, 1981. (1.5 feet; 50 cm)

438. Wahoo *Acanthocybium solanderi* (Cuvier)

D. XXI–XXVII + 12 + IX; A. II, 10 + IX; scales covering back of living specimens deep blue or green with prominent vertical black bars on sides; silvery blue between bars; silvery white on belly; first and second dorsal fins continuous. One of the few solitary scombrids, this fish is usually found far from shore and is a highly sought game and food fish. Individuals attain weights of over one hundred pounds (45 kg). Circumtropical, in the western Atlantic from New Jersey through the Caribbean to Colombia. (6 1/2 feet; 2 m)

439. Skipjack tuna (oceanic bonito) *Euthynnus pelamis* (Linnaeus)
D. XV–XVI + 12 +VIII; A. II, 12 +VII; scales well developed, covering anterior body; body silvery, greenish blue above with oblique dark lines on back and dark horizontal lines on lower sides and belly; dorsal fins set close, but not continuous; first dorsal with high anterior lobe. Also known as *Katsuwonus pelamis,* this species, which travels in large schools, has been caught well offshore off Port Isabel. Circumtropical, in the western Atlantic from Maine through the Caribbean to south Brazil. Matsumoto et al., 1984. (40 inches; 1 m)

440. Little tuna; bonito (false albacore) *Euthynnus alletteratus* (Rafinesque)
D. XIV–XVI + 12 +VIII; A. II, 12 +VII; scales forming corselet as in *E. pelamis;* back bluish green with oblique wavy lines; belly white with large, round black spots below pectoral fin; dorsal fins close-set; anterior dorsal lobed. This is the common bonito or "bone-eater" of Gulf sportfishermen. This species comes into shallower water than the other tunas and frequently feeds near the surface. It is a hard-hitting but small fish, generally regarded as an excellent game fish but not highly rated for its food value. Tropical Atlantic, in the west from the Gulf of Maine and Bermuda through the Caribbean to Brazil. De Sylva and Rathjen, 1961; Yoshida, 1979. (2 feet; 61 cm)

441. Bluefin tuna *Thunnus thynnus* (Linnaeus)
D XIII–XIV + 13 + IX–X; A. II, 12 +VIII–IX; Gr. on lower limb of first arch 25–28; entire body scaly; back dark blue to black; cheeks, sides, and belly silvery white; first and second dorsal fins dark; finlets yellow with black edges; anal fin and finlets silvery gray (finlets sometimes yellowish). The giant among tunas, Atlantic Ocean specimens of bluefin attain weights of over one thousand pounds (455 kg). Although they are rare in the north-western Gulf, there have been several caught off the Mississippi Delta and South Texas in deep water. This species was one of the few marine fishes considered rare or endangered by the National Marine Fisheries Service, and sportfishing for bluefin tuna has been under federal management since the 1970s. This is sometimes considered to be a single worldwide species, but the Pacific bluefin is currently placed in a separate species. The Atlantic bluefin occurs on both sides of the Atlantic Ocean, in the west from Newfoundland and Bermuda through the Caribbean to Brazil. Scott, et al., 1993. (14 feet; 4.25 m)

442. Blackfin tuna *Thunnus atlanticus* (Lesson)
D. XIII–XIV + 12–15 +VII–IX; A. II, 11–15 +VII–VIII; Gr. on lower limb 15–19; pectoral fin long, ending near second dorsal (not reaching end of first dorsal in *T. thynnus*); body fully scaled; bluish black above, silvery white on belly; pectoral, dorsal, and anal fins black; finlets yellow, edged with black. The commonest true tuna *(Thunnus)* in the northwestern Gulf, this fish is exceeded in abundance only by *Euthynnus alletteratus.* The blackfin

tuna is a popular sport and food fish. Massachusetts and Bermuda to Brazil. De Sylva, 1955. (40 inches; 1 m)

443. Yellowfin tuna *Thunnus albacares* (Bonneterre)
D. XIII–XV + 13–16 + VIII–XI; A. II, 12–15 + VIII–X; Gr. on lower limb 20–22; pectoral fin long, reaching second dorsal fin; body fully scaled, blue-black above, silvery white below; first dorsal and pectoral fins black, second dorsal and anal fins yellow and greatly elongated in older specimens. A popular food and game fish, the yellowfin is less common than the blackfin. Circumtropical; in the western Atlantic from Massachusetts to Brazil. Lang et al., 1994. (6.5 feet; 2 m)

444. Atlantic bonito *Sarda sarda* (Bloch)
D. XXI + I, 13 + VIII; A. I, 13 + VII; body fully scaled, back blue with oblique, almost horizontal dark lines; whitish below; spinous dorsal fin long, high for most of its length. This species is not common in the northwestern Gulf. Atlantic Ocean, in the west from Nova Scotia to Argentina. Collette and Chao, 1975; Yoshida, 1980. (3 feet; 90 cm)

445. King mackerel; kingfish *Scomberomorus cavalla* (Cuvier)
D. XV + I, 15 + VIII–IX; A. II, 15 + VIII; mouth with large, compressed teeth, about 30 on each side of jaw; sides silvery, greenish above; young fish with dull yellow or greenish spots; very small individuals (6 inches—15 cm) uniformly silver; dorsal fin uniformly dark; lateral line dipping suddenly below second dorsal and thereafter undulating. This is perhaps the most popular offshore game fish in the northwestern Gulf, where the appearance of kingfish is regarded as the marine harbinger of summer. Although some reach over one hundred pounds, those from our area average fifteen to twenty pounds. The king mackerel is generally found farther offshore than the Spanish mackerel. Gulf of Maine through the Caribbean to Brazil. Grimes et al., 1990; McEachran et al, 1980; Richardson and McEachran, 1981. (5.5 feet; 1.7 cm)

446. Spanish mackerel *Scomberomorus maculatus* (Mitchill)
D. XVII + I, 18 + VIII–IX; A. II, 17 + IX; mouth with 24–32 teeth in each jaw, somewhat smaller and more widely spaced than those in comparable size of *S. cavalla;* sides silvery with distinct yellow spots, brighter than those in king mackerel and retained at all sizes; lateral line gently curved beneath second dorsal; only anteriormost portion of dorsal fin dark, especially in juveniles; very small individuals (about 2 inches—5 cm) without spots, but spots acquired by length of 6 inches (15 cm). The young are common in the surf zone and even in low-salinity bays. The Spanish mackerel is a popular sport fish and is fished commercially in Florida. Both sides of the Atlantic (in the eastern Pacific *S. sierra* may also represent this species), from the Gulf of Maine and Bermuda to Brazil. McEachran et al., 1980; Richardson and McEachran, 1981; Fable et al., 1987. (2 feet; 61 cm)

447. Cero *Scomberomorus regalis* (Bloch)

D. XVI–XVIII + I, 15–16 + VIII–IX; A. II, 14 + VIII; mouth with about 30–40 teeth in each jaw; sides silvery with well-defined yellow spots and prominent yellow streaks; first dorsal fin light, with prominent black area at front; scales present on pectoral fins (the other two *Scomberomorus* species having scaleless pectoral fins); lateral line dipping gradually below second dorsal (as in Spanish mackerel). The cero is the least common of the mackerels in the northwestern Gulf. Because many anglers mistake young kingfish that still have spots for ceros, fishermen who think they may have caught a cero should have the identity of the specimen verified by a biologist. Massachusetts to Brazil, common throughout the Caribbean. Baughman, 1941b; Reed, 1941. (3 feet; 91 cm)

Xiphiidae

The swordfish is the sole member of this family. While superficially it resembles the istiophorids, with which it is often classed as a billfish, *Xiphias gladius* is quite distinct and only distantly related to the billfish. Swordfish possess a flattened, serrated bill and lack ventral fins. (Nakamura, 1985)

448. Swordfish *Xiphias gladius* Linnaeus

D. 41–48 + 4; A. 16–18 + 14; P. 15–18; upper jaw extended into a flattened, serrated sword. The swordfish is widely distributed both north and south of the equator. In the Gulf it is not seen at the surface, as it is in cooler waters. Spawning in the Gulf apparently occurs during a protracted period from late spring through late summer. The fish reaches considerable size; one from off Peru weighed 1,182 pounds (537 kg). A small fishery exists off the Mississippi Delta. Worldwide in cold temperate through tropical waters, although restricted to greater depths in the tropics; in the western Atlantic from Newfoundland to Argentina. Arata, 1954; Arnold, 1955; Eschmeyer, 1963; Kramer, 1950; Palko et al., 1981. (16 feet; 5 m)

Istiophoridae

The Istiophoridae or billfishes constitute a family of large, pelagic fishes characterized by their elongate upper jaws or bills. They differ from the swordfish (Xiphiidae) in their possession of ventral fins and in having a rounded instead of flattened bill. All species grow to a large size, though some greatly exceed others. The Indo-Pacific black marlin, *Makaira indica*, has been known to exceed two thousand pounds (900 kg), and the blue marlin, *M. nigricans*, reaches fifteen hundred pounds (680 kg) and may even outweigh the black marlin.

Relatively little is known of the life histories and biology of these species except for the barest of outlines. The billfishes are all apex predators, feeding at the top of the food chain, and they maintain fairly small, widely dispersed populations. The taxonomy of the istiophorids has been confused, with a great many more species described than probably exist. Recent work with specimens from the entire range of the species indicates that sailfish, at least, belong to a single species around the world. Similarly, blue marlins of the Atlantic and Pacific oceans may belong to the same species. There are five species of billfishes reported from the northwestern Gulf and four (perhaps more) extralimital species found elsewhere in the world. Although the black marlin is normally restricted to the Pacific Ocean, occasional individuals have been reported in the Atlantic. This species is distinguished from the blue marlins by possessing rigid pectoral fins. (De Sylva, 1974; Nakamura, 1974, 1985; Russo, 1981)

1 Adult fish greater than 24 inches (60 cm) in standard length 2
   Postlarval or juvenile fish 4–24 inches (10–60 cm) in standard length 6
2 Spinous dorsal greatly elevated its entire length, with middle rays longest; ventral fins with two or three rays . . . sailfish, *Istiophorus platypterus*.
   Spinous dorsal only moderately elevated, with middle rays not longest; ventral fins with only one ray 3
3 Anterior lobe of spinous dorsal low, pointed, with height less than depth of body; flesh pale . . . blue marlin, *Makaira nigricans*.
   Anterior lobe of spinous dorsal pointed, rounded, or blunt and higher than depth of body at dorsal fin origin 4
4 Spinous dorsal fin high throughout, with posterior rays almost as long as anterior rays; dorsal fin unspotted 5
   Spinous dorsal low posteriorly (except in young fish); anus less than one-half anal fin height from base of anal fin; dorsal fin spotted (fading somewhat after death) . . . white marlin, *Tetrapturus albidus*.
5 Anterior lobe of spinous dorsal pointed; anal fin pointed; anus in advance of anal fin base usually by more than height of first anal fin . . . longbill spearfish, *Tetrapturus pfluegeri*.
   Anterior lobe of spinous dorsal rounded or blunt; anal fin rounded; anus in advance of anal fin by less than one-half height of first anal fin . . . hatchet marlin, *Tetrapturus* sp.
6 Upper jaw much longer than lower; lateral line simple 7
   Upper jaw scarcely longer than lower; lateral line complex, consisting of reticulated pattern . . . blue marlin, *Makaira nigricans*.
7 Anus forward, about midway between bases of anal and ventral fins; pelvics short, not reaching base of anal fin; dorsal unspotted; dorsal spines 45–53 (49) . . . longbill spearfish, *Tetrapturus pfluegeri*.
   Anus close to anal fin origin; pelvics long, nearly reaching base of anal fin; dorsal fin spotted or unmarked; dorsal spines 38–49 8
8 Dorsal fin unmarked . . . hatchet marlin, *Tetrapturus* sp.
   Dorsal fin mottled or spotted 9

9   Dorsal mottled, with no distinct ocelli; dorsal with 37–49 (usually 43–45) spines … sailfish, *Istiophorus platypterus*.

Dorsal fin with four distinct ocelli near base; dorsal with 38–46 (usually 42) spines … white marlin, *Tetrapturus albidus*.

449. Sailfish *Istiophorus platypterus* (Shaw and Nodder)

D. 37–49 + 6–8; A. 8–16 + 5–8; P. 17–20; adults with the anteriormost rays of both the dorsal and the anal fins degenerate and covered by skin, resulting in lowered meristic counts; adults blue-black above, light blue to silver below; dorsal fin membrane dark blue with black spots; vertical rows of golden spots on sides of body; young uniformly lighter, with mottled dorsal fin membrane; lateral line simple. Morrow and Harbo (1969) place all sailfish in this single, cosmopolitan species. Formerly Atlantic sailfish were referred to as *I. americanus* (Cuvier) or *I. albicans* (Latreille). Off southern Texas, sailfish first appear in early May in most years and usually leave by November. They are present on the northern Gulf coast about one month later and leave one month earlier. Sailfish apparently avoid temperatures below 50°F (10°C), and their movements seem to be correlated with water temperatures in the 75°–80°F (24–27°C) range. Sailfish live only four or five years, with most of their growth occurring during the first two or three years. Circumtropical (to 40°N and S); in the western Atlantic from Rhode Island to Brazil. (De Sylva, 1957; Jolley, 1974; Morrow and Harbo, 1969; Voss, 1953. (8 feet; 2.4 m—but bigger in the Pacific)

450. Blue marlin *Makaira nigricans* Lacepède

D. 39–46 + 6–7; A. 14–17 + 6–7; P. 20–22; anteriormost rays of dorsal fin not greater than body depth at origin of dorsal fin; dorsal fin pointed; adults dark blue above, lighter below, with dark vertical stripes along sides, disappearing in larger fish; after death, more uniformly dark coloration; dorsal fin black or very dark blue; lateral line complex but often inconspicuous, forming reticulate pattern along sides of body; young with little or no noticeable bill, upper jaw being only slightly longer or no longer than lower. Blue marlin occur throughout the tropical oceans. Females attain a greater size than males, which seldom exceed three hundred pounds. The largest fish are usually caught around the middle of the season (July and August in the Gulf). Atlantic blue marlin were formerly referred to as *M. ampla* and Pacific blue marlin as *M. mazara* and *M.* (or *Istiompax*) *howardii*. *Makaira perezi* from the South Atlantic is also probably synonymous with *M. nigricans*. Circumtropical, in the western Atlantic from Massachusetts to Uruguay. (12 feet; 3.75 m—but bigger elsewhere)

451. White marlin *Tetrapturus albidus* Poey

D. 38–46 + 5–7; A. 12–18 + 5–7; P. 17–21; height of anterior rays of dorsal fin greater than body depth at origin of dorsal fin; dorsal fin lobe rounded; anus located near the origin of the anal fin; body silvery, only slightly darker above than below; dorsal fin spotted, especially evident in dorsal groove; series of iridescent spots above lateral line (called "spotlights" by Texas fishermen). White marlin seem to prefer water between 78° and 80°F (26–27°C). Their feeding grounds are characterized by bottom irregularities and fairly low levels of dissolved oxygen (4.8–5.5 mg/l). From this fact it would appear that marlin seek out areas of upwelling, where food would be expected to be plentiful. In the Gulf there is a concentration of fish off the mouth of the Mississippi in midsummer, followed by a dispersion to other parts of the Gulf in the later summer. Spawning occurs in late spring and early summer. Though they can reach as much as one hundred pounds (45 kg), white marlin seldom exceed sixty pounds (27 kg). This fish is much longer-lived than the sailfish, having a life of perhaps ten years. Atlantic Ocean, in the west from Nova Scotia to Brazil (45°N and S). De Sylva and Davis, 1963; Gibbs, 1957. (7 feet; 2.1 m—but bigger in the eastern Atlantic)

452. Longbill spearfish *Tetrapturus pfluegeri* Robins and De Sylva

D. 45–53 + 6–7; A. 12–18 + 6–8; P. 18–20; posterior dorsal nearly as high as anterior dorsal fin rounded; anus noticeably forward, about halfway between origins of anal and ventral fins; blue-black above, silvery below; vertical bands may be present on small specimens but are absent from larger fish. This species rarely exceeds sixty pounds (27 kg). It has only been reported once from Texas, but it is likely that it has been mistaken for small white marlin, which it closely resembles. Atlantic Ocean, in the west from 45°N to 35°S. Springer and Hoese, 1958; Swann, 1957. (6 feet; 2 m)

453. Hatchet marlin *Tetrapturus* sp.

The distinctive dorsal fin of this species, which resembles that of a small white marlin, should make its identification easier. The possible existence of an unknown species of billfish in the northern Gulf has been shown from photographs taken by Robert Ewing of Monroe, Louisiana. Fish believed to be the hatchet marlin have also been taken off Charleston, South Carolina. Sportfishermen catching fish they feel may be hatchet marlin should report their catches to scientists and, if possible, make arrangements to preserve the fish until they can be studied. The hatchet marlin possibly represents an undescribed species or a western race of the roundscale spearfish, *T. georgei,* from the eastern Atlantic and Mediterranean. De Sylva, 1974; Pristas, 1980; Robins, 1974. (7 feet; 2.3 m)

 Stromateidae

The butterfishes and the closely related fishes placed in the families Nomeidae, Centrolophidae, and Ariommatidae are open-water schooling fishes often consolidated into an expanded family Stromateidae. The juveniles of most species float among the plankton and are often associated with jellyfish. Although not universally accepted, the current opinion seems to be to recognize separate families (Horn, 1984; Nelson, 1994) within the stromateoid suborder. Adults commonly live near the bottom, sometimes in quite deep water. The stromateids are small to moderate-sized fish with small embedded scales and which lack ventral fins. (Haedrich, 1967; Horn, 1970)

> Body height more than 60 percent of standard length; no row of pores below anterior portion of dorsal fin; premaxillary teeth pointed, simple ... harvestfish, *Peprilus paru*.
> Body height less than 60 percent of standard length; row of pores below anterior portion of dorsal fin; premaxillary teeth usually with three cusps ... Gulf butterfish, *Peprilus burti*.

454. Harvestfish *Peprilus alepidotus* (Linnaeus)

D. 38–47; A. 35–45; P. 18–24; Gr. 20–23; body depth 60–88 percent of standard length; anterior profile moderately to strongly convex; eye diameter greater than length of snout; dorsal and anal fins falcate, with longest rays often six or more times longer than the shortest; silvery. Gulf populations named *P. alepidotus* may be considered conspecific with the Atlantic *P. paru* (Linnaeus), since the distinguishing characteristics are clinal. Massachusetts to Argentina. Horn, 1970; Mansueti, 1963. (10 inches; 25 cm)

455. Gulf butterfish *Peprilus burti* Fowler

D. 38–48; A. 35–43; P. 19–23; Gr. 21–26; body moderately elongate, depth 46–60 percent of standard length; anterior profile moderately convex; eye diameter greater than snout; dorsal and anal fins only slightly falcate. This species is somewhat more common in Louisiana. Records of *Peprilus* (or *Poronotus*) *triacanthus* in the Gulf refer to this species. There has been a small, irregular fishery for this delicious fish. West coast of Florida to Yucatán. Caldwell, 1961; Murphy and Chittenden, 1991; Perschbacher et al., 1979; Render and Allen, 1987. (1 foot; 30 cm)

Ariommatidae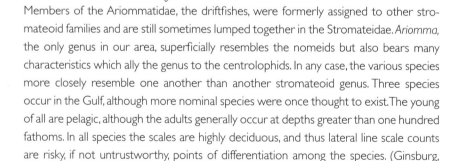

Members of the Ariommatidae, the driftfishes, were formerly assigned to other stromateoid families and are still sometimes lumped together in the Stromateidae. *Ariomma*, the only genus in our area, superficially resembles the nomeids but also bears many characteristics which ally the genus to the centrolophids. In any case, the various species more closely resemble one another than another stromateoid genus. Three species occur in the Gulf, although more nominal species were once thought to exist. The young of all are pelagic, although the adults generally occur at depths greater than one hundred fathoms. In all species the scales are highly deciduous, and thus lateral line scale counts are risky, if not untrustworthy, points of differentiation among the species. (Ginsburg, 1954; Haedrich, 1967; Haedrich and Horn, 1972; Horn, 1972)

1   Deep-bodied forms, with depth greater than 33 percent of standard length . . . spotted
     driftfish, *Ariomma regulus.*
     Slender-bodied forms, with depth less than 28 percent of standard length 2

2   Peritoneum dark, with many melanophores; scales small, 50–65 in lateral line . . . brown
     driftfish, *Ariomma melanum.*
     Peritoneum light, without or with few melanophores; scales large, 30–45 in lateral line . . .
     silver rag, *Ariomma bondi.*

456. Spotted driftfish *Ariomma regulus* (Poey)

D. XI + 1, 15–16; A. III, 15; P. 21–24; Gr. 7 + 16; teeth not cusped; body silvery, variously
spotted; first dorsal and pelvic fins darkening with age. Even small fish are more common at depths greater than one hundred fathoms. New Jersey to Cuba and the Gulf.
McKenny, 1961. (at least 8 inches; 20 cm)

457. Silver rag *Ariomma bondi* Fowler

D. XI–XII + 14–17; A. III, 12–16; P. 20–23; Gr. 8 + 15. The silver rag generally occurs in
water shallower than one hundred fathoms and so is ecologically somewhat different
from the other species of *Ariomma. Ariomma* (or *Cubiceps*) *nigroargenteus* Ginsburg is a
synonym. Gulf of Maine through the Caribbean to Uruguay; also off West Africa. Horn,
1972. (at least 8 inches; 20 cm)

458. Brown driftfish *Ariomma melanum* (Ginsburg)

D. XI–XII + 15–18; A. III, 13–16; P. 21–23; Gr. 9–11 + 17–20; color uniformly dusky brown.
This fish is a deep-shelf species, which generally occurs in one hundred to three hundred
fathoms. The young, however, are pelagic and may occur over the shelf at times. New
York to the Caribbean, including the Gulf; also off West Africa. Horn, 1972. (at least 8
inches; 20 cm)

Centrolophidae

The ruffs are pelagic, high seas fishes found near the edge of the continental shelf. The
adults of most species occur off the shelf in much greater depths. They are closely
related to the butterfishes (Stromateidae). Their geographic ranges are uncertain.
(Haedrich, 1967)

Spines of dorsal fin weakly developed . . . black ruff, *Centrolophus niger.*
Spines of dorsal short and stout . . . black driftfish, *Hyperoglyphe bythites.*

459. Black ruff *Centrolophus niger* (Gmelin)
D. 37–41; A. III, 20–23; P. 19–22; Gr. 5–6 + 13–16. This is apparently a single cosmopolitan species found in temperate waters. (3 feet; 91 cm)

460. Black driftfish *Hyperoglyphe bythites* (Ginsburg)
D. VII–VIII, 22–25; A. III, 16–17; P. 20–21; Gr. 6–7 + 16–17. The young of this driftfish occur near flotsam but rarely associate with medusae. Adults form large schools near the bottom in one hundred to two hundred fathoms. It is perhaps a synonym of *H. macrophthalma* (Miranda-Ribeiro) from Brazil; otherwise, it is known only from the northern Gulf. Dawson, 1971d. (30 inches; 76 cm).

Nomeidae

The nomeids are closely related to the butterfishes (Stromateidae), but they remain pelagic as adults and are often associated with animals, such as jellyfish—in the case of *Nomeus*, with the Portuguese man-of-war, *Physalia*—or with other objects. Only the man-of-war fish is normally found on the shelf.

1   Body elongate, depth less than 35 percent of standard length; origin of dorsal fin well behind (or, in small fish, above) insertion of pectoral fins 2
    Body deep, maximum depth usually greater than 40 percent of standard length; origin of dorsal before (or, in very large fish, directly above) insertion of pectoral fin 3
2   Anal count II, 14–16; pelvic fins inserted under or behind base of pectoral fins . . . bigeye cigarfish, *Cubiceps pauciradiatus.*
    Anal count III, 24–29; pelvic fins inserted before or under insertion of pectoral fins . . . man-of-war fish, *Nomeus gronovii.*
3   Dorsal IX–XI + 24–28; anal III, 24–28; small teeth in both jaws . . . freckled driftfish, *Psenes cyanophrys.*
    Dorsal XXI + III, 27–32; anal III, 26–31; knifelike teeth in lower jaw . . . bluefin driftfish, *Psenes pellucidus.*

461. Bigeye cigarfish *Cubiceps pauciradiatus* Günther
D. X–XI, I 15–17; A. II, 14–16; P. 17–20; Gr. 7–9 + 16–19. This elongate, finely scaled fish reaches considerable size. Worldwide between 40°N and S. Butler, 1979. (30 inches; 76 cm)

462. Man-of-war fish *Nomeus gronovii* (Gmelin)
D IX–XII + 24–28; A. III, 24–29; P. 21–23; Gr. 8–9 + 18–19; bright blue above, blotched and spotted on sides; dark blotches on median and pelvic fins (blotches may cover

nearly entire fin). This species commonly associates with *Physalia,* the Portuguese man-of-war, and has been observed feeding on the polyps. Apparently *Nomeus* is immune to the siphonophore's toxin. Numerous specimens have been collected from the Gulf, inshore waters, and occasionally more saline bays; these are probably juveniles of a deep-living fish. Circumtropical; in the western Atlantic from Bermuda and Massachusetts through the Caribbean to Brazil. (8 inches; 20 cm)

463. Freckled driftfish *Psenes cyanophrys* Valenciennes
D. IX–XI + 24–28; A. III, 24–28; P. 17–20; Gr. 8–9 + 20 (Gulf specimens having higher modal counts); numerous longitudinal streaks on body. Atlantic, Pacific, and Indian Oceans. Massachusetts to the Caribbean. (at least 8 inches; 20 cm)

464. Bluefin driftfish (black rag) *Psenes pellucidus* Lütken
D. XXI + III, 27–32; A. III, 29–31; P. 18–20; Gr. 8–9 + 15–17; body plain. A mid-water and deep-sea species found over shelf waters only rarely. Flabby musculature and knifelike teeth in the lower jaw characterize the species. Pacific and Indian oceans, in the Atlantic from New Jersey to the Gulf. (at least 8 inches; 20 cm)

Dactylopteridae

The flying gurnards, which do not really fly, are armored fishes with large pectoral fins. They are superficially like searobins, but they lack the free pectoral rays and have rectangular bodies.

465. Flying gurnard *Dactylopterus volitans* (Linnaeus)
D. II + IV, 8; A. 6; P. 28 + 6; first two dorsal spines free. The flying gurnard is a strangely armored tropical species rarely taken by shrimp trawlers. Tropical Atlantic, in the west from Massachusetts and Bermuda through the Caribbean to Argentina. (18 inches; 46 cm)

Triglidae

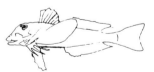

Searobins are peculiar armored fishes with large pectoral fins that can be spread like wings. Despite this illusion of wings, and the ability to glide in the water, searobins are found close to the bottom, at least at night. The lower pectoral rays are detached and are used as feelers or "legs" as the fish "walks" along the bottom. Searobins also produce sounds, especially during spawning.

The heads of searobins are armed with many spines, some of which change considerably with growth. Since these spines have been used to distinguish species, changes to or disappearance of the spines with growth can lead to confusion. Most of the species likely to be encountered are not too difficult to identify if sufficient care is taken. Life colors and habitat can also be used to separate many species. This group of fishes has the unusual distinction of having been revised independently by two researchers working in the same museum at the same time, with their results (Ginsburg, 1950; Teague, 1951) being published within months of each other. Unfortunately, confusing recent name changes involve common Gulf species. (Briggs, 1956; Chittenden and Moore, 1977; Miller and Kent, 1972; Miller and Richards, 1991a,b; Robins et al., 1986, 1991; Russell et al., 1992; Teague, 1952; Weiss et al., 1991)

1   Preorbital produced into spine extending beyond mouth . . . slender searobin, *Peristedion gracile.*
    Preorbital spine, if present, not extending beyond mouth 2
2   Dorsal spines usually XI, at least one filamentous 11
    Dorsal spines usually X, none filamentous 3
3   Posterior edge of pectoral fin emarginate, with middle rays shortest; chest largely scaled . . .
    Mexican sea robin, *Prionotus paralatus.*
    Posterior edge of pectoral straight or convex, with middle rays longest; chest largely
    naked 4
4   Nostril with large tentacle . . . bandtail searobin, *Prionotus ophryas.*
    Nostril without tentacle 5
5   Pectoral short, about same length as ventral fin . . . shortwing searobin, *Prionotus stearnsi.*
    Pectoral long, at least 1 1/4 times longer than ventral 6
6   Pectoral with many blue spots, usually persistent after preservation, although sometimes
    becoming dark . . . bluespotted searobin, *Prionotus roseus.*
    Pectoral without blue spots 7
7   Body depth 21 percent or less of standard length 10
    Body depth 22 percent or more of standard length 8
8   Lateral line scales 68–90; interorbital at least as large as eye, 7–11 percent of body length
    . . . bighead searobin, *Prionotus tribulus.*
    Lateral line scales 88–115; interorbital width 75 percent or less of eye diameter, 46 percent
    of body length 9
9   Black spot between fourth and fifth dorsal spine persistent; preopercular and opercular
    spines extend well beyond operculum margin; lateral line scales 88–106 . . . bigeye searobin,
    Prionotus longispinosus (formerly *rubio*).
    Black spot on dorsal fin disappears with age; preopercular and opercular spines extending
    barely if at all beyond opercular margin; lateral line scales 103–115 . . . blackwing searobin,
    Prionotus rubio (formerly *salmonicolor*).
10 Chest incompletely scaled; opercular flap scaled . . . leopard searobin, *Prionotus scitulus.*

Chest completely scaled; opercular flap naked ... northern searobin, *Prionotus carolinus.*

11   Lachrymal plate with hornlike process projecting anteriorly; first two dorsal spines filamentous ... horned searobin, *Bellator militaris.*

Lachrymal plate without hornlike process; not more than one filamentous dorsal spine 12

12   Scales 95–112 ... streamer searobin, *Bellator egretta.*

Scales 62–70 ... shortfin searobin, *Bellator brachychir.*

466. Slender searobin *Peristedion gracile* Goode and Bean

D.VIII + 20; A. I, 18; body slender, depth not more than 17 percent of standard length. The paired preorbital (rostral) spines extending anteriorly and the barbels on the maxilla are characteristic of this fish. A continental slope species, its juveniles are sometimes found on the outer shelf. A related species, *P. miniatum* Goode, may also be found there. These are sometimes placed in a separate family, the Peristediidae. New Jersey to the West Indies and probably the whole Gulf. Chittenden and Moore, 1977. (5 inches; 13 cm)

467. Mexican searobin *Prionotus paralatus* Ginsburg

D. X + 12; A. 10–12; P. 12–13; Sc. 93–103; body uniformly brown or red without distinct bands or spots; pectoral fin uniformly dark, sometimes with darker crossbands on upper part; dorsal spot on margin of fin between fourth and fifth spines, caudal fin sometimes with blackish margin. This is a common species on the outer Texas shelf, but less common off Louisiana. It is very closely related to and perhaps conspecific with *P. alatus,* the spiny searobin, which occurs from about the mouth of the Mississippi eastward to Florida and North Carolina. Hybrids occur off Mobile Bay. It is most easily distinguished from the other local species of *Prionotus* except *alatus* by the shape of its pectoral fin, and it is further distinguished from *P. alatus* by its longer pectoral fin (58–78 per cent of standard length vs. 40–53 percent of standard length in *P. alatus*). Louisiana to the Gulf of Campeche. McClure and McEachran, 1992. (6 inches; 15 cm)

468. Bandtail searobin *Prionotus ophryas* Jordan and Swain

D. X + 11–13; A. 10–11; P. 14; Sc. 93–105; body variably shaded without definite pattern; pectoral variable in color, brown-spotted, often bicolorate; spinous dorsal without definite spot; second dorsal with two broad, clear bands alternating with dark; caudal fin crossbanded, typically with dark areas at base, center of fin, and margin, light between. This is not a common species but is widely distributed across the shelf. Bahamas and Georgia and to Venezuela. (7 inches; 18 cm)

469. Shortwing searobin *Prionotus stearnsi* Jordan and Swain

D. X + 12–13; A. 10–11; P. 12–13; Sc. 78–93; uniformly dusky in preservative; usually silvery in life, without distinctive markings on body or fins. The shape of this fish departs radically from that seen in most other searobins and approaches that of a more typical fish. This more streamlined appearance makes the species unmistakable. A not uncommon species widely distributed across the shelf, it is usually not on the inner shelf. Georgia, Florida, and northern Gulf to Suriname. (5 inches; 13 cm)

470. Bluespotted searobin *Prionotus roseus* Jordan and Evermann
D. X + 11–13; A. 10–12; P. 12–14; Sc. 89–104; upper part of body lightly and irregularly marked; pectoral dusky to dark, crossbanded with darker areas, lower parts of fin with many bright blue spots standing out in live animals and usually persisting in preservative and with larger elongate spot between fifth and seventh rays (from top); dorsal spot not sharply marked, usually continuing diffusely forward and backward of fifth and sixth spines; soft dorsal dusky; anal fin clear. This is a middle shelf species, not common. North Carolina to Puerto Rico and Venezuela. (9 inches; 23 cm)

471. Bighead searobin *Prionotus tribulus* Cuvier
D. X + 11–12; A. 10–12; P. 12–14; Sc. 69–85; upper parts of body with short, oblique bands, one under soft dorsal fin being especially distinct; pectorals with dark crossbands; dorsal spot at margin of fin. This is the common inshore shelf and bay searobin and the only searobin with young in very low salinities. North Carolina to Florida and throughout the Gulf. (14 inches; 36 cm)

472. Bigeye searobin *Prionotus longispinosus* Teague
D. X + 12–13; A. 10–12; P. 12–13; Sc. 88–106; body darker dorsally, sometimes with a few faintly marked spots, often pinkish orange in life; pectoral fin with transverse rows of small light spots (orange) and with distinctive blue anterior edge and black spot posteriorly; first dorsal with irregular smoke-colored areas; smaller specimens with distinct ocellated dark spot between fourth and fifth dorsal spines; soft dorsal and anal dusky; inside of mouth orange red. This common species, which was formerly known as *P. rubio,* replaces the bighead robin in slightly deeper water out to near the shelf edge. It generally occurs farther inshore off southern Texas than off Louisiana, and small fish are sometimes found in the saltier bays. Whole Gulf to Cuba; perhaps in southern Caribbean. Cervigon, 1991. (12 inches; 30 cm)

473. Blackwing searobin *Prionotus rubio* Jordan
D. X + 12–13; A. 11–12; P. 12–13; Sc. 103–115; body uniformly shaded, sometimes with a few scattered spots; pectoral fins with lower parts uniformly dark but bright blue anterior edge without dark posterior spot, upper parts blotched or mottled; spinous dorsal without black spots; in small specimens, membranes between first, second, or third and fourth spines dusky. This is a fairly common inshore shelf searobin, previously known as *P. pectoralis* or *P. salmonicolor.* North Carolina to Florida and throughout the Gulf. (9 inches; 23 cm)

474. Leopard searobin *Prionotus scitulus* Jordan and Gilbert

D. X + 12–14; A. 11–13; P. 12–14; Sc. 123–132; chest incompletely scaled; upper part of body with many closely crowded spots, sometimes with diffuse, oblique dark bands on sides; pectoral usually uniformly dark; distinct spot on spinous dorsal between fourth and fifth spines, with another smaller and often more diffuse spot behind first spine; anal fin with clear margin. Specimens of this fish from the western Gulf are generally less well marked than those from elsewhere. A common inshore and bay searobin, it does not, however, occur in as low salinities as does *P. tribulus*. North Carolina to Venezuela. (8 inches; 20 cm)

475. Northern searobin *Prionotus carolinus* (Linnaeus)

D. X + 12–13; A. 11–13; P. 14–15; Sc. 99–106 chest completely scaled; upper part of body with elongate reddish brown spots; second dorsal and caudal with many small, diffuse spots; small fish (less than 2 1/3 inches—60 mm) with ill-defined crossbands (usually four); dorsal spot placed near margin of fin and not extending past fifth spine and usually partly ocellated; small, elongate dark spot frequently found behind first dorsal spine; pectoral fin dusky to nearly black, anal with dark margin; branchiostegal membranes dusky or with scattered melanophores. Populations of this Atlantic Coast species, perhaps left as relicts in the northern Gulf, are considered by some authorities to represent a separate species, *P. martis* Ginsburg. It is also closely related to *P. scitulus,* with which it has often been confused. Nova Scotia to Venezuela. (16 inches; 41 cm)

476. Horned searobin *Bellator militaris* (Goode and Bean)

D. XI + 11–12; A. 9–11; P. 12–13; Sc. 55–67. This peculiar robin with well-developed horns is primarily an outer shelf species. Two other species of this genus (see species key) but lacking the hornlike process are known from deep water in the northeastern Gulf. North Carolina to Florida and around the Gulf to Yucatán. Miller and Richards, 1991a. (5 inches; 13 cm)

Scorpaenidae

Scorpionfishes are colorful fishes with large spines capable of inflicting painful wounds and injecting a poison. The large spiny bone under the eye (preorbital or suborbital stay) and the small mail-like scales on the cheeks are characteristic of the group. Many species of *Sebastes,* commonly called redfish or rockfish, are of commercial importance in the northern Atlantic and Pacific oceans, but these species do not occur in the Gulf. In our area *S. plumieri,* the only species commonly encountered by anglers, is considered a dangerous nuisance. Deepwater scorpionfishes which occasionally venture upon the continental shelf are covered in greater detail by Eschmeyer (1969). These include the reef scorpionfish, *Scorpaenodes caribbaeus* Meek and Hildebrand (a common shallow-water species throughout the tropical Atlantic); the deepwater scorpionfish, *Setarches guentheri* Johnson; *Ectreposebastes imus* Garman (known from deep water off Louisiana); the Atlantic thornyhead, *Trachyscorpia cristulata* (Goode and Bean); and the longfin scorpionfish, *Scorpaena agassizi* Goode and Bean.

1 Lateral line a continuous channel, roofed by thin scales ... deepwater scorpionfish, *Setarches guentheri*.
   Lateral line scales tubed (normal appearance) 2
2 Dorsal spines 13 or more; pectoral rays 18–20 (19); one or more small spines below main row of suboribital spines ... reef scorpionfish, *Scorpaenodes caribbaeus*.
   Dorsal spines 12 3
3 Scales on body ctenoid 4
   Scales on body cycloid 7
4 Pectoral not wedge-shaped, longest rays near upper edge; pectoral rays 21–24 ... Atlantic thornyhead, *Trachyscorpia cristulata*.
   Pectoral fin wedge-shaped; pectoral rays usually 19 or fewer 5
5 Second preopercular spine longest; soft dorsal rays usually 11 or more ... blackbelly rosefish, *Helicolenus dactylopterus*.
   First preopercular spine longest; soft dorsal rays 10 or fewer 6
6 All pectoral rays unbranched ... longspine scorpionfish, *Pontinus longispinis*.
   Some pectoral rays branched ... spinycheek scorpionfish, *Neomerinthe hemingwayi*.
7 Preorbital bone with three or four spines (except in small juveniles) 8
   Preorbital bone with two spines 9
8 Pectoral axil with whitish or yellowish spot, 19–21 pectoral fin rays; pale caudal peduncle ... spotted scorpionfish, *Scorpaena plumieri*.
   Pectoral axil without spots; body mostly pale; 11–19 pectoral fin rays ... hunchback scorpionfish, *Scorpaena dispar*.
9 Pectoral fin with brown spots in axil; 50–60 scale rows; 23 brown spots behind head; occipital pits present ... barbfish, *Scorpaena brasiliensis*.
   Pectoral fin without brown spots, scale rows typically fewer than 50 10
10 Occipital pit absent; supplemental preopercular spine absent; pectoral fin with dark pigment in patches; 42–49 scale rows; one spot on head ... smoothhead scorpionfish, *Scorpaena calcarata*.
   Occipital pit present; supplemental preopercular spine (a small spine developing from the dorsal margin of the uppermost preopercular spine base) present ... longfin scorpionfish, *Scorpaena agassizi*.

477. Blackbelly rosefish *Helicolenus dactylopterus*
D. XII, 11–13 (12); A. III, 4–6 (5); P. 16–21; Sc. 55–80; Gr. 7–9 + 16–21. Red above, pinkish white below, peritoneum black; sides with (usually 6) diffuse red bands; smaller speci-

mens with black pigment near end of spinous dorsal; no slit behind fourth gill arch. This species is commonly taken by longliners and deep trawlers fishing for royal red shrimp in one hundred to three hundred fathoms (182–545 m). Western Pacific, Hawaii, and Nova Scotia to Venezuela, west in the Gulf at least to the Texas-Louisiana border. Eschmeyer, 1978. (8 inches; 20 cm)

478. Longspine scorpionfish *Pontinus longispinis* Goode and Bean
D. XII, 8–10 (usually 9); A. III, 5; P. 16–18 (usually 17); Sc. 45–50; Gr. 6–8 + 8–10; upper parts of head and body, soft dorsal fin, and caudal fin with dusky blotches on pale background; third dorsal spine noticeably elongate. This scorpionfish seems to prefer soft bottoms and is virtually unknown off Caribbean islands. It is common in water over fifty fathoms off the mouth of the Mississippi, with scattered records in seventy-five to ninety-one fathoms off Texas but usually outside of one hundred fathoms. South Carolina to Brazil, but rare from southern Gulf to Panama. (8 inches; 20 cm)

479. Spinycheek scorpionfish *Neomerinthe hemingwayi* Fowler
D. XII, 10 (rarely 9); A. III, 5; P. 16–17 (usually 17); third through seventh or eighth pectoral rays branched; Sc. 60–70; Gr. 6–7 + 9–12; no elongated dorsal spines; body reddish orange with numerous brown spots on body and fins; dark pigment on inside of pectoral fin. The coloration of this species resembles that of *Scorpaena brasiliensis;* however, the two species are otherwise quite distinct. Aside from possessing ctenoid scales (*Scorpaena* has cycloid scales), this species has a more pointed snout and a somewhat more terminal mouth. In the past it has frequently been misidentified as *Neomerinthe* (or *Pontinus*) *pollux* (Poey) or as *Pontinus castor* Poey. It usually occurs over the middle and outer shelf in thirty to one hundred fathoms. A similar deepwater species, the spotwing scorpionfish *N. beanorum* (Evermann and Marsh), with nine soft dorsal rays and an elongated third dorsal spine, has been reported from offshore Texas waters. Maryland to Florida and the northern Gulf. Eschmeyer, 1969. (12 inches; 30 cm)

480. Spotted scorpionfish *Scorpaena plumieri* Bloch
D. XII, 9; A. III, 5; P. 19–21; Sc. 42–49; Gr. 46 + 8–12; body and fins variously blotched, caudal peduncle somewhat pale; caudal fin with three vertical dark bars, white between; axil of pectoral fin dark with white or bright yellow spots on undersides, which are supposed to warn off intruders. This is the most common scorpionfish in the inshore area, but it is not very poisonous. It is usually found near jetties, oil platforms, and reefs out to thirty fathoms. *S. ginsburgi* Gunter is a synonym. Massachusetts through the Caribbean to Rio de Janeiro, Brazil. Eschmeyer, 1965 (12 inches; 30 cm)

481. Hunchback scorpionfish *Scorpaena dispar* Longley and Hildebrand
D. XII, 9; A. III, 5; P. 17–19; Sc. 42–47; Gr. 5 + 10–12. Apparently this is a deepwater species, replacing *S. calcarata* on the outer shelf (twenty to sixty-five fathoms). *S. similis*

Gunter is a synonym. North Carolina through the Caribbean to northeastern Brazil. Eschmeyer, 1965. (8 inches; 20 cm)

482. Barbfish *Scorpaena brasiliensis* Cuvier
D. XII, 9; A. III, 5; P. 18–20; Sc. 50–60; Gr. 4–5 + 8–10; colorful, usually redder than *S. plumieri;* caudal peduncle somewhat paler than rest of body, especially in juveniles, with dark brown spots in axil of pectoral fin (white spots in *plumieri*). Although it is more toxic than other species of *Scorpaena,* the barbfish is not common in our area but is common off the Florida panhandle. Elsewhere it prefers shallow bays and harbors, but it also occurs out to thirty fathoms. Virginia through the Caribbean to Brazil. Eschmeyer, 1965. (8 inches; 20 cm)

483. Smoothhead scorpionfish *Scorpaena calcarata* Goode and Bean
D. XII, 9; A. III, 5; P. 19–21; Sc. 42–49; Gr. 4–5 + 7–11. This is the most common scorpionfish on the inshore shelf and is often taken by shrimp trawlers. It is rarely found in the bays. *S. russula atlantica* Nichols and Breder is a synonym. North Carolina through the Caribbean to northeastern Brazil. Eschmeyer, 1965. (4 inches; 10 cm)

Bothidae

The Bothidae comprise the "left-handed" flatfishes—that is, flatfishes with their eyes and coloration on the left side. The tonguefishes of the family Soleidae are also lefthanded but are further distinguished by a preopercle covered by skin; in the bothids the preopercle is not covered. The three subfamilies recognized here follow Gutherz, 1967. Some recent authors recognize these as separate families (Hensley and Ahlstrom, 1984; Nelson, 1994). All commercial flounders that occur south of Cape Hatteras through the Gulf are bothids, primarily of the genus *Paralichthys.* Most other species of bothids remain small even when fully grown. These small species occur frequently in shrimp catches and are often incorrectly thought of as baby flounders.

Flatfishes, like other fishes, begin life with normally arranged eyes, one on either side of the head. When the larvae are still less than one inch long, metamorphosis occurs as one eye migrates to the other side, the mouth usually shifts to one side, and a rearrangement of internal organs, gills, and associated parts completes the asymmetry of the fish. Occasionally "reversed" specimens occur in which the external features are on the wrong side, but internally these reversed fishes resemble their correctly arranged relatives. In some Pacific bothids, reversal is as common as 30–40 percent of a population; however, it is quite rare in local species. Ambicoloration and partial or complete albinism are other abnormalities in flatfishes. Normally, the blind side is white or nearly so, but ambicolored fish, which are often reversed, exhibit varied amounts of color on the blind side. As one would expect, bothids, like other flatfish, are primarily bottom fish; most species lie buried in the bottom when they are at rest. They are famous for their ability to change the intensity of their skin coloration. Many species normally appear brown, but under respective backgrounds they range from almost white to dark brown, with many intermediate mottled phases. Dead fish are usually dark, whereas living ones are beautifully patterned.

In general, the life histories of most bothids are not well known. Accounts of collections in various localities contain information on different species, but there are few works concentrating on particular species or on bothids alone. Among the latter are papers by Fraser (1971), Gartner (1986), Hensley (1977), Landry and Johnson (1977), Matlock (1991), Prentice (1989), and Swingle (1971b). Systematic work by Gutherz (1967) has provided a good understanding of the taxonomy of the group. (Leslie and Stewart, 1986; Norman, 1934; Topp and Hoff, 1972)

1   Bases of pelvic fins symmetrical 2
    Bases of pelvic fins asymmetrical (subfamily Bothinae) . . . two spot flounder, *Bothus robinsi.*
2   Bases of both pelvic fins short, not extending forward onto urohyal; ocular side pelvic fin may or may not be on median line of body (subfamily Paralichthinae) 3
    Bases of both pelvic fins long, extending forward onto urohyal (subfamily Scophthalminae) . . . windowpane flounder, *Scophthalmus aquosus.**
3   Pectoral fin present on blind side 4
    Pectoral fin absent from blind side . . . deepwater flounder, *Monolene sessilicauda.*
4   Lateral line with high arch over pectoral fin on ocular side 5
    Lateral line without high arch over pectoral fin on ocular side 11
5   Three or four prominent ocellated spots on ocular side of body; additional spotting may be present 6
    Body spotting may be present or absent; if present, not with three or four prominent ocellated spots 8
6   Three large, ocellated spots present 7
    Four large, ocellated spots present . . . ocellated flounder, *Ancylopsetta quadrocellata.*
7   Anterior dorsal fin rays elongate; pelvic fin on ocular side longer than that on blind side . . . three-eye flounder, *Ancylopsetta dilecta.*
    Anterior dorsal fin rays not elongate; pelvic fins equal in length . . . Gulf flounder, *Paralichthys albigutta.***

---

*   The windowpane flounder, *Scophthalmus aquosus* (Mitchill), is included here based on one doubtful record listed by Baughman (1950a) from Galveston. The species normally occurs on the Atlantic Coast of the United States and is otherwise unknown from the Gulf of Mexico.

**   *Paralichthys triocellatus*, with 67–69 anal rays and 8–9 gill rakers on the lower limb of the first arch, reported by Springer and Bullis (1956) from "Oregon Station 1086" eighteen fathoms off the South Texas coast, may refer to *P. albigutta. P. triocellatus* Ribero, according to Ginsburg (1952c), is probably a synonym of *Pseudorhombus isosceles,* which has not been reported north of the Brazilian coast, and all earlier reports of *P. triocellatus* are also from South American waters. Cervigon (1966) reports neither from Venezuela.

8   Pelvic fin on ocular side not inserted on median line; lateral line well developed on both sides 9

Pelvic fin on ocular side inserted on median line; lateral line poorly developed or lacking on blind side 10

9   Body depth greater than 47 percent (usually 50 percent) of standard length; blind side dusky in large individuals; lateral line scales 104–117 ... broad flounder, *Paralichthys squamilentus*.

Body depth less than 47 percent (usually 44 percent) of standard length; blind side immaculate or dusky; lateral line scales 78–100 ... southern flounder, *Paralichthys lethostigma*.

10 Upper jaw short, 20–25 percent of head length; spines present on interorbital ridge; tentacles on eyes ... spiny flounder, *Engyophrys senta*.

Upper jaw moderate, 32–45 percent of head length; no interorbital spines or tentacles on eyes ... sash flounder, *Trichopsetta ventralis*.

11 Large round spots on dorsal, anal, and caudal fin, or body with five or six broad bars 12

No large spots or bars on body or fins 13

12 Large black spot in center of caudal fin; three smaller spots on dorsal edges of caudal (may be absent); large black blotch on distal edge of pectoral fin on ocular side, with no blotch under this fin; distal edge of pectoral fin truncate; pectoral rays on ocular side 11 or 12 ... spotfin flounder, *Cyclopsetta fimbriata*.

No large black spot in center of caudal fin, but three distinct spots along distal edge of caudal fin; no blotch on ocular pectoral fin, but with black blotch on body under this fin; distal edge of pectoral fin oblique; (instead of spots and blotches on body and fins there may be five or six broad bars); pectoral fin rays 14–16 ... Mexican flounder, *Cyclopsetta chittendeni*.

13 Upper jaw very short, 25 percent of head length; maxillary extending only to anterior margin of lower eye 14

Upper jaw moderate to long, maxillary longer than 35 percent of head length, usually extending past middle of lower eye 17

14 Scales without secondary squamation (small, microscopic scales on each primary scale) ... fringed flounder, *Etropus crossotus*.

Scales with secondary squamation 15

15 Primary body scales with only one row of secondary scale 16

Primary body scales densely covered with secondary scales ... smallmouth flounder, *Etropus microstomus*.

16 Scales on blind side ctenoid; scales on snout extending forward of a line connecting eyed and blind-side nostrils; sides plain, without ring-shaped marks ... gray flounder, *Etropus rimosus*.

Scales on blind side cycloid; scales on snout not extending forward of a line connecting eyed and blind-side nostrils; sides often with 5 or 6 ring-shaped marks (may be indistinct) .... shelf flounder, *Etropus cyclosquamata*.

17 Gill rakers short and stout with 6–9 on lower limb or long and stout with 67 on lower limb (total gill rakers 8–12) 18

Gill rakers long and slender with 9–13 on lower limb (total 13–22) 19

18 Body depth usually greater than 48 percent of standard length (45–53 percent); 46 to 55

scales in lateral line; gill rakers long and stout, 2–4 on upper limb and 6–8 on lower limb …
shoal flounder, *Syacium gunteri.*

Body depth usually 45 percent of standard length or less (40–46 percent); 47–68 scales in lateral line; gill rakers short and stout, 2 + 8 … dusky flounder, *Syacium papillosum.*

19 Cephalic spines on snout and anterior orbital rim … male horned whiff, *Citharichthys cornutus.*
No cephalic spines on snout or orbitals 20

20 Body and fins profusely covered with regularly arranged spots and blotches … spotted whiff, *Citharichthys macrops.*

Body and fins not profusely covered with regularly arranged spots and blotches 21

21 Eye diameter usually 30 percent of head length or greater; pectoral fin on ocular side usually greater than 20 percent of standard length … female horned whiff, *Citharichthys cornutus.* Eye diameter usually 25 percent of head length or less; pectoral fin on ocular side about 15 percent of standard length … bay whiff, *Citharichthys spilopterus.*

484. Twospot flounder *Bothus robinsi* Topp and Hoff

D. 78–90; A. 59–68; P. 8–11 (on ocular side); Gr. short, 27 + 59; Sc. 70–77; ocular side dark brown, generally with no spotting, but may be light tan with spotting or mottling; two large dark spots on median rays of caudal fin, one anterior to other; interorbital width greater in males. In most areas it occurs together with the closely related species *B. ocellatus* in depths of less than twenty-five fathoms. *Bothus ocellatus* differs from the spottail flounder by having the two spots on the caudal fin in a vertical line instead of a horizontal line. *B. ocellatus* occurs in the northeastern and southern Gulf, but we have been unable to verify its existence west of the delta. New York to Brazil. Moore, 1975b. (6 inches; 15 cm)

485. Deepwater flounder *Monolene sessilicauda* Goode

D. 92–107; A. 76–84; P. 11–14 on ocular side, no pectoral fin on blind side; Gr. 8–10; Sc. 88–94; body elongate (for a flounder), light tan often with darker crossbars; caudal fin usually with dark central spot; other dark spots along bases of dorsal and anal fins, lower distal portion of pectoral fin darkened, anterior lateral line arched over pectoral fin, with arch distinctly shaped, more square than curved. In our area this last character is found only in species of *Monolene* and *Trichopsetta.* This fish is known from relatively deep water (fifty to one hundred fathoms). Massachusetts to Brazil. (6 inches; 15 cm)

486. Ocellated flounder *Ancylopsetta quadrocellata* Gill

D. 67–76; A. 54–61; P. 10–12 on ocular side; Gr. 2–3 + 6–7; Sc. 80–90; ocular side dark brown with four larger ocellated spots; anteriormost rays of dorsal fin somewhat elongated. This flounder is common in bays and the shallow Gulf from two to ninety fathoms, with the largest specimens in deeper water. North Carolina to Jupiter, Florida, and from Cape Sable, Florida, to Campeche. Gutherz, 1966. (12 inches; 30 cm)

487. Three-eye flounder *Ancylopsetta dilecta* (Goode and Bean)

D. 68–79; A. 53–60; P. 10–12 on ocular side; Gr. 1–3 + 6–9; Sc. 73–82; ocular side tan or pale brown with numerous blotches and patches; three large, ocellated spots on ocular side, arranged triangularly; ventral fin on ocular side and anteriormost dorsal rays noticeably elongate. This species is more common in deeper water (thirty-two to two hundred fathoms) than is *A. quadrocellata*. North Carolina to Yucatán. (7 inches; 18 cm)

488. Gulf flounder *Paralichthys albigutta* Jordan and Gilbert

D. 71–85; A. 53–63; P. on ocular side 10–12; Gr. 2–4 (usually 2–3) + 9–12 (usually 10–11); Sc. 78–83; body depth usually 39–47 percent of standard length; ocular side either dark or light brown with numerous blotches and spots; three conspicuous ocellated spots (sometimes faint) arranged in triangular pattern; other spots fainter and not ocellated. As in other Texas species of *Paralichthys,* the young of this species are found in the bays during the spring and summer and migrate to the Gulf with the onset of colder weather, but Gulf flounder are more common in Florida. Ginsburg called this species the sand flounder, since the adults appeared to be more common on hard, sandy bottoms. In the bays the young are found in grass flats. North Carolina at least to southern Texas and the Bahamas. Enge and Mulholland, 1985; Ginsburg, 1952c; Stokes, 1977. (15 inches; 38 cm)

489. Broad flounder *Paralichthys squamilentus* Jordan and Gilbert

D. 76–85; A. 59–65; P. on ocular side 11–12; Gr. 3–5 (usually 3 or 5) + 9–12 (usually 10–12); Sc. 104–117; body depth usually 48–59 percent of standard length; eyed side brown, with numerous nonocellated spots; body tending to darken with age and increased size; broad area along dorsal and ventral edges of eyed side characteristically sprinkled with pigment, but center of ocular side virtually devoid of pigment; blind side frequently dusky. As in other *Paralichthys,* the young of this species occur inshore during the warmer months; however, the adults occur deeper than those of either *P. albigutta* or *P. lethostigma,* at depths of 60–120 fathoms. North Carolina to Mexico. (16 inches; 41 cm)

490. Southern flounder *Paralichthys lethostigma* Jordan and Gilbert

D. 80–95; A. 63–74; P. on ocular side 11–13; Gr. 2–3 (usually 2) + 8–11 (usually 9–10); Sc. 85–100. Body depth 39–47 percent of standard length; eyed side light or dark brown with diffuse nonocellated spots and blotches, which tend to disappear in the larger specimens; blind side immaculate or dusky. Young *P. lethostigma* are found in shallow bays, even in low salinities. The larger fish leave the bays for the open Gulf during the fall in order to spawn. A severe norther causes a mass migration, resulting in excellent floundering or gigging, while a moderate or warm winter causes the departure of the larger flounders to be spread over a greater period, resulting in decreased catches. The southern flounder has sustained a steady commercial and sport fishery. This fish has been called the "mud flounder." In the Gulf as well as in the bays, it is often more common over the softer mud bottoms. Large individuals are often called "halibut." North Carolina to Florida, in the Gulf from Florida to northern Mexico. Enge and Mulholland, 1985; Fox and White, 1969; Ginsburg, 1952c; Matlock, 1991; Prentice, 1989; Stokes, 1977. (3 feet; 91 cm)

491. Spiny flounder *Engyophrys senta* Ginsburg

D. 74–83; A. 60–67; P. on ocular side 8–10 (usually 9); Gr. short, 0–3 + 4–7; Sc. 50; ocular side dark tan or brownish with darker blotches along lateral line and edges of body; usually three blotches on lateral line, with center one being largest; blind side of mature males with three to seven (usually five) vertical, diffuse bars on anterior portion of body; blind side of females and immature males immaculate. This is the smallest bothid occurring in these waters. Its common name is derived from the interorbital spines. Both sexes also possess short tentacles extending from the posterior margin of the eyes, but these become reduced in males and may be absent in large males. This fish is common in twenty to one hundred fathoms of water. Northern Gulf and Bahamas through the Caribbean to Brazil. Anderson and Lindner, 1951; Hensley, 1977. (3 inches; 8 cm)

492. Sash flounder *Trichopsetta ventralis* (Goode and Bean)

D. 89–95; A. 69–75; P. on ocular side 12–13, on blind side 7–10; Gr. moderately long and slender, 0 + 9–11; Sc. 63–68; ocular side brownish with limited spotting on body and fins; three blotches along lateral line, with anteriormost being most distinct (these possibly indistinct or lacking); males having greatly elongate pelvic fin rays on blind side, with pectoral fin on blind side frequently longer than that on ocular side. Little is known of the life history of this fish, which is found between eighteen and sixty fathoms. Three additional species of *Trichopsetta* occur in the Caribbean. Throughout the Gulf. Anderson and Gutherz, 1967. (6 inches; 15 cm)

493. Spotfin flounder *Cyclopsetta fimbriata* (Goode and Bean)

D. 78–87; A. 59–67; P. on ocular side 11–12, on blind side 9–10; Gr. 3–4 + 9–10; Sc. 65–75; ocular side brown with several large black spots on dorsal, anal, and caudal fins; large black spot on distal portion of pectoral fin; caudal fin with large spot in center and sometimes with three smaller spots along posterior edge; pectoral fin on ocular side with truncate margin. While it occurs in 10–125 fathoms, in the northwestern Gulf this species is not as common as *C. chittendeni*. North Carolina through the West Indies to British Guiana. (15 inches; 38 cm)

494. Mexican flounder *Cyclopsetta chittendeni* Bean

D. 82–90; A. 63–69; P. on ocular side 13–16, on blind side 11–13; Gr. 3–5 + 8–9; Sc. 74–80; ocular side brown with several large spots on dorsal, anal, and caudal fins and large black spot under pectoral fin; caudal fin with three large black spots on distal edge, none in center of fin; canine teeth large (larger than in *C. fimbriata*). *Cyclopsetta decussata* Gunter, based on one mounted specimen, is a color variant in which the black spots are merged into five or six broad bands extending across the body and fins, a color pattern sometimes seen in live animals. *C. chittendeni* is a common fish, occurring in ten to seventy-five fathoms. Northern Gulf through the Caribbean to Brazil. Dawson, 1968. (13 inches; 33 cm)

495. Fringed flounder *Etropus crossotus* Jordan and Gilbert
D. 75–85; A. 58–68; P. on ocular side 8–10, on blind side 7–9; Gr. 4–5 + 6–9 (usually 7–8); Sc. 41–47; ocular side brown; no spotting on body; dorsal, anal, and caudal fins with dusky blotches; caudal sometimes edged with black; body scales deciduous, with no secondary squamation. Of the three species with secondary squamation, *E. rimosus* Goode and Bean is known east but not west of the Mississippi Delta, also occurring off Yucatán (see species key), and the Atlantic species *E. microstomus* (Gill) is erroneously reported from the Gulf. The fringed flounder is generally found in shallow water of five to thirty-five fathoms, entering the bays during the warmer months of the year. In the northwestern Gulf it occurs mostly in water shallower than seventeen fathoms. Chesapeake Bay through the Caribbean to French Guiana. (7 inches; 18 cm)

496. Shelf flounder *Etropus cyclosquamata* Leslie and Stewart
D. 70–82 (73–80); A. 54–64 (56–61); P. 8–11 (9–10); Gr. 4–8 + 3–6; Sc. 36–45 (34 42). Snout not scaled forward of line between nostrils on blind and eyed sides. Color dusky gray to brown, often with discrete dark rings in two rows, above and below lateral line. A deepwater species, sometimes taken inside one hundred fathoms. Cape Hatteras to Florida and northern Gulf west to Mississippi. Leslie and Stewart, 1986; Retzer, 1990. (6 inches; 15 cm)

497. Shoal flounder *Syacium gunteri* Ginsburg
D. 74–85; A. 59–68; P. on ocular side 9–11 (usually 11); Gr. moderately long and thick, 2–4 (usually 3) + 6–8 (usually 7); Sc. 46–55; ocular side tan, sometimes with numerous circular or ocellated spots or blotches on body and median fins, generally with large, diffuse blotch on caudal peduncle; blind side immaculate. Found in five to fifty fathoms, but generally most abundant in water ten to forty fathoms deep, this is the most abundant flatfish, and indeed the most abundant fish caught on the brown shrimp grounds of Texas. For distinctions between *S. gunteri* and *S. papillosum,* see the discussion under the latter species. Florida and the Gulf through the Caribbean to French Guiana. (11 inches; 28 cm)

498. Dusky flounder *Syacium papillosum* (Linnaeus)
D. 82–94; A. 64–75; P. on ocular side 11–12 (usually 11); Gr. short and stout, 2 + 8–9 (usually 8); Sc. 47–60; ocular side brown with little if any spotting; large males with pigment lines from upper eye to snout, along dorsal, and on lips, mandible, and lower jaw; blind side dusky in large males, immaculate or slightly "dirty" in females and immature

males. Found from seven to seventy-five fathoms, this species is less abundant in the northwestern Gulf than *S. gunteri,* but the situation is reversed east of the Mississippi. In general, large specimens (over three inches, or 8 cm, in standard length) of *Syacium* from the Gulf can readily be separated by the greater interorbital width of *S. gunteri*. This difference is not apparent in smaller fish (less than three inches) but becomes more pronounced with increasing size. *S. micrurum* Ranzani, often reported from the Gulf, is a problem and we have not been able to verify its presence here. It seems to have the coloration of *gunteri* but a body shape and meristics closer to those of *papillosum*. North Carolina through the Caribbean to Brazil. Fraser, 1971. (11 inches; 28 cm)

499. Horned whiff *Citharichthys cornutus* (Günther)
D. 74–83; A. 59–66; P. on ocular side 10–11; Gr. moderately long and slender 3–5 + 11–15; Sc. 40–45; ocular side brown; ocular pectoral with dark area in axil, sometimes with dark crossbars; adult males show pronounced cephalic spination, with single large spine projecting horizontally beyond margin of head as well as several smaller spines along anterior edge of upper eye. The horned whiff is found in relatively deep water (15–200 fathoms, generally exceeding 75 fathoms). The only reports from the northwestern Gulf are from 103 fathoms. Georgia and Bahamas through the Caribbean to Brazil. (4 inches; 10 cm)

500. Spotted whiff *Citharichthys macrops* Dresel
D. 80–85; A. 56–64; P. on ocular side 9–12; Gr. long and slender, 5–6 + 13–16; Sc. 37–44; ocular side brown with numerous spots and blotches on body and median fins, becoming indistinct when highly deciduous scales are lost. This flatfish is rare to uncommon off Texas and Louisiana but abundant on the shrimp grounds off Campeche and in the northeastern Gulf because it has a preference for hard, coarse, sand-shell bottoms, which are rare in the northwestern Gulf but common in those other areas. South Carolina to Florida and throughout the Gulf. (6 inches; 15 cm)

501. Bay whiff *Citharichthys spilopterus* Günther
D. 75–84; A. 56–63; P. on ocular side 9–10; Gr. of moderate length and stoutness, 4–5 + 9–15; Sc. 41–49; ocular side brownish after death, varying from light to dark in life; two dark spots on caudal peduncle; light spot under pectoral. Found inshore to depths of forty fathoms, rarely exceeding twenty fathoms in the Gulf, this species moves into the bays and shallow Gulf during the warmer months of the year. It is one of the commonest small flatfish in this area. Atlantic Ocean, in the west from New Jersey through the Caribbean to Brazil. Kuhn, 1977. (6 inches; 15 cm)

Achiridae

The American soles are commonly represented by only three species in our area, although two others may also occur. These are short-bodied, nearly round fishes with their eyes on the right side. They can use the blind side to adhere to hard objects such as aquarium walls, an attribute which is said to have choked a hog. Although these soles are right-handed, recent work has shown them to be closely related to left-handed tonguefishes and the right-handed Old World soles (Soleidae), with which they are sometimes combined (Nelson, 1994; Robins et al., 1991)

1 Body covered with well-developed scales; upper eye in advance of lower eye; margin of ventral fin on blind side free 2

Body not scaled; skin loose; upper eye vertically in line with lower eye; margins of both ventral fins attached to body 3

2 Pectoral fins small, present on at least right (ocular) side ... lined sole, *Achirus lineatus.*

Pectoral fins wholly lacking on both sides ... hogchoker, *Trinectes maculatus.*

3 Number of pores in third accessory sensory line less than 42; number of stripes originating on dorsal margin usually over 30 ... fringed sole, *Gymnachirus texae.*

Number of pores in third accessory sensory line more than 42; number of stripes originating on dorsal margin usually under 30 ... naked sole, *Gymnachirus melas.*

502. Fringed sole (zebra sole) *Gymnachirus texae* (Gunter)

D. 57–66; A. 41–48; C. 14–17 (usually 16); P. on ocular side 1–3 (usually 2), sometimes not externally evident; right and left ventral fins enclosed in common fleshy envelope; body covered by scaleless, loose skin with distinct black and white stripes; blind side creamy, dusky, or with considerable pigment, especially about edges of median fins. There is a narrow zone of overlap between this species and the related naked sole, *G. melas* (plate 502b), which replaces it in the eastern Gulf as well as on the Atlantic Coast. Similarly patterned, *G. melas* has broader stripes. Fairly common in the shallow Gulf, preferring mud bottoms, *G. texae* normally is collected in water thirty to fifty fathoms deep. The young are not uncommon in even shallower water during the summer and may go into saltier bays. It overlaps in the southern Gulf with *G. nudus* of the tropics. The name *Gymnachirus williamsoni* (Gunter), which has been reported from Texas and Louisiana, has been used for both species. Alabama west and south to the Campeche Banks and the west coast of Yucatán. Caldwell and Briggs, 1957b; Dawson, 1964. (5 inches; 13 cm)

503. Lined sole (cover) *Achirus lineatus* (Linnaeus)

D. 50–58; A. 38–48; P. on ocular side 5–6; body with eight narrow bands that fade with age; median fins with small dark spots, especially distinct on caudal. Records of *Achirus*

achirus (Linnaeus) refer to this species, a small, tan flatfish covered with spots and diffuse lines. It is fairly common in the shallow Gulf and bays, especially during the summer. South Carolina to Uruguay. (5 inches; 13 cm)

504. Hogchoker (cover) *Trinectes maculatus* (Bloch and Schneider)
D. 50–56; A. 36–42; P. lacking; ventral on right side 3, on left 1; Sc. 66–75; ocular side usually dark gray-green to brown with seven or eight darker vertical bars. The hogchoker generally resembles *Achirus lineatus* but lacks the spotting. It is common in the bays and shallow Gulf (out to twenty-five fathoms). This species is apparently more tolerant of brackish waters than is *A. lineatus* and is correspondingly more common in the bays. Young run up rivers, which makes them practically catadromous. Young hogchokers are frequently sold in aquarium stores as "freshwater flounder." In early literature this species is often referred to as *Achirus fasciatus* Lacepède. Massachusetts to Panama. (6 inches; 15 cm)

Cynoglossidae

The tonguefishes are represented by only one genus *(Symphurus)* in the northwestern Gulf. In this genus one of the key characters is the number of caudal rays. Since the caudal fin is continuous with both the dorsal and anal fins, some care must be taken to distinguish the caudal rays from those of the other fins. Generally the bases of the caudal rays lie on a more or less straight line and are more closely spaced than those of the dorsal or anal fins, and the outermost caudal rays (both top and bottom) have broadened bases, often with a projecting burr. Species of *Symphurus* are markedly selective in their depth distributions, which also aids in identification. All are small-mouthed, bottom animals, which feed on small invertebrates such as worms. (Ginsburg, 1951b)

1 Distinct black spot with surrounding clearer area covering much of caudal fin . . . spottail tonguefish, *Symphurus urospilus*.
No such spot on caudal 2
2 Caudal rays 10 3
Caudal rays 12 5
3 Teeth in upper jaw on eyed side extending no more than half length of jaw (or may be absent); teeth absent or few in lower jaw 4
Teeth nearly completely filling both jaws on eyed side of head ... pygmy tonguefish, *Symphurus parvus*.
4 Large black spots on posterior portions of dorsal and anal fins, or these regions quite dark; no spot on opercle; teeth absent from both jaws on eyed side of head ... spottedfin tonguefish, *Symphurus diomedianus*.

Large black spots lacking on fins, which are pale, sometimes with small, diffuse spots; distinct black patch on opercle; teeth absent from lower jaw on eyed side of head, present for only about one-half length of upper jaw . . . blackcheek tonguefish, *Symphurus plagiusa*.

5   Teeth present in both jaws on eyed side of head, covering one-half to all of upper jaw 6
Teeth absent from both jaws . . . offshore tonguefish, *Symphurus civitatus*.

6   Dorsal rays 85 or more; anal rays 72 or more; found in over 50 fathoms . . . deepwater tonguefish, *Symphurus piger*.
Dorsal rays fewer than 82; anal rays fewer than 68; fish living in 20–50 fathoms . . . longtail tonguefish, *Symphurus pelicanus*.

505. Spottail tonguefish *Symphurus urospilus* Ginsburg
D. 84–86; A. 68–71; C. 11. Scattered specimens of this distinctive fish have been taken in coarse sediments at mid-depths. Mexico to Florida. Dennis and Bright, 1988a. (3 2/3 inches; 9 cm)

506. Pygmy tonguefish *Symphurus parvus* Ginsburg
D. 78–84; A. 64–68; C. 10 (rarely 11); Sc. 86–98; teeth in jaws on eyed side few or absent; body uniformly brown, with one to four dark spots on posterior portion of dorsal and anal fins, or these portions of fins uniformly dark. This fish is found from eight to fifty fathoms, and usually in water deeper than fifteen fathoms. North Carolina to Brazil. (3 inches; 8 cm)

507. Spottedfin tonguefish *Symphurus diomedianus* (Goode and Bean)
D. 89–93; A. 73–78; C. 10 (rarely 11); Sc. 86–98; teeth on eyed side usually absent, or with only a few at top of upper jaw and middle of lower jaw; uniformly brown with one to four distinct round spots on posterior dorsal and anal fins. This species is usually caught in fifteen to twenty-five fathoms. North Carolina to Brazil. (8 inches; 20 cm)

508. Blackcheek tonguefish; patch *Symphurus plagiusa* (Linnaeus)
D. 85–92; A. 69–76; C. 9–11 (almost always 10); Sc. 71–86; teeth covering about half length of upper jaw on eyed side; teeth absent from lower jaw; color variable, with crossbands present or not, but generally with dark spot on opercle (possibly faded in preserved specimens or absent entirely). The most common inshore species of *Symphurus*, rarely found deeper than twenty fathoms, this is the only species so far reported from brackish water. Long Island to Yucatán. (8 inches; 20 cm)

509. Offshore tonguefish; patch *Symphurus civitatus* Ginsburg
D. 87–92; A. 70–77; C. 12 (rarely 11); Sc. 69–80; teeth not extending over anterior one-half of upper jaw on eyed side; teeth absent from lower jaw; crossbands on body absent or faint; no black spots on fins or opercle. This fish is usually found inshore in four to thirty fathoms. North Carolina to Florida and the whole Gulf. (6 inches; 15 cm)

510. Deepwater tonguefish *Symphurus piger* (Goode and Bean)

D. 85–88; A. 72–73; C. 12; Sc. 69–74; teeth extending over anterior three-fourths of both jaws on eyed side; body pale, with contrasting narrow crossbands. This tonguefish occurs in deep water from fifty to over one hundred fathoms. Gulf of Mexico and West Indies. (6 inches; 15 cm)

511. Longtail tonguefish *Symphurus pelicanus* Ginsburg

D. 80–81; A. 63–67; C. 12; Sc. 61–74; teeth small, extending entire length of jaws on eyed side; body uniformly brownish or irregularly shaded; black peritoneum often showing through skin behind head. This midshelf species occurs in twenty-five to fifty fathoms. Gulf of Mexico and West Indies. (3 inches; 8 cm)

Balistidae

These fishes, well armored with long dorsal spines, were formerly separated into two families, the triggerfishes (Balistidae) and the filefishes (Monacanthidae), and are so considered by Nelson (1994). The combined family has been given the common name leatherjackets in reference to their heavy skins. Most live around hard substrates, to which they are well adapted with small mouths for browsing on small attached organisms. Young of many balistid species associate with sargassum and other floating objects. Many species are observed by divers, but their hard mouths make them resistant to capture with hook and line. (Berry and Vogele, 1961; Böhlke and Chaplin, 1968, 1993; Moore, 1967; Randall et al., 1978; Tyler, 1980)

1 Three dorsal spines; large, platelike scales 2
  Two dorsal spines; scales small 7

2 Two large canines in upper and lower jaws; dark but never black 3
  Teeth even, more incisorlike; almost entirely black . . . black durgon, *Melichthys niger.*

3 One or more bony plates behind gill openings 4
  Ordinary scales behind gill openings 5

4 Head with two blue stripes; 29–31 soft dorsal rays; 26–28 anal rays . . . queen triggerfish, *Balistes vetula.*
  Head without blue stripes; 27–29 soft dorsal rays; 23–26 anal rays . . . gray triggerfish, *Balistes capriscus.*

5 Cheek with narrow parallel grooves; chin projecting . . . sargassum triggerfish, *Xanthichthys ringens.*
  Cheek without grooves, closely scaled; chin not projecting 6

6 Body without pale spots; dorsal rays 27; anal rays 24 or 25 . . . ocean triggerfish, *Canthidermis sufflamen.*

Body typically with pale spots; dorsal rays 24; anal rays 22 ... rough triggerfish, *Canthidermis maculata.*

7 Pelvic bone with no evident external spine; gill openings at 45-degree angle 8
   Pelvic bone with large external spine; gill openings nearly vertical 11
8 Dorsal rays 43–50; anal rays 46–52 9
   Dorsal rays 32–41; anal rays 33–44 10
9 Caudal peduncle longer than high; distance from eye to dorsal spine 7–8 percent of standard length ... scrawled filefish, *Aluterus scriptus.*
   Caudal peduncle higher than long; distance from eye to dorsal spine 5–6.7 percent of standard length ... unicorn filefish, *Aluterus monoceros.*
10 Dorsal spine with small barbs only at base; live specimens with orange spots ... orange filefish, *Aluterus schoepfi.*
   Dorsal spine with large barbs extending to tip; live specimens with purple lines ... dotterel filefish, *Aluterus heudeloti.*
11 Deep groove behind dorsal spine where spine can be inserted 12
   No deep groove behind dorsal spine 13
12 Two pairs of strong spines on each side of caudal peduncle; pectoral rays usually 14; gill rakers 29–35 ... whitespotted filefish, *Cantherhines macrocerus.*
   No strong spines on caudal peduncle, pectoral rays usually 13; gill rakers 34–46 ... orangespotted filefish, *Cantherhines pullus.*
13 Caudal peduncle with two to four pairs of enlarged spines (recurved in males); individual scales with unbranched spines; no elongated dorsal rays ... fringed filefish, *Monacanthus ciliatus.*
   Caudal peduncle without spines; scales with branched spines in specimens greater than one-half inch (13 mm); dorsal rays elongated in adult males 14
14 Dorsal rays 31–34 (29–35); anal rays 31–34 (30–35) ... planehead filefish, *Monacanthus hispidus.*
   Dorsal rays 27–29 (27–30); anal rays 27–29 (26–30) ... pygmy filefish, *Monacanthus setifer.*

512. Black durgon; black triggerfish *Melichthys niger* (Bloch)
D. III + 32–34; A. 28–31; P. 16–17; Gr. 36–37; entirely black. This is a secretive but not uncommon fish on some offshore reefs. Probably circumtropical; in the western Atlantic from Massachusetts and Bermuda through the Caribbean to Brazil. (15 inches; 38 cm)

513. Queen triggerfish *Balistes vetula* Linnaeus
D. III + 29–31; A. 26–28; P. 15–16; Gr. 35–38; dorsal, anal, and caudal fins with produced rays; two broad blue bands on face; broad blue band on caudal peduncle. This is an occasional fish on offshore reefs. Massachusetts to Brazil as well as the eastern Atlantic. (20 inches; 51 cm)

514. Gray triggerfish *Balistes capriscus* Gmelin

D. III + 27–29; A. 23–26; P. 15; Gr. 31–35; body grayish with irregular dark markings; small blue spots on upper sides and spinous dorsal membranes. This very common fish is found near reefs, oil rigs, and jetties; the young are found inshore. *B. carolinensis* is a synonym. Atlantic Ocean, in the west from Nova Scotia and Bermuda through the Caribbean to Argentina. Johnson and Salomon, 1984. (1 foot; 30 cm)

515. Sargassum triggerfish *Xanthichthys ringens* (Linnaeus)

D. III + 26–30; A. 23–27; P. 13; Gr. 36–37. The parallel grooves in the cheek and slightly protruding skin of this triggerfish are characteristic. The young associate with *Sargassum*, while the adults occur in deep water, usually over one hundred feet. Recently confirmed in the western Gulf by Dennis and Bright (1988b). Circumtropical. Randall et al., 1978. (10 inches; 25 cm)

516. Ocean triggerfish *Canthidermis sufflamen* (Mitchill)

D. III + 26–27; A. 24; P. 16; Gr. 32–36; body gray with dark spot in axil of pectoral fin; outer caudal rays prolonged; dorsal and anal fins falcate, but not so extreme as those of *Balistes vetula*. The ocean triggerfish is fairly common on offshore reefs. Massachusetts and Bermuda through the Caribbean and Gulf to the Lesser Antilles. Bright and Cashman, 1974; Moore, 1967; Sonnier et al., 1976. (2 feet; 61 cm)

517. Rough triggerfish *Canthidermis maculata* (Bloch)

D. 23–25; A. 20–22; P. 13–15. Body brown or gray, usually with many light spots on sides and venter; dorsal and anal fin membranes dark, frequently spotted; depth 36–45 percent of standard length. Small (.5–.8 inches; 10–20 mm) specimens with three dark papillae above lateral line on caudal peduncle. Circumtropical, in the Western Atlantic from New Jersey to Argentina. (13 inches; 33 cm)

518. Scrawled filefish *Aluterus scriptus* (Osbeck)

D. II + 43–49; A. 46–52; P. 13–15; Gr. 32–42; body elongate, depth 22–34 percent of standard length; snout long, upturned, projecting; body olive with dark scrawls. This is a rare fish on the offshore reefs, but the young are commonly taken inshore, especially in grass beds. Circumtropical; in the western Atlantic from Massachusetts and Bermuda through the Caribbean to Brazil. (16 inches; 41 cm)

519. Unicorn filefish *Aluterus monoceros* (Linnaeus)

D. II+ 46–50; A. 47–52; P. 14; color uniform gray with many small round spots. Probably circumtropical, in the western Atlantic from Massachusetts to Brazil, occasional in the northern Gulf. (2 feet; 61 cm)

520. Orange filefish *Aluterus schoepfi* (Walbaum)

D. II + 32–39; A. 35–41; P. 11–14; Gr. 21–27; depth 19–48 percent of standard length (smaller fish more elongate); profile of snout generally flattened; body plain, either orange or black or with orange spots in life, which soon fade. The orange filefish is widespread on the offshore reefs; the young are common inshore. Nova Scotia and Bermuda through the Caribbean to Brazil. (16 inches; 41 cm)

521. Dotterel filefish *Aluterus heudeloti* Hollard

D. II + 36–41; A. 39–44; P. 13–15; depth 28–48 percent of standard length; body colored like *A. scriptus*. This fish is only rarely reported from the coast; its status is uncertain. Bermuda and Massachusetts to Brazil. Bullis and Thompson, 1965. (10 inches; 25 cm)

522. Whitespotted filefish *Cantherhines macrocerus* (Hollard)

D. II + 34–36; A. 29–32; P. 13–14 (14); Gr. 29–35; sides of body with large white spots; 2–3 pairs of enlarged spines on caudal peduncle (not always apparent in juveniles); caudal fin dark. Northern Gulf of Mexico, Florida, and Bermuda through the Caribbean to Brazil. Sonnier et al., 1976 (16 inches; 41 cm)

523. Orangespotted filefish *Cantherhines pullus* (Ranzani)

D. II + 33–36; A. 29–32; P. 12–14; Gr. 34–46; body usually with indistinct light and dark stripes on sides and scattered orange spots; white spot on upper side of caudal peduncle. A rare fish from offshore reefs, this species is sometimes placed in the genus *Amanses*. Atlantic Ocean, in the west from Bermuda, Florida, and the northern Gulf of Mexico through the Caribbean to Brazil. (6 inches; 18 cm)

524. Fringed filefish *Monacanthus ciliatus* (Mitchill)

D. II + 29–37; A. 28–36; P. 11; Gr. 15–23; depth 40–56 percent of standard length; color variable. This fish occurs irregularly west of the Mississippi River, but juveniles are common in the grass beds of the Chandeleur Islands. Atlantic Ocean, in the west from Newfoundland and Bermuda through the Caribbean to Brazil. (5 inches; 13 cm)

525. Planehead filefish *Monacanthus hispidus* (Linnaeus)

D. II + 29–35; A. 30–35; P. 12–14; body light tan or gray with irregular dark markings. This is the most common inshore filefish over most of the shelf, the young often entering bays. Atlantic Ocean, in the west from Nova Scotia and Bermuda to Brazil. (9 inches; 23 cm)

526. Pygmy filefish *Monacanthus setifer* Bennett

D. II + 27–30; A. 26–30; P. 11–13; body tan or gray with distinct rows of dark spots on sides and two distinct bars on caudal fin, with these markings becoming more obscure with age. North Carolina, Bahamas, and Bermuda throughout the Gulf of Mexico and Caribbean. Bright and Cashman, 1974. (5 inches; 13 cm)

Ostraciidae

Boxfishes or trunkfishes are peculiarly shaped fishes, their bodies protected by rigid, bony plates often supplied with protuberances. Because of the shell, the fish can move only by use of the dorsal, anal, and pectoral fins, but they are still fairly fast swimmers. Two species are known to occur, but the possibility of three more tropical species exists. The shell is sometimes sold as a curio. (Tyler, 1965)

> Body with spines projecting in front of eyes; two spines projecting in front of anal fin (other tropical species of *Lactophrys* also have these spines before anal fin but lack head spines; very small cowfish lack all spines, but also lack body markings found in *Lactophrys*) . . . scrawled cowfish, *Lactophrys quadricornis.*
> Body without spines . . . smooth trunkfish, *Lactophrys triqueter.*

527. Scrawled cowfish *Lactophrys quadricornis* (Linnaeus)
Dorsal, anal, and caudal fins all with 10 rays; P. usually 11; Gr. 13–17; spine in front of each eye as well as pair of posteriorly directed spines in front of anal fin; body yellowish with blue spots; irregular blue markings on body, caudal peduncle, and fins; two to four horizontal blue bands on cheek under eye. This is the common trunkfish over much of the shelf as well as in the saltier bays. *Lactophrys* (=*Acanthostracion*) *tricornis* is a synonym. Atlantic Ocean, in the west from Massachusetts and Bermuda through the Caribbean to Brazil. (18 inches; 46 cm)

528. Smooth trunkfish *Lactophrys triqueter* (Linnaeus)
Dorsal, anal, and caudal fins each with 10 rays; P. 12; Gr. 8–9; no spines on head or before anal fin (although other species of *Lactophrys* have spines); carapace and caudal peduncle with dark hexagonal patterns; dark spot at base of dorsal and pectoral fins; margins of caudal and anal fins dark. Records of *L. trigonus* probably refer to this species, which is common on the offshore reefs. Massachusetts and Bermuda through the Caribbean to Brazil. Reed, 1941. (11 inches; 28 cm)

Tetraodontidae

The puffers differ from the porcupinefishes or burrfishes (family Diodontidae) by possessing a median division in each half of the beak (resulting in four "teeth" in the tetraodontids as opposed to two in the diodontids) and by having small prickles instead of large spines on the body. Both families are capable of inflating their stomachs with air or water. In combination inflation and the spines and prickles protect the fish against predators.

Confusion has existed about the identity of the common puffer on the Texas and Louisiana coast, described as a new species, *S. parvus*. Northwestern Gulf references in the literature to *S. nephelus, marmoratus, maculatus,* and, *spengleri* probably refer to this species, although the latter species is also known to occur there. The occurrence of the bluntnose puffer, *Sphoeroides pachygaster* (Müller and Troschel), offshore in the northwestern Gulf is based on three specimens originally identified as *Liosaccus cutaneus* and collected at one hundred fathoms. Unlike most puffers, it has a smooth skin and a white-tipped caudal.

Some Gulf puffers and members of closely related families are known to be poisonous to some degree, but some species are eaten. The poison is usually restricted to the viscera and skin, and fortunately most fish poisoning occurs in the tropics. (Halstead, 1967, 1978; Shipp, 1974; Shipp and Yerger, 1969)

1	Dorsal and anal each with 12–15 rays . . . smooth puffer, *Lagocephalus laevigatus*.	
	Dorsal and anal each with 6–8 or 9–10 rays	2
2	Dorsal rays 10; anal rays 8–9 . . . sharpnose puffer, *Canthigaster rostrata*.	
	Dorsal and anal rays 6–8	3
3	Small fleshy tabs (lappets) present on dorsal surface, with either one pair behind eyes or many over posterior of body	4
	Small fleshy tabs absent	5
4	Single pair of black lappets behind eyes . . . marbled puffer, *Sphoeroides dorsalis*.	
	Many tan lappets on posterior portion of body . . . bandtail puffer, *Sphoeroides spengleri*.	
5	Body uniformly dark, except for a few scattered spots; skin smooth . . . bluntnose puffer, *Sphoeroides pachygaster*	
	Body variously mottled; skin with prickles, at least on back	8
6	One or two distinct, white interorbital bars, often with white circular markings behind eyes . . . checkered puffer, *Sphoeroides testudineus*.	
	One vague, black interorbital bar; body mottled but without white circular marks behind eye	7
7	Distinct dark spot in axil of pectoral fin . . . southern puffer, *Sphoeroides nephelus*.	
	No distinct dark spot in axil of pectoral fin . . . least puffer, *Sphoeroides parvus*.	

529. Smooth puffer *Lagocephalus laevigatus* (Linnaeus)

D. 14; A. 12; skin smooth; silvery with black blotches. This large puffer is generally found on the inner and middle shelf, although it is known to enter the saltier bays. The oceanic puffer, *L. lagocephalus,* with a blue back and extended lower caudal lobe, may occur offshore. Cape Cod to Brazil. (12 inches; 30 cm)

530. Sharpnose puffer *Canthigaster rostrata* (Bloch)

D. 10; A. 9; P. 16–18; body high, moderately compressed; brown on top; sides white, sometimes with faint blue spots; blue lines on head radiating from eye; upper and lower edges of caudal peduncle and caudal fin black. This puffer occurs commonly on offshore reefs. Atlantic Ocean, in the west from Bermuda, Bahamas, northern Gulf and Florida through the Caribbean to Colombia. (4 inches; 10 cm)

531. Marbled puffer *Sphoeroides dorsalis* Longley

D. 8; A. 7; P. 15; pair of small black lappets on either side of dorsal midline; pale, irregular scrawls on face and lower sides of body. North Carolina and Bahamas through the Caribbean to Suriname (Dutch Guiana). (7 inches; 18 cm)

532. Bandtail puffer *Sphoeroides spengleri* (Bloch)

D. 8; A. 7; P. 14; sides usually with small lappets; body olive brown with numerous black spots as large as eye; spot in axil of pectoral most distinctive; caudal fin distinctly barred. In Texas waters it occurs on 7 1/2-Fathom Reef and other offshore reefs, but it is more common in the northeastern Gulf. Atlantic Ocean, in the west from Bermuda and Massachusetts through the Caribbean to Brazil. (6 inches; 15 cm)

533. Checkered puffer *Sphoeroides testudineus* (Linnaeus)

D. 8; A. 6; P. 14; body olivaceous with white curved lines running over body; large irregular dark spots on sides, creating a checkered pattern. There are rare records from Texas bays which we have not verified, but this puffer is to be expected more often about offshore reefs. Rhode Island through the Caribbean to Brazil. (3 inches; 8 cm)

534. Southern puffer *Sphoeroides nephelus* (Goode and Bean)

D. 7; A. 6; P. 14; body brown with numerous darker and lighter spots and blotches; interorbital with dark bar; distinct dark spot in axil of pectoral fin. This is the common puffer in the northeastern Gulf. East coast of Florida to the Chandeleur Islands and off Yucatán, perhaps in South America. (8 inches; 20 cm)

535. Least puffer *Sphoeroides parvus* Shipp and Yerger

D. 8–9; A. 6–8; P. 13–16; body small, usually less than 4 inches (10 cm) in standard length; body tan with irregular dark and light markings on sides and back, but no prominent dark spot in axil of pectoral fin. This is the common bay and inshore puffer off the Louisiana and Texas coasts. Apalachicola Bay, Florida, westward to Texas and south to Yucatán. (3 inches; 8 cm)

Diodontidae

Porcupinefishes and burrfishes are inflatable fishes, like the puffers, but they have longer spines and a strange beak for crushing armored prey. They are often dried and sold as curiosities. Other tropical species may occur offshore. (Leis, 1978)

1 Spines fixed erect, most with three roots; body striped. . . striped burrfish, *Chilomycterus schoepfi*.

   Spines able to fold back, most with two roots; body spotted 2

2 Forehead spines shorter than those behind pectoral fin; spots about same diameter as spines . . . porcupinefish, *Diodon hystrix*.

   Forehead spines longer than those behind pectoral fin; most spots two or more times larger than spine diameter . . . balloonfish, *Diodon holocanthus*.

536. Striped burrfish *Chilomycterus schoepfi* (Walbaum)

D. 12; A. 10; large individuals light-colored with dark, wavy, roughly parallel lines and large dark spots on body and fins; young fish considerably different, having much darker (dark green) bodies, with lines and spots set much closer together. Burrfish are hardy animals and make excellent aquarium pets. Most will learn to accept food from the hand. Burrfish are common in the salty bays and shallow Gulf, especially in summer. The tropical web burrfish, *C. antillarum* Jordan and Rutter, with a network of intersecting lines, has been taken on the Florida panhandle. New England through the Caribbean to Brazil, but rare in the tropics. (10 inches; 25 cm)

537. Porcupinefish *Diodon hystrix* Linnaeus

D. 15–17; A. 15–16; P. 25; spines on body shorter than those of balloonfish, about 20 in row between snout and origin of dorsal; light green on back, white underneath; numerous small spots on head, body, and fins. Circumtropical; in the western Atlantic from Massachusetts through the Caribbean to Brazil. Baughman, 1950b; Guillory et al., 1985. (2 feet; 61 cm)

538. Balloonfish *Diodon holocanthus* Linnaeus

D. 13–14; A. 13–14; P. 22–23; spines on body long and movable, about 15 in row between snout and origin of dorsal fin; light brown on back, white underneath; dark brown bar passing through eye; scattered brown spots, smaller than eye, on sides and back. Circumtropical; in the western Atlantic from the Bahamas, Florida, and the northern Gulf of Mexico to Brazil. (1 foot; 30 cm)

Molidae

The strange ocean sunfishes or headfishes are rarely seen, solitary surface fishes with a high, flattened body continuous with the head, giving them a chopped-off appearance. Specimens are occasionally harpooned or found dead on the beach. They reach great size, some exceeding seven feet (2 m) in length and height. Another worldwide genus, *Ranzania,* with a very long, slender body, may also occur in the area. (Fraser-Brunner, 1951; Dawson, 1965)

1   Eye nearer tip of snout than gill opening; caudal with rounded lobe in middle . . . sharptail mola, *Mola oxyuropterus.*
    Eye almost between tip of snout and gill openings; caudal without large central lobe . . . ocean sunfish, *Mola mola.*

539. Sharptail mola *Mola oxyuropterus* (Bleeker)
The sharptail mola is rarely taken anywhere, sometimes known as *M. lanceolata* Liénard, the differing names for each sex. A model of a specimen formerly on display at the Louisiana Wildlife and Fisheries Commission Museum in New Orleans is presumed to have come from the area. It is also known from deep water off South Texas. Perhaps worldwide, but not known in the eastern Pacific. (7 feet; 2 m)

540. Ocean sunfish *Mola mola* (Linnaeus)
The ocean sunfish is a wide-ranging species which is apparently not rare far offshore. Occasional individuals come inshore. Worldwide in temperate and tropical waters; in the western Atlantic from Newfoundland to Argentina. Kemp, 1957. (10 feet; 3 m)

Appendixes

Appendix 1.
Temperate and Subtropical Species Occurring in Either the Northeastern Gulf or the Southeastern U.S. Atlantic but Not Confirmed in the Northwestern Gulf

	NE Gulf	SE U.S. Atlantic		NE Gulf	SE U.S. Atlantic
Petromyzon marinus		X	Floridichthys carpio	X	
Alosa pseudoharengus		X	Fundulus heteroclitus		X
Alosa sapidissima		X	Fundulus confluentus	X	X
Alosa aestivalis		X	Urophycis earlli		X
Alosa mediocris		X	Carapus bermudensis	X	
Brevoortia tyrannus		X	Otophidium omostigmum	X	X
Brevoortia smithi	X	X	Ophidion marginatum	?	X
Anchoa lamprotaenia	X		Opsanus tau		X
Saurida normani	X		Antennarius ocellatus	X	X
Muraena retifera	X	X	Ogcocephalus parvus	X	X
Gymnothorax saxicola	X	X	Ogcocephalus corniger	X	
Ariosoma impressa	X	X	Acentronura dendritica	X	
Callechelys muraena	X		Syngnathus springeri	X	X
Letharchus velifer	X	X	Cosmocampus elucens	X	
Gordiichthys irretitus	X		Cosmocampus hildebrandi	X	X
Bascanichthys scuticaris	X	X	Cosmocampus albirostris	X	X
Ophichthus puncticeps	X	X	Menidia menidia		X
Rhyncoconger gracilior	X		Holocentrus bullisi	X	
Strongylura notata	?		Corniger spinosus	X	

	NE Gulf	SE U.S. Atlantic		NE Gulf	SE U.S. Atlantic
Phaeoptyx xenus	X	X	Prionotus evolans		X
Astropogon alutus	X	X	Prionotus alatus	X	X
Centropristis striata	X	X	Bellator egretta	X	
Echeneis neucratoides		X	Bellator brachychir	X	
Lutjanus mahogoni		X	Opistognathus macrognathus	X	
Hemanthias aureorubens	X		Dactyloscopus tridigitatus	X	X
Decapterus macarellus		X	Astroscopus guttatus		X
Decapterus tabl	X	X	Paraclinus marmoratus	X	
Haemulon chrysargenteum	X		Paraclinus fasciatus	X	
Cynoscion regalis		X	Peprilus triacanthus		X
Calamus penna	X		Bothus ocellatus	X	X
Stenotomus chrysops		X	Paralichthys dentatus		X
Tautoga onitis		X	Etropus rimosus	X	X
Tautogolabrus adspersus		X	Etropus microstomus	X	X
Nicholsina usta	X		Gymnachirus melas	X	X
Doratonotus megalepis	X		Parahollardia lineata	X	X
Gobionellus stigmaticus	X	X	Sphoeroides maculatus		X
Gobiosoma ginsburgi		X	Chilomycterus antillarum	X	
Coryphopterus glaucofraenum		X			

Appendix 2.
Rarely Caught Species of the Outer Shelf and Continental Slope Not Covered in Species Accounts

sevengilled shark	Heptranchias perlo
sixgilled shark	Hexanchus griseus
bramble shark	Echinorhinus brucus
bigeye sand tiger	Odontaspis noronhai
bigeye thresher	Alopias superciliosus
oceanic whitetip shark	Carcharhinus longimanus
night shark	Carcharhinus signatus
pelagic stingray	Dasyatis violacea
longnose lanceletfish	Alepisaurus ferox
spaghetti eel	Moringua edwardsi
collared eel	Kaupichthys nuchalis
viper moray	Enchelycore nigricans
chestnut moray	Enchelycore carychroa

conger eel	*Conger oceanicus*
bandtooth conger	*Ariosoma balearicum*
tusky eel	*Aplatophis chauliodus*
indifferent eel	*Ethadophis akkistikos*
pike conger	*Hoplunnis tenuis*
pike conger	*Hoplunnis diomedianus*
orangespot sardine	*Sardinella brasiliensis*
redear sardine	*Harengula humeralis*
false pilchard	*Harengula clupeola*
striated argentine	*Argentina striata*
longnose greeneye	*Parasudis truculenta*
shortnose greeneye	*Chlorophthalmus agassizi*
tricorn batfish	*Zalieutes mcgintyi*
bandwing flyingfish	*Cypselurus exsiliens*
fourwing flyingfish	*Hirundichthys affinis*
codlets	*Bregmaceros* spp.
metallic codling	*Physiculus fulvus*
marlin-spike	*Nezumia bairdi*
American john dory	*Zenopsis ocellata*
deepbody boarfish	*Antigonia capros*
keelcheek bass	*Synagrops spinosus*
misty grouper	*Epinephelus mystacinus*
Bulleye	*Cookeolus japonicus*
moustache jawfish	*Opistognathus lonchurus*
yellowhead jawfish	*Opistognathus aurifrons*
glasseye snapper	*Priacanthus cruentatus*
longspine snipefish	*Macrorhamphosus scolopax*
lowfin pomfret	*Brama dussumieri*
pomfret	*Taractes rubescens*
freckled stargazer	*Gnathagnus egregius*
goby flathead	*Bembrops gobioides*
lancer dragonet	*Paradiplogrammus bairdi*
goldspot goby	*Gnatholepis thompsoni*
island goby	*Lythrypnus nesiotes*
bluegold goby	*Lythrypnus spilus*
rusty goby	*Quisquilius hipoliti*
tusked goby	*Risor ruber*
snake mackerel	*Gempylus serpens*
oilfish	*Ruvettus pretiosus*
greenblotch parrotfish	*Sparisoma atomarium*
midnight parrotfish	*Scarus coelestinus*

redband parrotfish	*Sparisoma aurofrenatum*
redtail parrotfish	*Sparisoma chrysopterum*
redfin parrotfish	*Sparisoma rubripinne*
armored searobin	*Peristedion miniatum*
shortfin searobin	*Bellator brachychir*
streamer searobin	*Bellator egretta*
longfin scorpionfish	*Scorpaena agassizi*
reef scorpionfish	*Scorpaenodes caribbaeus*
deepwater scorpionfish	*Setarches guentheri*
scorpionfish	*Ectretosebastes imus*
Atlantic thornyhead	*Trachyscorpia cristulata*
highfin scorpionfish	*Pontinus rathbuni*
blunthead puffer	*Sphoeroides pachygaster*

Appendix 3.
Freshwater Fishes Likely to be Found in Marine Waters

This list is not at all complete since nearly any species might wash out to sea, but these are the more regular strays. Freshwater species that normally tolerate salt water are included in the text.

paddlefish	*Polyodon spathula*
pallid sturgeon	*Scaphirhynchus albus*
shovelnose sturgeon	*Scaphirhynchus platorhynchus*
shortnose gar	*Lepisosteus platostomus*
bowfin	*Amia calva*
chain pickerel	*Esox niger*
grass pickerel	*Esox americanus*
carp	*Cyprinus carpio*
golden shiner	*Notemigonus crysoleucas*
blacktail shiner	*Notropis venustus*
bullhead minnow	*Pimephales vigilax*
river carpsucker	*Carpiodes carpio*
smallmouth buffalo	*Ictiobus bubalus*
flathead catfish	*Pylodictis olivaris*
channel catfish	*Ictalurus punctatus*
black bullhead	*Ictalurus melas*
yellow bullhead	*Ictalurus natalis*
tadpole madtom	*Noturus gyrinus*
pirate perch	*Aphredoderus sayanus*

golden topminnow	*Fundulus chrysotus*
brook silverside	*Labidesthes sicculus*
yellow bass	*Morone mississippiensis*
largemouth bass	*Micropterus salmoides*
banded pygmy sunfish	*Elassoma zonatum*
bluegill	*Lepomis macrochirus*
redear sunfish	*Lepomis microlophus*
spotted sunfish	*Lepomis punctatus*
warmouth	*Lepomis gulosus*
white crappie	*Pomoxis annularis*
black crappie	*Pomoxis nigromaculatus*
freshwater drum	*Aplodinotus grunniens*

Appendix 4.
Marine Fishes That Regularly Invade Northern Gulf Coastal Fresh Water

Hubbs et al. (1991) list expected species, including a few whose occurrence in fresh water we believe to be only coincidental. Listing *Brevoortia gunteri* rather than *B. patronus*, based on Gunter is in error—see Gunter and Christmas (1960) and Hoese (1965).

bull shark	*Carcharhinus leucas*
Atlantic stingray	*Dasyatis sabina*
Atlantic sturgeon*	*Acipenser oxyrhynchus*
ladyfish	*Elops saurus*
tarpon	*Megalops atlanticus*
American eel**	*Anguilla rostrata*
Alabama shad*	*Alosa alabamae*
skipjack herring*	*Alosa chrysochloris*
Gulf menhaden	*Brevoortia patronus*
bay anchovy	*Anchoa mitchilli*
sea catfish	*Arius felis*
Atlantic needlefish	*Strongylura marina*
sheepshead minnow	*Cyprinodon variegatus*
saltmarsh topminnow	*Fundulus jenkinsi*
bayou killifish	*Fundulus pulvereus*
Gulf killifish	*Fundulus grandis*
rainwater killifish	*Lucania parva*
tidewater silverside	*Menidia beryllina*
Gulf pipefish	*Syngnathus scovelli*
striped bass*	*Morone saxatilis*

jack crevalle	*Caranx hippos*
mojarras	see species accounts
gray snapper	*Lutjanus griseus*
sheepshead	*Archosargus probatocephalus*
pinfish	*Lagodon rhomboides*
spotted seatrout	*Cynoscion nebulosus*
sand seatrout	*Cynoscion arenarius*
spot	*Leiostomus xanthurus*
Atlantic croaker	*Micropogonias undulatus*
red drum	*Sciaenops ocellatus*
mountain mullet**	*Agonostomus monticola*
striped mullet**	*Mugil cephalus*
white mullet	*Mugil curema*
violet goby	*Gobioides broussoneti*
freshwater goby	*Gobionellus shufeldti*
naked goby	*Gobiosoma bosc*
clown goby	*Microgobius gulosus*
lyre goby	*Evorthodus lyricus*
spinycheek sleeper	*Eleotris pisonis*
bigmouth sleeper	*Gobiomorus dormitor*
river goby	*Awaous tajasica*
bay whiff	*Citharichthys spilopterus*
southern flounder	*Paralichthys lethostigma*
hogchoker**	*Trinectes maculatus*
lined sole	*Achirus lineatus*
least puffer	*Sphoeroides parvus*

*Anadromous
**At least part of population catadromous

Appendix 5.
Common Fish Species with Protracted Spawning Seasons

Year-round Spawners

bay anchovy	*Anchoa mitchilli*

Spring through Fall Spawners

finetooth shark	*Carcharhimus isodon*
bonnethead	*Sphyrna tiburo*

striped anchovy	*Anchoa hepsetus*
Gulf killifish	*Fundulus grandis*
longnose killifish	*Fundulus similis*
sheepshead minnow	*Cyprinodon variegatus*
rough silversides	*Membras martinica*
naked goby	*Gobiosoma bosc*
harvestfish	*Peprilus paru*
least puffer	*Sphoeroides parvus*

Fall-Winter Spawners

| striped mullet | *Mugil cephalus* |

Winter-Spring Spawners

| pigfish | *Orthopristis chrysoptera* |
| black drum | *Pogonias cromis* |

Spring Spawners

lesser electric ray	*Narcine brasiliensis*
ladyfish	*Elops saurus*
inshore lizardfish	*Synodus foetens*
skilletfish	*Gobiesox strumosus*
silver perch	*Bairdiella chrysoura*
sheepshead	*Archosargus probatocephalus*
white mullet	*Mugil curema*
bighead searobin	*Prionotus tribulus*

Summer Spawners

Atlantic sharpnose shark	*Rhizoprionodon terraenovae*
blacktip shark	*Carcharhinus limbatus*
scalloped hammerhead	*Sphyrna lewini*
roundel skate	*Raja texana*
Atlantic stingray	*Dasyatis sabina*
scaled sardine	*Harengula jaguana*
sea catfish	*Arius felis*
gafftopsail catfish	*Bagre marinus*
Gulf toadfish	*Opsanus beta*

cobia	*Rachycentron canadum*
Florida pompano	*Trachinotus carolinus*
crevalle jack	*Caranx hippos*
bumper	*Chloroscombrus chrysurus*
dolphin	*Coryphaena hippurus*
red snapper	*Lutjanus campechanus*
sand seatrout	*Cynoscion arenarius*
spotted seatrout	*Cynoscion nebulosus*
spadefish	*Chaetodipterus faber*
great barracuda	*Sphyraena barracuda*
guaguanche	*Sphyraena guachancho*
Spanish mackerel	*Scomberomorus maculatus*
sailfish	*Istiophorus platypterus*
hogchoker	*Trinectes maculatus*

Fall Spawners

red drum	*Sciaenops ocellatus*
bluefish	*Pomotomus saltatrix*
silver seatrout	*Cynoscion nothus*
king mackerel (?)	*Scomberomorus cavalla*

Winter Spawners

speckled worm eel	*Myrophis punctatus*
Gulf menhaden	*Brevoortia patronus*
round herring	*Etrumeus teres*
southern hake	*Urophycis floridanus*
spot	*Leiostomus xanthurus*
croaker	*Micropogonias undulatus*
pinfish	*Lagodon rhomboides*
butterfish	*Peprilus burti*
southern flounder	*Paralichthys lethostigma*

Spring and Fall Spawners

bull shark	*Carcharhinus leucas*
midshipman	*Porichthys plectrodon*
tidewater silverside	*Menidia beryllina*
southern kingfish	*Menticirrhus americanus*

crested cusk-eel	*Ophidion welshi*
blackedge cusk-eel	*Lepophidium brevibarbe*

Appendix 6.
Some French (Cajun) Common Names for Marine Fish

See also Read (1931). Zaneveld (1983) gives an interesting list in several languages.

Cajun Name	Translation	AFS Common Name
requin	shark	shark
ange	angel	skate
terre	earth	stingray
poisson armé	armoredfish	gar
sardine	sardine	menhaden
*salop**	probably trash?	shad
grande écaille	bigscale	tarpon
banane	banana	ladyfish
congo	?	American eel
*mashwadan** (mâchoirans)	jaw	sea catfish
tête dur	hardhead	sea catfish
mashwadan passe*	jaw	gafftopsail
anguille	eel	American eel
serpent mer	sea serpent	other eels
aiguille	needle	needlefish
poisson huître	oyster fish	toadfish
cochon	pig	cod
docteur	doctor	searobin
patassa l'eau sale*	saltwater perch	striped bass
vielle	old lady	grouper
petit groupe	small grouper	grouper
poissonbleu	bluefish	bluefish
limon	lemon	cobia
dauphin	dolphin	dolphin
papino	pompano	pompano
cochon	pig	pigfish
poisson beurre	butterfish	pinfish
truite gris	gray trout	spotted seatrout
truite blanc	white trout	sand seatrout
*sandigas**	?	spot

Cajun Name	Translation	AFS Common Name
poisson rouge	redfish	red drum
tambour	drum	black drum
robal	robalo	kingfish
poisson blanche	whitefish	silver perch
mulle	mullet	mullet
poisson électricité	electric fish	stargazer
maquereau	mackerel	mackerel
plie	flounder	flounder
ferre aupasse	file	filefish
cornard	horny	triggerfish
crapaud mer	sea toad	puffer

* Phonetic spelling

Appendix 7.
Some Spanish (Mexican) Common Names for Important Species of Marine Fish

FAO publications (Fischer, 1978, and the numerous publications in the FAO Fisheries Synopsis series) as well as Zaneveld, 1983, include Spanish common names for many fishes.

Spanish Name	Translation	AFS Common Name
tiburón	shark	shark
carconetta	?	(small sharks, mostly *Carcharhinus*)
cornuda (cornua)	hammerhead	hammerhead and bonnethead
raya	ray	Atlantic stingray
catan	gar	gar
machete	machete	ladyfish
matajuelo real	royal little killer	ladyfish
lisa francesca	French mullet	ladyfish
savanilla	little (grass)	flat tarpon
sábalo	shad	tarpon
chile	chili pepper	inshore lizardfish
bagre de mar	sea catfish	sea catfish
bandera	flag	gafftopsail catfish

Spanish Name	Translation	AFS Common Name
signatido	pencil	pipefish
róbalo	snook	snook
cabra mora	Moorish goat	rock hind
mero	grouper	large grouper
aguaji	gag	gag
bacalao	codfish	scamp
pámpano	pompano	pompano
jurel	jack	jack crevalle
coronado	crowned one	amberjack
dorado	golden one	dolphin
pargo mulato	black porgy	gray snapper
pargo prieto	dark porgy	gray snapper
huachinango	red porgy	red snapper
pargo colorado	red porgy	red or dog snapper
pargo criolla	creole porgy	mutton snapper
manchego	spotted one	lane snapper
cagón de lo alto	coward	vermilion snapper
mojarra	mojarra	(any large mojarra, *Diapterus*)
chopa espina	spined bream	pinfish
pargo	porgy	sheepshead
tambor	drum	black drum
ronco amarillo	yellow grunt	silver perch
corvina	corvina	red drum or other member of drum family
pesca colorado	redfish	red drum
gurrubato	little boy	(*Micropogonias furnieri*)
roncador	croaker	croaker or sand drum
trucha de mar	sea trout	spotted seatrout
trucha blanca	white trout	sand seatrout
lisa	mullet	mullet
chopa blanca	white bream	Bermuda chub
peto	breast plate	wahoo
caballa	mare	king mackerel
sierra	mountain	Spanish mackerel
atún	tuna	tuna

Spanish Name	Translation	AFS Common Name
espadon	?	blue marlin and other billfish
volador	flier	sailfish
lenguad	flounder	flounder

Appendix 8.
Deeper-Dwelling Families Occasionally Found over the Continental Shelf

These outline drawings may be used to identify families of fishes that normally dwell in deeper water but sometimes may occur over the shelf.

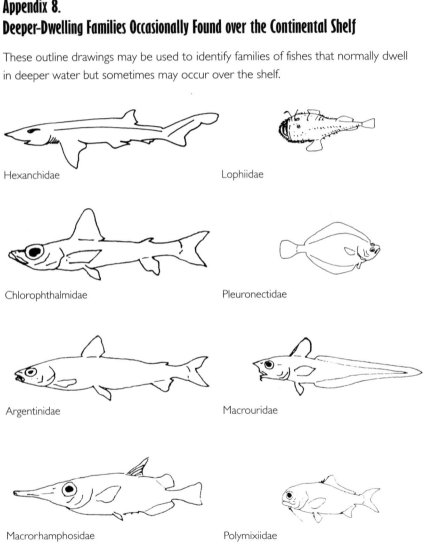

Hexanchidae

Lophiidae

Chlorophthalmidae

Pleuronectidae

Argentinidae

Macrouridae

Macrorhamphosidae

Polymixiidae

Caproidae

Zeidae

Percophidae

Triacanthodidae

Callionymidae

Merlucciidae

Glossary

ACUMINATE. Somewhat pointed, but not as extreme as lanceolate.

ABDOMINAL. Referring to the belly region.

ACCESSORY SENSORY LINE. One or more series of sensory pores that diverge from the main lateral line. In soles of the genus *Gymnachirus* these occur at right angles to the main lateral line on the right (eyed) side.

ADIPOSE. Referring to fatty tissue. For example, adipose eyelid—a transparent covering over the eye of some fishes—or adipose fin (see FIN).

ADNATE. Attached.

AIR BLADDER. Swim bladder, a gas-filled membranous organ responsible for buoyancy in many fishes. Some fish use their air bladder as a lung, and some others use it as a sound-producing organ.

AMBICOLORATE. In the flatfishes, part or all of the blind side having the same or similar pigment as the eyed side.

ANADROMOUS. Living in the sea but entering fresh water to spawn.

ANAL FIN. See FIN (fig. 7).

ANGULATE. Having definite corners, forming an angle, with at least one point.

ANTITROPICAL. Distributed in both northern and southern temperate zones, but not common in the tropics.

AXIL. The rear side of the pectoral fin base; the "armpit."

AXILLARY SCALE (AXILLARY PROCESS). An elongate structure at the base of the pectoral or ventral fins in some fish (fig. 7).

BARBEL. A threadlike structure on the head; usually sensory (fig. 7).

BATHYPELAGIC. Pertaining to or living in the deep waters of the open ocean (depths usually greater than 1000 m).

BENTHIC. Referring to the sea bottom.

BIFURCATE. Branching into two lobes or sections.

BONY STAY. A prominent bony ridge running from a suborbital bone to the preopercle.

BRANCHIOSTEGAL MEMBRANE. A membrane connecting the gill cover or opercle with the throat (figs. 8 and 9).

BRANCHIOSTEGAL RAY. Slender bones in the branchiostegal membrane.

BUCKLER. Large, multispined structure in the skin of batfishes.

CANINE. A slender, rounded, pointed tooth for holding or tearing.

CATADROMOUS. Living in fresh water but entering the sea to spawn.

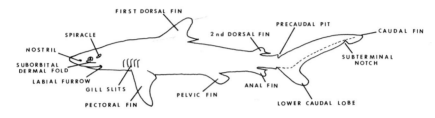

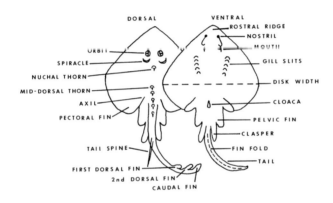

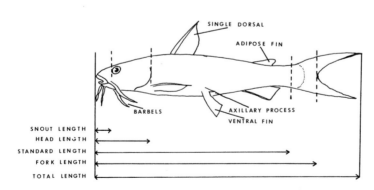

Fig. 7. Features important in fish identification

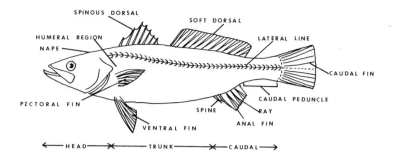

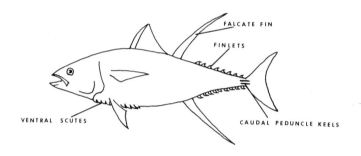

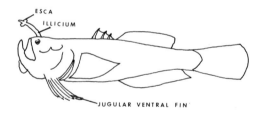

(Fig. 7 continued)

CAUDAL FIN. See FIN (fig. 7).

CAUDAL PEDUNCLE. The region between the last ray of the anal fin and the base of the caudal fin.

CHEST. The ventral area just behind the throat.

CIGUATERA. A disease of the nervous system caused by eating certain tropical fishes.

CIRCUMTROPICAL. Occurring around the world, in all oceans, in the warm areas extending from the equator to approximately 20° to 30°N and S.

CIRRUS. A fleshy appendage, usually on the head or tips of the fins.

COMPRESSED. Laterally flattened.

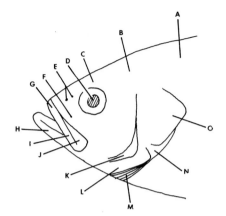

A. NAPE   H. MANDIBLE

B. OCCIPUT   I. MAXILLARY

C. INTERORBITAL   J. SUPRAMAXILLARY

D. EYE   K. PREOPERCLE

E. NOSTRILS   L. INTEROPERCLE

F. PREORBITAL   M. BRANCHIOSTEGALS

G. PREMAXILLARY   N. SUBOPERCLE

                         O. OPERCLE

Fig. 8. Head of a typical fish

CORSELET. Covering of enlarged, thick scales on the anterior body of some scombrids (mackerel and tuna).

CTENOID SCALE. See SCALE (fig. 11).

CUSP. The base of a tooth, the region where it is attached.

CUTANEOUS FOLD. A low, finlike fold on the tails of rays.

CYCLOID SCALES. See SCALE (fig. 11).

DECIDUOUS. Tending to shed or break off.

DENTICLE. See SCALE (fig. 11).

DISC LAMELLAE. In remoras, the flattened, overlapping folds in the sucker, actually modified dorsal rays.

DISTAL. Remote from the point of origin or attachment.

DORSAL. Referring to the back.

DORSAL FIN. See FIN (fig. 7).

DORSUM. The upper (or dorsal) portion of the fish's body.

ELECTROPHORESIS. One of several molecular techniques used to demonstrate genetic similarities or differences between organisms.

EMARGINATE. Having the margin indented, but not so deeply as to be forked (fig. 12).

ENTIRE. Whole, complete, or smooth.

EPIPELAGIC. Pertaining to or living in the surface waters of the open ocean (depths usually greater than 200 m)

ESCA. The fleshy "bait" at the end of the illicium of frog-, goose-, and batfishes.

ESTUARY. An area where fresh water meets sea water.

EURYHALINE. Capable of withstanding large changes in salinity (salt concentration).

EXSERTED. Extending beyond an otherwise even margin.

EXTRALIMITAL. Distributed outside the range. The term may be applied to the range of a species or other taxonomic group or to the coverage of a book, paper, or other report.

FALCATE. Sickle shaped (fig. 12).

FIN. Median or paired structure, usually membranous and supported by soft rays or spines. Fins may be variously modified into other structures such as sucking discs or "fishing poles." Different fins exist as follows (fig. 7):

Adipose. A fleshy median dorsal fin without spines or rays.

Anal. A median fin on the ventral surface between the anus and the base of the tail.

Caudal. The tail fin; the median fin at the base of the tail (fig. 12)

Dorsal. A median fin on the dorsal surface; it may be single or divided into two or more fins.

Finlets. Detached median fins following the dorsal or anal.

Pectoral. Paired fins on either side of the body, usually near or just behind the gill opening; these correspond to the arm or foreleg of terrestrial vertebrates.

Pelvic or *Ventral.* Paired fins below or behind the pectorals, near the anus (abdominally inserted), under the pectorals (thoracically inserted), or in advance of the pectorals (jugular).

FINLET. Typically found in fast swimming fishes, they are thought to improve the hydrodynamics of these species. See FIN (fig. 7).

FORKED. Divided into two parts or branches.

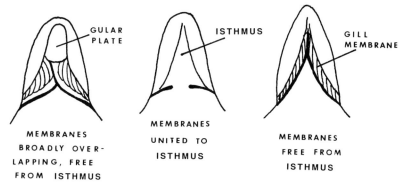

GULAR PLATE

ISTHMUS

GILL MEMBRANE

MEMBRANES BROADLY OVER-LAPPING, FREE FROM ISTHMUS

MEMBRANES UNITED TO ISTHMUS

MEMBRANES FREE FROM ISTHMUS

Fig. 9. Attachment of branchiostegal membranes

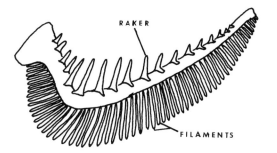

RAKER

FILAMENTS

Fig. 10. Gill arch

FUSIFORM. Streamlined "cigar shape" typical of most fishes.

GANOID SCALE. See SCALE (fig. 11).

GILL ARCH. Unit of respiratory structures on either side of the pharynx (fig. 10).

GILL FILAMENT. Slender respiratory structures that compose the posterior part of the gill arch where gas exchange occurs (fig. 10).

GILL MEMBRANE. See BRANCHIOSTEGAL MEMBRANE (fig. 9).

GILL RAKERS. Usually stiff projections on the inner or anterior surfaces of the gill arch, used for straining food (fig. 10).

GULAR PLATE. A bony median plate between the lower jaws of some fishes (fig. 9).

HEAD (HEAD LENGTH). The region from the tip of the snout to the posterior edge of the gill cover (fig. 7).

HETEROCERCAL TAIL. See TAIL (fig. 12).

HOMOCERCAL TAIL. See TAIL (fig. 12).

HUMERAL. Pertaining to the shoulder region, just behind and above the pectoral fin in most marine fishes.

HYOID. Of or pertaining to the tongue.

HYPURAL PLATE. Posterior end of the vertebral column, noticeable as a vertical crease when the tail of the fish is bent forward.

ILLICIUM. Modified dorsal spine that serves as the "fishing rod" in angling fishes; see also ESCA.

INCISOR. A long but sharp-edged tooth for scraping or cutting.

INTERHAEMAL. Bones connecting the ventral vertebral arches.

INTERORBITAL. Region (or bone) on top of the head between the eyes (fig. 8).

INTROMITTENT ORGAN. A modified structure (fin) in the male of fishes with internal fertilization that is used for transfer of sperm to the female.

ISOCERCAL TAIL. See TAIL (fig. 12).

ISTHMUS. Fleshy region extending forward on the throat between the gills (fig 9).

JUGULAR. Of or pertaining to the throat.

KEEL. A raised ridge, often on a scale or on the caudal peduncle.

LACHRYMAL PLATE. In searobins, a bone under the eye and above the maxilla.

LANCEOLATE. Tapering to a long, lancelike point (fig. 12).

LATERAL LINE (LATERAL LINE SCALES). A line of modified scales with pores in them connected by tubes usually running the length of the fish from behind the gill opening to the base of the caudal fin. The pressure-sensitive pores, but not the scales of the lateral line, usually extend onto the head of the fish and sometimes onto the caudal fin as well. The position, shape, and number of scales in the lateral line is of taxonomic importance in many fishes.

LATERAL SCALE ROWS (VERTICAL SCALE ROWS). The number of scales in a verti- cal row between the gill opening and the base of the caudal fin, used instead of the lateral line scale count in fishes that lack a lateral line.

LENGTH. Measured in various ways (fig. 7):

Fork length. From the tip of the snout to the fork of the caudal fin.

Standard length (SL). From the tip of the snout to the tip of the hypural plate.

Total length (TL). From the tip of the snout to the tip of the caudal fin.

LEPTOCEPHALUS. A laterally flattened, transparent larval stage of eels, bonefish, tarpon, and ladyfish. It has a small head and decreases considerably in size and body depth during metamorphosis.

LUNATE. Deeply forked, with curved branches (fig. 12).

MANDIBLE. Lower jaw (fig. 8).

MAXILLA (MAXILLARY). One of the bones comprising the upper jaw (figs. 8 and 13).

MEDIAL. Near the centerline of the body.

MELANOPHORE. A dark-colored pigment cell.

MERISTIC. Pertaining to the number of serial parts, for example, fin rays or lateral line scales.

MESOPELAGIC. Pertaining to or living in the midwaters of the open ocean (depths usually 200–1000 m).

MOLAR. A short, blunt tooth for crushing.

NAPE. The posteriormost part of the head just before the dorsal fin.

NICTITATING MEMBRANE. A lid in the lower or back corner of the eye that can be used to cover the eye.

NUCHAL. Of or pertaining to the nape.

OBSOLETE. Disappearing with age or growth.

OCCIPUT. The posterior portion of the head behind the eyes but anterior to the nape.

OCELLUS. A round spot surrounded by a lighter region; the word *ocellus* means eye.

OPERCLE (OPERCULUM). A gill cover, composed of the opercular bones (fig. 8).

ORBIT. The socket of the eye.

PALATINE. One of a pair of bones, often with teeth, on the anterior roof of the mouth posterior to and often fused to the vomer (fig. 13).

PECTORAL. Referring to the shoulder region; for example, pectoral fin.

PEDUNCLE. See CAUDAL PEDUNCLE.

PELVIC. Referring to the region of the pelvic girdle; for example, pelvic fins.

PERITONEUM. The membrane lining the body cavity, often visible through the outer layer of skin.

PHARYNGEAL. Referring to the throat or gill region; for example, pharyngeal arches.

PREDORSAL. Referring to the area immediately before the dorsal fin; for example, predorsal length, measured from the snout to the dorsal fin, or predorsal midline, a line on the predorsal region.

PREOPERCLE. One of the bones of the opercular series (fig. 8).

PREORBITAL. A large bone just anterior to the eye (fig. 8).

PREMAXILLARY (PREMAXILLA). The anteriormost bone of the upper jaw, often protrusible (figs. 8 and 13).

PROXIMAL. Near to the origin or point of attachment.

PSEUDOBRANCHIUM (pl. -IAE). Small, gill-like structures on the inner surface of the gill cover; they may be covered by skin or absent in some species.

PTERYGOID. Pair of bones on posterior roof of mouth. Often bearing teeth (fig. 13).

PYLORIC CAECA. Fingerlike projections or pockets of the intestine where it joins the stomach.

RAYS. Any support of fins, whether spinous, segmented, or unsegmented; the term usually refers to a jointed, flexible support, usually branched unless rudimentary, and having a ladderlike appearance when viewed in reflected light.

RELICT. A population left behind as conditions change and most of the population moves; for example, as North America warmed in the Pleistocene, cold-adapted fish moved up the East Coast, leaving small populations as relicts in deep, cool portions of the Gulf of Mexico.

RETICULATE PATTERN. A network, a repeated intercrossing of lines on a background color.

ROSTRAL SPINES. Spines on the snout of searobins and similar fishes.

ROSTRUM. A snout resembling a beak or bill.

SEGMENTED RAY. See RAY.

SCALE. A small, bony plate in the skin, occurring in various shapes and with various compositions (fig. 11)

    Scale counts often used in fish taxonomy are:

    Lateral line scales or *Lateral scale count.* The number of pored scales or scales where the lateral line should be.

    Above lateral line. The number of scale rows from the base of the dorsal fin to the lateral line.

    Below lateral line. The number of scale rows from the lateral line to the base of the anal fin. The scales of the lateral line are not included in these last two counts.

SCUTE   DENTICLE   GANOID   CTENOID   CYCLOID

Fig. 11. Scale types

SCUTE. A modified scale, usually keeled, or in sturgeon an ossification imbedded in the skin.

SERRATE. Notched or with small saw teeth.

SETIFORM. Comblike.

SNOUT. The region from the top of the head to the front of the eye (fig. 7)

SOFT RAY. See RAY.

SPIRACLE. A small hole just behind the eye in some sharks and rays by which water may be passed out of the gill cavity.

SPINOUS FIN. A portion of a fin, especially the dorsal, supported by spines.

SQUAMATION. Development of scales. Primary squamation is development of the main body scales; secondary squamation is development of small scales located on top of the primary row.

STENOHALINE. Inability to withstand large changes in salinity (salt concentration).

SUBEQUAL. Relatively similar but not equal in size.

SUBORBITAL STAY. Prominent longitudinal ridge, sometimes spiny, under the eye in searobins and scorpionfish.

SUPRAMAXILLARY (SUPAMAXILLA). A small bone lying along the upper posterior margin of the maxillary in some fishes.

SWIM BLADDER. See AIR BLADDER.

SYNONYM. An invalid scientific name of a species proposed later than the accepted name.

TAIL. Caudal region (fig. 12).

TELEOST. The most advanced group of bony fishes. Includes all bony fishes in this work except gars and sturgeons.

THORACIC. Of or pertaining to the chest; the region below the pectoral fins in most fishes.

TRUNCATE. Squared off (fig. 12).

TUBERCLE. A small prominence elevated above the surrounding area.

UNSEGMENTED RAY. Found in codlike and blennoid fishes; see RAY.

UROHYAL. A modified branchiostegal located posteriorly and ventrally in the hyoid apparatus under the throat.

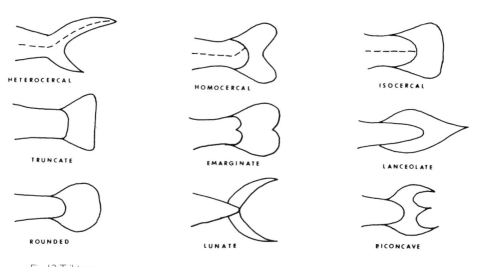

HETEROCERCAL

HOMOCERCAL

ISOCERCAL

TRUNCATE

EMARGINATE

LANCEOLATE

ROUNDED

LUNATE

BICONCAVE

Fig. 12. Tail types

VENTER. The ventral area.

VENTRAL. Pertaining to the lower side of the body.

VENTRAL FIN. See FIN.

VILLIFORM. Slender, closely packed projections like the teeth of a brush.

VOMER. A thin, flat bone anterior in the upper roof of the mouth (fig. 13).

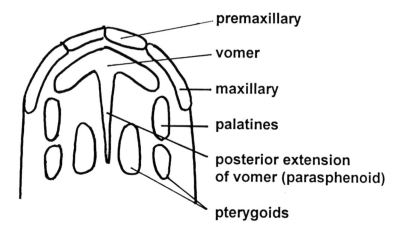

Fig. 13. Tooth-bearing bones of the roof of the mouth

Bibliography

Many of the relevant scientific publications covering the fishes of the area are mentioned with the family or species descriptions, but a few are general works of special importance that include regional lists of fishes (the more recent of them often more specialized, giving fuller detail on fewer species). These works include:

For Texas: Baughman, 1950a, b; Baughman and Springer, 1950; Bonin, 1977; Breuer, 1957, 1962; Causey, 1969; Gunter, 1945a, 1950; Hildebrand, 1954, 1955; Hoese, 1958a, 1965; Hook, 1991; Johnson, 1977; King, 1971; Matlock 1992a; McEachron et al., 1977; McEachron et al., 1994; Miller, 1965; Moore, 1978; Murdy, 1983; Murdy et al., 1983; Parker, 1965; Parker and Bailey, 1979; Pezold and Edwards, 1983; Putt, 1982; Reid, 1957; Renfro, 1960; Retzer, 1991; Robinson, 1969; Sheridan, 1983; Sheridan and Trimm, 1983; Sheridan, Trimm, and Baker, 1984; Simmons, 1957; Travis, 1994; Yoshiyama et al., 1982.

For Louisiana: Behre, 1950; Cowan and Shaw, 1988; Darnell, 1958; Dawson, 1966a; Deegan and Thompson, 1985; Ditty, 1986; Dugas, 1970; Dunham, 1972; Fontenot and Rogillio, 1970; Gonovi, 1993; Gowanloch, 1933; Guillory et al., 1985; Gunter, 1938a, b; Gunter and Shell, 1958; Hastings, 1987; Hastings et al., 1987; Hein et al., 1996; Herke, 1971; Morton, 1973; Norden, 1966; Perret and Caillouet, 1974; Perret et al., 1971; Perry and Carter, 1979; Putt et al., 1986; Russell, 1977; Stanley and Wilson, 1990; Suttkus et al., 1953–54; Thomas, Wagner, and Loesch, 1971; Weaver and Holloway, 1974.

For Mississippi: Christmas, 1973; Cliburn, 1974; Franks, 1970; Franks et al., 1972; Modde and Ross, 1983; Modde, 1983; Peterson and Ross, 1991.

For Alabama: Boschung, 1957, 1992; Swingle, 1971a; Swingle and Bland, 1974.

For the northwest coast of Florida: Bailey et al., 1954; Briggs, 1958; Darovec, 1983; Hastings, 1972; Hastings, 1979; Joseph and Yerger, 1956; Kilby, 1955; Moe and Martin, 1965; Naughton and

Saloman, 1977; Ogren and Brusher, 1977; Reid, 1954; Smith, 1976; Smith et al., 1975; Springer and Woodburn, 1960.

For the east coast of Mexico: Castro-Aguirre, 1978; Darnell, 1962; Dickerson, 1908; Flores-Coto et al., 1983; Hildebrand, 1954, 1955, 1958, 1969; Jordan and Alvarez, 1970; Medina, 1970, 1971; Nakamura, 1976; Salmeron and Ruiz-Luna, 1985; Yáñez-Arancibia and Sanchez-Gil, 1986.

Important general works including more than one state: Bortone, Hastings, and Collard, 1977; Branstetter, 1981; Bullis and Thompson, 1965; Chittenden and Moore, 1977; Christmas et al., 1960; Darnell and Kleypas, 1987; Darnell et al., 1983; Dennis and Bright, 1988a, b; Fowler, 1945; Moore et al., 1970; Murdy et al., 1982; Nelson, 1992; Parker, Moore, and Galloway, 1975; Rezak et al., 1985; Rezak et al., 1990; Richards et al., 1993; Roithmayr, 1965; Sheridan et al., 1984; Springer and Bullis, 1956; Topp and Ingle, 1972; Walls, 1975. An upcoming multivolume work by John McEachran to be published by the University of Texas Press will cover the whole Gulf.

For offshore fishes: LaMonte, 1946, 1952; Neil, 1996; Norman and Fraser, 1949; and Russo (1981) include those important as game and commercial fishes. The monumental work of Jordan and Evermann, 1896–1900, is essential as a rich source of information. It led to two more popular works: Jordan and Evermann, 1923; Breder, 1948. Many of the continental slope fishes can be found in Goode and Bean, 1895. Both nineteenth-century works are out of date, but until the completion of the progressing "Fishes of the Western North Atlantic" in the Sears Foundation Memoir no. 1 (parts 1–9 complete), which contains the work of various authors cited throughout this book, Jordan and Evermann's early work remains the most complete compendium of information on New World marine fishes of the Atlantic. Two field guides to Atlantic species are Boschung et al., 1983, and Robins et al., 1986, the latter being the most complete list of American Atlantic fishes.

Pertinent extralimital works: Beebe and Tee-Van, 1933; Bigelow and Schroeder, 1953a; Breder, 1948; Cervigon, 1966, 1991–94; Dahlberg, 1975; Longley, 1941; Meek and Hildebrand, 1923–25; Smith, 1907; Perlmutter, 1961; and Uyeno et al., 1983. Two works essential for identifying western Atlantic tropical marine species not included here are Böhlke and Chaplin, 1968, and Randall, 1968, 1983. The Bölke and Chaplin work has been reprinted (1993). In addition, a very useful book for tropical species is Humann, 1994. The recent revision of the classic work on Chesapeake Bay fishes, originally published by Hildebrand and Schroeder (1928) by Murdy et al. (1997), is an essential reference to the cool temperate fish fauna north of Cape Hatterras which occasionally finds its way into our waters.

For freshwater fishes that regularly enter estuaries during floods: Blair et al., 1968; Carr and Goin, 1959; Cook, 1959; Douglas, 1974; Eddy and Underhill, 1977; Hubbs and Lagler, 1958; Hubbs et al., 1991; Knapp, 1953; Lee et al., 1980; and Page and Burr, 1991. Hubbs and Lagler, 1958, present the most complete information on the way to study a fish taxonomically. A useful summary is also shown in Standard Methods (American Public Health Association, 1992). There are now very good guides to many southern states, which include species that may enter our area.

Journals of most importance to the study of fishes of the area are *Contributions in Marine Science* (formerly *Publications of the Institute of Marine Science of the University of Texas*); *Gulf Research Reports; Copeia; Transactions of the American Fisheries Society; Alabama Marine Resources Bulletin; Northeast Gulf Science; Technical Bulletin of the Louisiana Wildlife and Fisheries Commission; Bulletin of Marine Science* (formerly *Bulletin of Marine Science of the Gulf and Caribbean*); *Journal of Marine Science; Texas Journal of Science; Transactions of the Louisiana Academy of Sciences; Florida Scientist* (formerly *Quarterly Journal of the Florida Academy of Science*); and bulletins and technical reports issued by the Texas Parks and Wildlife Commission and the Florida Board of Natural Resources (now Environmental Protection).

The preceding listings are not complete, and do not include unpublished reports such as the annual reports of the various conservation agencies, but by using the literature cited in each paper, the student of fishes should be able to find nearly all works on Gulf of Mexico temperate fishes.

General and Popular Works

Allen, G. R., 1979. *Butterfly and angelfishes of the world.* Vol. 2, *Atlantic Ocean, Caribbean Sea, Red Sea, Indo-Pacific.* New York: J. Wiley and Sons. Pp. 149–352.

American Public Health Association. 1992. Fishes. In *Standard Methods,* ed. A. E. Greenberg, L. S. Clesceri, A. D. Eaton, and M. A. H. Franson. Pp. 10–67 to 10–81.

Anonymous. 1917. The salt water fish of Louisiana. *Bull. La. Conserv. Comm.* 3.

Anonymous. 1996. Shark mother: sextuplets times 50! 1996. *National Geographic.* "Geographica" section. 190(3): unpaginated.

Bailey, R. M., J. E. Fitch, E. S. Herald, E. A. Lachner, C. C. Lindsey, C. R. Robins, and W. B. Scott. 1970. *A list of common and scientific names of fishes from the United States and Canada (3d ed.).* Am. Fish. Soc. Spec. Publ. no. 6. Washington, D.C. 150 pp.

Baughman, J. L., and S. Springer. 1950. Biological and economic notes on the sharks of the Gulf of Mexico, with especial reference to those of Texas, and with a key for their identification. *Am. Midl. Nat.* 44 (1):96–152.

Beebe, W., and J. Tee-Van. 1933. *Field book of the shore fishes of Bermuda and the West Indies.* New York: G. P. Putman's Sons. Reprint 1970, New York: Dover. 337 pp.

Bigelow, H. B., and W. C. Schroeder. 1953a. Fishes of the Gulf of Maine. 2d ed., rev. of Bigelow and Welsh, 1925. U.S. Fish Wildl. Serv. Fish. Bull. 74. 577 pp.

Bigelow, H. B., and W. W. Welsh. 1925. Fishes of the Gulf of Maine. Bull. U.S. Bur. Fish. 40. 567 pp.

Blair, W. F., A. P. Blair, P. Brodkorb, F. R. Cagle, and G. A. Moore. 1968. *Vertebrates of the United States.* 2d ed. New York: McGraw-Hill. 819 pp.

Böhlke, J. E., and C. C. G. Chaplin. 1968. *Fishes of the Bahamas and adjacent tropical waters.* Wynnewood, Pa.: Livingston.

Böhlke, J. E., and C. C. G. Chaplin. 1993. *Fishes of the Bahamas and adjacent tropical waters.* 2d ed., with nomenclatural changes and additions by E. B. Böhlke and W. F. Smith-Vaniz. Austin, Tex.: University of Texas Press. 771 pp.

Bone, Q., N. B. Marshall, and J. H. S. Blaxter. 1995. *Biology of fishes.* 2d ed. London: Chapman and Hall. 332 pp.

Boschung, H.T., Jr. 1992. Catalog of freshwater and marine fishes of Alabama. *Bull. Al. Mus. Nat. Hist.* 14. 266 pp.

Boschung, H.T., Jr., J. D. Williams, D. W. Gotshall, D. K. Caldwell, and M. K. Caldwell. 1983. *The Audubon Society field guide to North American fishes, whales, and dolphins.* New York: A. A. Knopf. 843 pp.

Breder, C. M., Jr. 1948. *Fieldbook of marine fishes of the Atlantic coast from Labrador to Texas.* 2d ed. New York: G. P. Putman's Sons. 332 pp.

Briggs, J. C. 1975. *Marine zoogeography.* New York: McGraw-Hill. 475 pp.

Britton, J.C. and B. Morton, 1989. *Shore ecology of the Gulf of Mexico,* Austin: University of Texas Press. 387 pp.

Burgess, W. E. 1978. *Butterflyfishes of the world: a monograph of the butterflyfishes (Family Chaetodontidae).* Jersey City, N.J.: T.F.H. Publ. 832 pp.

Burr, J. G. 1932. Fishes of Texas. Bull. Texas Game, Fish, and Oyster Comm. 5. 41 pp.

Carr, A., and C. J. Goin. 1959. *Guide to the reptiles, amphibians and fresh water fishes of Florida.* Gainesville: Univ. of Fla. Press. 341 pp.

Castro, J. I. 1983. *The sharks of North American waters.* College Station: Texas A&M Univ. Press. 180 pp.

Castro-Aguirre, J. L. 1978. *Catálogo sistemático de los peces marinos que penetran a las aquas continentales de México con aspectos zoogeográficos y ecológicos.* México: Div. Gen. del Inst., Nac. de Pesca. Ser. Cien. 19. 298 pp.

Cervigón, M. F. 1966. *Los peces marinos de Venezuela.* Monografia no. 11. 2 vols. Caracas: Fundación La Salle de Ciencias Naturales. 951 pp.

———. 1991–94. *Los peces marinos de Venezuela.* 3 vols. Caracas: Fundación LaSalle de Científica Naturales. 2d ed. 1,219 pp.

Cliburn, J. W. 1974. A key to the fishes of Mississippi Sound and adjacent waters. Mimeographed. Ocean Springs, Miss.: Gulf Coast Res. Lab. 36 pp.

Compagno, L. J.V. 1988. *Sharks of the order Carcharhiniformes.* Princeton Univ Press. 485 pp.

Cook, F.A. 1959. *Freshwater fishes in Mississippi.* Jackson: Miss. Game and Fish. Comm. 239 pp.

Dahlberg, M. D. 1975. *Guide to coastal fishes of Georgia and nearby states.* Athens: Univ. of Georgia Press. 186 pp.

Douglas, N. H. 1974. *Freshwater fishes of Louisiana,* Baton Rouge, La.: Claitor's Bookstore. 443 pp.

Eddy, S. and J. E. Underhill 1978. *How to know the freshwater fishes.* 3d ed. Dubuque, Iowa: Wm. C. Brown. 296 pp.

Eschmeyer, W. N., and R. M. Bailey. 1990. *Catalog of the genera of recent fishes.* San Francisco: Calif. Acad. Sci. 697 pp.

Fisk, H. N. 1944. Geological investigation of the alluvial valley of the Lower Mississippi River. *J. Geology* 59:333–56.

Gilligan, M. R. 1989. *An illustrated field guide to the fishes of Gray's Reef National Marine Sanctuary.* NOAA Tech. Mem. NOS MEMD 25. Washington D.C.: U.S. Dept. Commerce.

Goode, G. B., and T. H. Bean. 1895. *Oceanic ichthyology.* Smithson. Contrib. Knowl. no. 981. Washington, D.C.: Smithsonian Inst. 553 pp.

Gowanloch, J. N. 1933. *Fishes and fishing in Louisiana.* La. Dep. Conserv. Bull. no. 23. 638 pp. Reprint 1965, Baton Rouge: Claitor's Bookstore.

Greenberg, I. 1992. *Guía de corales y Pesca.* Miami, Fla.: Seahawk Press. 64 pp.

Guitart, D. J. 1974–78. Sinopsis de los Peces Marinos de Cuba. *Acad. Cien. Cuba Inst. de Ocean.*

Halstead, B. W. 1967. *Poisonous and venomous marine animals of the world.* Vol. II. *Vertebrates.* U.S. Govt. Printing Off. 1070 pp.

———. 1978. *Poisonous and venomous marine animals of the world* (revised ed.). Princeton, N.J.: Darwin Press. 1326 pp.

Hardisty, M. W. 1979. *Biology of the Cyclostomes.* London: Chapman and Hall. 428 pp.

Heemstra, P. C. 1965. A field key to the Florida sharks. Fla. State Board Conserv. Tech. Ser. no. 45. 11 pp.

Hein, S., G. Adkins, M. Bourgeois, and E. Moss. 1996. *A fishermen's guide to common coastal fishes of Louisiana and adjacent offshore waters.* Baton Rouge: La. Sea Grant Coll. Prog. 49 pp.

Hildebrand, S. F., and W. C. Schroeder. 1928. *Fishes of Chesapeake Bay.* Bull. U.S. Bur. Fish. 43. 366 pp. Reprint 1972, Jersey City, N.J.: T.F.H. Publ.

Hubbs, C. L., R. J. Edwards, and G. P. Garrett. 1991. An annotated checklist of the freshwater fish of Texas with keys to identification of species. *Tex. J. Sci.* 43(4):1–56.

Hubbs, C. L., and K. F. Lagler. 1958. *Fishes of the Great Lakes region.* 2d ed. Ann Arbor: Univ. of Mich. Press. 213 pp.

Humann, P. 1994. *Reef fish identification: Florida, Caribbean, Bahamas.* 2d ed. Jacksonville, Fla.: New World Publ. 396 pp.

Jones, P. W., F. D. Martin, and J. D. Hardy, Jr. 1978. *Development of fishes of the Mid-Atlantic Bight: an atlas of egg, larval and juvenile stages.* U.S. Dep. Int. Fish Wildl. Serv., Off. Biol. Serv. 78-12. Vols. 1–6.

Jordan, D. S., and W. B. Evermann. 1896–1900. *The fishes of North and Middle America.* 4 vols. Bull. U.S. Natl. Mus. 47. 3,313 pp. Reprint 1963, Jersey City, N.J.: T.F.H. Publ.

———. 1923. *American food and game fishes.* New York: Doubleday, Page and Co. Reprint 1969, New York: Dover. 574 pp.

Knapp, F. T. 1953. *Fishes found in the freshwaters of Texas.* Brunswick, Ga.: Ragland. 166 pp.

Lagler, K. F., J. E. Bardach, R. R. Miller, and D. R. M. Passino. 1977. *Ichthyology.* 2d ed. New York: John Wiley and Sons. 506 pp.

LaMonte, F. 1946. *North American game fishes.* Garden City, N.Y.: Doubleday and Co. 202 pp.

———. 1952. *Marine game fishes of the world.* Garden City, N.Y.: Doubleday and Co. 190 pp.

Lee, D. S., C. R. Gilbert, C. H. Hocutt, R. E. Jenkins, and D. E. McAllister. 1980 et seq. *Atlas of North American freshwater fishes.* N. Carolina. Biol. Surv. Publ. 180. 867 pp.

Leim, A. H., and W. B. Scott. 1966. *Fishes of the Atlantic coast of Canada.* Bull. Fish. Res. Board of Canada no. 155. 485 pp.

Longley, W. H. 1941. *Systematic catalogue of the fishes of Tortugas, Florida.* Ed. S. F. Hildebrand. Papers Tortugas Lab. no. 34. Carnegie Inst. Wash. Pub. 535. 331 pp.

Manooch, C.S., III. 1984. *Fisherman's guide to the southeastern United States.* Raleigh: North Carolina State Mus. Nat. Hist. 362 pp.

Marshall, N. B. 1966. *The life of fishes.* Cleveland and New York: World Publ. Co. 402 pp.

Marshall, N. B. 1971. *Explorations in the life of fishes.* Cambridge, Mass.: Harvard Univ. Press. 204 pp.

Meek, S. E., and S. F. Hildebrand. 1923–25. *The marine fishes of Panama.* Publ. no. 215. Chicago: Field Mus. Nat. Hist. 1,045 pp.

Moser, H. G., W. J. Richards, D. M. Cohen, M. P. Fahay, A. W. Kendall, Jr., and S. L. Richardson (eds.). 1984. *Ontogeny and systematics of fishes.* Spec. Publ. no. 1., Amer Soc. Ich. Herp. 760 pp.

Moyle, P. B. *Fishes: an enthusiast's guide.* Berkeley: Univ. of Calif. Press. 272 pp.

Moyle, P. B., and J. J. Cech, Jr. 1988. *Fishes: an introduction to ichthyology*. 2d ed. Englewood Cliffs, N.J.: Prentice-Hall. 559 pp.

Murdy, E. O. 1983. *Saltwater fishes of Texas: a dichotomous key*. Texas A&M Sea Grant. TAMU G-SG-83-607. 220 pp.

Murdy, E. O., R. S. Birdsong, and J. A. Musick. 1997. *Fishes of Chesapeake Bay*. Washington D.C.: Smithsonian Institution Press. 324 pp.

Nakamura, I. 1976. *Catalogo des Peces Marinos de Mexicanos*. México: Sec. de Ind. y Com. Subsec. Pesca. Inst. Nac. de Pesca. 462 pp.

Nelson, J. S. 1994. *Fishes of the world*. 3d ed. New York: John Wiley & Sons. 600 pp.

Nikolskii, G. V. 1963. *The ecology of fishes*. London and N.Y.: Academic Press. 352 pp.

Norman, J. R., and F. C. Fraser. 1949. *Field book of giant fishes*. New York: G. P. Putman's Sons. 375 pp.

Norman, J. R., and P. H. Greenwood. 1975. *A history of fishes*. 3d ed. London: Ernest Bonn. 467 pp.

Organisation for Economic Co-operation and Development. 1990. *Multilingual dictionary of fish and fish products*. Oxford: Fishing News Books. 442 pp.

Page, L. M. and B. M. Burr. 1991. *A field guide to freshwater fishes*. Boston: Houghton Mifflin. 432 pp.

Parker, J. C., D. R. Moore, and B. J. Galloway. 1975. *Keys to the estuarine and marine fishes of Texas*. 2d ed. College Station: Texas A&M University Agricultural Extension Service.

Patrick, R. 1994. *Rivers of the United States*. Vol. I. *Estuaries*. New York: John Wiley and Sons. 825 p.

Perlmutter, A. 1961. *Guide to marine fishes*. New York: New York Univ. Press. 431 pp.

Pew, P. 1954. *Food and game fishes of the Texas coast*. Tex. Game and Fish Comm. Bull. no 33. 68 pp.

Potts, D. T., and J. S. Ramsey. 1987. A preliminary guide to demersal fishes of the Gulf of Mexico Continental Slope (100–600 f). Ala. Sea Grant. Ext. Serv.

Randall, J. E. 1968. *Caribbean reef fishes*. Jersey City, N.J.: T.F.H. Publ. 318 pp.

————. 1983. *Caribbean reef fishes*. 2d ed. Neptune City, N.J.: T.F.H. Publ. 350 pp.

Reed, C. T. 1941. *Marine life in Texas Waters*. San Angelo: Tex. Acad. Sci. 88 pp.

Read, W. 1931. Louisiana French. *L.S.U. University Studies*. 253 pp.

Robins, C. R., R. M. Bailey, C. E. Bond, J. R. Brooker, E. A. Lachner, R. N. Lea, and W. B. Scott. 1980. *A list of common and scientific names of fishes from the United States and Canada*. 4th ed. Amer. Fish. Soc. Spec. Publ. no. 12. Bethesda Md. 174 pp.

————. 1991. *A list of common and scientific names of fishes from the United States and Canada*. 5th ed. Amer. Fish. Soc. Spec. Publ. no 20. Bethesda Md. 183 pp.

Robins, C. R., G. C. Ray, and J. Douglass, 1986. *A field guide to Atlantic coast fishes of North America*. Boston: Houghton Mifflin. 324 pp.

Salmeron, L. A. P., and C. A. Ruiz-Luna. 1985. *Los animales comestibles de importancia comercial en aquas mexicanos*. Com Ed. Cont. Mex. 46 pp.

Scott, W. B., and M. G. Scott. 1988. *Atlantic fishes of Canada*. Can. Bull. Fish. Aquatic Sci. 219. 731 pp.

Shipp, R. L., 1986. *Dr. Bob Shipp's guide to fishes of the Gulf of Mexico*. Dauphin Island, Ala.: Marine Environmental Sciences Consortium. 256 pp.

Smith, C. L. 1994. *Fish watching: an outdoor guide to freshwater fishes*. Ithaca, N.Y.: Cornell Univ. Press. 216 pp.

Smith, H. M. 1907. *The fishes of North Carolina*. Vol. 2. Raleigh: North Carolina Geol. Econ. Surv. 453 pp.

Springer, S., and H.T. Bullis. 1956. *Collections by the* Oregon *in the Gulf of Mexico*. U.S. Fish Wildl. Serv. Spec. Sci. Rept. Fish. no 196. 134 pp.

Stickney, R. R., 1984. *Estuarine ecology of the southeastern United States and Gulf of Mexico.* College Station: Texas A&M University Press. 310 p.

Thresher, R. E. 1980. *Reef fish: behavior and ecology on the reef and in the aquarium*. St. Petersburg: Palmetto Publ. Co. 171 pp.

Topp, R.W., and R. M. Ingle. 1972. Annotated list of post 1950 literature pertaining to distribution of Gulf of Mexico fishes. Fla. Dept. Nat. Res. Spec. Sci. Rep. no. 33. 17 pp.

Travis, N. T. (ed.). 1994. *Freshwater and marine fishes of Texas and the northwestern Gulf of Mexico*. Tex. Sys. Nat. Lab. Index Ser. No. FTX/NWGM-94. 270 pp.

Ursin, M. J. 1977. *A guide to fishes of the temperate Atlantic coast*. New York: E. P. Dutton. 262 pp.

Viosca, P, Jr. 1942. Untapped fishery resources of Louisiana. *Trans. N. Amer. Wildl. Conf.* 7:423–25.

Wahlquist, H. 1966. A field key to the batoid fishes (sawfishes, guitarfishes, skates, and rays) of Florida and adjacent waters. Fla. State Board Conserv. Tech. Ser. no. 50. 20 pp.

Walls, J. G. 1975. *Fishes of the northern Gulf of Mexico*. Neptune City, N.J.: T.F.H. Publ. 432 pp.

Wilson, R., and J. Q. Wilson. 1992. *Pisces guide to watching fishes: understanding coral reef fish behavior*. Houston: Gulf Publ. Co. 275 pp.

Wooton, R. J. 1990. *Ecology of teleost fishes*. New York: Chapman and Hall. 404 pp.

———. 1992. *Fish ecology*. New York: Chapman and Hall. 212 pp.

Zaneveld, J. S. 1983. *Caribbean fish life*. Leiden: E. J. Brill. 163 pp.

Zim, H. S., and H. H. Shoemaker. 1955. *Fishes: a guide to fresh- and salt-water species*. New York: Golden Press, Golden Nature Guide. 160 pp.

Specialized Works

Able, K. W., D. C. Twichell, C. B. Grimes, and R. S. Jones. 1987. Tilefishes of the genus *Caulolatilus* construct burrows on the sea floor. *Bull. Mar. Sci.* 40(1):1–10.

Adkins, G. 1993. A comprehensive assessment of bycatch in the Louisiana shrimp fishery. *La. Dept. Wildl. Fisher. Tech. Bull.* 42:1–71.

Allen, G. R. 1985. *FAO species catalogue*. Vol. 6, *Snappers of the world; an annotated and illustrated catalogue of lutjanid species known to date*. FAO Fisheries Synopsis no. 125. 189 pp.

Anderson, W. D., Jr. 1966. A new species of *Pristipomoides* (Pisces: Lutjanidae) from the tropical western Atlantic. *Bull. Mar. Sci.* 16(4):814–26.

———. 1967. Field guide to the snappers (Lutjanidae) of the eastern Atlantic. U.S. Fish Wildl. Serv. Circ. no. 252. 14 pp.

———. 1981. A new species of Indo-West Pacific *Etelis* (Pisces: Lutjanidae) with comments on other species of the genus. *Copeia* (4):820–25.

Anderson, W.W., J. W. Gehringer, and F. H. Berry. 1966a. Field guide to the Synodontidae (lizard-fishes) of the western Atlantic Ocean. U.S. Fish Wildl. Serv. Circ. no. 245. 12 pp.

Anderson, W. D., Jr., and P. C. Heemstra. 1980. Two new species of western Atlantic *Anthias* (Pisces: Serranidae): redescription of *A. asperilingus* and review of *Holanthias martinicensis*. *Copeia* (1):72–87.

Anderson, W.W., and E. J. Gutherz. 1967. Revision of the flatfish genus *Trichopsetta* (Bothidae) with descriptions of three new species. *Bull. Mar. Sci.* 17 (4):892–913.

Anderson, W.W., and M. J. Lindner. 1951. Notes on the flatfish, *Engyophrys sentus* Ginsburg. *Copeia* (1):23–27.

Anderson, W. W., J. W. Gehringer, and F. H. Berry. 1966b. Family Synodontidae. In *Fishes of the western North Atlantic*. Memoir Sears Found. Mar. Res. no. 1, pt. 5, pp. 30–102. New Haven.

Arata, G. F. 1954. A contribution to the life history of the swordfish, *Xiphias gladius* Linnaeus, from the South Atlantic coast of the United States and the Gulf of Mexico. *Bull. Mar. Sci. Gulf Caribb.* 4:183–243.

Armstrong, N. E. 1979. Effects of altered freshwater inflow on estuarine systems. *Proc. Gulf of Mexico Coast. Ecosys. Workshop*. U.S. Fish Wild. Serv. FWS/OBS-80/30, pp. 17–31.

———. 1982. Responses of Texas estuaries to freshwater inflows. In *Estuarine comparisons*, ed. V. S. Kennedy, pp. 103–20. New York: Academic Press.

Armstrong, N. E., and G. H. Ward, Jr. 1981. Effects of alterations of freshwater inflows into Matagorda Bay, Texas. *Proc. Nat. Symp. Freshwater Inflow Est.* U.S. Fish Wildl. Serv. FWS/OBS-81/04. 1:179–96.

Arnold, C. R, G. J. Holt, and P.Thomas. 1988. Red drum aquaculture. *Contr. mar. sci.* suppl. 30:1–197.

Arnold, C. R., J. M. Wakeman, T. D. Williams, and G. D. Treece. 1978. Spawning of the red snapper, *Lutjanus campechanus*, in captivity. *Aquaculture* 15:301–302.

Arnold, E. L., Jr. 1955. Notes on the capture of young sailfish and swordfish in the Gulf of Mexico. *Copeia* (1):150–51.

Avault, J. W. Jr., C. L. Birdsong, and W. G. Perry, Jr. 1969. Growth, survival, food habits, and sexual development of croaker, *Micropogon undulatus*, in brackish water ponds. *Proc.Ann. Conf. Southeastern Assoc. Game and Fish Comm.* 23:251–55.

Avent, R. M., M. E. King, and R. H. Gore. 1977. Topographic and faunal studies of shelf-edge prominences off the central eastern Florida coast. *Int. Revue Ges. Hydrobiol.* 62:185–208.

Azzarello, M. Y. 1991. Some questions concerning the Syngnathidae broodpouch. *Bull. Mar. Sci.* 49(3):741–47.

Backus, R. H., S. Springer, and E. L. Arnold. 1956. A contribution to the natural history of the whitetip shark, *Pterolamiops longimanus* (Poey). *Deep-Sea Res.* 3:178–88.

Bailey, R. M., H. E. Winn, and C. L. Smith. 1954. Fishes from the Escambia River, Alabama and Florida, with ecologic and taxonomic notes. *Proc. Acad. Nat. Sci. Philadelphia.* 106:109–64.

Baird, R. C. 1965. Ecological implications of the behavior of the sexually dimorphic goby, *Microgobius gulosus* (Girard). *Publ. Inst. Mar. Sci. Univ.Tex.* 10:1–8.

Baird, S., and C. Girard. 1854. Descriptions of new species of fishes collected by John H. Clark on the U.S. and Mexican boundary survey, and in Texas, by Captain Stewart Vliet, U.S.A. *Proc. Acad. Nat. Sci. Philadelphia.* 7:2–29.

Banford, H. M., and B. B. Collette. 1993. *Hyporhamphus meeki,* a new species of halfbeak (Teleostei: Hemirhamphidae) from the Atlantic and Gulf coasts of the United States. *Proc. Biol. Soc.Wash.* 106(2):369–84.

Barger, L. W. 1990. Age and growth of bluefish, *Pomatomus saltatrix,* from the northern Gulf of Mexico and U.S. south Atlantic coast. *Fish. Bull, U.S.* 88:805–9.

Barlow, G.W., 1975. On the sociobiology of hermaphroditic serranid fishes, the hamlets, in Puerto Rico. *Marine Biology* 33: 295–300.

Baughman, J. L. 1941a. On the occurrence in the Gulf Coast waters of the United States of the triple tail, *Lobotes surinamensis*, with notes on its natural history. *Am. Nat.* 75:569–79.

———. 1941b. Scombriformes, new, rare, or little known in Texas waters with notes on their natural history and distribution. *Trans. Tex. Acad. Sci.* 24:14–26.

———. 1941c. On a heavy run of dolphin, *Coryphaena hippurus*, off the Texas coast. *Copeia* (1):117.

———. 1943a. Notes on the sawfish, *Pristis perottei* Müller and Henle, not previously reported from the waters of the U.S. *Copeia* (1):43–48.

———. 1943b. Some serranid fishes of Texas: the Centropomidae, Moronidae, and Epinephelidae. *Am. Midl. Nat.* 30(3):769–73.

———. 1943c. The lutjanid fishes of Texas. *Copeia* (4):212–15.

———. 1943d. Additional notes on the occurrence and natural history of the triple tail *Lobotes surinamensis*. *Am. Midl. Nat.* 29(2):365–70.

———. 1947. Fishes not previously reported from Texas, with miscellaneous notes on the species. *Copeia* (4):280.

———. 1950a. Random notes on Texas fishes. Part 1. *Tex. J. Sci.* 2(1):117–138.

———. 1950b. Random notes on Texas fishes. Part 2. *Tex. J. Sci.* 2(2):242–63.

———. 1952. The marine fisheries of the Mayas as given in Diego de Landa's "Relacion de las cosas de Yucatan," with notes on probable identification of fishes. *Tex. J. Sci.* 4(4):432–59.

———. 1955. The oviparity of the whale shark, *Rhineodon typus*, with records of this and other fishes in Texas waters. *Copeia* (1):54–55.

Beckman, D. W. 1989. Age and growth of red drum, *Sciaenops ocellatus*, and black drum, *Pogonias cromis*, in the northern Gulf of Mexico. Ph. D. diss., Louisiana State Univ., Baton Rouge. 159 pp.

Beckman, D. W., A. L. Stanley, J. H. Render, and C. A. Wilson. 1990. Age and growth of black drum in Louisiana waters of the Gulf of Mexico. *Trans. Am. Fish. Soc.* 119(3):537–44.

———. 1991. Age and growth rate estimation of sheepshead, *Archosargus probatocephalus*, in Louisiana waters using otoliths. *Fish. Bull., U.S.* 89(1):1–8.

Beckman, D. W., C. A. Wilson, and A. L. Stanley. 1989. Age and growth of red drum, *Sciaenops ocellatus*, from offshore waters of the northern Gulf of Mexico. *Fish. Bull., U.S.* 87(1):17–28.

Bedinger, C. A., Jr. (ed.). 1981. Ecological investigations of petroleum production platforms in the central Gulf of Mexico. *Southwest Res. Inst. Exec. Sum.* (3):1–29.

Behre, E. H. 1950. Annotated list of the fauna of the Grand Isle region. Occas. Pap. no. 6, Mar. Lab., Louisiana State Univ. 66 pp.

Bellinger, J. W., and J. W. Avault, Jr. 1970. Seasonal occurrence, growth, and length-weight relationships of juvenile pompano, *Trachinotus carolinus*, in Louisiana. *Trans. Am. Fish. Soc.* 99(2):353–58.

———. 1971. Food habits of juvenile pompano. *Trachinotus carolinus*, in Louisiana. *Trans. Am. Fish. Soc.* 100(3):486–94.

Benefield, R. L., A. W. Moffett, and L. W. McEachron. 1977. Occurrence of striped bass *(Morone saxatilis)* in coastal waters of Texas. *Tex. J. Sci.* 28:357–58.

Berry, F. H. 1959. Young jack crevalles (*Caranx* species) off the southeastern Atlantic coast of the United States. *Fish. Bull., U.S.* 59(152):417–535.

Berry, F. H. 1964. Review and emendation of family Clupeidae. *Copeia* (4):720–30.

Berry, F. H. 1968. A new species of carangid fish *(Decapterus tabl)* from the western Atlantic. *Contrib. Mar. Sci.* 13:145–67.

Berry, F. H., and W. W. Anderson. 1961. Stargazer fishes from the western North Atlantic (family Uranoscopidae). *Proc. U.S. Natl. Mus.* 112(3448):563–86.

Berry, F. H., and I. Barrett. 1963. Gillraker analysis and speciation in the thread herring, genus *Opisthonema*. *Inter-Am. Trop. Tuna Comm. Bull.* 7(2):111–90.

Berry, F. H., and L. R. Rivas. 1962. Data on six species of needlefishes (Belonidae) from the western Atlantic. *Copeia* (1):152–60.

Berry, F. H., and L. F. Vogele. 1961. Filefishes (Monacanthidae) of the western North Atlantic. *Fish. Bull., U.S.* 61(181):61–109.

Bigelow, H. B. 1963. Bony fishes: Superclass, class, subclass, and orders. In *Fishes of the western North Atlantic*. Memoir Sears Found. Mar. Res. no. 1, pt. 3, pp. 1–19. New Haven.

Bigelow, H. B., and W. C. Schroeder. 1948. Sharks. In *Fishes of the western North Atlantic*. Memoir Sears Found. Mar. Res. no. 1, pt. 1, pp. 59–547. New Haven.

———. 1953. Sawfishes, guitarfishes, skates, and rays. In *Fishes of the western North Atlantic*. Memoir Sears Found. Mar. Res. no. 1, pt. 2, pp. 1–514. New Haven.

———. 1958. Four new rajids from the Gulf of Mexico. *Bull. Mus. Comp. Zool.* 119(2):201–33.

———. 1965. A further account of batoid fishes from the western Atlantic. *Bull. Mus. Comp. Zool.* 132(5):443–77.

Birdsong, R. S. 1981. A review of the gobiid fish genus *Microgobius* Poey. *Bull. Mar. Sci.* 31(2):267–306.

Bishop, J. M., and J. V. Miglarese. 1978. Carnivorous feeding in adult striped mullet. *Copeia* (4):705–707.

Boesch, D. F. and N. N. Rabalais. 1987. *Long-term environmental effects of offshore oil and gas development.* New York: Elsevier Applied Science. 708 pp.

Boesch, D. F., and R. E. Turner. 1984. Dependence of fishery species on salt marshes: the role of food and refuge. *Estuaries.* 7(4A):460–68.

Böhlke, J. E., and E. B. Böhlke. 1980. The identity of the moray, *Gymnothorax conspersus* Poey, and description of *G. kolpos*, n. sp., from the western Atlantic ocean. *Proc. Acad. Nat. Sci. Philadelphia* 132:218–27.

Böhlke, J. E., and J. H. Caruso, 1980. *Ophichthus rex*: a new giant snake eel from the Gulf of Mexico (Anguilliformes: Ophichthidae). *Proc. Acad. Nat. Sci. Philadelphia* 132:239–44.

Böhlke, J. E. and J. E. Randall, 1968. Five new species of Western Atlantic cardinalfishes of the genus *Apogon* with a key to the shallow water western Atlantic members of the family. *Proc. Acad. Nat. Sci. Philadelphia* 120:175–206.

Böhlke, J. E., and V. G. Springer. 1961. A review of the Atlantic species of the clinid fish genus *Starksia*. *Proc. Acad. Nat. Sci. Philadelphia* 113(3):29–60.

Bonin, R. E. 1977. Juvenile marine fishes of Harbor Island, Texas. M. S. thesis, Texas A&M Univ, College Station.

Boothby, R. N., and J. W. Avault. 1971. Food habits, length-weight relationship, and condition factor of the red drum *(Sciaenops ocellata)* in southeastern Louisiana. *Trans. Am. Fish. Soc.* 100(2): 290–95.

Bortone, S. A. 1977. Revision of the sea basses of the genus *Diplectrum* (Pisces: Serranidae). NOAA Tech. Rept. NMFS Cir. 404. 49 pp.

Bortone, S. A., P. A. Hastings, and S. B. Collard. 1977. The pelagic-*Sargassum* ichthyofauna of the Gulf of Mexico. *Northeast Gulf Sci.* 1(2):60–67.

Boschung, H. T., Jr. 1957. The fishes of Mobile Bay and the Gulf coast of Alabama. Ph.D. thesis, Univ. Alabama, Montgomery. 626 pp.

Bradbury, M. G. 1967. The genera of batfishes (family Ogcocephalidae). *Copeia* (2):399–422.

———. 1980. A revision of the fish genus *Ogcocephalus* with descriptions of new species from the western Atlantic Ocean (Ogcocephalidae: Lophiiformes). *Proc. Calif. Acad. Sci.* 42(7):229–85.

Bradley, E., and C. F. Bryan III. 1975. Life history and fishery of the red snapper *(Lutjanus campechanus)* in the northwestern Gulf of Mexico: 1970–1974. *Proc. Gulf and Caribb. Fish. Inst.* 27:77–106.

Branstetter, S. 1981. Biological notes on the sharks of the northcentral Gulf of Mexico. *Contrib. Mar. Sci.* 24:13–34.

———. 1982. Problems associated with the identification and separation of the spinner shark, *Carcharhinus brevipinna,* and the blacktip shark, *Carcharhinus limbatus. Copeia* (2):461–65.

———. 1987a. Age and growth validation of newborn sharks held in laboratory aquaria, with comments on the life history of the Atlantic sharpnose shark, *Rhizoprionodon terraenovae. Copeia* (2):291–300.

———. 1987b. Age, growth and reproductive biology of the silky shark, *Carcharhinus falciformis,* and the scalloped hammerhead, *Sphyrna lewini,* from the northwestern Gulf of Mexico. *Environ. Biol. Fishes* 19(3):161–73.

———. 1987c. Age and growth estimates for blacktip, *Carcharhinus limbatus,* and spinner, *Carcharhinus brevipinna,* sharks from the northwestern Gulf of Mexico. *Copeia* (4):964–74.

Branstetter, S., and J. D. McEachran. 1983. A first record of the bigeye thresher, *Alopias superciliosus,* the blue shark, *Prionace glauca,* and the pelagic stingray, *Dasyatis violacea,* from the Gulf of Mexico. *Northeast Gulf Sci.* 6(1):59–61.

———. 1986. A first record of *Odontaspis norohai* (Lamniformes: Odontaspididae) for the western North Atlantic, with notes on two uncommon sharks from the Gulf of Mexico. *Northeast Gulf Sci.* 8(2):153–58.

Branstetter, S., J. A. Musick, and J. A. Colvocoresses. 1987. A comparison of age and growth of the tiger shark, *Galeocerdo cuvier,* from off Virginia and from the northwestern Gulf of Mexico. *Fish. Bull., U.S.* 85:269–79.

Branstetter, S., and R. Stiles. 1987. Age and growth estimates of the bull shark, *Carcharhinus leucas,* from the northern Gulf of Mexico. *Environ. Biol. Fishes* 20(3):169–81.

Brasseaux, C. A., and H. D. Hoese. 1991. Close encounter with a creature "of the finny tribe": Louisiana's sea monster sighting of 1856. *Gulf Coast Hist. Rev.* 7(1):7–17.

Breder, C. M. 1938. A contribution to the life histories of the Atlantic ocean flyingfishes. *Bull. Bingham Oceanogr. Collect.* 6(5). 126 pp.

Breuer, J. P. 1954. The littlest biggest fish. *Tex. Game and Fish* 12(2):4–5, 29.

———. 1957. An ecological survey of Baffin and Alazan bays, Texas. *Publ. Inst. Mar. Sci. Univ. Tex.* 4(2):134–55.

———. 1962. An ecological survey of the lower Laguna Madre of Texas 1953–1959. *Publ. Inst. Mar. Sci. Univ. Tex.* 8:153–83.

Briggs, J. C. 1955. A monograph of the clingfishes (order Xenopterygii). Stanford Ichthyol. Bull. no. 6. 224 pp.

———. 1956. Notes on the triglid fishes of the genus *Prionotus. Q. J. Fla. Acad. Sci.* 9(2–3):99–103.

———. 1958. A list of Florida fishes and their distribution. *Bull. Fla. State Mus. Biol. Sci.* 2(8):223–318.

———. 1964. The graysby, *Petrometopon cruentatum* (Lacepède), first occurrence in the northern Gulf of Mexico. *Tex. J. Sci.* 26(4):451–52.

Briggs, J. C., and D. K. Caldwell. 1957. *Acanthurus randalli,* a new surgeon fish from the Gulf of Mexico. *Bull. Fla. State Mus. Biol. Sci.* 2(4):43–51.

Briggs, J. C., H. D. Hoese, W. F. Hadley, and R. S. Jones. 1964. Twenty-two new marine fish records for the northwestern Gulf of Mexico. *Tex. J. Sci.* 16(1):113–16.

Bright, T. J. 1977. Coral reefs, nepheloid layers, gas seeps and brine flows on hard banks in the northwestern Gulf of Mexico. *Proc. 3d Int. Coral Reef Symp.* (Univ. of Miami, Fla.): 39–46.

Bright, T. J., and C. W. Cashman. 1974. Fishes. In *Biota of the West Flower Garden Bank,* ed. T. J. Bright and L. H. Pequegnat, pp. 340–409. Houston: Gulf Publ. Co.

Bright, T. J., and R. Rezak, 1976. A biological and geological reconnaissance of selected topographic features on the Texas continental shelf. Final Report to U.S. Dept. of the Interior, Bureau of Land Management Contract #08550-075-4 NTIS Order No. PB80-166036. 377 pp.

Bright, T. J., J. W. Tunnell, L. H. Pequegnat, T. E. Burke, C. W. Cashman, D. A. Cropper, J. P. Ray, R. C. Tresslar, J. Teerling, and J. B. Wills. 1974. Biotic zonation on the West Flower Garden Bank. In *Biota of the West Flower Garden Bank,* ed. T. J. Bright and L. H. Pequegnat, pp. 3–63. Houston: Gulf Publ. Co.

Brongersma-Sanders, M. 1957. Mass mortality in the sea. *Mem. Geol. Soc. Am.* 1(67):94–1010.

Brown-Peterson, N., P. Thomas, and C. R. Arnold. 1988. Reproductive biology of the spotted seatrout, *Cynoscion nothus,* in south Texas. *Fish. Bull., U.S.* 86(2):373–378.

Brown-Peterson, N. B., and M. S. Peterson. 1990. Comparative life history of female mosquitofish, *Gambusia affinis,* in tidal freshwater and oligohaline habitats. *Environ. Biol. Fishes* 27(1): 33–42.

Bruun, A. F. 1935. Flyingfishes (Exocoetidae) of the Atlantic, systematic and biological studies. *Dana-Rep. Carlsbergfondets* no. 6. 106 pp.

Bryan, C. E. 1971. An ecological survey of the Arroyo Colorado, Texas 1966–1969. Tech. Bull. Texas Parks and Wildl. Dept. 10. 28 pp.

Bryan, C. E., T. Cody, and G. C. Matlock. 1982. Organisms captured by the commercial shrimp fleet on the Texas brown shrimp (*Penaeus aztecus* Ives) grounds. Tech. Bull. Texas Parks and Wildl. Dept. 31. 26 pp.

Bullis, H. T., and J. R. Thompson. 1965. Collections by the exploratory fishing vessels *Oregon, Silver Bay, Combat,* and *Pelican* made during 1956 to 1960 in southwestern North Atlantic. U.S. Fish Wildl. Serv. Spec. Sci. Rept. Fish. no. 510. 130 pp.

Bullock, L. H., and M. F. Godcharles. 1982. Range extensions of four sea basses (Pisces: Serranidae) from the eastern Gulf of Mexico, with a color note of *Hemianthus leptus* (Ginsburg). *Northeast Gulf Sci.* 5(2):53–56.

Bullock, L. H., M. D. Murphy, M. F. Godcharles, and M. E. Mitchell. 1992. Age, growth and reproduction of jewfish, *Epinephelus itajara,* in the eastern Gulf of Mexico. *Fish. Bull., U.S.* 90(2):243–49.

Bullock, L. H., and G. B. Smith. 1991. Seabasses (Pisces: Serranidae). *Mem. Hourglass Cruises* 8(2). 243 pp.

Burgess, G. H., and S. Branstetter. 1985. Status of *Neoscopelus* (Neoscopelidae) in the Gulf of Mexico, with distributional notes on *Caulolatilus chrysops* (Branchiostegidae) and *Etelis oculatus* (Lutjanidae). *Northeast Gulf Sci.* 7(2):157–62.

Burgess, G. H., F. F. Snelson, S. J. Walsh, S. Clark, K. G. Abbott, L. E. Barton, and W. S. Otwell. 1989. Biological, fishery and product assessments of the keoghfish, an underutilized and unmanaged Gulf of Mexico resource. Report to Natl. Mar Fish. Serv. Mar. Fish. Init (MARFIN). 108 pp.

Burgess, W. E. 1974. Evidence for the evaluation to family status of the angelfishes (Pomacanthidae) previously considered to be a subfamily of the butterflyfish family, Chaetodontidae. *Pac. Sci.* 28(1):57–71.

Burke, J. S., D. S. Peters, and P. J. Hanson. 1993. Morphological indices and otolith microstructure of Atlantic croaker, *Micropogonias undulatus,* as indicators of habitat quality along an estuarine pollution gradient. *Environ. Biol. Fishes* 35:25–33.

Buskey, E. J., and C. J. Hyatt. 1995. Effects of the Texas "brown tide" alga on planktonic grazers. *Mar. Ecol. Prog. Ser.* 126(1–3):285–92.

Butler, J. L. 1979. The nomeid genus *Cubiceps* (Pisces) with a description of a few species. *Bull. Mar. Sci.* 29(2):226–41.

Butter, M. E., M. Wapstra, and E. van Dijk. 1980. *Meandrina meandrites* and *Emblemariopsis diaphana,* first record of an association between a stony coral and a fish, similar to anemone/fish relationships. *Bijdr. Dierk* 50(1): 87–95.

Caillouet, C. W. Jr., W. S. Perret, and B. J. Fontenot, 1969. Weight, length, and sex ratio of immature bull sharks, *Carcharhinus leucas,* from Vermilion Bay, Louisiana. *Copeia* (1):196–97.

Caldwell, D. K. 1955a. Distribution of the longspined porgy *Stenotomus caprinus. Bull. Mar. Sci. Gulf Caribb.* 5(2):230–39.

———. 1955b. Notes on the distribution, spawning, and growth of the spottailed pinfish, *Diplodus holbrooki. Q. J. Fla. Acad. Sci.* 18(2):73–83.

———. 1957. The biology and systematics of the pinfish, *Lagodon rhomboides* (Linnaeus). *Bull. Fla. State Mus. Biol. Sci.* 2(6):77–173.

———. 1961. Populations of the butterfish, *Poronotus triacanthus* (Peck), with systematic comments. *Bull. South. Calif. Acad. Sci.* 60(1):19–31

———. 1962a. Western Atlantic fishes of the family Priacanthidae. *Copeia* (2):417–24.

———. 1962b. Development and distribution of the short bigeye *Pseudopriacanthus altus* (Gill) in the western North Atlantic. *Fish. Bull., U.S.* 62(203):103–50.

———. 1965. Systematics and variation in the sparid fish *Archosargus probatocephalus. Bull. South. Calif. Acad. Sci.* 64(2):89–100.

Caldwell, D. K., and J. C. Briggs. 1957b. Range extensions of western North Atlantic fishes with notes on some soles of the genus *Gymnachirus. Bull. Fla. State Mus. Biol. Sci.* 2(1):1–11.

Caldwell, M. C. 1962. Development and distribution of larval and juvenile fishes of the family Mullidae of the western North Atlantic. *Fish. Bull., U.S.* 62(213):403–57.

Camber, C. I. 1955. A survey of the red snapper fishery of the Gulf of Mexico, with special reference to the Campeche Banks. Fla. State Board Conserv. Tech. Ser. no. 12. 64 pp.

Campbell, R. P., C. Hons, and L. M. Green. 1991. Trends in finfish landings of sport-boat anglers in Texas marine waters, May 1974–May 1990. Texas Parks Wildl. Dept. Manag. Ser.

Carpenter, J. S. 1965. A review of the Gulf of Mexico red snapper fishery. U.S. Fish Wildl. Serv. Circ. no. 208. 35 pp.

Causey, B. D. 1969. The fishes of Seven-and-one-half Fathom Reef. M.S. thesis, Texas A&I Univ., Kingsville. 110 pp.

Cervigón, F., and E. Velasquez. 1966. Las especies del genero *Mycteroperca* de las costas de Venezuela. *Mem. Soc. Cienc. Nat. La Salle* 26(74):77–143.

Chernoff, B., J. V. Conner, and C. F. Bryan. 1981. Systematics of the *Menidia beryllina* complex (Pisces: Atherinidae) from the Gulf of Mexico and its tributaries. *Copeia* (2):319–36.

Chittenden, M. E., and J. D. McEachran. 1976. Composition, ecology, and dynamics of demersal fish communities on the northwestern Gulf of Mexico continental shelf, with a similar synopsis for the entire Gulf. Tex. A & M Univ. Sea Grant Publ. TAMU-SG-76-208:1–104.

Chittenden, M. E., and D. Moore. 1977. Composition of the ichthyofauna inhabiting the 110-meter contour of the Gulf of Mexico, Mississippi River to Rio Grande. *Northeast Gulf Sci.* 1(2):106–14.

Christmas, J.Y. (ed.). 1973. Cooperative Gulf of Mexico estuarine inventory and study, Mississippi. Jackson: Miss. Mar. Conserv. Comm. 433 pp.

Christmas, J. Y., and G. Gunter. 1960. Distribution of menhaden, genus *Brevoortia*, in the Gulf of Mexico. *Trans. Amer. Fish. Soc.* 89(4):338–43.

Christmas, J. Y., J. T. McBee, R. S. Waller, and F. C. Sutter III. 1982. Habitat suitability index models: Gulf menhaden. U.S. Fish and Wildl. Serv. FWS/OBS-82-10.23. 23 pp.

Christmas, J.Y., G. Gunter, and E. C. Whatley. 1960. Fishes taken in the menhaden fishery of Alabama, Mississippi, and eastern Louisiana. U.S. Fish Wildl. Serv. Spec. Sci. Rept. Fish. no. 339. 10 pp.

Clark, E., and K. von Schmidt. 1965. Sharks of the central Gulf coast of Florida. *Bull. Mar Sci.* 15(1): 13–83.

Clark, R. B. (ed.). 1982. *The long-term effects of oil pollution on marine populations, communities, and ecosystems.* London: Royal Society. 259 pp.

Cohen, D. M.; T. Inada; T. Iwamoto; and N. Scialabba. 1990. *FAO species catalog.* Vol. 10, *Gadiform fishes of the world (Order Gadiformes). An annotated and illustrated catalogue of cods, hakes, grenadiers and other gadiform fishes known to date.* FAO Fisheries Synopsis no. 125. 442 pp.

Cohen, D. M., and J. G. Nielsen. 1978. Guide to the identification of genera of the fish order Ophidiiformes with a tentative classification of the order. NOAA Tech. Rept. NMFS Circ. 417. 72 pp.

Colin, P. L., and D. W. Arenson. 1978. Aspects of the natural history of the Swordtail Jawfish, *Lonchopisthus micrognathus*, off southwestern Puerto Rico (Pisces: Opistognathidae). *Journal of Natural History (London)* 12:689–97.

Colin, P. L., and J. B. Heiser. 1973. Associations of two species of cardinalfishes (Apogonidae: Pisces) with sea anemones in the West Indies. *Bull. Mar. Sci.* 23 (3):521–24.

Collette, B. B. 1978. Scombridae. In *FAO Species identification sheets for fishery purposes. Western Central Atlantic (Fishing Area 31)*, ed. W. Fischer. Vol 4. Roma: FAO.

Collette, B. B., and F. H. Berry. 1965. Recent studies on the needlefishes (Belonidae): an evaluation. *Copeia* (3):386–92.

Collette, B. B., and L. N. Chao. 1975. Systematics and morphology of the bonitos *(Sarda)* and their relatives (Scombridae, Sardini). *Fish. Bull., U.S.* 73(3):516–625.

Collette, B. B., and C. E. Nauen. 1983. *FAO species catalog.* Vol. 2, *Scombrids of the world. An annotated and illustrated catalogue of tunas, mackerels, bonitos and related species known to date.* FAO Fisheries Synopsis no. 125. 137 pp.

Collette, B. B., and J. C. Russo. 1984. Morphology, systematics, and biology of the Spanish mackerels *(Scomberomorus*, Scombridae). *Fish. Bull., U.S.* 82(4):545–692.

Collins, L. A., J. H. Finucane, and L. E. Barger. 1979. Description of larval and juvenile red snapper, *Lutjanus campechanus. U.S. Natl. Mar. Fish. Serv. Fish Bull.* 77(4):965–74.

Compagno, L. J.V. 1984a. *FAO species catalogue.* Vol. 4, *Sharks of the world.* Part 1, Hexanchiformes to Lamniformes. FAO Fisheries Synopsis no. 125. 249 pp.

————. 1984b. *FAO species catalogue.* Vol. 4, *Sharks of the world.* Part 2, Carcharhiniformes. FAO Fisheries Synopsis no 125. 655 pp.

Conn, C. H., and D. L. Belcher. 1996. Reproductive strategy in a population of *Gobiosoma bosci* (Osteichthyes: Gobiidae) with slow and fast maturing individuals. *Gulf Res. Rept.* 9(3):177–82.

Connell, C. H., and J. B. Cross. 1950. Mass mortality of fish associated with the protozoan *Gonyaulax* in the Gulf of Mexico. *Science* 112(2909):359–63.

Cooley, N. R. 1978. An inventory of the estuarine fauna in the vicinity of Pensacola, Florida. *Publ. Fl. Dep. Nat. Res. Mar. Res. Lab.* 31:1–119.

Copeland, B. J. 1966. Effects of decreased river flow on estuarine ecology. *J. Water Pollut. Control Fed.* 38(11):1831–39.

Cordova, F. G., 1986. Distribution of the coney, *Epinephelus fulvus,* in the northwestern Gulf of Mexico. *Northeast Gulf Sci.* 8(2):161–62.

Courtenay, W. R., Jr. 1961. Western Atlantic fishes of the genus *Haemulon* (Pomadasyidae): Systematic status and juvenile pigmentation. *Bull. Mar. Sci. Gulf Caribb.* 11(1):66–149.

————. 1967. Atlantic fishes of the genus *Rypticus* (Grammistidae). *Proc. Acad. Nat. Sci. Philadelphia* 119(6):241–93.

Cowan, J. H. Jr., and R. F. Shaw. 1988. The distribution, abundance, and transport of larval sciaenids collected during winter and early spring from the continental shelf waters off west Louisiana. *Fish. Bull., U.S.* 86(1):129–42.

Cowan, J. H. Jr, R. F. Shaw, and J. G. Ditty. 1989. Occurrence, age and growth of two morphological types of sand seatrout *(Cynoscion arenarius)* larvae in the winter and early spring coastal waters off west Louisiana. *Contrib. Mar. Sci.* 32:39–50.

Cross, J. C., and H. B. Parks. 1937. Marine fauna and sea-side flora of the Nueces River basin and the adjacent islands. *Bull. Tex. Coll. A&I* 8(3). 36 pp.

Crowe, B. J. 1984. Distribution, length-weight, and length-frequency data of southern kingfish, *Menticirrhus americanus,* in Mississippi. *Fish. Bull., U.S.* 82(2):427–34.

Curran, H. W. 1942. A systematic revision of the gerrid fishes referred to the genus *Eucinostomus,* with a discussion of their distribution and speciation. Ph.D. diss., Univ. of Mich., Ann Arbor. 183 pp.

Dahlberg, M. D. 1970. Atlantic and Gulf of Mexico menhadens, genus *Brevoortia* (Pisces: Clupeidae). *Bull. Fla. State Mus. Biol Sci.* 15(3):91–162.

Daly, R. J. 1970. Systematics of southern Florida anchovies (Pisces:Engraulidae). *Bull. Mar. Sci.* 20(1): 70–104.

Darcy, G. H. 1983a. Synopsis of biological data on the grunts *Haemulon aurolineatum* and *H. plumieri* (Pisces: Haemulidae). FAO Fisheries Synopsis 133, NOAA Tech Rep. NMFS Circ. 448. 37 pp.

————. 1983b. Synopsis of biological data on the pigfish *Orthopristis chrysopterus* (Pisces: Haemulidae). FAO Fisheries Synopsis 134, NOAA Tech. Rep. NMFS Circ. 449. 23 pp.

————. 1985a. Synopsis of biological data on the spottail pinfish, *Diplodus holbrooki* (Pisces: Sparidae). NOAA Tech. Rep. NMFS Circ. 19. 11 pp.

————. 1985b. Synopsis of biological data on the pinfish, *Lagodon rhomboides* (Pisces: Sparidae). NOAA Tech. Rept. NMFS Circ. 23. 32 pp.

————. 1985c. Synopsis of biological data on the sand perch, *Diplectrum formosum* (Pisces: Serranidae). NOAA Tech. Rept. NMFS Circ. 26. 21 pp.

———. 1986 Synopsis of biological data on the porgies, *Calamus arctifrons* and *C. proridens* (Pisces: Sparidae). NOAA Tech. Rept. NMFS Circ. 44. 19 pp.

Darcy, G. H., and E. J. Gutherz. 1984. Abundance and density of demersal fishes on the west Florida shelf, January 1978. *Bull. Mar. Sci.* 34(1):81–105.

Darnell, R. M. 1958. Food habits of fishes and larger invertebrates of Lake Pontchartrain, Louisiana, an estuarine community. *Publ. Inst. Mar. Sci. Univ Tex.* 5:353–416.

———. 1962. Fishes of the Rio Tamesi and related coastal lagoons in east central Mexico. *Publ. Inst. Mar. Sci. Univ. Tex.* 8:299–365.

Darnell, R. M., and P. Abramoff. 1968. Distribution of the gynogenetic fish, *Poecilia formosa,* with remarks on the evolution of the species. *Copeia* (2):354–61.

Darnell, R. M., R. E. Defenbaugh, and D. Moore. 1983. Northwestern Gulf shelf bio-atlas. A study of the distribution of demersal fishes and penaeid shrimp of soft bottoms of the continental shelf from the Rio Grande to the Mississippi River delta. U.S. Dep. Int. Min. Manag. Serv. Open file rep. 82-04. 438 pp.

Darnell, R. M., and J. A. Kleypas. 1987. Eastern Gulf shelf bio-atlas. A study of the distribution of demersal fishes and penaeid shrimp of soft bottoms of the continental shelf from the Mississippi River to the Florida Keys. U.S. Dep. Int. Min. Manag. Serv. Study. MMS86-0041. 548 pp.

Darovec, J. E., Jr, 1983. Sciaenid fishes (Osteichthyes: Perciformes) of western peninsular Florida. *Mem. Hourglass Cruises* 6(3). 76 pp.

Davis, J. T., B. J. Fontenot, C. E. Hoenke, A, M, Williams, and J. S. Hughes. 1970. Ecological factors affecting anadromous fishes of Lake Pontchartrain and its tributaries. La. Wild Life Fish. Comm. Fish. Bull. no. 9. 63 pp.

Dawson, C. E. 1962a. New records and notes on fishes from the north-central Gulf of Mexico. *Copeia* (2):442–44.

———. 1962b. A new gobioid fish, *Microdesmus lanceolatus,* from the Gulf of Mexico with notes on *M. longipinnis* (Weymouth). *Copeia* (2):330–36.

———. 1964. A revision of the western Atlantic flatfish genus *Gymnachirus* (the naked soles). *Copeia* (4):646–65.

———. 1965. Records of two headfishes (family Molidae) from the north central Gulf of Mexico. *Proc. La. Acad. Sci.* 28:86–89.

———. 1966a. Additions to the known marine fauna of Grand Isle, Louisiana. *Proc. La. Acad. Sci.* 21:175–80.

———. 1966b. Observations on the anacanthine fish *Bregmaceros atlanticus,* in the north central Gulf of Mexico. *Copeia* (3):604–605.

———. 1966c. *Gunterichthys longipenis,* a new genus and species of ophidioid fish from the northern Gulf of Mexico. *Proc. Biol Soc. Wash.* 79:205–14.

———. 1966d. Studies on the gobies (Pisces: Gobiidae) of Mississippi Sound and adjacent waters: I. *Gobiosoma. Am. Midl. Nat.* 76(2):379–409.

———. 1967. Contributions to the biology of the cutlassfish *(Trichiurus lepturus)* in the northern Gulf of Mexico. *Trans. Am. Fish. Soc.* 96(2):117–21.

———. 1968. Contributions to the biology of the Mexican flounder, *Cyclopsetta chittendeni,* in the northern Gulf of Mexico. *Trans. Am. Fish. Soc.* 97(4):504–507.

———. 1969. Studies on the gobies of Mississippi Sound and adjacent waters. Vol. 2, An illustrated key to gobioid fishes. Pub. no. 1. Ocean Springs, Miss.: Gulf Coast Res. Lab. Mus. 59 pp.

————. 1970. A Mississippi population of the opossum pipefish, *Oostethus lineatus* (Syngnathidae). *Copeia* (4):772–73.

————. 1971a. Supplemental observations on *Gunterichthys longipenis*, a northern Gulf of Mexico brotulid fish. *Copeia* (1):164–67.

————. 1971b. Records of the pearlfish, *Carapus bermudensis*, in the northern Gulf of Mexico and of a new host species. *Copeia* (4):730–31.

————. 1971c. Occurrence and description of prejuvenile and early juvenile Gulf of Mexico cobia, *Rachycentron canadum. Copeia* (1):65–71.

————. 1971d. Notes on juvenile black driftfish, *Hyperoglyphe bythites*, from the northern Gulf of Mexico. *Copeia* (4):732–35.

————. 1972. Nektonic pipefishes (Syngnathidae) from the Gulf of Mexico off Mississippi. *Copeia* (4):844–48.

————. 1982a. Atlantic sand stargazers (Pisces: Dactyloscopidae), with description of one new genus and seven new species. *Bull. Mar. Sci.* 32(1):14–85.

————. 1982b. Order Gasterosteiformes, suborder Syngnathoidei, Syngnathidae. In *Fishes of the western North Atlantic.* Memoir Sears Found. Mar. Res. no. 1, pt. 8. 198 pp. New Haven.

————. 1984. Revision of the genus *Microphis* Kaup (Pisces: Syngnathidae). *Bull. Mar. Sci.* 35(2):117–81.

Day, J. W. Jr., C. S. Hopkinson, and W. H. Conner. 1982. An analysis of environmental factors regulating community metabolism and fisheries production in a Louisiana estuary. In *Estuarine comparisons,* ed. V. S. Kennedy, pp. 121–36. New York: Academic Press.

Deckert, G. D. 1973. A systematic revision of the genera *Diapterus* and *Eugerres*: with the description of a new genus, *Shizopterus* (Pisces: Gerreidae). M.S. thesis, Univ. of Northern Ill., DeKalb. 74 pp.

Deckert, G. D., and D. W. Greenfield. 1987. A review of the western Atlantic species of the genera *Diapterus* and *Eugerres* (Pisces: Gerreidae). *Copeia* (1):182–94.

Deegan, L. A., and B. A. Thompson. 1985. The ecology of fish communities in the Mississippi River plain. In *Fish communities in estuaries and coastal lagoons: towards an ecosystem integration,* ed. A. Yáñez-Arancibia, pp. 35–56. DR (R) Universidad Nacional autónoma de México.

Dennis, G. D., and T. J. Bright. 1988a. New records of fishes in the northwestern Gulf of Mexico, with notes on some rare species. *Northeast Gulf Sci.* 10(1):1–18.

————. 1988b. Reef fish assemblages on hard banks in the northwestern Gulf of Mexico. *Bull. Mar. Sci.* 43(2):280–307.

Dentzau, M. W., and M. E. Chittenden, Jr. 1990. Reproduction, movements, and apparent population dynamics of the Atlantic threadfin, *Polydactylus octonemus,* in the northern Gulf of Mexico. *Fish. Bull., U.S.* 88(3):439–62.

de Sylva, D. P. 1955. The osteology and phylogenetic relationship of the blackfin tuna, *Thunnus atlanticus* (Lesson). *Bull. Mar. Sci. Gulf Caribb.* 5(1):1–41.

————. 1957. Studies on the age and growth of the Atlantic sailfish, *Istiophorus americanus* (Cuvier), using length-frequency curves. *Bull. Mar. Sci. Gulf Caribb.* 7(1):1–20.

————. 1963. Systematics and life history of the great barracuda, *Sphyraena barracuda* (Walbaum). *Stud. Trop. Oceanogr.* 1:1–179.

————. 1974. A review of the world sport fishery for billfishes (Istiophoridae and Xiphiidae). Nat. Mar. Fish. Serv. Spec. Sci. Rep. Fish. no. 675. 233 pp.

de Sylva, D. P., and W. P. Davis. 1963. White marlin, *Tetrapturus albidus,* in the Middle Atlantic Bight, with observations on the hydrography of the fishing grounds. *Copeia* (1):81–99.

de Sylva, D. P., and W. F. Rathjen. 1961. Life history notes on the little tuna, *Euthynnus alletteratus*, from the southeastern United States. *Bull. Mar. Sci Gulf Caribb.* 11(2):161–90.

DeVries, D. A., and M. E. Chittenden, Jr. 1982. Spawning, age determination, longevity, and mortality of the silver seatrout, *Cynoscion nothus. Fish. Bull., U.S.* 80(3):487–500.

Ditton, R.B., A. J. Fedler, and R. T. Christian. The evolution of recreational fisheries management in Texas. *Ocean and Shoreline Management* 17:169–181.

Ditty, J. G. 1986. Ichthyoplankton in neritic waters of the northern Gulf of Mexico off Louisiana: composition, relative abundance, and seasonality. *Fish. Bull., U.S.* 84(4):935–46.

———. 1989. Separating early larvae of sciaenids from the western north Atlantic: a review and comparison of larvae off Louisiana and Atlantic coast of the U.S. *Bull. Mar. Sci.* 44(3):1083–1105.

Ditty, J. G., M. Bourgeois, R. Kasprzak, and M. A. Konikoff. 1991. Life history and ecology of sand seatrout *Cynoscion arenarius* Ginsburg, in the northern Gulf of Mexico: a review. *Northeast Gulf Sci.* 12(1):35–47.

Ditty, J. G., and R. F. Shaw. 1992. Larval development, distribution and ecology of cobia, *Rachycentron canadum* (Family Rachycentridae) in the northern Gulf of Mexico. *Fish. Bull., U.S.* 90(3):668–77.

———. 1994. Larval development of tripletail, *Lobotes surinamensis* (Pisces: Lobotidae), and their spatial and temporal distribution in the northern Gulf of Mexico. *Fish Bull., U.S.* 92:33–45.

Ditty, J. G., R. F. Shaw, and J. S. Cope. 1994. A re-description of Atlantic spadefish larvae, *Chaetodipterus faber* (family: Ephippidae), and their distribution, abundance, and seasonal occurrence in the Gulf of Mexico. *Fish.. Bull., U.S.* 92(2):262–74.

Ditty, J. G., R. F. Shaw, C. B. Grimes, and J. S. Cope. 1994. Larval development,distribution, and abundance of common dolphin, *Coryphaena hippurus,* and pompano dolphin, *C. equisetis,* (family: Coryphaenidae) in the Gulf of Mexico. *Fish. Bull., U.S.* 92(2):275–91.

Ditty, J. G., G. C. Zieske, and R. F. Shaw. 1988. Seasonality and depth distribution of larval fishes in the northern Gulf of Mexico above latitude 26°00'N. *Fish. Bull., U.S.* 86(4):811–23.

Divita, R., M. Creel, and P. F. Sheridan. 1982. Foods of coastal fishes during brown shrimp, *Penaeus aztecus,* migrations from Texas estuaries (June–July 1981). *Fish. Bull., U.S.* 81(2):396–404.

Dokken, Q. R., G. C. Matlock, and S. Cornelius. 1984. Distribution and composition of larval fish populations within Alazan Bay, Texas. *Contrib. Mar. Sci.* 27:205–22.

Domeier, M. L. 1994. Speciation in the serranid fish *Hypoplectrus. Bull. Mar. Sci.* 54(1):103–41.

Domeier, M. L., and M. E. Clarke. 1992. A laboratory produced hybrid between *Lutjanus synagris* and *Ocyurus chrysurus* and a probable hybrid between *Lutjanus griseus* and *Ocyurus chrysurus*(Perciformes: Lutjanidae). *Bull. Mar. Sci.* 50(3):501–507.

Dooley, J. K. 1972. Fishes associated with the pelagic sargassum complex, with a discussion of the sargassum community. *Contrib. Mar. Sci.* 16:1–32.

———. 1974. Systematic revision and comparative biology of the tilefishes (Perciformes: Branchiostegidae and Malacanthidae). Ph.D. diss., Univ. North Carolina, Chapel Hill. 301 pp.

———. 1978. Systematics and biology of the tilefishes (Perciformes: Branchiostegidae and Malacanthidae), with descriptions of two new species. NOAA Tech. Rep. Circ. 411. 78 pp.

———. 1981. A new species of tilefish (Pisces: Branchiostegidae) from Bermuda with a brief discussion of the genus *Caulolatilus. Northeast Gulf Sci.* 5(1):39–44.

Dooley, J. K., and F. H. Berry. 1977. A new species of tilefish (Pisces: Branchiostegidae) from the western tropical Atlantic. *Northeast Gulf Sci.* 1(1):8–13.

Dugas, R. J. 1970. An ecological study of Vermilion Bay, 1968–1969. M.S. thesis, Univ. Southwestern Louisiana, Lafayette. 105 pp.

Dunham, F. 1972. A study of commercially important estuarine-dependent industrial fishes. La. Wild Life Fish. Comm. Tech. Bull. no. 4. 63 pp.

Dunstan, P., B. H. Lidz, and E. A. Shinn. 1991. Impact of exploratory wells, offshore Florida: a biological assessment. *Bull. Mar. Sci.* 48(1):94–124.

Echelle, A. A., and D. T. Mosier. 1982. *Menidia clarkhubbsi,* n. sp. (Pisces: Atherinidae), an all female species. *Copeia.* (3):533–40.

Edwards, R. J., E. Marsh, and F. B. Stevens, Jr. 1978. The utility of the air bladder position in determining specific relationships in the atherinid genus *Menidia. Contrib. Mar. Sci.* 21:1–7.

Edwards, R. J., T. S. Sturdivant, and C. S. Linskey. 1986. The river goby, *Awaous tajasica* (Osteichthyes: Gobiidae) confirmed from the lower Rio Grande, Texas and Mexico. *Tex. J. Sci.* 38:191–92.

Elvers, D., and J. B. Johnston. 1976. Identification and mapping of fishing banks on the outer continental shelf of the Gulf of Mexico. *Proc. Gulf Carib. Fish. Inst.* 28:35–48.

Emery, A. R. 1968. A new species of *Chromis* (Pisces: Pomacentridae) from the western North Atlantic. *Copeia* (1):49–55.

———. 1973a. Comparative ecology and functional osteology of fourteen species of damselfish (Pisces: Pomacentridae) at Alligator Reef, Florida Keys. *Bull. Mar. Sci.* 23(3):649–770.

———. 1973b. Atlantic bicolor damselfish (Pomacentridae): a taxonomic question. *Copeia* (3): 590–92.

Emery, A. R., and W. E. Burgess. 1974. A new species of damselfish *(Eupomacentrus)* from the western Atlantic with a key to known species of that area. *Copeia* (4):879–86.

Emery, A. R., and W. F. Smith-Vaniz. 1982. Geographic variation and redescription of the western Atlantic damselfish *Chromis enchrysurus* Jordan and Gilbert (Pisces: Pomacentridae). *Bull. Mar. Sci.* 32(1):151–65.

Enge, K. M. and R. Mulholland 1985. Habitat suitability index models: Southern and Gulf Flounder. U.S. Fish Wildl. Serv. Biol. Rep. 82 (10.92). 25 pp.

Eschmeyer, W. N. 1963. A deepwater-trawl capture of two swordfish *(Xiphias gladius)* in the Gulf of Mexico. *Copeia* (3):590.

———. 1965. Western Atlantic scorpionfishes of the genus *Scorpaena,* including four new species. *Bull. Mar. Sci.* 15(1):84–164.

———. 1969. A systematic revision of the scorpion fishes of the Atlantic Ocean (Pisces: Scorpaenidae). Occas. Pap. Calif. Acad. Sci. no. 79. 143 pp.

———. 1978. Scorpaenidae. In *FAO Species identification sheets for fishery purposes. Western Central Atlantic (Fishing Area 31),* ed. W. Fischer. Vol 4. Roma: FAO.

Eschmeyer, W. N., and R. M. Bailey. 1990. *Catalog of the genera of recent fishes.* San Francisco: Calif. Acad. Sci. 697 pp.

Evermann, W. B., and W. C. Kendall. 1894. The fishes of Texas and the Rio Grande Basin, considered chiefly with reference to their geographic distribution. *Bull. U.S. Fish. Comm.* 12(1892):57–126.

Fable, W. A., Jr. 1980. Tagging studies of red snapper, *Lutjanus campechanus,* and vermilion snapper, *Rhomboplites aurorubens,* off the South Texas coast. *Contrib. Mar. Sci.* 23:115–21.

Fable, W.A. Jr., A. G. Johnson, and L. E. Barger. 1987. Age and growth of Spanish mackerel, *Scomberomorus maculatus,* from Florida and the Gulf of Mexico. *Fish. Bull., U.S.* 85(4):777–83.

Fahay, M. P., and D. F. Markle. 1984. Gadiformes: development and relationships. In *Ontogeny and*

Systematics of Fishes, ed. H. G. Moser et al., pp. 265–83. Spec. Publ. no. I, Amer Soc. Ich. Herp.

Feddern, H. A. 1968. Hybridization between the western Atlantic angelfishes, *Holacanthus isabelita* and *H. ciliaris. Bull. Mar. Sci.* 18(2):351–82.

Feddern, H. A. 1972. *Field guide to the angelfishes (Pomacanthidae) in the western Atlantic.* Natl. Mar. Fish. Serv. Circ. no. 369. 10 pp.

Felley, J. D., M. Vecchione, G. R. Gaston, and S. M. Felley. 1989. Habitat selection by demersal nekton: analysis of videotape data. *Northeast Gulf Sci.* 10(2):69–84.

Fields, H. M. 1962. Pompanos (*Trachinotus* spp.) of South Atlantic coast of the United States. *U.S. Fish Wildl. Serv. Fish. Bull.* 62(207):189–222.

Fischer, E. A. 1980. Speciation in hamlets *(Hypoplectrus unicolor)*—a continuing enigma. *Copeia* (4):649–59.

Fischer, W. (ed.). 1978. *FAO species identification sheets for fishery purposes. Western Central Atlantic (fishing area 31).* Vols. 1–7. Roma: FAO.

Fitzhugh, G. R., B. A. Thompson, and T. G. Snider III. 1993. Ovarian development, fecundity, and spawning frequency of black drum, *Pogonias cromis,* in Louisiana. *Fish. Bull., U.S.* 91(2):244–53.

Flores-Coto, C., F. Barba-Torres, and Jesus Sanchez-Robles. 1983. Seasonal diversity, abundances, and distribution of ichthyoplankton in Tamiahua Lagoon, western Gulf of Mexico. *Trans. Am. Fish. Soc.* 112:247–56.

Fontenot, B. J. Jr., and H. E. Rogillio. 1970. A study of estuarine sportfishes in the Biloxi Marsh Complex, Louisiana. Baton Rouge: La. Wild Life and Fish. Comm. 172 pp.

Fore, P. L. 1971. The distribution of the eggs and larvae of the round herring *Etrumeus teres* in the northern Gulf of Mexico. *Assoc. Southeast. Biol. Bull.* 18(2):34.

Forman, W. W. 1968b. Notes on the ecology of six species of cyprinodontid fishes from Grand Terre, Louisiana. *Proc. La. Acad. Sci.* 31:39–40.

Foster, N. R., and L. A. Fuiman. 1987. Notes on the behavior and early life history of captive lyre gobies, *Evorthodus lyricus. Bull. Mar. Sci.* 41(2):27–35.

Fowler, H. W. 1933. Notes on Louisiana fishes. *Proc. Biol. Soc. Wash.* 46:57–64.

Fowler, H. W. 1945. A study of the fishes of the Southern Piedmont and Coastal Plain. Monograph no. 7. Philadelphia: Acad. Nat. Sci. Philadelphia. 408 pp.

Fox, L. S., and C. J. White. 1969. Feeding habits of the southern flounder, *Paralichthys lethostigma,* in Barataria Bay, Louisiana. *Proc. La. Acad. Sci.* 32:31–38.

Frank, K. T., and W. C. Leggett. 1994. Fisheries ecology in the context of ecological and evolutionary theory. *Ann. Rev. Ecol. Sys.* 25:401–22.

Franks, J. S. 1970. An investigation of the fish population within the inland waters of Horn Island, Mississippi, a barrier island in the northern Gulf of Mexico. *Gulf Res. Rept.* 3(1):3–104.

Franks, J. S., J. Y. Christmas, W. L. Siler, R. Coombs, R. Waller, and C. Bums. 1972. A study of nektonic and benthic faunas of the shallow Gulf of Mexico off the State of Mississippi. *Gulf Res. Rept.* 4(1):1–148.

Fraser, T. H. 1971. Notes on the biology and systematics of the flatfish genus *Syacium* (Bothidae) in the straits of Florida. *Bull. Mar. Sci.* 21(2):491–509.

Fraser, T. H., and C. R. Robins. 1970. A new Atlantic genus of cardinalfishes with comments on some species from the Gulf of Guinea. *Stud. Trop. Oceanogr.* 4(2):302–15.

Fraser-Bruner, A. 1951. The ocean sunfishes. *Bull. Br. Mus. (Nat. Hist.) Zool.* 1(6):89–121.

Fritchey, R. 1994. *Wetland riders.* New Orleans: New Moon Press. 393 pp.

Fritzsche, R. A. 1976. A review of the cornetfishes, genus *Fistularia* (Fistulariidae), with a discussion of intrageneric relationships and zoogeography. *Bull. Mar. Sci.* 26(2): 196–204.

Fritzsche, R. A., and G. D. Johnson. 1981. *Pseudopriacanthus* Bleeker a synonym of the priacanthid genus *Pristigenys* Agassiz. *Copeia* (2):490–92.

Fruge, D. J., and F. M. Truesdale. 1978. Comparative larval development of *Micropogon undulatus* and *Leiostomus xanthurus* (Pisces: Sciaenidae) from the northern Gulf of Mexico. *Copeia* (4):643–48.

Fry, B. 1983. Fish and shrimp migrations in the northern Gulf of Mexico analyzed using stable C, N, and S isotope ratios. *Fish. Bull., U.S.* 81(4):789–801.

Fuiman, L. A. 1993. Water quality and the early life stages of fishes. *Amer. Fish. Soc. Symp.* 14:172.

Fuiman, L. A., and D. R. Ottey. 1993. Temperature effects on spontaneous behavior of larval and juvenile red drum, *Sciaenops ocellatus*, and implications for foraging. *Fish. Bull., U.S.* 91(1):23–35.

Funicelli, N. A. 1984. Assessing and managing effects of reduced freshwater inflow to two Texas estuaries. In *The estuary as a filter*, ed. V. S. Kennedy, pp. 435–556. New York: Academic Press.

Garrick, J. A. F. 1964. Additional information on the morphology of an embryo whale shark. *Proc. U.S. Natl. Mus.* 115 (3476):1–8.

———. 1967a. Revision of sharks of genus *Isurus* with description of a new species (Galeoidea, Lamnidae). *Proc. U.S. Natl. Mus.* 118 (3537):663–90.

———. 1967b. A taxonomic synopsis of the hammerhead sharks (family Sphyrnidae). In *Sharks, skates, rays,* eds. P. W. Gilbert, R. F. Mathewson, and D. P. Rall, pp. 69–77. Baltimore: Johns Hopkins Univ. Press.

———. 1982. Sharks of the genus *Carcharhinus*. NOAA Tech. Rept. NMFS Circ. 445. 194 pp.

———. 1985. Additions to a revision of the shark genus *Carcharhinus*: synonymy of *Aprionodon* and *Hypoprion,* and a description of a new species of *Carcharhinus (Carcharhinidae)*. NOAA Tech. Rep. NMFS 34. 26 pp.

Garrick, J. A. F., T. H. Backus, and R. H. Gibbs, Jr. 1964. *Carcharhinus floridanus,* the silky shark, a synonym of *C. falciformis*. *Copeia* (2):369–75.

Gartner, J. V. J. 1986. Observations on anomalous conditions in some flatfishes (Pisces: Pleuronectiformes), with a new record of partial albinism. *Environ. Biol. Fishes* 17(2):141–52.

Garwood, G. P. 1968. Notes on the life histories of the silversides, *Menidia beryllina* (Cope) and *Membras martinica* (Valenciennes) in Mississippi Sound and adjacent water. *Proc. Ann. Conf. Southeastern Assoc. Game and Fish Comm.* 22:314–23.

Garzón F. J., and A. Acero P. 1986. Notes on the fish *Synagrops trispinosus* (Perciformes: Acropomatidae) from the Colombian Caribbean. *Japanese Journal of Ichthyology* 33(3):316–18.

Geoghegan, P., and M. E. Chittenden, Jr. 1982. Reproduction, movement and population dynamics of the longspine porgy, *Stenotomus caprinus*. *Fish. Bull., U.S.* 80(3):523–40.

Gibbs, R. H., Jr. 1957. Preliminary analysis of the distribution of white marlin, *Makaira albida* (Poey), in the Gulf of Mexico. *Bull. Mar. Sci. Gulf Caribb.* 7(4):360–69.

———. 1959. A synopsis of the postlarvae of western Atlantic lizardfishes *(Synodontidae)*. *Copeia* (3):232–36.

Gibbs, R. H. Jr., and B. B. Collette. 1959. On the identification, distribution, and biology of the dolphins, *Coryphaena hippurus* and *C. equisetis*. *Bull. Mar. Sci. Gulf Caribb.* 9(2):117–52.

Gibbs, R. H. Jr., and B. B. Collette. 1967. Comparative anatomy and systematics of the tunas, genus *Thunnus*. *Fish. Bull., U.S.* 66:65–130.

Gilbert, C. R. 1961. First record for the hammerhead shark, *Sphyrna tudes*, in United States waters. *Copeia* (4):480.

———. 1966. Western Atlantic sciaenid fishes of the genus *Umbrina*. *Bull. Mar. Sci.* 16(2):230–58.

———. 1967. A revision of the hammerhead sharks (family: Sphyrnidae). *Proc. U.S. Natl. Mus.* 119 (3539):1–88.

———. 1971. Two new Atlantic clinid fishes of the genus *Starksia*. *Q. J. Fla. Acad. Sci.* 33(3):193–206.

———. 1977. The gobiid fish *Palatogobius paradoxus* in the northern Gulf of Mexico. *Northeast Gulf Sci.* 1(1):48–51.

———. 1986. Species profiles: life histories and environmental requirements of coastal fishes and invertebrates (South Florida). *U.S. Fish Wildl. Serv. Biol. Rep.* 82(11:54):1–2.

———. 1992. *Rare and endangered biota of Florida*. Vol. II. *Fishes*. Gainesville: Univ. Press of Florida. 247 pp.

———. 1993. Geographic distribution of the striped mullet *(Mugil cephalus)* in the Atlantic and eastern Pacific Ocean. *Fl. Sci.* 56(4):1–10.

Gilbert, C. R., and K. P. Kelso. 1971. Fishes of the Tortuguero area, Caribbean Costa Rica. *Bull. Fl. State Mus. Biol. Sci.* 16(1):1–54.

Gilbert, C. R., and J. E. Randall. 1979. Two new western Atlantic species of the gobiid fish genus *Gobionellus* with remarks on characteristics of other species. *Northeast Gulf Sci.* 3(1):27–47.

Gilmore, R. G. 1977. Notes on the opossum pipefish, *Oostethus lineatus*, from the Indian River lagoon and vicinity, Florida, *Copeia* (4):781–83.

———. 1983. Observation on the embryos of the longfin mako *Isurus paucus* and the bigeye thresher *Alopias superciliosus*. *Copeia* 1983(2):375–82.

Gilmore, R. G., L. H. Bullock, and F. H. Berry. 1978. Hypothermal mortality in marine fishes of south central Florida, January, 1977. *Northeast Gulf Sci.* 2(2):77–97.

Gilmore, R. G., J. W. Dodrill, and P. A. Linley. 1983. Reproduction and embryonic development of the sand tiger shark, *Odontaspis taurus* (Rafinesque). *Fish. Bull., U.S.* 81(2):201–26.

Gilmore, R. G., and R. S. Jones. 1982. *Lipogramma flavescens*, a new grammid fish from the Bahama Islands, with descriptions and distributional notes on *L. evides* and *L. anabantoides*. *Bull. Mar. Sci.* 42(3):435.

———. 1992. Color variation and associated behavior in the epinepheline grouper, *Mycteroperca microlepis* (Goode and Bean), and *Mycteroperca phenax* Jordan and Swain. *Bull. Mar. Sci.* 51(1):83–103.

Ginsburg, I. 1931. On the differences in the habitat and size of *Cynoscion arenarius* and *Cynoscion nothus*. *Copeia* (3):144.

———. 1932. A revision of the genus *Gobionellus* (family Gobiidae). *Bull. Bingham Oceanogr. Collect.* 4(2):3–51.

———. 1933. A revision of the genus *Gobiosoma* (family Gobiidae) with an account of the genus *Garmannia*. *Bull. Bingham Oceanogr. Collect.* 4(5):1–59.

———. 1937. A review of the seahorses *(Hippocampus)* found on the coasts of the American continents and of Europe. *Proc. U.S. Natl. Mus.* 83(2997):497–594.

———. 1942. Seven new American fishes. *J. Wash. Acad. Sci.* 32(12):364–70.

———. 1948. Some Atlantic populations related to *Diplectrum radiale* (Serranidae) with description of a new subspecies from the Gulf coast of the United States. *Copeia* (4):266–70.

———. 1950. Review of the western Atlantic Triglidae (fishes). *Tex. J. Sci.* 2(4):489–527.

————. 1951a. The eels of the northern Gulf coast of the United States and some related species. *Tex. J. Sci.* 3(3):431–85.

————. 1951b. Western Atlantic tonguefishes with descriptions of six new species. *Zoologica* (N.Y.) 36(3):185–201.

————. 1952a. Eight new fishes from the Gulf coast of the United States with two new genera and notes on geographic distribution. *J. Wash. Acad. Sci.* 42(3):84–101.

————. 1952b. Fishes of the family Carangidae of the northern Gulf of Mexico and three related species. *Publ. Inst. Mar. Sci. Univ. Tex.* 2(2):43–117.

————. 1952c. Flounders of the genus *Paralichthys* and related genera in American waters. *Fish. Bull., U.S.* 52(71):267–351.

————. 1954. Four new fishes and one little known species from the east coast of the United States including the Gulf of Mexico. *J. Wash. Acad. Sci.* 44(8):256–64.

Girard, C. 1858. Notes upon various new genera and new species of fishes in the Museum of the Smithsonian Institution, and collected in connection with the United States and Mexican Boundary Survey, Major William Emory, Commissioner. *Proc. Acad. Nat. Sci. Philadelphia* 10:167–71.

————. 1859. United States and Mexican Boundary Survey under the order of Lt. Col. W. H. Emory, Major First Cavalry, and United States Commissioner. Ichthyology of the Boundary. In *Report of the U.S. and Mexican Boundary Survey,* vol. 2, Washington, D.C., pp. 1–85.

Gittings, S. R., T. J. Bright, and E. N. Powell. 1984. Hard-bottom macrofauna of the East Flower Garden brine seep: impact of a long-term, sulfurous brine discharge. *Contrib. Mar. Sci.* 27:105–25.

Gittings, S. R., T. J. Bright, W. W. Schroeder, W. W. Sager, J. S. Laswell, and R. Rezak. 1992. Invertebrate assemblages and ecological controls on topographic features in the northeast Gulf of Mexico. *Bull. Mar. Sci.* 50(3):435–55.

Gonovi, J. J. 1993. Flux of larval fishes across frontal boundaries: examples from the Mississippi River plume front and the western Gulf Stream front in winter. *Bull. Mar. Sci.* 53(2):538–66.

Gonovi, J. J., D. E. Hoss, and D. R. Colby. 1989. The spatial distribution of larval fishes about the Mississippi River Plume. *Limnol. Oceanogr.* 34(1):178–87.

Gonovi, J. J., J. E. Onley, D. F. Markle, and W. Curtsinger. 1984. Observations on structure and evolution of possible formations of the vexillum in larval Carapidae (Ophidiiformes). *Bull. Mar. Sci.* 34(1):60–70.

Goode, G. B. 1879. A revision of the American species of the Genus *Brevoortia,* with a description of a new species from the Gulf of Mexico. *Proc. U.S. Natl. Mus.* 1:30–42.

Goodwin, J. M. IV, and A. G. Johnson. 1986. Age, growth and mortality of blue runner, *Caranx crysos,* from the northern Gulf of Mexico. *Northeast Gulf Sci.* 8(2):107–14.

Gosline, W. A. 1968. The suborders of perciform fishes. *Proc U.S. Natl. Mus.* 124(3647):1–78.

Gowanloch, J. N. 1950. Fisheries effects on Bonnet Carré spillway opening. *La. Conserv.* 2(6):12–13, 24–25.

Graves, J. E., and R. H. Rosenblatt. 1980. Genetic relationships of the color morphs of the serranid fish *Hypoplectrus unicolor. Evolution* 34:240–45.

Greeley, M. S., Jr. 1984. Spawning by *Fundulus pulvereus* and *Adinia xenica* (Cyprinodontidae) along the Alabama Gulf coast is associated with the semilunar tidal cycles. *Copeia* (3):797–800.

Greenfield, D. W. 1975. *Centropomus poeyi* from Belize, with a key to the western Atlantic species of *Centropomus. Copeia* (3):582–83.

Greenfield, D. W., and R. K. Johnson. 1981. The blennioid fishes of Belize and Honduras, Central America, with comments on their systematics, ecology and distribution *(Blennidae, Chaenopsidae, Labrisomidae, Tripterygiidae). Fieldiana Zoology* new ser. 8. 106 pp.

Greenwood, P. H. 1977. Notes on the anatomy and classification of elopomorph fishes. *Bull. Brit. Mus. Nat. Hist. (Zool.)* 32(4):65–102.

Greenwood, P. H., D. E. Rosen, S. H. Weitzman, and G. Myers. 1966. Phyletic studies of teleostean fishes, with a provisional classification of living forms. *Bull. Am. Mus. Nat. Hist.* 131(4):339–456.

Grimes, C. B., J. H. Finucane, L. A. Collins, and D. A. DeVries. 1990. Young king mackerel, *Scomberomorus cavalla,* in the Gulf of Mexico: a summary of the distribution and occurrence of larvae and juveniles, and spawning dates for Mexican juveniles. *Bull. Mar. Sci.* 46(3):640–54.

Grimes, C. B., C. S. Manooch, and G. R. Huntsman. 1982. Reef and rock outcropping fishes of the outer continental shelf of North Carolina and South Carolina, and ecological notes on the red porgy and vermilion snapper. *Bull. Mar. Sci.* 32:277–89.

Grove, R. S., and C. A. Wilson (eds.). 1994. Fifth international conference on aquatic habitat enhancement, 3–7 November, 1991. *Bull. Mar. Sci.* 55(2–3):1–1359.

Gruber, S. H., and L. J. V. Compagno. 1982. Taxonomic status and biology of the bigeye thresher, *Alopias superciliosus* (Lowe, 1839). *Fish. Bull., U.S.* 79(4):617–40.

Gudger, E. W. 1916. The gaff-topsail *(Felichthys felis),* a sea catfish that carries its eggs in its mouth. *Zoologica* 2(5):125–58.

Guest, W. C., and G. Gunter. 1958. The seatrout or weakfishes (genus *Cynoscion*) of the Gulf of Mexico. Gulf States Mar. Fish. Comm. Tech. Summ. no. 1. 40 pp.

Guillen, G., P. J. Hanson, D. Steinman, and S. Marx. 1994. Characteristics of demersal nekton populations inhabiting an industrialized coastal bayou. *Amer. Fish. Soc. Ann. Meet.* 124(Abs.):95.

Guillory, V. 1982a. An annotated checklist of the marine fish fauna of Grand Isle, Louisiana. *La. Dept. Wildl. Fish. Tech. Bull.* 35:1–13.

————. 1982b. A comparison of fish populations in baseline and dredged areas in Lake Pontchartrain. *La. Dept. Wildl. Fish. Tech. Bull.* 35:63–67.

Guillory, V., K. Foote, and E. Melancon. 1985. Additions to the Grande Isle, Louisiana fish fauna. *Proc. La. Acad. Sci.* 48:82–85.

Guillory, V., and G. Hutton. 1982. A survey of bycatch in the Louisiana Gulf menhaden fishery. *Proc. Ann. Conf. Southeastern Assoc. Game and Fish Comm.* 36:213–23.

Gunter, G. 1935. Records of fishes rarely caught in shrimp trawls in Louisiana. *Copeia* (1):39–45.

————. 1936. Studies on the destruction of marine fish by shrimp trawlers in Louisiana. *La. Conser. Rev.* 5:18–24, 45–46.

————. 1938a. Seasonal variations in abundance of certain estuarine and marine fishes in Louisiana, with particular references to life histories. *Ecol. Monogr.* 8(3):313–46.

————. 1938b. The relative numbers of marine fishes on the Louisiana coast *Am. Nat.* 72:77–83.

————. 1938c. Notes on invasion of fresh waters by fishes of the Gulf of Mexico with special reference to the Mississippi-Atchafalaya river system. *Copeia* (2):69–72.

————. 1941. Relative numbers of shallow water fishes of the northern Gulf of Mexico, with some records of rare fishes from the Texas coast. *Am. Midl. Nat.* 26(1):194–200.

————. 1944. A perpetuated error concerning the capitaine, *Lachnolaimus maximus* (Walbaum) in Texas waters. *Copeia* (1):55–56.

————. 1945a. Studies on marine fishes of Texas. *Publ. Inst. Mar. Sci. Univ. Tex.* 1(1):1–190.

————. 1945b. Some characteristics of ocean waters and the Laguna Madre. *Tex. Game and Fish* 3(11):7, 19, 21–22.

————. 1950. Distributions and abundance of fishes on the Aransas National Wildlife Refuge with life history notes. *Publ. Inst. Mar. Sci. Univ. Tex.* 1(2):89–102.

————. 1951. Mass mortality and dinoflagellate blooms in the Gulf of Mexico. *Science* 113 (2931):250–51.

————. 1952a. The import of catastrophic mortalities for marine fisheries along the Texas coast. *J. Wildl. Manag.* 16(1):63–69.

————. 1952b. Historical changes in the Mississippi River and the adjacent marine environment. *Publ. Inst. Mar. Sci. Univ. Tex.* 2(2):118–39.

————. 1953. Observations on fish turning flips over a line. *Copeia* (3):188–90.

————. 1957. Predominance of the young among marine fishes found in fresh water. *Copeia* (1):13–16.

————. 1961. Some relations of estuarine organisms to salinity. *Limnol. Oceanogr.* 6(2):182–90.

————. 1963. The fertile fisheries crescent. *J. Miss. Acad. Sci.* 9:286–90.

Gunter, G., and J. Y. Christmas. 1960. A review of literature on menhaden with special reference to the Gulf of Mexico menhaden, *Brevoortia patronus* Goode. *U. S. Fish Wildl. Serv., Spec. Sci. Rep. Fish.* 363:1–31.

Gunter, G., and H. H. Hildebrand. 1951. Destruction of fishes and other organisms on the south Texas coast by the cold wave of January 28–February 3, 1951. *Ecology* 32(4):731–36.

Gunter, G., and L. Knapp. 1951. Fishes, new, rare or seldom recorded from the Texas coast. *Tex. J. Sci.* 3(1):134–38.

Gunter, G., and W. E. Shell, Jr. 1958. A study of an estuarine area with water level control in the Louisiana marsh. *Proc. La. Acad. Sci.* 21:5–34.

Gunter, G., R. H. Williams, C. C. Davis, and F. G. Walton Smith. 1948. Catastrophic mass mortality of marine animals and coincident phytoplankton bloom on the west coast of Florida, November 1946–August 1947. *Ecol. Monogr.* 18(3):309–24

Gutherz, E. J. 1966. Revision of the flounder genus *Ancylopsetta* (Heterosomata: Bothidae) with descriptions of two new species from the Antilles and the Caribbean Sea. *Bull. Mar. Sci.* 16(3):445–79.

————. 1967. Field guide to the flatfishes of the family Bothidae in the western North Atlantic. U.S. Fish Wildl. Serv. Circ. no. 263. 47 pp.

Gutherz, E. J., W. R. Nelson, and G. M. Russell. 1987. Range extension of *Polymyxia nobilis* Lowe 1938 (Polymixiidae) into the northwestern Gulf of Mexico. *Northeast Gulf Sci.* 9(2):143–45.

Haburay, K., R. W. Hastings, D. DeVries, and J. Massey. 1974. Tropical marine fishes from Pensacola, Florida. *Fla. Sci.* 37(2):105–109.

Haedrich, R. L. 1967. The stromateoid fishes: systematics and classification. *Bull. Mus. Comp. Zool.* 135(2):31–139.

Haedrich, R. L., and M. H. Horn. 1972. A key to the stromateoid fishes. Woods Hole Oceanogr. Inst. Tech. Rept. WHO 1-72-15. 46 pp.

Hairston, N. G. 1989. Ecological Experiments, Purpose, Design, Execution. Cambridge: Cambridge Univ. Press. 370 pp.

Hammerschmidt, P. C., M. F. Osborn, and H. H. Martin, 1992. Status of black drum in Texas. *Proc. Gulf and Carib. Fisher. Inst.* 41:382–402.

Hanks, B. G., and M. J. McCoid. 1988. First record for the least killifish, *Heterandria formosa* (Pisces: Poeciliidae) in Texas. *Tex. J. Sci.* 40(4):447–48.

Harding, S. M., and M. E. Chittenden, Jr. 1987. Reproduction, movements and population dynamics of the southern kingfish, *Menticirrhus americanus*, in the northwestern Gulf of Mexico. NOAA Tech. Rept. NMFS Circ. 49. 21 pp.

Harper, D. E. Jr., L. D. McKinney, R. D. Salzer, and R. J. Case. 1981. The occurrence of hypoxic bottom water off the upper Texas coast and its effects on the benthic biota. *Contr. Mar. Sci.* 24:53–79.

Harris, S. A. and P. F. Darensbourg. 1992. Coastal Louisiana takes it on the chin. *La. Conser.* 44(6): 8–12.

Hastings, P. A. 1978. First North American continental record of *Gobionellus pseudofasciatus* (Pisces: Gobiidae). *Northeast Gulf Science* 2(2):140–44.

Hastings, P. A., and S. A. Bortone. 1980. Observations on the life history of the belted sandfish, *Serranus subligarius* (Serranidae). *Environ. Biol. Fishes* 5(4):365–74.

Hastings, P. A., and R. L. Shipp. 1980. A new species of pikeblenny (Pisces: Chaenopsidae) from the Western Atlantic. *Proc. Biol. Soc. Wash.* 93(4):875–86.

Hastings, R. W. 1972. The origin and seasonality of the fish fauna on a new jetty in the northeastern Gulf of Mexico. Ph.D. diss., Florida State Univ., Tallahassee. 555 pp.

———. 1973. Biology of the pygmy sea bass, *Serraniculus pumilio* (Pisces: Serranidae). *Fish. Bull., U.S.* 71(1):235–42.

———. 1977. Notes on the occurrence of the silver anchovy, *Engraulis eurystole*, in the northern Gulf of Mexico. *Northeast Gulf Sci.* 1(2):116–18.

———. 1979. The origin and seasonality of the fish fauna on a new jetty in the northeastern Gulf of Mexico. *Bull. Fla. State. Mus. Biol. Sci.* 24(1):1–124.

———. 1983. Redescription of *Gobulus myersi* (Pisces: Gobiidae) *Northeast Gulf Sci.* 6(2):191–96.

———. 1987. Fishes of the Manchac Wildlife Management Area, Louisiana. *Proc. Louisiana Acad. Sci.* 50:21–26.

Hastings, R. W., L. H. Ogren, and M. T. Mabry. 1976. Observations on the fish fauna associated with offshore platforms in the northeastern Gulf of Mexico. *Fish. Bull., U.S.* 74(2):387–402.

Hastings, R. W., and C. W. Petersen. 1986. A novel sexual pattern in serranid fishes: simultaneous hermaphrodites and secondary males in *Serranus fasciatus*. *Env. Biol. Fish* 15(1):59–68.

Hastings, R. W., D. A. Turner, and R. G. Thomas. 1987. The fish fauna of Lake Maurepas, an oligohaline part of the Lake Pontchartrain estuary. *Northeast Gulf Sci.* 9(2):89–98.

Hein, S., and J. Shepard. 1979. Spawning of spotted seatrout in a Louisiana estuarine ecosystem. *Proc. Ann. Conf. Southeast Assoc. Fish Wildl. Agencies* 33:451–65.

Heemstra, P. C. 1973. A revision of the shark genus *Mustelus* (Squaliformes: *Carcharhinidae*). Ph.D. diss., Univ. of Miami, Coral Gables. 187 pp.

———. 1993. *FAO species catalogue.* Vol. 16, *Groupers of the world.* FAO Fisheries Synopsis no. 125. 382 pp.

Henley, D. E., and D. G. Rauschuber. 1981. Freshwater needs of fish and wildlife resources in the Nueces-Corpus Christi Bay area. U.S. Fish Wildl. Serv. FWS/OBS. 80/10. 410 pp.

Hensley, D. A. 1977. Larval development of *Engyophrys senta* (Bothidae) with comments on intermuscular bones in flatfishes. *Bull. Mar. Sci.* 27(4):681–703.

Hensley, D. A., and E. H. Ahlstrom. 1984. Pleuronectiformes: relationships. In *Ontogeny and systematics of fishes*, ed. H. G. Moser et al., pp. 670–87. Spec. Publ. no. 1, Amer. Soc. Ich. Herp.

Hensley, D. A., and G. B. Smith. 1977. Additional data on the pomacentrid fish, *Chromis scotti*. *Copeia* (2):391–93.

Henwood, T. A., P. Johnson, and R. Heard. 1978. Feeding habits and food of the longspine porgy, *Stenotomus caprinus* Bean. *Northeast Gulf Science* 2: 133–37.

Herald, E. S. 1942. Three new pipefishes from the Atlantic coast of North and South America, with a key to the Atlantic American species. *Stanford Ichthyol. Bull.* 2(4):125–34.

———. 1965. Studies on the Atlantic American pipefishes with descriptions of new species. *Proc. Calif. Acad. Sci.*, 4th ser., 32:363–75.

Herke, W. H. 1968. Weirs, potholes, and fishery management. In *Proc. Marsh and Estuarine Management Symposium,* ed. J. D. Newsom, pp. 193–211. Baton Rouge: Div. Cont. Educ., La. State Univ.

———. 1969. An unusual inland collection of larval ladyfish, *Elops saurus,* in Louisiana. *Proc. La. Acad. Sci.* 32:29–30.

———. 1971. Use of natural, and semi-impounded, Louisiana tidal marshes as nurseries for fishes and crustaceans. Ph.D. diss., La. State Univ., Baton Rouge.

Hildebrand, H. H. 1954. A study of the fauna of the brown shrimp *(Penaeus aztecus* Ives) grounds in the western Gulf of Mexico. *Publ. Inst. Mar. Sci. Univ. Tex.* 3(2):233–366.

———. 1955. A study of the fauna of the pink shrimp (*Penaeus duorarum* Burkenroad) grounds in the Gulf of Campeche. *Publ. Inst. Mar. Sci. Univ. Tex.* 4(1):169–232.

———. 1958. Estudios biológicos preliminares sobre la Laguna Madre de Tamaulipas. *Ciencia* (Mexico City) 17(7–9):151–73.

———. 1969. Laguna Madre, Tamaulipas: Observations on its hydrography and fisheries. In *Lagunas Costeras, un Simposio,* Mem. Simp. Intern. Lagunas Costeras UNAM-UNESCO, Nov. 28–30, Mexico, D.F., pp. 679–86.

Hildebrand, H. H., H. Chavez, and H. Compton 1964. Aporte al conocimiento de los peces del Arrecife Alacranes, Yucatán (Mexico). *Ciencia* (Mexico City) 23(3):107–34.

Hildebrand, S. F. 1963. Families Elopidae and Albulidae. In *Fishes of the western North Atlantic*. Memoir Sears Found. Mar. Res. no. 1, pt. 3, pp. 111–47. New Haven.

———. 1964a. Family Engraulidae. In *Fishes of the western North Atlantic*. Memoir Sears Found. Mar. Res. no. 1, pt. 3, pp. 152–249. New Haven.

———. 1964b. Review and emendation of family Clupeidae. *Copeia* (4):720–30.

Hildebrand, S. F., and L. E. Cable. 1934. Reproduction and development of whitings or kingfishes, drum, spot, croaker, and weakfishes or sea trouts, family Sciaenidae, of the Atlantic coast of the United States. *Bull. U.S. Bur. Fish.* 48:41–117.

Hildebrand, S. F., L. R. Rivas, and R. R Miller. 1963. Family Clupeidae. In *Fishes of the western North Atlantic*. Memoir Sears Found. Mar. Res. no. 1, pt. 3, pp. 259–454. New Haven.

Hjort, J. 1914. Fluctuations in the great fisheries of northern Europe viewed in the light of biological research. *Rapp. Procès-Verb, Cons. intern. Explor. Mer.* 20. 229 pp.

Hoar, P., J. Hoey, J. Mance, C. Nelson (eds.). 1992. A research plan addressing finfish bycatch in the Gulf of Mexico and South Atlantic shrimp fisheries. Tampa, Fla.: Gulf and S. Atlantic Dev. Found. 114 pp.

Hoese, H. D. 1958a. A partially annotated checklist of the marine fishes of Texas. *Publ. Inst. Mar. Sci. Univ. Tex.* 5:312–52.

———. 1958b. The case of the pass. *Tex. Game and Fish* 16(6):16–18.

————. 1960. Biotic changes in a bay associated with the end of a drought. *Limnol. Oceanogr.* 5(3):326–36.

————. 1965. Spawning of marine fishes in the Port Aransas, Texas, area as determined by the distribution of young and larvae. Ph.D. diss., Univ. of Texas, Austin. 144 pp.

————. 1966a. Ectoparasitism by juvenile sea catfish, *Galeichthys felis. Copeia* (4):880–81.

————. 1966b. Habitat segregation in aquaria between two sympatric species of *Gobiosoma. Publ. Inst. Mar. Sci. Univ. Tex.* 11:7–11.

————. 1981. Some effects of fresh water on the Atchafalaya Bay system. In *Proc. Nat. Symp. Freshwater Inflow Est.,* pp. 110–24. Biol. Serv. Prog. U.S. Fish. Wildl. Serv. FWS/OBS 81/04. Vol. 2.

————. 1985. Jumping mullet: the internal diving bell hypothesis. *Environ. Biol. Fishes* 13(4):309–14.

Hoese, H. D., B. J. Copeland, F. N. Moseley, and E. D. Lane. 1968. Fauna of the Aransas Pass Inlet. III. Diel and seasonal variations in trawlable organisms of the adjacent area. *Tex. J. Sci.* 20:33–60.

Hoese, H. D., and R. B. Moore. 1958. Notes on the life history of the bonnetnose shark, *Sphyrna tiburo. Tex. J. Sci.* 10(1):69–72.

Hoffman, W., T. H. Fritts, and R. P. Reynolds. 1981. Whale sharks associated with fish schools off south Texas. *Northeast Gulf Sci.* 5(1):55–57.

Holt, S. A., and C. R. Arnold. 1982. Growth of juvenile red snapper, *Lutjanus campechanus,* in the northwestern Gulf of Mexico. *Fish. Bull., U.S.* 80(3):644–48.

Holt, S. A., and G. J. Holt. 1983. Cold death of fishes at Port Aransas, Texas: January 1982. *Southwest. Nat.* 28(4):464–66.

Holt, Š. A., Č. L. Kitting, and C. R. Arnold. 1983. Distribution of young red drums among different sea-grass meadows. *Trans. Amer. Fish. Soc.* 112:267–71.

Hood, P. B., and R. A. Schlieder. 1992. Age, growth, and reproduction of gag, *Mycteroperca microlepis* (Pisces: Serranidae), in the eastern Gulf of Mexico. *Bull. Mar. Sci.* 51(3):337–52.

Hook, J. H. 1991. Seasonal variation in relative abundance and species diversity of fishes in South Bay. *Contrib. Mar. Sci.* 32:127–41.

Horn, M. H. 1970. Systematics and biology of the stromateid fishes of the genus *Peprilus. Bull. Mus. Comp. Zool.* 140(5):165–261.

————. 1972. Systematic status and aspects of the ecology of the elongate ariommid fishes (suborder Stromateoidei) in the Atlantic. *Bull. Mar. Sci.* 22(3):537–558.

————. 1984. Stromateoidei: development and relationships. In *Ontogengy and systematics of fishes,* eds. H. G. Moser, et al., pp. 620–28. Spec. Publ. No. 1, Amer. Soc. Ich. Herp.

Horst, J. W. 1976. Aspects of the biology of the striped bass, *Roccus saxatilis,* (Walbaum), of the Atchafalaya Basin, Louisiana. M.S. thesis, La. State Univ., Baton Rouge. 68 pp.

Houde, E. D. 1977a. Abundance and potential yield of the round herring, *Etrumeus teres,* and aspects of its early life history in the eastern Gulf of Mexico. *Fish. Bull., U.S.* 75(1):61–90.

————. 1977b. Abundance and potential yield of the Atlantic thread herring, *Opisthonema oglinum,* and aspects of its early life history in the eastern Gulf of Mexico. *Fish. Bull., U.S.* 75(3):493–512.

————. 1977c. Abundance and potential yield of the scaled sardine, *Harengula jaguana,* and aspects of its early life history in the eastern Gulf of Mexico. *Fish. Bull., U.S.* 75(3):613–28.

Houde, E. D., 1981. Distribution and abundance of four types of codlet (Pisces: Bregmacerotidae) larvae from the Gulf of Mexico. *Biological Oceanography* 1(1): 81–104.

Hubbs, C. 1964. Interactions between a bisexual fish species and its gynogenetic sexual parasite. *Bull. Tex. Memorial Mus.* no. 8. 72 pp.

Hubbs, C. L. 1939. The characters and distribution of the Atlantic coast fishes referred to the genus *Hypsoblennius. Pap. Mich. Acad. Sci. Arts Lett.* 24(2):153–57.

———. 1963. *Chaetodon aya* and related deep-dwelling butterflyfishes: their variations, distribution and synonymy. *Bull. Mar. Sci. Gulf Caribb.* 13(1):133–192.

Huntsman, G. R., 1992. Population characteristics of the red porgy, *Pagrus pagrus,* stock off the Carolinas. *Bull. Mar. Sci.* 50(1):1–20.

———. 1994. Endangered marine finfish: neglected resources or beasts of fiction? *Fisheries (Bethesda)* 19(7):8–15.

International Game Fish Association. (Annual.) *World Record Game Fish.* Coral Gables, Fla.

Irwin, R. J. 1970. Geographical variation, systematics, and general biology of shore fishes of the genus *Menticirrhus,* family Sciaenidae. Ph.D. diss., Tulane Univ., New Orleans. 295 pp.

Johnson, A. G., and C. H. Salomon. 1984. Age, growth, and mortality of gray triggerfish, *Balistes capriscus,* from the northeastern Gulf of Mexico. *Fish. Bull., U.S.* 82(3):483–92.

Johnson, G. D. 1984. Percoidei: development and relationships. In *Ontogeny and systematics of fishes,* eds. H. G. Moser et al., pp. 464–98. Spec. Publ. No. 1, Amer. Soc. Ich. Herp.

Johnson, G. D., and W. D. Anderson, Jr. (eds.). 1993. Proceedings of the symposium on phylogeny of Percomorpha. *Bull. Mar. Sci.* 52(1): 626 pp.

Johnson, G. D., and P. Keener. 1984. Aid to identification of American grouper larvae. *Bull. Mar. Sci.* 34(1):106–34.

Johnson, M. S. 1975. Biochemical systematics of the atherinid genus *Menidia. Copeia* (4):662–91.

Johnson, R. B., Jr. 1977. Fishery survey of Cedar Lakes and the Brazos and San Bernard River estuaries. Tex. Parks Wildl. Dept. Tech. Ser. 23. 65 pp.

Johnson, R. K. and D. W. Greenfield. 1983. Clingfishes (Gobiescosidae) from Belize and Honduras, Central America, with a redescription of *Gobiesox barbatulus* Starks. *Northeastern Gulf Sci.* 6(1):33–49.

Jolley, J. W., Jr. 1974. On the biology of Florida east coast Atlantic sailfish *(Istiophorus platypterus).* Natl. Mar. Fish. Serv. Spec. Sci. Rep. Fish. no. 675, pp. 81–88.

Jones, R. S., E. J. Gutherz, W. R. Nelson, and G. C. Matlock. 1989. Burrow utilization by yellowedge grouper, *Epinephelus flavolimbatus,* in the northwestern Gulf of Mexico. *Environ. Biol. Fishes* 26:277–84.

Jordan, D. S., and M. C. Dickerson. 1908. Notes on a collection of fishes from the Gulf of Mexico at Vera Cruz and Tampico. *Proc. U.S. Natl. Mus.* 34:11–22.

Jordan, D. S., and C. H. Gilbert. 1883. Notes on fishes observed about Pensacola, Florida, and Galveston, Texas, with description of new species. *Proc. U.S. Natl. Mus.* 5:241–307.

Joseph, E. B., and R. W. Yerger. 1956. The fishes of Alligator Harbor, Florida, with notes on their natural history. Fla. State Univ. Stud. no. 22. *Pap. Oceanogr. Inst.* no. 2, pp. 111–56.

Joutel, H. 1714. *A journal of the last voyage performed by Monsr. de la Sale, to the Gulph of Mexico.* Reprint 1962, London: Corinth. 187 pp.

Kanazawa, R. H. 1958. A revision of the eels of the genus *Conger* with descriptions of four new species. *Proc. U.S. Natl. Mus.* 108:219–67.

———. 1961. *Paraconger,* a new genus with three new species of eels (family Congridae). *Proc. U.S. Natl. Mus.* 113:1–14.

Katz, S. J., C. B. Grimes, and K. W. Able. 1983. Delineation of tilefish, *Lopholatilus chamaeleonticeps,* stocks along the United States east coast and Gulf of Mexico. *Fish. Bull., U.S.* 81(1):41–50.

Kemp, R. J., Jr. 1957. Occurrences of the ocean sunfish, *Mola mola* (Linnaeus), in Texas. *Copeia* (3):250–51.

Kilby, J. D. 1955. The fishes of two Gulf coastal marsh areas of Florida. *Tulane Stud. Zool.* 2(8):176–247.

Killam, K., and G. Parsons. 1986. First record of the longfin mako, *Isurus paucus*, in the Gulf of Mexico. *Fish. Bull., U.S.* 84(3):748–49.

King, B. D., III. 1971. Study of migratory patterns of fish and shellfish through a natural pass. Tex. Parks Wildl. Dept. Tech. Ser. no. 9. 54 pp.

King, T. L., P. C. Hammerschmidt, and E. D. Young. 1991. Identification of Gulf of Mexico sciaenids by isoelectric focusing. *Proc. Ann. Conf. Southeastern Assoc. Game and Fish Comm.* 45:307–10.

Klawe, W. L., and B. M. Shimada. 1959. Young scombroid fishes from the Gulf of Mexico. *Bull. Mar. Sci. Gulf Caribb.* 9(1):100–115.

Knudsen, E. E., and W. H. Herke. 1978. Growth rate of marked juvenile Atlantic croakers, *Micropogon undulatus,* and length of stay in a coastal marsh nursery in southwest Louisiana. *Trans. Amer. Fish. Soc.* 107(1):12–20.

Kramer, D. 1950. A record of the swordfish, *Xiphias gladius* Linnaeus, from the Texas coast. *Copeia* (1):65.

Kuentzler, E. J. 1974. Mangrove swamp systems. In *Coastal ecological systems of the United States,* vol. 1, ed. H. T. Odum, B. J. Copeland, and E. A. McMahan, pp. 346–71. Washington, D.C.: Conservation Foundation.

Kuhn, N. A. 1977. Occurrence and distribution of larval flatfish (Pleuronectiformes) of the southeast Louisiana coast during four cruises, including brief descriptions of the early larvae of *Citharichthys spilopterus* and *Etropus crossotus.* M. S. thesis, La. State Univ., Baton Rouge.

Lachner, E. A. 1966. Family *Echeneidae:* diskfishes. In *Fishes of the Marshalls and Marianas,* eds. L. P. Schultz, L .P. Woods, and E. A. Lachner. *Bull U.S. Natl. Mus.* 202(3):76–80.

Lackey, R. T. 1994. Ecological risk assessment. *Fisheries.* 19(9):14–18.

Landry, A. M. Jr., and K. W. Johnson. 1977. An ambicolorate windowpane *(Scophthalmus aquosus)* with notes on other anomalous flatfish. *Tex. J. Sci.* 28(1–4):362–66.

Lane, E. D. 1967. A study of the Atlantic midshipmen, *Porichthys porosissimus,* in the vicinity of Port Aransas, Texas. *Contrib. Mar. Sci.* 12:1–53.

Lane, E. D., and K. W. Stewart. 1968. A revision of the genus *Hoplunnis* Kaup (Apodes, Muraenesocidae) with a description of a new species. *Contrib. Mar. Sci.* 13:51–64.

Lang, K. L., C. B. Grimes, and R. F. Shaw. 1994. Variation in the age and growth of yellowfin tuna larvae, *Thunnus albacares,* collected along the Mississippi River plume. *Environ. Biol. Fishes* 39: 259–70.

Laroche, W. A. 1977. Description of larval and early juvenile vermilion snapper, *Rhomboplites aurorubens. Fish. Bull., U.S.* 73(3):547–59.

Laska, A. L. 1973. Fishes of the Chandeleur Islands, Louisiana. Ph.D. diss., Tulane Univ., New Orleans. 260 pp.

Lauder, G. V., and K. F. Liem. 1983. The evolution and interrelationships of the actinopterygian fishes. *Bull. Mus. Comp. Zoo.* 105:95–197.

Leary, T. R. 1956. The occurrence of the parrotfish, *Sparisoma radians,* in a Texas Bay. *Copeia* (4): 249–50.

———. 1957. The bonefish, *Albula vulpes,* in Texas. *Copeia* (3):248–49.

Lefler, D. L., and R. F. Shaw. 1992. Age validation, growth and mortality of larval Atlantic bumper (Carangidae: *Chloroscombrus chrusurus*) in the northern Gulf of Mexico. *Fish. Bull., U.S.* 90(4): 711–19.

Leiby, M. M. 1979. Leptocephalus larvae of the eel family Ophichthidae. I. *Ophichthus gomesi* Castelnau. *Bull. Mar. Sci.* 29(3):329–43.

———. 1981. Larval morphology of the eels, *Bascanichthys bascanium, B. scuticaris, Ophichthys melanoporus* and *O. ophis* (Ophichthidae), with a discussion of larval identification methods. *Bull. Mar. Sci.* 31(1):46–71.

Leiby, M. M., and R. W. Yerger. 1980. The genus *Bascanichthys* (Pisces: Ophichthidae) in the Gulf of Mexico. *Copeia* (3):402–408.

Leis, J. M. 1978. Systematics and zoogeography of the porcupine fishes *(Diodon, Diodontidae, Tetra-dontiformes)*, with comments on egg and larval development. *Fish. Bull., U. S.* 76(3):535–67.

Leslie, A. J. Jr., and D. J. Stewart. 1986. Systematics and distributional ecology of *Etropus* (Pisces, Bothidae) on the Atlantic coast of the United States with description of a new species. *Copeia* (1):140–56.

Lester, G. 1981. Plants and animals of special concern in the Louisiana coastal zone. La. Nat. Hert. Prog. La. Dept. Wildl. Fisher. Spec. Publ. 2. 291 pp.

Lindeman, K. C. 1986. Development of larvae of the french grunt, *Haemulon flavolimbatus*, and comparative development of twelve species of western Atlantic *Haemulon* (Percoidei: Haemulidae). *Bull. Mar. Sci.* 39(3):673–716.

Lindquist, D. G., and R. M. Dillaman. Trophic morphology of four western Atlantic blennies (Pisces: Blenniidae). *Copeia* (1):207–13.

Lipcius, R. N., and C. B. Subrahmanyam. 1986. Temporal factors influencing killifish abundance and recruitment in Gulf of Mexico salt marshes. *Estuarine, Coastal and Shelf Science* 22:101–14.

Livingston, R. J. 1971. Circadian rhythms in the respiration of eight species of cardinal fishes (Pisces: Apogonidae): Comparative analysis and adaptive significance. *Mar. Biol.* 9(3):253–66.

Lochmann, S. E. 1990. Mechanisms of transport of estuarine related larval fishes and invertebrates through tidal passes of the Texas coast. Ph.D. diss., Texas A&M Univ.

Lochmann, S. E., and W. S. Alevizon, 1989. Mechanisms of coloration of the Atlantic trumpetfish *Aulostomus maculatus. Copeia* (4):1072–74.

Loftus, W. F. 1992. *Lutjanus ambiguus* (Poey), a natural intergeneric hybrid of *Ocyurus chrysurus* (Bloch) and *Lutjanus synagris* (L.). *Bull. Mar. Sci.* 50(3):489–500.

Lyczkowski-Schultz, J., D. C. Ruple, S. L. Richardson, and J. H. Cowan, Jr. 1990. Distribution of fish larvae relative to time and tide in a Gulf of Mexico barrier island pass. *Bull. Mar. Sci.* 46(3): 563–77.

Manooch, C. S. III, and C. A. Barans. 1982. Distribution, abundance, and age and growth of the tomtate, *Haemulon aurolineatum* along the southeastern United States coast. *Fish. Bull., U.S.* 80(1):1–19.

Mansueti, A. J., and J. P. Hardy. 1967. *Development of fishes of the Chesapeake Bay region*. College Park: Nat. Res. Inst., Univ. Md. 202 pp.

Mansueti, R. 1963. Symbiotic behavior between small fishes and jellyfishes with new data on that between the stromateoid, *Peprilus alepidotus*, and the scyphomedusa, *Chrysaora quinquecirrha. Copeia* (1):40–80.

Markle, D. F., and J. E. Onley 1980. A description of the vexillifer larvae of *Pyramodon ventralis* and

Snyderia carena (Pisces: Carapidae) with comments on classification. *Pac. Sci.* 34(2):173–80.

————. 1990. Systematics of the pearlfishes (Pisces: Carapidae). *Bull. Mar. Sci.* 47(2):269–410.

Marshall, A. R. 1958. A survey of the snook fishery of Florida, with studies on the biology of the principal species, *Centropomus undecimalis* (Bloch). Fla. State Board Conserv. Tech. Ser. no. 22. 37 pp.

Marshall, N. B., and D. M. Cohen. 1973. Anacanthini (Gadiformes). In *Fishes of the western North Atlantic*. Memoir Sears Found. Mar. Res. no. 1, pt. 6, pp. 479–665. New Haven.

Martin, J. H., and T. L. King. 1991. Occurrence of fat snook *(Centropomus parallelus)* in Texas: evidence for a range extension. *Contrib. Mar. Sci.* 32:123–26.

Matheson, R. E., Jr. 1981. The distribution of the flagfin mojarra, *Eucinostomus melanopterus* (Pisces: Gerreidae) with ecological notes on Texas and Florida populations. *Northeast Gulf Sci.* 5(1): 63–66.

Matheson, R. E. Jr., and J. D. McEachran. 1984. Taxonomic studies of the *Eucinostomus argenteus* complex (Pisces: Gerreidae): preliminary studies of external morphology. *Copeia* (4):893–902.

Matlock, G. C. 1987. The role of hurricanes in determining year class strength. *Contrib. Mar. Sci.* 30:39–47.

————. 1991. Growth, mortality, and yield of southern flounder in Texas. *Northeast Gulf Sci.* 12(1): 61–65.

————. 1992a. Growth of five fishes in Texas bays in the 1960's. *Fish. Bull., U.S.* 90(2):407–11.

————. 1992b. Life history aspects of seahorses, *Hippocampus,* in Texas. *Tex. J. Sci.* 44(2):213–22.

Matlock, G. C., and M. A. Garcia. 1983. Stomach contents of selected fishes from Texas bays. *Contrib. Mar. Sci.* 26:95–110.

Matlock, G. C., and H. R. Osburn. 1987. Demise of the snook fishery in Texas. *Northeast Gulf Sci.* 9(1):53–58.

Matlock, G. C., J. E. Weaver, and A. W. Green. 1977. Trends in spotted seatrout and red drum abundance in Texas coastal waters influenced by commerical netting. *Proc. Ann. Conf. Southeastern Assoc. Game and Fish Comm.* 31:477–83.

————. 1982. Sampling nearshore estuarine fishes with rotenone. *Trans. Amer. Fish. Soc.* 111: 326–31.

Matsui, T. 1967. Review of the mackerel genera *Scomber* and *Rastrelliger* with descriptions of a new species of *Rastrelliger. Copeia* (1):71–83.

Matsumoto, W. M., R. A. Skillman, and A. E. Dizon. 1984. Synopsis of biological data on skipjack tuna, *Katsuwonus pelamis.* NOAA Tech. Rept. NMFS Circ. 45. 92 pp.

May, E. D. 1973. Extensive oxygen depletion in Mobile Bay. *Limnol. Oceanogr.* 18(3): 353–66.

McClure, M. R., and J. D. McEachran. 1992. Hybridization between *Prionotus alatus* and *Prionotus paralatus* in the northern Gulf of Mexico. *Copeia* (4):1039–46.

McCosker, J. E. 1973. The osteology, classification, and relationships of the eel family Ophichthidae (Pisces: Anguilliformes). Ph.D. thesis, Univ. of Calif., San Diego. 289 pp.

McCosker, J. E., E. B. Böhlke, and J. E. Böhlke. 1989. Family *Ophichthidae.* Snake eels and worm eels. In *Fishes of the Western North Atlantic.* Memoir Sears Found. Mar. Res., no. 1, pt. 9, pp. 254–412, New Haven.

McEachran, J. D. 1977. Variation in *Raja garmani* and the status of *Raja lentiginosa* (Pisces: Rajidae). *Bull. Mar. Sci.* 27(3):423–39.

McEachran, J. D., J. H. Finucane, and L. S. Hall. 1980. Distribution, seasonality, and abundance of king and spanish mackerel larvae in the northeast Gulf of Mexico (Pisces: Scombridae). *Northeast Gulf Sci.* 4(1):1–16.

McEachran, J. D., and J. A. Musick. 1975. Distribution and relative abundance of seven species of skates (Pisces: Rajidae) which occur between Nova Scotia and Cape Hatteras. *Fish. Bull., U.S.* 73(1):110–136.

McEachron, L. W., G. C. Matlock, C. E. Bryan, P. Unger, T. J. Cody and J. H. Martin. 1994. Winter mass mortality of animals in Texas bays. *Northeast Gulf Sci.* 13(2):121–38.

McEachron, L. W., C. R. Shaw, and A. W. Moffett. 1977. A fishery survey of Christmas, Drum and Bastrop bays, Brazoria County, Texas. Tex. Parks Wildl. Dept. Tech. Ser. 20. 83 pp.

McKenny, T. W. 1961. Larval and adult stages of the stromateoid fish *Psenes regulus* with comments on its classification. *Bull Mar. Sci. Gulf Caribb.* 11:210–36.

McMichael, R. H. Jr., and S. T. Ross. 1987. The relative abundance and feeding habits of juvenile kingfish (Sciaenidae: *Menticirrhus*) in a Gulf of Mexico surf zone. *Northeast Gulf Sci.* 9(2): 109–23.

Mead, G. W. 1957. On the bramid fishes of the Gulf of Mexico. *Zoologica* (N.Y.) 42(2):51–62.

Mead, G. W., and G. E. Maul. 1958. *Taractes asper* and the systematic relationships of the Steinegeriidae and Trachyberycidae. *Bull. Mus. Comp. Zool.* 119(6):391–418.

Medina, A. R. 1970. Estudio de los peces de la Laguna de Tamiahua, Veracruz, México. *An. Inst. Biol. Univ. Nal. Auton. Mexico. Ser. Cienc. del mar* 41(1):79–146.

———. 1971. Peces colectados en el arrecife La Blanquilla, Veracruz, Mexico. *An. Inst. Biol. Univ. Nal. Auton. Mexico. Ser. Cienc. del mar* 42(1):7–30.

Mericas, D. 1981. Feeding habits of the Atlantic cutlassfish, *Trichiurus lepturus,* in the Gulf of Mexico. *Northeast Gulf Sci.* 4(2):137–40.

Middaugh, D. P., M. J. Hemmut, and Y. Lamadrid-Rose. 1986. Laboratory spawning cues in *Menidia beryllina* and *Menidia peninsulae* (Pisces: Atherinidae) with notes on survival and growth of larvae at different salinities. *Environ. Biol. Fishes* 15(2):107–17.

Miliken, D. M. and E. D. Houde. 1984. A new species of Bregmacerotidae (Pisces), *Bregmacerotus cantori,* from the western Atlantic Ocean. *Bull. Mar. Sci.* 35: 11–19.

Miller, A. C., and D. M. Kent. 1972. Redescription of *Prionotus beani* (Pisces: Triglidae). *Q. J. Fla. Acad. Sci.* 34(3):223–42.

Miller, G. C. and W. J. Richards, 1979. Reef fish habitat, faunal assemblages, and factors determining distributions in the South Atlantic Bight. *Proc. Gulf Carib. Fish Inst.* 32:114–30.

———. 1991a. Nomenclatural changes in the genus *Prionotus* (Pisces: Triglidae). *Bull. Mar. Sci.* 48(3):757–62.

———. 1991b. Revision of the western Atlantic and eastern Pacific genus *Bellator* (Pisces: Triglidae). *Bull. Mar. Sci.* 48(3):635–56.

Miller, G. C., and L. P. Woods. 1988. A new species of sciaenid fish, *Paraeques iwamotoi,* from the western Atlantic with color descriptions of prejuvenile and juvenile *Pareques acuminatus* and *Pareques umbrosus. Bull. Mar. Sci.* 43(1):88–92.

Miller, J. M. 1965. A trawl survey of the shallow Gulf fishes near Port Aransas, Texas. *Publ. Inst. Mar. Sci. Univ. Tex.* 10:80–107.

Miller, R. J. 1959. A review of the seabasses of the genus *Centropristes* (Serranidae). *Tulane Stud. Zool.* 7(2):35–68.

Miller, R. R. 1945. *Hyporhamphus partis,* a new species of hemiramphid fish from Sinaloa, Mexico, with an analysis of the generic characters in *Hyporhamphus* and *Hemiramphus. Proc. U.S. Natl. Mus.* 96(3195):185–93.

———. 1960. Systematics and biology of the gizzard shad *(Dorosoma cepedianum)* and related fishes. *U.S. Fish. Wildl. Serv. Fish. Bull.* 60(173):371–92.

Millican, T., D. Turner, and G. Thomas. 1984. Checklist of the species of fishes in Lake Maurepas, Louisiana. *Proc. La. Acad. Sci.* 47:30–33.

Modde, T. 1980. Growth and residency of juvenile fishes within a surf zone habitat in the Gulf of Mexico. *Gulf Res. Rept.* 6(4):377–85.

———. 1983. Trophic relationships of fishes occurring within a surf zone habitat in the northern Gulf of Mexico. *Northeast Gulf Sci.* 6(2):109–20.

Modde, T., and S. T. Ross. 1981. Seasonality of fishes occupying a surfzone habitat in the northern Gulf of Mexico. *Fish. Bull., U.S.* 78(4):911–22.

Moe, M. A. 1968. First Gulf of Mexico record for *Lutjanus cyanopterus. Q. J. Fla. Acad. Sci.* 29(4) 285–86.

———. 1969. Biology of the red grouper *Epinephelus morio* (Valenciennes) from the eastern Gulf of Mexico. Prof. Pap. Ser. no. 10. Fla. Dept. Nat. Resour. Mar. Res. Lab. 85 pp.

Moe, M.A., and G.T. Martin. 1965. Fishes taken in monthly trawl samples offshore of Pinellas County, Florida, with new additions to the fish fauna of the Tampa Bay area. *Tulane Stud. Zool.* 12(4): 129–51.

Mook, D. 1977. Larval and osteological development of the sheepshead, *Archosargus probatocephalus* (Pisces: Sparidae) *Copeia* (1):126–33.

Moore, D. 1962. Development, distribution, and comparison of rudder fishes, *Kyphosus sectatrix* (Linnaeus) and *K. incisor* (Cuvier) in the western North Atlantic. *U.S. Fish. Wildl. Serv. Fish. Bull.* 61(196):451–80.

———. 1967. Triggerfishes (Balistidae) of the western Atlantic. *Bull. Mar. Sci.* 17(3):689–722.

Moore, D., H. A. Brusher, and L. Trent. 1970. Relative abundance, seasonal distribution, and species composition of demersal fishes off Louisiana and Texas, 1962–1964. *Contrib. Mar. Sci.* 15:45–70.

Moore, R. H. 1974. General ecology, distribution, and relative abundance of *Mugil cephalus* and *Mugil curema* on the South Texas coast. *Contrib. Mar. Sci.* 18:241–55.

———. 1975a. Occurrence of tropical marine fishes at Pt. Aransas, Texas, 1967–1973, related to sea temperatures. *Copeia* (1):170–72.

———. 1975b. New records of three marine fish from Texas waters with notes on some additional species. *Tex. J. Sci.* 26(1–2):155–63.

———. 1976. Observations on fishes killed by cold at Port Aransas, Texas, 11–12 January, 1973. *Southwestern Naturalist* 20(4): 461–66.

———. 1978. Variations in diversity of summer estuarine fish populations in Aransas Bay, Texas, 1966–1973. *Est. Coast. Mar. Sci.* 6:495–501.

———. 1992. Low-salinity back bays and lagoons. In *Biodiversity of the southeastern United States—aquatic communities,* ed. C.T. Hackney, S. M. Adams, and W. H. Martin, pp. 541–614. New York: John Wiley and Sons.

Morrow, J. E., and S. J. Harbo. 1969. A revision of the sailfish genus *Istiophorus. Copeia* (1):34–44.

Morton, T. 1973. The ecological effects of water-control structures on an estuarine area, White Lake, Louisiana. M.S. thesis, Univ. Southwestern La., Lafayette. 43 pp.

Moseley, F. N. 1966a. Notes on fishes from the snapper banks off Port Aransas, Texas. *Tex. J. Sci.* 18(1):75–79.

———. 1966b. Biology of the red snapper, *Lutjanus aya* Bloch of the northwestern Gulf of Mexico. *Publ. Inst. Mar. Sci. Univ. Tex.* 11:90–101.

Motta, P. J. 1989. Dentition patterns among Pacific and western Atlantic butterfishes (Perciformes, Chaetodontidae): relationship to feeding, ecology, and evolutionary history. *Environ. Biol. Fishes* 25(1–3):159–70.

Munroe, T. A. 1991. Western Atlantic tonguefishes of the *Symphurus plagusia* complex (Cynoglossidae: Pleuronectiformes) with descriptions of two new species. *Fish. Bull., U.S.* 89(2):247–787.

Murdy, E. O., R. E. Matheson Jr., J. D. Fechhelm, and M. J. McCold. 1983. Midwater fishes of the Gulf of Mexico collected from the *R/V Alaminos*, 1965–1973. *Texas J. Sci.* 35:109–27.

Murphy, M. D., and M. E. Chittenden, Jr. 1991. Reproduction, age, growth, and movements of the Gulf butterfish, *Peprilus burti*. *Fish. Bull., U.S.* 89(1):101–16.

Nakamura, I. 1974. Some aspects of the systematics and distribution of billfishes. In *Proceedings of the International Billfish Symposium, Kailua-Kona, Hawaii, 9–12 August, 1972*, ed. R. S. Shomura and F. Williams, part 2, Review and contributed papers, pp. 45–53. U.S. Dept. Comm., NOAA Tech. Rep NMFS/SSRF-675.

———. 1985. *FAO species catalogue.* Vol. 5, *Billfishes of the world*. FAO Fisheries Synopsis no. 125. 65 pp.

Nakamura, I., and N. V. Parin. 1993. *FAO species catalog.* Vol. 15, *Snake mackerels and cutlassfishes of the world*. FAO Fisheries Synopsis no. 125. 136 pp.

Naughton, S. P., and C. H. Saloman. 1977. Fishes of the nearshore zone of St. Andrew Bay, Florida, and adjacent coast. *Northeast Gulf Sci.* 2(1):43–55.

Nelson, D. M. (ed.). 1992. *Distribution and abundance of fishes and invertebrates in Gulf of Mexico estuaries.* Vol. 1, *Data summaries*. Rockville, Md.: ELMR Rep. No. 10 NOAA/NOS Strategic Environmental Assessments Division. 273 pp.

Nelson, G. 1986. Identity of the anchovy *Engraulis clarki* with notes on the species-groups of *Anchoa*. *Copeia* (4):891–902.

Nelson, R. S. 1985. Growth, mortality and condition of cottonwick in the Gulf of Mexico. *Proc. Ann. Conf. Southeastern Assoc. Game and Fish Comm.* 39:34–44.

———. 1988. A study of the life history, ecology and population dynamics of four sympatric reef predators *(Rhomboplites aurorubens, Lutjanus campechanus,* Lutjanidae; *Haemulon melanurum* Haemulidae; and *Pagrus pagrus* Sparidae) on the East and West Flower Garden Banks, Northwestern Gulf of Mexico. Ph.D. diss., North Carolina State Univ., Raleigh. 197 pp.

Nelson, R. S., and C. S. Manooch, III. 1982. Growth and mortality of red snappers in the west-central Atlantic Ocean and northern Gulf of Mexico. *Trans. Am. Fish. Soc.* 111:465–75.

Nelson, W. R., and D. W. Ahrenholz. 1975. Population and fishery characteristics of Gulf menhaden, *Brevoortia patronus*. *Fish. Bull., U.S.* 84(2):311–25.

Nelson, W. R., and J. S. Carpenter. 1968. Bottom longline explorations in the Gulf of Mexico. A report on *Oregon II's* first cruise. *Comm. Fish. Rev.* 30(10):57–62.

Nichols, J. T., and C. M. Breder, Jr. 1922. *Otophidium welshi*, a new cusk eel, with notes on two others from the Gulf of Mexico. *Proc. Biol. Soc. Wash.* 35:13–15.

———. 1924. New Gulf races of a Pacific *Scorpaena* and *Prionotus*, with notes on other Gulf of Mexico fishes. *Proc. Biol. Soc. Wash.* 37:21–23.

Nieland, D. L., and C. A. Wilson. 1993. Reproductive biology and annual variation of reproductive variables of black drum in the northern Gulf of Mexico. *Trans. Amer. Fish. Soc.* 122(3):318–27.

Nixon, S. W. 1981. Freshwater inputs and estuarine productivity. In *Proc. Nat. Symp. Freshwater Inflow Est.,* pp. 31–57. U.S. Fish Wildl. Serv. FWS/OBS-81/04(1).

Norden, C. R. 1966. The seasonal distribution of fishes in Vermilion Bay, Louisiana. *Wis. Acad. Sci. Arts Lett.* 55:119–37.

Nordlie, F. G. 1987. Salinity tolerance and osmoregulation in the diamond killifish, *Adinia xenica. Environ. Biol. Fishes* 20(3):229–32.

Norman, J. R. 1934. *A systematic monograph of the flatfishes (Heterosomata).* Vol. 1, Psettodidae, Bothidae, Pleuronectidae. London: British Mus. Nat. Hist. 459 pp.

Notarbartolo-di-sciara, G. 1987. A revisionary study of the genus *Mobula* Rafinesque, 1810 (Chondrichthyes: Mobulidae) with the description of a new species. *Zool. J. Linn. Soc.* 91:1–91.

O'Connor, C. R. 1987. An overview of U.S. management of large pelagic resources in the Atlantic, Gulf of Mexico, and Caribbean. *Proc. Gulf Carib. Fish. Inst.* 40:37–42.

Ogren, L. H., and H. A. Brusher. 1977. The distribution and abundance of fishes caught with a trawl in the St. Andrew Bay system, Florida. *Northeast Gulf Sci.* 1(2):83–105.

Onley, J. E., and D. F. Markle, 1979. Description and occurrence of vexillifer larvae of *Echiodon* (Pisces: Carapidae) in the western North Atlantic and notes on other carapid vexillifers. *Bull. Mar. Sci.* 29:369–79.

Overstreet, R. M., and C. H. Lyles. 1974. A rubber band around an Atlantic croaker. *Gulf Res. Rept.* 4(3):476–78.

Palko, B. J., G. L. Beardsley, and W. J. Richards. 1981. Synopsis of the biology of the swordfish, *Xiphias gladius* Linnaeus. FAO Fisheries Synopsis 127, NOAA Tech. Rep. NMFS Circ 441. 21 pp.

———. 1982. Synopsis of biological data on dolphin-fishes, *Coryphaena hippurus* Linnaeus and *Coryphaena equisetis* Linnaeus. FAO Fisheries Synopsis 130, NOAA Tech Rep. NMFS Circ. 443. 28 pp.

Parker, F. R. Jr., and C. M. Bailey. 1979. Massive aggregations of elasmobranchs near Mustang and Padre islands, Texas. *Tex. J. Sci.* 31(3):255–66.

Parker, J. C. 1965. An annotated checklist of the fishes of the Galveston Bay system, Texas. *Publ. Inst. Mar. Sci. Univ. Tex.* 10:201–20.

Parker, R. O. Jr., D. R. Colby, and T. D. Willis. 1983. Estimated amount of reef habitat on a portion of the United States South Atlantic and Gulf of Mexico continental shelf. *Bull. Mar. Sci.* 33(4):935–40.

Parsons, G. R. 1982. The reproductive biology of the Atlantic sharpnose shark, *Rhizoprionodon terraenovae* (Richardson). *Fish. Bull., U.S.* 81(1):61–73.

———. 1985. Growth and age estimate of the Atlantic sharpnose shark, *Rhizoprionodon terraenovae;* a comparison of techniques. *Copeia* (1):80–85.

Pavela, J. S., J. L. Ross, and M. E. Chittenden, Jr. 1983. Sharp reductions in abundance of fishes and benthic macroinvertebrates in the Gulf of Mexico associated with hypoxia. *Northeast Gulf Sci.* 6(2):167–73.

Pearson, J. C. 1929. Natural history and conservation of redfish and other commercial sciaenids on the Texas coast. *Bull. U.S. Bur. of Fish.* 44:129–214.

Perez, K. T. 1969. An orthokinetic response to rates of salinity change in two estuarine fishes. *Ecology* 50(3):454–57.

Perret, W. S. 1971. *Cooperative Gulf of Mexico estuarine inventory and study, Louisiana.* Phase 1, area description; phase IV, biology. Baton Rouge: La. Wild Life and Fish. Comm. 175 pp.

Perret, W. S., and C. W. Caillouet, Jr. 1974. Abundance and size of fishes taken by trawling in Vermilion Bay, Louisiana. *Bull. Mar. Sci.* 24(1):52–75.

Perret, W. S., J. E. Roussell, J. F., Burden, and J. F. Pollard. 1993. Long term trends of some trawl caught estuarine species in Louisiana. In *Proc. 8th Symp. Coastal Ocean Manag,* ASCE New Orleans, pp. 3459–73.

Perret, W. S., J. E. Weaver, R. O. Williams, P. L. Johansen, T. D. McIlwain, R. C. Raulerson, and W. M. Tatum. 1971. *Fishery profiles of red drum and spotted seatrout.* Gulf States Mar. Fish. Comm., Ocean Springs 6:1–60.

Perry, W. G., Jr. 1968. Distribution and relative abundance of blue catfish, *Ictalurus furcatus,* and channel catfish, *Ictalurus punctatus,* with relation to salinity. *Proc. Ann. Conf. Southeastern Assoc. Game and Fish Comm.* 21:436–44.

———. 1969. Food habits of blue and channel catfish collected from a brackish water habitat. *Prog. Fish Cult.* 31(1):47–50.

Perry, W. G. Jr., and B. J. Carter. 1979. Seasonal occurrence of fishes collected from beach seining, southwest Lousiana. *Proc. La. Acad. Sci.* 43:24–38.

Perry, W. G. Jr., and A. Williams. 1985. A note on the brackish water striped bass program in southwest Louisiana. *Proc. La. Acad. Sci.* 48:55–58.

Perschbacher, P. W., K. J. Sulak, and F. J. Schwartz. 1979. Invasion of the Atlantic by *Peprilus burti* (Pisces: Stromateidae) and possible implications. *Copeia* (3):538–41.

Peters, K. M. 1981. Reproductive biology and of the Florida blenny, *Chasmodes saburrae* (Pisces: Blenniidae). *Northeast Gulf Sci.* 4(2):79–98.

Peters, R. H. 1991. *A Critique for Ecology.* Cambridge: Cambridge Univ. Press. 366 pp.

Peterson, M. S., and S. T. Ross. 1991. Dynamics of littoral fishes and decapods along a coastal river-estuarine gradient. *Est. Coast. Shelf Sci.* 33:467–83.

Pew, P. 1957. Occurrence of young dolphin, *Coryphaena hippurus,* in a Texas bay. *Copeia* (4):300.

Pezold, F. L., and R. C. Cashner. 1983. A character analysis of *Gobionellus boleosoma* and *G. shufeldti* (Pisces: Gobiidae) from the north-central Gulf of Mexico. *Northeast Gulf Sci.* 6(1):71–77.

Pezold, F. L., and R. D. Edwards. 1983. Additions to the Texas marine ichthyofauna, with notes on the Rio Grande Estuary. *Southwest. Nat.* 28(1):102–105.

Pezold, F. L., and J. M. Grady. 1989. A morphological and allozymic analysis of species in the *Gobionellus oceanicus* complex (Pisces: Gobiidae). *Bull. Mar. Sci.* 45(3):648–63.

Pietsch, T. W., and D. B. Grobecker. 1987. *Frogfishes of the world.* Palo Alto: Stanford Univ. Press. 420 pp.

Polovina, J. J., and S. Ralston., 1987. *Tropical snappers and groupers: biology and fisheries management.* Bloulder, Colo.: Westview Press. 659 pp.

Powell, C. R., and K. Strawn. 1963. Notes on the fringed pipefish, *Micrognathus crinigerus,* from the west coast of Florida. *Publ. Inst. Mar. Sci. Univ. Tex.* 9:112–16.

Powell, G. L. 1977. Estuarine fishery dynamics and freshwater inflow in the San Antonio Bay system, Texas. *Proc. Ann. Conf. Southeast Assoc. Fish Wildl. Ag.* 31:498–504.

Pratz, le Page du. 1774. *The history of Louisiana.* Reprint 1975, Louisiana State Univ. Press, Baton Rouge. 405 pp.

Prentice, J. A. 1989. Low-temperature tolerance of southern flounder in Texas. *Trans. Amer. Fish. Soc.* 118(1):30–35.

Price, W. A. 1952. Reduction of maintenance by proper orientation of ship channels through tidal inlets. In *Proc. Second Conf. Coastal Eng.* Louisiana State Univ., 1951, pp. 243–55. Baton Rouge.

Pristas, P. 1980. A possible hatchet marlin *(Tetrapturus* sp.) from the Gulf of Mexico. *Northeast Gulf Sci.* 4(1):51–56.

Pristas, P. J., and A. M. Avrigan. 1991. Big game fishing in the Gulf of Mexico. NOAA Tech. Mem. NMFS-SEFC-289. 28 pp.

Putt, R. E., Jr. 1982. A quantitative study of fish populations associated with a platform within Buccaneer Oil Field, northwestern Gulf of Mexico. M.S. thesis, Texas A&M Univ., College Station.

Putt, R. E. Jr., D. A. Gettleson, and N. W. Phillips. 1986. Fish assemblages and benthic biota associated with natural hard-bottom areas in the northwestern Gulf of Mexico. *Northeast Gulf Sci.* 8(1): 51–81.

Ragan, J. G., E. J. Melancon, A. H. Harris, R. N. Falgout, J. D. Gann, and J. H. Green. 1978. Bottomfishes of the continental shelf off Louisiana. Prof. Pap. Ser. (Biol.) Nicholls State Univ. 2. 34 pp.

Randall, J. E. 1956. A revision of the surgeon fish genus *Acanthurus. Pac. Sci.* 10(2):159–235.

———. 1963. Review of the hawkfishes (family Cirrhitidae). *Proc U.S. Natl. Mus.* 114(3472):389–451.

Randall, J. E., and J. E. Böhlke. 1965. Review of the Atlantic labrid fishes of the genus *Halichoeres. Proc. Acad. Nat. Sci Philadelphia* 117(7):235–59.

Randall, J. E., and D. K. Caldwell. 1966. A review of the sparid fish genus *Calamus,* with descriptions of four new species. Bull. Los Angeles County Mus. Nat. Hist. Sci. no. 2. 47 pp.

Randall, J. E., K. Matsuura, and A. Zamora. 1978. A revision of the triggerfish genus *Xanthichthys,* with description of a new species. *Bull. Mar. Sci.* 28(4):688–706.

Randall, J. E., and R. Vergara R. 1978. Sparidae. In *FAO Species identification sheets for fishery purposes. Western Central Atlantic (Fishing Area 31),* ed. W. Fischer. Vol. 5. Rome: FAO.

Rauch, T. J. III. 1995. Effect of size and prior residence on dominance in *Parablennius marmoreus* (Osteichthyes: Blenniidae). M.S. thesis, La. State Univ., Baton Rouge. 30 pp.

Raymond, R. I. 1905. The fishes of Louisiana. M.S. thesis, Tulane Univ., New Orleans.

Reid, G. K. 1954. An ecological study of the Gulf of Mexico fishes in the vicinity of Cedar Key, Florida. *Bull. Mar. Sci. Gulf Caribb.* 4(1):1–94.

———. 1957. Biologic and hydrographic adjustment in a disturbed Gulf coast estuary. *Limnol. Oceanogr.* 2(3):198–212.

Relyea, K. 1983. A systematic study of two species complexes of the genus *Fundulus* (Pisces: Cyprinodontidae). *Bull. Florida State Mus., Biol. Sci.* 29(1):1–64.

Renaud, M. L. 1986. Hypoxia in Louisiana coastal waters during 1983: implications for fisheries. *Fish. Bull., U.S.* 84(1):19–26.

Render, J. H., and R. L. Allen. 1987. The relationship between lunar phase and Gulf butterfish, *Peprilus burti* catch rate. *Fish. Bull., U.S.* 84(4):817–19.

Renfro, W. C. 1959. Survival and migration of freshwater fishes in salt water. *Tex. J. Sci.* 11(2):172–80.

———. 1960. Salinity relations of some fishes in the Aransas River, Texas. *Tulane Stud. Zool.* 8(3): 83–91.

———. 1963. Gas-bubble mortality of fishes in Galveston Bay, Texas. *Trans. Am. Fish. Soc.* 92(3): 320–22.

Retzer, M. E. 1990. New records and range extensions of twelve species of fishes in the Gulf of Mexico. *Northeast Gulf Sci.* 11(2):137–43.

———. 1991. Life-history aspects of four species of cusk-eels (Ophidiidae: Ophidiiformes) from the northern Gulf of Mexico. *Copeia* (3):703–10.

Rezak, R., T. J. Bright, and D. W. McGrail. 1985. *Reefs and banks of the northwestern Gulf of Mexico: their geological, biological, and physical dynamics*. New York: John Wiley and Sons. 259 pp.

Rezak, R., S. R. Gittings, and T. J. Bright. 1990. Biotic assemblages and ecological controls on reefs and banks of the northwest Gulf of Mexico. *Amer. Zool.* 30:23–35.

Richards, W. J., M. F. McGowan, T. Leming, J. T. Larkin, and S. Kelley. 1993. Larval fish assemblages at the loop current boundary in the Gulf of Mexico. *Bull. Mar. Sci.* 53(2):475–537.

Richardson, S. L., and J. D. McEachran. 1981. Identification of small (< 3 mm) larvae of king and Spanish mackerel, *Scomberomorus cavalla* and *Scomberomorus maculatus*. *Northeast Gulf Science* 5(1):75–79.

Riley, C. M., S. A. Holt, G. J. Holt, E. J. Buskey, and C. R. Arnold. 1989. Mortality of larval red drum *(Sciaenops ocellatus)* associated with a *Ptychodiscus brevis* red tide. *Contr. Mar. Sci.* 31:137–46.

Rivas, L. R. 1950. A revision of the American clupeid fishes of the genus *Harengula*, with descriptions of four new subspecies. *Proc. U.S. Natl. Mus.* 100:275–309.

———. 1951. A preliminary review of the western North Atlantic fishes of the family Scombridae. *Bull. Mar. Sci. Gulf Caribb.* 1(3):209–30.

———. 1960. The fishes of the genus *Pomacentrus* in Florida and the western Bahamas. *Q. J. Fla. Acad. Sci.* 23(2):130–62.

———. 1962. The Florida fishes of the genus *Centropomus*, commonly known as snook. *Q. J. Fla. Acad. Sci.* 25:53–64.

———. 1964. Key to the Atlantic Ocean tuna fishes of the genus *Thnnus*. In *Proc. symp. scombroid fishes*, pt. 1, pp. 427–28. Mar. Biol. Assoc. India.

———. 1966. Review of the *Lutjanus campechanus* complex of red snappers. *Q. J. Fla. Acad. Sci.* 29 (2):117–36.

———. 1970. Snappers of the western North Atlantic. *Commer. Fish. Rev.* 32(1):41–44.

———. 1986. Systematic review of the perciform fishes of the genus *Centropomus*. *Copeia* (3):579–611.

Rivas, L. R., and D. B. McClellan. 1982. Shark investigations by the National Marine Fisheries Service, Miami Laboratory. *Fla. Sci.* 45(1):40–45.

Roberts, C. D. 1993. Comparative morphology of spined scales and their significance in the Teleostei. *Bulletin of Marine Science* 52(1):60–113.

Robinette, H. R. 1983. Species Profiles: Life histories and environmental requirements of coastal fishes and invertebrates. (Bay anchovy and striped anchovy). U.S. Fish Wildl. Serv. Biol. Rep. FWS/OBS-82/11.14. 15 pp.

Robins, C. H., and C. R. Robins. 1970. The eel family Dysommidae (including the Dysomminidae and Nettodaridae), its osteology and composition, including a new genus and species. *Proc Acad. Nat. Sci. Philadelphia* 122(6):293–335.

———. 1989. Family Synaphobranchidae. In *Fishes of the Western North Atlantic*. Memoir Sears Found. Mar. Res. no. 1, pt. 9, pp. 207–53. New Haven.

Robins, C. R. 1957. Effects of storms on the shallow water fish fauna of southern Florida with new records of fishes from Florida. *Bull. Mar. Sci. Gulf Caribb.* 7(3):266–75.

———. 1974. The validity and status of the round-scale spearfish, *Tetrapturus georgei*. Natl. Mar. Fish. Ser. Spec Sci. Rep. Fish. no. 675, pp. 54–61.

———. 1986. The status of the ophidiid fishes *Ophidium brevibarbe* Cuvier, *Ophidium graellsi* Poey and *Lepophidium profundorum* Gill. *Proc. Biol. Soc. Wash.* 99(3):384–87.

Robins, C. R., and W. A. Starck II. 1961. Materials for a revision of *Serranus* and related fish genera. *Proc Acad. Nat. Sci. Philadelphia* 113(11):259–314.

Robinson, M. C 1969. Elasmobranch records and range extensions for the Texas Gulf coast. *Tex. J. Sci.* 21(2):235–36.

Rogers, C., C. Roden, R. Lohoefener, K. Mullin, and W. Hoggard. 1990. Behavior, distribution and relative abundance of cownose ray schools, *Rhinoptera bonasus,* in the northern Gulf of Mexico. *Northeast Gulf Sci.* 11(1):69–76.

Roithmayr, C. M. 1965. Industrial bottomfish fishery of the northern Gulf of Mexico, 1959–1963. U.S. Fish. Wildl. Serv. Spec. Sci. Rep. Fish. no. 18. 23 pp.

Rosen, D. E. 1973. Suborder Cyprinodontoidei. In *Fishes of the western North Atlantic.* Memoir Sears Found. Mar. Res. no. 1, pt. 6, pp. 229–62. New Haven.

Ross, J. L., J. S. Pavela, and M. E. Chittenden, Jr. 1983. Seasonal occurrence of the black drum, *Pogonias cromis,* and red drum, *Sciaenops ocellatus,* off Texas. *Northeast Gulf Sci.* 6(1):67–70.

———. 1989. Food habits of the rock sea bass, *Centropristis philadelphica,* in the western Gulf of Mexico. *Northeast Gulf Science* 10(2): 139–52.

Russell, M. 1977. Apparent effects of flooding on distribution and landings of industrial bottomfish in the Gulf of Mexico. *Northeast Gulf Sci.* 1(2):77–82.

Russell, M., M. Grace, and E. J. Gutherz. 1992. Field guide to the searobins *(Prionotus* and *Bellator)* in the western North Atlantic. NOAA Tech. Rep. NMFS Circ. 107. 26 pp.

Russell, S. J. 1993. Shark bycatch in the northern Gulf of Mexico tuna longline fishery, 1988–91, with observations on the nearshore directed shark fishery. In *Conservation biology of fishes,* ed. S. Branstetter, pp. 19–29. NOAA Tech. Rep. NMFS Circ. 115.

Russo, J. L. 1981. Field guide to fishes commonly taken in longline operations in the western North Atlantic Ocean. NOAA Tech. Rep. NMFS Circ. 435. 51 pp.

Sabins, D. S., and F. M. Truesdale. 1975. Diel and seasonal occurrence of immature fishes in a Louisiana tidal pass. *Proc. Ann. Conf. Southeastern Assoc. Game and Fish Comm.* 28:161–71.

Sage, M., R. G. Jackson, W. L. Klesch, and V. L. deVlaming. 1972. Growth and seasonal distribution of the elasmobranch *Dasyatis sabina. Contrib. Mar. Sci.* 16:71–74.

Saksena, V. P., and W. J. Richards. 1986. A new species of gadiform fish, *Bregmaceros houdei,* from the western north Atlantic. *Bull. Mar. Sci.* 38(2):285–92.

Saucier, M. H., and D. M. Baltz. 1993. Spawning site selection by spotted seatrout, *Cynoscion nebulosus,* and black drum, *Pogonias cromis,* in Louisiana. *Environ. Biol. Fishes* 36:257–72.

Schaldach, W. J. Jr. N.d. Checklist of the marine and littoral fishes of the coast of the Tuxtla region. Unpublished ms.

Schlicht, F. G. 1959. First records of the mountain mullet, *Agonostomus monticola* (Bancroft), in Texas. *Tex. J. Sci.* 11(2):181–82.

Schultz, L. P. 1957. The frogfishes of the family Antennariidae. *Proc. U.S. Natl Mus.* 107(3383):47–105.

———. 1958, Three new serranid fishes genus *Pikea,* from the western Atlantic. *Proc. U.S. Natl. Mus.* 108(3405):321–29.

Schultz, L. P., L. P. Woods, and E. A. Lachner. 1966. Fishes of the Marshall and Marianas Islands: Families Kraemeriidae through Antennariidae. *Bull. U. S. Natl. Mus.* 202(3):1–176.

Scott, G. P., S. C. Turner, C. B. Grimes, W. J. Richards, and E. B. Brothers. 1993. Indices of larval bluefin tunas, *Thunnus thynnus,* abundance in the Gulf of Mexico; modeling variability in growth, mortality, and gear selectivity. *Bull. Mar. Sci.* 53(2):912–29.

Shaffer, R. V., and E. L. Nakamura. 1989. Synopsis of biological data on the cobia, *Rachycentron canadum* (Pisces-Rachycentricae). NOAA Tech. Rep. NMFS 82. 21 pp.

Shaw, R. F., J. H. Cowan, Jr., and T. L. Tillman. 1985. Distribution and density of *Brevoortia patronus* (Gmelin) eggs and larvae in the continental shelf waters of Louisiana. *Bull. Mar. Sci.* 26(1):96–103.

Shaw, R. F., and D. L. Drullinger. 1990. Early-life-history profiles, seasonal abundance and distribution of four species of carangid larvae off Louisiana. NOAA Tech. Rep. NMFS Circ. 89. 37 pp.

Shaw, R. F., W. J. Wiseman, Jr., R. E. Turner, L. H. Rouse, Jr., and R. E. Condrey. 1985. Transport of larval gulf menhaden *Brevoortia patronus* in continental shelf waters of western Louisiana: a hypothesis. *Trans. Amer. Fish. Soc.* 114(4):452–60.

Sheridan, P. F. 1983. Abundance and distribution of fishes in the Galveston Bay system, 1963–64. *Contrib. Mar. Sci.* 26:143–64.

Sheridan, P. F., and D. L. Trimm. 1983. Summer foods of Texas coastal fishes relative to age and habitat. *Fish. Bull., U.S.* 81(3):643–47.

Sheridan, P. F., D. L. Trimm, and B. M. Baker. 1984. Reproduction and food habits of seven species of northern Gulf of Mexico fishes. *Contrib. Mar. Sci.* 27:175–204.

Sherrod, C. L, and C. McMillan. 1985. The distributional history and ecology of mangrove vegetation along the northern Gulf of Mexico coastal region. *Contrib. Mar. Sci.* 28:129–40.

Shipp, R. L. 1974. The pufferfishes (Tetraodontidae) of the Atlantic Ocean. *Publ. Gulf Coast Res. Lab.* 4:1–162.

———. 1975. Pirates in the northern Gulf of Mexico. *Mar. Aquar.* 6(7):16–20.

———. 1991. Endangered marine fishes of Alabama: are there any? *J. Al. Acad. Sci.* 62(1):14–17.

———. 1992. Biogeography of Alabama's marine fishes. In Catalog of freshwater and marine fishes of Alabama, ed. H. T. Boschung, Jr., pp. 7–9. Bull. Alabama Mus. Nat. Hist. No. 14.

Shipp, R. L., and R. W. Yerger. 1969. A new pufferfish, *Sphoeroides parvus,* from the western Gulf of Mexico, with a key to species of *Sphoeroides* from the Atlantic and Gulf coasts of the United States. *Proc. Biol. Soc. Wash.* 82:477–88

Shlossman, P. A., and M. E. Chittenden, Jr. 1982. Reproduction, movements, and population dynamics of the sand seatrout, *Cynoscion arenarius. Fish. Bull., U.S.* 79(4):649–70.

Simmons, E. G. 1957. An ecological survey of the upper Laguna Madre of Texas. *Publ. Inst. Mar. Sci. Univ. Tex.* 4(2):156–200.

Simmons, E. G., and J. P. Breuer. 1962. A study of redfish, *Sciaenops ocellata* Linnaeus, and black drum, *Pogonias cromis* Linnaeus. *Publ. Inst. Mar. Sci. Univ. Tex.* 8:184–211.

Simoneaux, L. P. 1979. The distribution of menhaden, genus *Brevoortia,* with respect to salinity, in the upper drainage of Barataria Bay, Louisiana. M.S. thesis, La. State Univ. 96 pp.

Simpson, D. G., and G. Gunter. 1956. Notes on habits, systematic characters and life histories of Texas saltwater Cyprinodontes. *Tulane Stud. Zool.* 4(4):115–34.

Sindermann, C. J. 1979. Pollution associated diseases and abnormalities of fish and shellfish: a review. *Fish. Bull., U.S.* 76(4):717–50.

Smith, C. L. 1964. Hermaphroditism in Bahama groupers. *Nat. Hist.* 73 (6):42–47.

———. 1965. The patterns of sexuality and the classification of serranid fishes. *Am. Mus. Novit.* (2207):1–20.

————. 1971. A revision of the American groupers: *Epinephelus* and allied genera. *Bull. Am. Mus. Nat Hist.* 146(2):67–241.

Smith, C. L., and J. C. Tyler, 1969. Observations on the commensal relationships of western Atlantic pearlfish *Carapus bermudensis* and holothurians. *Copeia* (1):206–208.

Smith, C. L., J. C. Tyler, and M. N. Feinberg, 1981. Population ecology and biology of the pearlfish *(Carapus bermudensis)* in the lagoon at Bimini, Bahamas. *Bull. Mar. Sci.* 31(4):876–902.

Smith, D. G. 1980. Early larvae of the tarpon, *Megalops atlantica* Valenciennes (Pisces: Elopidae), with notes on spawning in the Gulf of Mexico and Yucatan Channel. *Bull. Mar. Sci.* 30(1):136–41.

————. 1989a. Family Congridae. Conger eels In *Fishes of the Western North Atlantic.* Memoir Sears Found. Mar. Res. no. 1, pt. 9, pp. 460–567. New Haven.

————. 1989b. Family Nettastomatidae. Duckbill eels or sorcerers. In *Fishes of the Western North Atlantic.* Memoir Sears Found. Mar. Res. no. 1, pt. 9, pp. 568–612. New Haven.

————. 1989c. Order Anguilliformes. Family Anguillidae. Freshwater eels. In *Fishes of the Western North Atlantic.* Memoir Sears Found. Mar. Res. no. 1, pt. 9, pp. 25–47. New Haven.

Smith, D. G., and P. H. J. Castle. 1972. The eel genus *Neoconger* Girard: Systematics, osteology, and life history. *Bull. Mar. Sci.* 22(1):196–249.

Smith, G. B. 1976. Ecology and distribution of eastern Gulf of Mexico reef fishes. Fla. Mar. Res. Publ. no. 19. 78 pp.

Smith, G. B., H. M. Austin, S. A. Bortone, R. W Hastings, and L. H. Ogren. 1975. Fishes of the Florida Middle Ground with comments on ecology and zoogeography. *Fla. Mar. Res. Publ.* no. 9. 14 pp.

Smith, P. J. 1986. Low genetic variation in sharks (Chondrichthyes). *Copeia* (1):203–206.

Smith, S. L., and G. Guillan. 1994. Utilization of a field necropsy based health assessment index in southeast Texas estuarine systems. *Amer. Fish. Soc. Ann. Meeting* 124(Abs.):62.

Smith-Vaniz, W. F. 1980. Revision of western Atlantic species of the blenniid fish genus *Hypsoblennius.* *Proc. Acad. Nat. Sci. Philadelphia* 132:285–305.

Smith-Vaniz, W. F., and A. R. Emery, 1980. Redescription and synonymy of the western Atlantic damselfish *Chromis flavicauda* (Günther). *Bull. Mar. Sci.* 30:204–12.

Soileau, D. M, J. D. Brown, and D. W. Fruge. 1985. Mitigation banking: a mechanism for compensating unavoidable fish and wildlife habitat losses. *Trans. N. Amer. Wildl. Nat. Res. Conf.* 50:465–74.

Sonnier, F., J. Teerling, and H. D. Hoese. 1976. Observations on the offshore reef and platform fish fauna of Louisiana. *Copeia* (1):105–11.

Southeast Fisheries Science Center. 1992. Status of fishery resources off the southeast U.S. for 1991. NOAA Tech. Mem. NMFS-SEFSC-306. 75 pp.

Springer, S. 1950a. Notes on the sharks of Florida. *Proc. Fla. Acad. Sci.* 3:141.

————. 1950b. Natural history notes on the lemon shark, *Negaprion brevirostris. Tex. J. Sci.* 2(3):349–59.

————. 1960. Natural history of the sandbar shark, *Eulamia milberti. U.S. Fish Wildl. Serv. Fish. Bull., U.S.* 61(178):1–38.

————. 1979. A revision of the catsharks, family Scyliorhinidae. NOAA Tech Rep. NMFS Circ. 422. 152 pp.

Springer, S., and R. H. Lowe. 1963. A new smooth dogfish, *Mustelus higmani,* from the equatorial Atlantic coast South America. *Copeia* (2):245–51.

Springer, V. G. 1958. Systematics and zoogeography of the clinid fishes of the subtribe Labrisomini Hubbs. *Publ. Inst. Mar. Sci. Univ. Tex.* 5:417–92.

————. 1959. Blenniid fishes of the genus *Chasmodes*. *Tex. J. Sci.* 11(3):321–34.

————. 1960. A new gobiid fish from the eastern Gulf of Mexico. *Bull Mar. Sci. Gulf Caribb.* 10(2): 237–40.

————. 1964. A revision of the carcharhinid shark genera *Scoliodon, Loxodon,* and *Rhizoprionodon. Proc. U.S Natl. Mus.* 115(3493):559–632.

Springer, V. G., and H. D. Hoese. 1958. Notes and records of marine fishes from the Texas coast. *Tex. J. Sci.* 10(3):343–48.

Springer, V. G., and J. P. Joy. 1989. *Sharks in question: the Smithsonian answer book.* Washington, D.C.: Smithsonian Institution Press. 187 pp.

Springer, V. G., and K. D. Woodburn. 1960. An ecological study of the fishes of the Tampa Bay area. Fla. State Board Conserv. Mar Res. Lab. Prof. Pap. Ser. no. 1. 104 pp.

Staiger, J. C. 1965. Atlantic flyingfishes of the genus *Cypselurus,* with descriptions of juveniles. *Bull. Mar. Sci.* 15(3):672–725.

Stanley, D. R., and C. A. Wilson. 1991. Factors affecting the abundance of selected fishes near oil and gas platforms in the northern Gulf of Mexico. *Fish. Bull., U.S.* 89(1):149–59.

————. 1990. A fishery dependent based study of fish species composition and associated catch rates around oil and gas structures off Louisiana. *Fish. Bull., U.S.* 88(4):719–30.

Starck, W. A. II, and W. R. Courtenay, Jr. 1962. *Chlorististium eukrines,* a new serranid fish from Florida, with notes on related species. *Proc. Biol. Soc. Wash.* 75:159–67.

Starnes, W. C. 1988. Revision, phylogeny, and biogeographic comments on the circumtropical marine percoid fish family Pricanthidae. *Bull. Mar. Sci.* 43(2):117–203.

Steen, R. C., 1977. *Butterfly and angelfishes of the world.* Vol. 1, *Australia.* New York: J. Wiley and Sons. Pp. 1–148.

Stephens, J. S. 1963. A revised classification of the blennioid fishes of the American family Chaenopsidae. *Univ. Calif. Publ. Zool.* 68:1–133.

————. 1970. Seven new chaenopsid blennies from the western Atlantic. *Copeia* (2):280–309.

Stickney, R. R., and M. L. Cuenco. 1982. Habitat suitability models: Spot. U.S. Fish Wildl. Ser. FWS/OBS-82/10.20. 12 pp.

Stokes, G. M. 1977. Life history studies of southern flounder *(Paralichthys lethostigma)* and Gulf flounder *(Paralichthys albigutta)* in the Aransas Bay area of Texas. Tex. Parks Wildl. Dept. Tech. Bull. 25. 37 pp.

Strawn, K. 1958. Life history of the pygmy seahorse, *Hippocampus zosterae* Jordan and Gilbert, at Cedar Key Florida. *Copeia* (1):16–22.

Strusaker, P. 1969. Demersal fish resources: composition, distribution and commercial potential of the continental stocks of the southeastern United States. *U.S. Fish Wildl. Serv. Fish. Industr. Resr.* 4(7): 261–300.

Summers, J. K., and K. A. Rose. 1987. The role of interactions among environmental conditions in controlling historical fisheries variability. *Estuaries* 10:255–66.

Sundararaj, B. I., and R. D. Suttkus. 1962. Fecundity of the *Cynoscion nebulosus* (Cuvier), from Lake Borgne area, Louisiana. *Trans. Amer Fish. Soc.* 9(1):84–88.

Suttkus, R. D. 1954. Seasonal movement and growth of Atlantic croaker *(Micropogon undulatus)* along the east Louisiana coast. *Proc. Gulf Carib. Fish. Inst.* 7:1–7.

————. 1956a. Early life history of the Gulf menhaden, *Brevoortia patronus,* in Louisiana. *Proc. N. Amer. Wildl. Conf.* 21:390–407.

————. 1956b. First record of the mountain mullet, *Agonostomus monticola* (Bancroft) in Louisiana. *Proc. La. Acad. Sci.* 19:43–46.

————. 1963. Order Lepisostei. In *Fishes of the western North Atlantic.* Memoir Sears Found. Mar. Res. no. 1, pt. 3, pp. 61–88. New Haven.

Suttkus, R. D., R. M. Darnell, and J. H. Darnell. 1953–54. *Biological study of Lake Pontchartrain.* Ann. Rept. New Orleans: Zool. Dept., Tulane Univ.

Svetovidov, A. N. 1948. Fauna of the U.S.S.R.: Pisces, Gadiformes. *Zool. Ins. Acad. Sci. U.S.S.R.* 9(4):1–304. Trans. 1962, Washington, D.C.: U.S. Dept. of Commerce.

Swann, R. 1957. A stranger takes the bait. *Tex. Game and Fish.* 15(12):15, 28.

Swingle, H. A. 1971a. Biology of Alabama estuarine areas: cooperative Gulf of Mexico estuarine inventory. *Ala. Mar. Res. Bull.* 5:1–123.

————. 1971b. A color variation of the Mexican flounder, *Cyclopsetta chittendeni* Bean, 1895, and a revision of the taxonomic status of *Cyclopsetta decussata* Gunter. *Copeia* (2):335–36.

Swingle, H. A., and D. G. Bland. 1971. A study of fishes of the coastal watercourses of Alabama. *Ala. Mar. Res. Bull.* 10:17–102.

Tavolga, W. N. 1971. Acoustic orientation in the sea catfish, *Galeichthys felis. Ann. N.Y. Acad. Sci.* 188:80–97.

Taylor, D. D., and T. J. Bright. 1973. The distribution of heavy metals in reef-dwelling groupers in the Gulf of Mexico and Bahama Islands. Texas A&M Univ. Sea Grant Publ. TAMU-SCI-73-208. 249 pp.

Teague, G. W. 1951. The sea robins of America: a revision of the triglid fishes of the genus *Prionotus. Comm. Zool. Museo Hist. Nat. de Montevideo.* 3(61):1–53.

————. 1952. The "Mercator" sea robins: a revision of the triglid fishes of the genus *Prionotus* collected off the east coast of America, during the ninth cruise (1936) of the Belgian ship "Mercator," together with a review of those taken on a subsequent voyage (1939). *Bull. Inst. R. Sci. Nat. Belg.* 28(59):1–18.

Thomas, J., P. Wagner, and H. Loesch. 1971. Studies on the fishes of Barataria Bay, an estuarine community. *Coastal Stud. Bull. La. State Univ.* 61:56–66.

Thomerson, J. E., T. B. Thorson, and R. L. Hempel. 1977. The bull shark, *Carcharhinus leucas,* from the upper Mississippi River near Alton, Illinois. *Copeia* (1):166–68.

Thompson, B. A., and Fitzhugh 1985. Synthesis and analysis of Lake Pontchartrain environments, influencing factors and trends. Louisiana State Univ., Baton Rouge. LSU-CFI-84-28. 238 pp.

Thompson, B. A., and L. A. Deegan. 1982. Distribution of ladyfish *(Elops saurus)* and bonefish *(Albula vulpes)* leptocephali in Louisiana. *Bull. Mar. Sci.* 32(4):936–39.

Thompson, B. A., and S. J. Russell. 1995. Capture of the Bramble shark in the Gulf of Mexico. Ann. Meet. ASIH (abs.)

————. In Press. Pomfrets (family Bramidae) of the Gulf of Mexico and nearby waters. Spec. Publ. Boletin del Inst. Nac. Oceanogr. VIII Congress Soc. Eur. Ichthy.

Thomson, J. M. 1978. Mugilidae. In *FAO species identification sheets for fishery purposes: Western Central Atlantic (fishing area 31),* ed. W. Fischer. Vol. 3. Rome: FAO.

Thresher, R. E. 1975. Atlantic *Chromis. Mar. Aquar.* 6(8):23–32.

————. 1978. Polymorphism, mimicry, and the evolution of the hamlets *(Hypoplectrus,* Serranidae). *Bull. Mar. Sci.* 28(2):345–53.

Tolley, S. G., and E. B. Peebles. 1987. Occurrences of *Gunterichthys longipenis* (Osteichthyes: Bythitidae) in a southwest Florida estuary. *Northeast Gulf Sci.* 9(1):43–45.

Topp, R. W., and F. H. Hoff, Jr. 1972. Flatfishes (Pleuronectiformes). *Mem. Hourglass Cruise* 4(2). 135 pp.

Trimm, D. L., and T. S. Searcy. 1989. Occurrence of black snapper, *Apsilus dentatus,* in the Gulf of Mexico. *Northeast Gulf Sci.* 10(2):157–58.

Trott, L.B., and J. E. Onley, 1986. Carapidae. In *Fishes of the North-eastern Atlantic and Mediterranean,* ed. P. J. P. Whitehead, M-L Bauchot, J-C Hureau, J. Nielsen, and E. Tortone, vol. 3, pp. 1172–76. Paris UNESCO.

Turner, R. E., and N. N. Rabalais. 1991. Changes in Mississippi River water quality in this century. *Bioscience* 43(3):140–47.

Tyler, J. C. 1965. The trunkfish genus *Acanthostracion* (Ostraciontidae: Plectognathi) in the western Atlantic: Two species rather than one. *Proc. Acad. Nat. Sci. Philadelphia* 117:1–18.

————. 1980. Osteology, phylogeny, and higher classification of the fishes of the order Plectognathi (Tetradontiformes). NOAA Tech. Rep. NMFS Cir. 434. 422 pp.

Uchida, R. N. 1981. Synopsis of biological data on frigate tuna, *Auxis thazard* and bullet tuna, *A. rochei.* NOAA Tech. Rep. NMFS Cir. 436. 63 pp.

Uyeno, T, K. Matsuura, and E. Fujii. 1983. *Fishes trawled off Suriname and French Guiana.* Japan Marine Fishery Resource Research Center. 519 pp. Tokyo.

Vari, R. P. 1982. Subfamily Hippocampinae. The sea horses. In *Fishes of the Western North Atlantic.* Memoir Sears Found. Mar. Res. no. 1, pt. 8, pp. 173–89. New Haven.

Vaughan, D. S. 1987. Stock assessment of the Gulf menhaden, *Brevoortia patronus,* fishery. NOAA Tech. Rep. NMFS Cir. 58. 18 pp.

Vergara, R. 1978. Lutjanidae. In *FAO species identification sheets for fishery purposes. Western Central Atlantic (fishing area 31),* ed. W. Fischer, vol. 3. Rome: FAO.

Vetter, R. D. 1982. Seasonal metabolic compensation in sympatric seatrout: adaptation to the estuary. *Trans. Amer. Fish. Soc.* 111:193–98.

Viola, T. L. 1992. Occurrence of Gulf pipefish, *Syngnathus scovelli,* in a freshwater Texas reservoir. *Tex. J. Sci.* 44(3):361.

Vladykov, V. D. 1955. A comparison of Atlantic sea sturgeon with a new subspecies from the Gulf of Mexico *(Acipenser oxyrhynchus desotoi). J. Fish. Res. Board. Can.* 12(5):754–61.

Vladykov, V. D., and J. R. Greeley. 1963. Order Acipenseroidei. In *Fishes of the western North Atlantic.* Memoir Sears Found. Mar. Res. no. 1, pt. 3, pp. 24–60. New Haven.

Vladykov, V. D., and E. Kott. 1980. First record of the sea lamprey, *Petromyzon marinus* L., in the Gulf of Mexico. *Northeast Gulf Sci.* 4(1):49–50.

von Schmidt, K. 1969. *Remorina albescens* in the Gulf of Mexico, with a note on pigmentation. *Copeia* (1):194–95.

Voss, G. L. 1953. A contribution to the life history and biology of the sailfish *Istiophorus americanus* Cuv. and Val. in Florida waters. *Bull. Mar. Sci. Gulf Caribb.* 3:206–40.

Wagner, P. R. 1973. Seasonal biomass, abundance, and distribution of estuarine dependent fishes in the Caminada Bay system of Louisiana. Ph.D. diss., La. State Univ., Baton Rouge.

Wakeman, J. M., C. R. Arnold, D. E. Wohlschlag, and S. C. Rabalais. 1979. Oxygen consumption, energy expenditure, and growth of the red snapper *(Lutjanus campechanus). Trans. Amer. Fish. Soc.* 108(3):288–92.

Wakeman, J. M., P. R. Ramsey, and J. G. Stanley. 1990. Population dynamics of the black drum *(Pogonias cromis)* in the Gulf of Mexico. *Proc. La. Acad. Sci.* 53:5–12.

Wakeman, J. M., and D. E. Wohlschlag. 1977. Salinity stress and swimming performance of spotted sea trout. *Proc. Ann. Conf. Southeastern Assoc. Game and Fish Comm.* 31:357–61.

———. 1982. Least cost swimming speeds and transportation costs in some pelagic estuarine fishes. *Fisher. Res.* 1:117–27.

———. 1983. Time course of osmotic adaptation with respect to blood serum osmolality and oxygen uptake in the euryhaline teleost, *Sciaenops ocellatus* (red drum). *Contrib. Mar. Sci.* 26:165–77.

Walls, J. G. 1973. Noteworthy marine fishes from eastern Louisiana. *Q. J. Fla. Acad. Sci.* 35(2):109–12.

Walters, V., and C. R. Robins. 1961. A new toadfish (Batrachoididae) considered to be relict in the West Indies. *Am. Mus. Novit.* no. 2047. 124 pp.

Ward, C. H., M. E. Bendert, D. J., Reish, Eds. 1979. The offshore ecology investigation. Effects of oil drilling and production in a coastal environment. *Rice Univ. Stud.* 65(4–5):1–589.

Ward, J. W. 1957. The reproduction and early development of the sea catfish, *Galeichthys felis,* in the Biloxi (Mississippi) Bay. *Copeia* (4):295–98.

Warlen, S. M. 1988. Age and growth of larval Gulf menhaden, *Brevoortia patronus,* in the northern Gulf of Mexico. *Fish. Bull., U.S.* 86(1):77–90.

Watts, N. H., and G. J. Pellegrin, Jr. 1982. Comparisons of shrimp and finfish catch rates and ratios for Texas and Louisiana. *Mar. Fisher. Rev.* 44(9–10):44–49.

Weaver, J. E., and L. F. Holloway. 1974. Community structure of fishes and macrocrustaceans in ponds of a Louisiana tidal march [sic] influenced by weirs. *Contrib. Mar. Sci.* 18:57–69.

Weinstein, M. P., and R. W. Yerger. 1976. Protein taxonomy of the Gulf of Mexico and Atlantic Ocean seatrouts, genus *Cynoscion. Fish. Bull., U.S.* 74(3):599–607.

Weiss, J. A., M. K. Rylander, and R. C. Harrel. 1991. The distribution and depth preference of searobins (Teleostei: Triglidae) in the northwestern Gulf of Mexico. *Tex. J. Sci.* 43(1):39–44.

Welsh, W. W., and C. M. Breder, Jr. 1923. Contributions to the life histories of the Sciaenidae of the eastern United States coast. *Bull. U.S. Bur. Fish.* 39:141–201.

Weymouth, F. W. 1910. Notes on a collection of fishes from Cameron, Louisiana. *Proc. U. S. Natl. Mus.* 38(1734):1–35.

Whatley, E. C. 1962. Occurrence of breeding Gulf pipefish, *Syngnathus scovelli,* in the inland freshwaters of Louisiana. *Copeia* (1):220.

———. 1969. A study of *Syngnathus scovelli* in freshwaters of Louisiana and salt waters of Mississippi. *Gulf Res. Rep.* 2(4):437–74.

White, C. J., and W. S. Perret. 1974. Short term effects of the Toledo Bend project on Sabine Lake, Louisiana. *Proc. Ann. Conf. Southeast. Assoc. Game and Fish Comm.* 27:710–17.

Whitehead, P. J. P. 1963. A revision of the recent round herrings (Pisces: Dussumieriidae). *Bull. Br. Mus. (Nat. Hist.) Zool.* 10(6):305–80.

———. 1973. The clupeoid fishes of the Guianas. *Bull. Br. Mus. (Nat. Hist.) Zool., Suppl.* 5:1–227.

———. 1985. *FAO species catalogue.* Vol. 7, *Clupeoid fishes of the world.* Part 1, Chirocentridae, Clupeidae, and Pristigasteridae. FAO Fisheries Synopsis no. 125. Pp. 1–303.

Whitehead, P. J. P., G. J. Nelson, and T. Wongratana. 1988. *FAO species catalogue.* Vol. 7, *Clupeoid fishes of the world (Suborder Clupeoidei).* Part 2, Engraulidae. FAO Fisheries Synopsis no. 125. Pp. 305–579.

Williams, J. E., J. E. Johnson, D. A. Hendrickson, S. Contreras-Balderas, J. D. Williams, M. Navarro-

Mendoza, D. E. McAllister, and J. E. Deacon. 1989. Fishes of North America endangered, threatened, or of special concern. *Fisheries* 14(6):2–20.

Williams, J. T. 1983. Taxonomy and ecology of the genus *Chasmodes* (Pisces: Blenniidae) with a discussion of its zoogeography. *Bull. Florida State Mus. Bio. Sci.* 26(2):65–101.

Williams, J. T., and R. L. Shipp. 1980. Observations on fishes previously unknown or rarely encountered in the northeast Gulf of Mexico. *Northeast Gulf Sci.* 4(1):17–27.

———. 1982. A new species of the genus *Echiodon* (Pisces: Carapidae) from the eastern Gulf of Mexico. *Copeia* (4):845–51.

Woods, L. P. 1942. Rare fishes from the coast of Texas. *Copeia* (3):191–92.

———. 1955. Western Atlantic species of the genus *Holocentrus*. *Fieldiana Zool.* 37:91–119.

———. 1965. A new squirrelfish, *Adioryx poco*, of the family Holocentridae from the Bahama Islands. *Notulae Naturae Acad. Nat. Sci. Philadelphia* no. 377, pp. 1–5.

Woods, L. P., and P. M. Sonoda. 1973. Order Berycomorphi (Beryciformes). In *Fishes of the western North Atlantic*. Memoir Sears Found. Mar. Res. no 1, pt. 6, pp. 263–396. New Haven.

Wooten, M. C., K. T. Scribner L. P. Woods, and M. H. Smith. 1988. Genetic variability and systematics of *Gambusia* in the southeastern United States. *Copeia* (2):283–89.

Yáñez-Arancibia, A., and P. Sanchez-Gil. 1986. Los peces demersales de la plataforma continental del sur del Golfo de Mexico. 1. Caracterizacion ambiental, ecologia y evaluacion de las especies, poblaciones y comunidades. Inst. Cienc. del mar y Limnol., Univ. Nal. Auton. Mexico, Publ. Esp. 9. 229 pp.

Yerger, R. E. 1961. Additional records of marine fishes from Alligator Harbor, Florida, and vicinity. *Q. J. Fla. Acad. Sci.* 24(2):111–16.

Yoshida, H. O. 1980a. Summary of biological data on tunas of the genus *Euthynnus*. NOAA Tech. Rep. NMFS Circ. 429. 57 pp.

———. 1980b. Summary of biological data on bonitos of the genus *Sarda*. NOAA Tech. Rep. NMFS Circ. 432. 50 pp.

Yoshiyama, R. M., J. Holt, S. Holt, R. Godbout, and D. E. Wohlschlag. 1982. Abundance and distribution patterns of demersal fishes on the south Texas outer continental shelf: a statistical description. *Contrib. Mar. Sci.* 25:61–84.

Index